Survival
Stories

ALSO BY KATHRYN RHETT

Near Breathing

Survival

Stories

MEMOIRS OF CRISIS

edited by

Kathryn Rhett

ANCHOR BOOKS
DOUBLEDAY
New York London Toronto Sydney Auckland

AN ANCHOR BOOK
PUBLISHED BY DOUBLEDAY
a division of Bantam Doubleday Dell Publishing Group, Inc.
1540 Broadway, New York, New York 10036

ANCHOR BOOKS, DOUBLEDAY, and the portrayal of an anchor
are trademarks of Doubleday, a division of Bantam Doubleday Dell
Publishing Group, Inc.

Survival Stories: Memoirs of Crisis was originally published
in hardcover by Doubleday in 1997. The Anchor Books edition
is published by arrangement with Doubleday.

Book Design by F. J. Levine

The Library of Congress has cataloged the Doubleday hardcover edition
of this book as follows

Survival stories : memoirs of a crisis / edited by Kathryn Rhett
p.   cm.
1. Biography—20th century. 2. Life change events—Psychological aspects.
3. Stress (Psychology) I. Rhett, Kathryn, 1962– .
CT120.S85   1997
155.9′3—dc21   96-52427
CIP

ISBN 0-385-48450-X
Printed in the United States of America
First Anchor Books Trade Paperback Edition: August 1998

1   3   5   7   9   10   8   6   4   2

For Jacob, Cade, and Fred

Acknowledgments

My profound thanks to Jennifer Rudolph Walsh, and to Arabella Meyer, Siobhan Adcock, and Jay Mandel. From the Iowa Summer Writing Festival, I thank Peggy Houston and Amy Margolis as well as the participants in the memoirs of crisis workshops.

Thanks to the following people, who were so generous with advice and assistance: Mary Allen, Carol Ascher, Amy Bloom, Richard Burgin, Carol Cloos, Peter H. Davies, Robert Fogarty, Patricia Foster, Pat de Groot, Lee Gutkind, Colin Harrison, A. M. Homes, Barbara Jones, Brigit Pegeen Kelly, Ann Lauterbach, Don Lee, Andrew Levy, James McConkey, George Packer, W. S. di Piero, Kathleen Peirce, Lynne Raughley, Rodney Sappington, Lynne Sharon Schwartz, Debra Spark, Alix Kates Shulman, Evelyn Somers, Peter Stitt, Deborah Treisman, and Joanna Wos.

As always, my gratitude to Fred Leebron.

Contents

Introduction

KATHRYN RHETT

The idea for this anthology came out of a workshop I teach at the Iowa Summer Writing Festival on memoir of crisis. I used to teach a standard memoirs workshop, and though I enjoyed the family stories of midwestern farms and the coming-of-age accounts, I was most compelled by the memoirs about crises: depression, loss of friendship, divorce, illness, and death. The stories were taut, focused, and illuminating. Each created its own rules for structure and style, because each expressed—with its inclusion of present and past, narrative and digression—the crux of an individual's experience. In terms of urgency, these writers were reporting back from the front lines of personal wars. I liked the urgency, which felt akin to poetry, of work that absolutely needed to be written. Crisis memoirs not only represented, but presented for the first time to both writer and reader, discoveries essential to the writer's life.

So I proposed a new course, which the festival encourages, and read my catalog copy, and wondered nervously if I had crossed the bounds of literary good taste. I usually taught poetry and memoir—what was this course, with a TV-movie-of-the-week tinge to it? "Our life-writing is a passage through grief to knowledge." I'm a conventional teacher, not a guru, not a drum beater or spiritual diviner, not a therapist. The course filled, to my surprise, and in my spring welcome letter I wrote sternly that the workshop would concentrate on matters of text, such as tone, pace, structure, and style. On a Sunday night I met the group, and we pulled chairs into a circle to discuss our projects. What are you writing about, I asked. "A benign brain tumor." "A malignant brain tumor." "My cousin who died of AIDS." "My infertility." "My mother's death." "A hospital's incompetence that led to me having to abort my baby." Everyone began with a composed expression, but as they elaborated on their goals for the week, a few cried. People quietly held hands and said, "I'm sorry." Many had never spoken of their difficulties to anyone outside their families. Oh, God, I thought, what have I assembled here? Group hysteria seemed a possibility, not to mention the personal comments that cause me to behave like a police officer: Get back on the road ma'am, we were discussing the clarity of page two, not cancer treatment in general. With a notepad on my knee, a class list at my side, handout material at my feet, I glanced over at the square window in the exit door.

As we proceeded around the circle, I had to tell my story too. How had I come to create this workshop? As much as crisis memoirs interested me, I would not have read so widely in the genre, or developed this course, if I had not had a crisis story of my own. At the moment when I began talking, I felt that maybe I never should have proposed it. Why not remain in the realm of academic tradition, of safety? And I felt simultaneously that I should be *taking* the class rather than teaching it, which was alarming considering that I was supposed to be in charge of this unwieldy mass of writers and their writing. When my little girl was born, I started to explain, she was sick. She was full-term but there were delivery complications, and her respiratory system shut down. How had my students neatly encapsulated their crises? In the classroom, I felt close to tears. How was it that though my crisis had technically ended, now that my daughter was a healthy two-year-old, I seemed to be still in the midst of it?

I continued, describing how I had begun writing a record of the birth experience and hospitalization so as not to forget the facts and feelings, how I tried writing a bit every morning, and found that I wasn't finished after two months, that I seemed, in fact, to be writing a book, which felt strange, since I usually wrote poetry, and had a history of struggling to meet the length requirements for graduate school papers. Other crises had occurred in my life and hadn't caused a persistent writing effort. Where was all this stuff coming from? And where, exactly, was it going?

All the while I was writing my account, I was reading. If one can track state of mind through choice of reading material, then denial of the impact of a difficult birth was in full force as I read Paul Theroux's *The Happy Isles of Oceania* and Ronald Wright's *Time Among the Maya*. I read them while nursing my daughter, and escaped into distant worlds. I was beginning to face up to emotional hardship with Brett Millier's biography of Elizabeth Bishop, and I confronted disaster with William Loizeaux's *Anna: A Daughter's Life*, which chronicles the birth, illness, and death of a baby. (I still remember the day I found it, in a Mill Valley, California, bookstore, how I might have clutched it to my chest in gratitude if I were prone to such gestures, and how I tried to read it slowly and quickly at once.) It was around this time that I realized I was writing a book, and wanted it to be good. I looked for writing to admire, and for sustenance in my sleep-deprived life. I needed these memoirs for my writing, and for my life. Stories like mine.

I wished there were a section in bookstores for memoirs about bad times. You had to search through biography in most stores, and then sometimes under subjects; the unhealthy baby stories, for example, were mixed in with all the parenting and baby-care books. My reading desires were not restricted by subject—I wanted to read about people at jarring moments in their lives, and cared more about quality of thought and writing than about topic. At times I felt alone, and these books kept me company. One night I read the medical records our attorney had recommended we get, and I reentered our drama from the hospital's point of view. There were lab reports, nurses' notes, respiratory therapists' notes, doctors' daily notes. The notes told a story grimmer than I'd realized, and I found I was holding my breath when I read through the part where they took our baby off the respirator at three A.M. because nothing was working. Though my husband sat next to me on the couch, we were totally separate, existing momentarily across a distance not unlike the distance between us and parents with good birth experiences. We could be isolated from other parents, and even from each other. The memoirs I could lay my hands on articulated thoughts that were massed like senseless clouds in my head, and they made me feel—what is the opposite of alone?—befriended.

I said some of this to the class, and I said that finding published memoirs of crisis let me feel that there were friends, thinkers, and role models out there for me. Reading also led me to know that writing these stories was a necessary act for their authors. The need to write my memoir exerted itself forcefully and mysteriously at a particular time, and I found that many writers of crisis memoir had the same experience—they didn't expect to write anything, and then one day they were writing, and then after that they wondered what the hell they were doing and if anyone else was doing it, and if they could be doing it better. The need sprang from a traumatic event outside the writer's control. The need was to recognize the impact of the event and reconcile it with the rest of the writer's life.

Anyway, I said, I felt that people were doing this urgent writing work, and that perhaps, since crisis was isolating in itself, and crisis writing might be a new experience for some writers, convening these memoirists to discuss craft would be a good idea. It may be that my voice sounded doubtful at this point. It may be that I thought we should all go back to our desks at home. But everyone distributed manuscripts and I assigned readings, and no one stepped in and shut down the class, and so we began.

I've taught the class for three summers now, and there's always a mood of uncertainty at the beginning. The writers arrive, hand out their work, and wait, apprehensive. They have a question: Will it be like group therapy? They haven't signed up for group therapy, haven't paid money and dragged themselves to Iowa in July for therapy. No, they want criticism, advice about technique. When the workshop begins on Monday, almost everyone is relieved: I don't bring a box of tissues to class. This is a workshop like any other, just as these memoirs are writing, like any writing. The crisis memoir has distinguishing characteristics, and we enjoy being in the company of people engaged in work similar to our own. Over the course of the week, we discuss the commonalities of our work, in its varied shapes and qualities and desires.

The writers and readers of crisis memoirs are survivors, the ones left to tell the story, the ones left to live. To survive means "to live on," beyond someone else, beyond any familiar idea of oneself and one's fate.

Many of the memoirs collected here are about someone who has died, and the writers of these in particular confront the creative and destructive powers of writing. In identifying a person, creating an identity, one simultaneously destroys all of the unwritten possibilities. Annie Dillard has written, "If you prize your memories as they are, by all means avoid—eschew—writing a memoir." Just as a photograph replaces a memory with its fixed image, so a memoir limits its subject. Rick Moody creates a series of vignettes about his sister (who worked in a photo lab, generating endless prints), urgent litanies with a kind of mania in the insistence on detail, the repetitions building toward exhaustion. After each vignette there is a pause, then a willful, jerky start-up, as if the narrator can't rest until it's all been said, until we've seen every last picture. Self-recriminatory at the end, he laments his writerly choices, the ways in which he has summed her up. And Richard McCann, watching his mother make a scrapbook of his brother's life, thinks, "Tonight, I want only the singular, precise moments of everything that remains unfixed, unsorted, not yet pasted to its final page." McCann evokes those singular moments in imagistic writing, and certainly to recall through re-creating a sensory reality is a means of resurrection. What's fixed and perfect is inhuman, abstract. Writing a memoir about his father, Patton Hollow comments, "is about the assignation of meaning, transfiguring the incomprehensible concrete into fathomable abstraction." To transform a person into significance is both to raise and erase.

Alan Shapiro, describing the rituals and behavior of his family as they attend his dying sister, wonders if there *is* an objective, observable identity, or whether Beth has become "but a blank page written over by what each of us—out of our own particular relationship to her— was predisposed to write." The imposition of, as Hollow puts it, "a closing narrative" is uncomfortable for the writer, meaning being "an endless branching of associations" that can come all too easily, failing to lead to any actual truth. This is the seduction of language, which leads us on with sound and texture and forward motion. The structure of a story, Maxine Scates says, is of a beginning, middle, and end, but "we lived in the middle." To what extent does the shape of a story distort what happened? As Scates summons up incomplete recollections, she wonders, Am I "simply looking for the incident that will mark the turning point in my own story?" She distrusts the logical progression of story, telling hers in multiple sections and voices. "The Dreaming Back" begins in present tense, in a rush of shocking statements all delivered flat in a single paragraph. Time collapses in a cycle in which everything keeps happening. Space collapses—her body is indistinguishable from her father's. The reader is relieved to reach the orderly past tense of the second section, which presents a history and a geography unfolding in the normal way.

The mix of past and present tense can push the limits of narrative, letting stories shimmer and expand. Nearly every writer here claims, at one point or another, a present time from which to speak. William Van Wert uses, in effect, three tenses: a present tense for his current thinking as he composes the memoir of his mother, a past tense for the narrative summary of what happened, and a present tense for the scenes in Florida before his mother's death. The summary cast in the past is like Van Wert's sober north, "where the cold sorts out all extraneous thoughts." The scenes in the present give the piece a vivid tropical reality in which his mother lives, cracking jokes and buying muumuus and ordering liver and onions. Van Wert's present-tense thinking about his mother, which is the memoir's frame, raises a new life—his own, with his late-discovered earthly joy. Lauren Slater begins with a memory of making snow angels as a child, set in the present tense. William Loizeaux, working in journal form, contains the finite narrative of his child's life within the infinite present of each day's meditation. The journal form emphasizes the passage of time, with the reader feeling the possibilities and limits of each day's entry: this amount of remembrance, this insight, and then the day closes. Laura Benedict intersperses present-tense scenes of her courtship, marriage, and divorce in a chronological narrative. As Frances Mayes comments, "Present acts constantly rearrange the past, that sliding scale." Nancy Mairs writes about her husband's adultery, and how it shifts the whole history of a marriage. She incorporates journal entries from years before to reconstruct how she felt in her marriage then, and comments on how she perceives the past now that she knows about the affair.

On the other hand, Don Snyder's "Winter Work: Diary of a Day Laborer" resolutely does *not* circle to the present to fill us in with current wisdom, but keeps us in the painful moments of his learning, for example, that a carpenter is supposed to *equip* and not just *strap on* a tool belt before coming to work. We're trapped in a past tense moving inexorably forward, in which we feel part of each scene. William Styron's chapter of *Darkness Visible* illustrates the suspense of chronological narrative, as he prepares for suicide by discarding his writing notebook, wrapping it elaborately and burying it in the garbage can, after which, he writes, "I felt my heart pounding wildly, like that of a man facing a firing squad, and I knew I had made an irreversible decision."

The crisis memoir arises from an event, or series of events. The question of how to enrich a chronological narrative is answered in many ways in this collection. The crisis writer has a subject—now how can it be shaped, and how can the complex consciousness of the narrator be evoked? Many writers use associative structure, ordering memory according to connections among images and ideas as well as chronology. "My memory," Isabel Allende writes, "is like a Mexican mural in which all themes are simultaneous." Frances Mayes begins with an image of something she desired as a child: "On the frontispiece of childhood, a white goat pulls a painted cart." The goat is described, and a vision of the narrator "standing up in it wearing a sundress: a little charioteer of Delphi." After considering what she knew of goats ("that black bar for a pupil. Did it see in blocks, like looking through a crack in the wall?"), she tells what her parents gave her instead: "a green parakeet named Tweedle. They thought my fear of birds was silly and I should get over it." The memoir, full of detail, its explanations often elided, evokes a childhood in which Mayes was alone with her imagination. Lauren Slater creates images of angels that echo and resonate throughout her memoir: snow angels, the shadow of a bird's wing, a friend pressing a cool cloth to her forehead, a transcendent part of the self, God's messenger angels. Her insistent metaphors are poetic and even frightening—in a chain of transformation, is the original link to reality lost? She speculates that her obsessive compulsive disorder "had something to do with deep disconnection and too much awe." Metaphorical, sensory language embodies that idea.

The shape of a story represents experience as well. Jane Bernstein's memoir of caring for her retarded daughter is enfolded within the story of her cousins' caring for a difficult elderly uncle. Connections between the stories amplify her ideas about a crisis that won't end. The enclosure of her story within a story (with the addition of a tiny story at the end, as if we are in a set of nesting boxes) expresses the sensation of being trapped. Natalie Kusz structures her memoir in five sections, each different in atmosphere, time, and point of view. The sections are not ordered chronologically. She begins with "I was always waking up, in those days, to the smell of gauze soaked with mucus and needing to be changed." Kusz comments, "I've heard my father, and other immigrant survivors of World War II, speak of behavior peculiar to people under siege, of how they live not in terms of years but of moments, and this was certainly true of our lives." Her inhabitance of the moment is enacted by the use of sensory detail to govern the shape of the story.

Kusz also expands her memoir by incorporating her mother's perspective in two of the sections, a technique that Maxine Scates employs as well when she interviews her father about his war experiences. Jamaica Kincaid posits a second-person perspective in her work, a "you" who is the reader, a typical visitor to her childhood home of Antigua, a "you" who becomes implicated in the island's British Colonial history. "The Antigua that I knew, the Antigua in which I grew up, is not the Antigua you, a tourist, would see now," she writes. "That Antigua no longer exists."

The techniques of multiple verb tenses, associative structure, and expansive points of view reflect the fact that memoir is about the complex connection between an old self and a new one; the essayist Thomas Larson says that "all writing about the self is a tale of two selves told by one who lives now about one who lived then." The sensation of two selves applies especially to crisis memoirists, who are writing about radical, transformative events. Isabel Allende, examining a photograph of herself taken just before her daughter fell ill, notes the manicured nails and confident smile and says, "I don't know that woman." Floyd Skloot, suffering from chronic fatigue syndrome, comments, "In certain moods, I cannot help but see healing as transformation or feel that I must somehow reinvent myself in order to get well." Reynolds Price instructs that you "must find your way to be somebody else, the next viable you." Christopher Davis, who constructs an entire autobiography in the wake of his brother's murder, presents serial versions of a self. Describing his teenage years, he writes, "By draping my obese body in a green army trench coat and driving into Hollywood, to the Whiskey A-Go-Go, to pogo to Devo, I could worship the loser, the outcast, the monster: myself." The self is progressively a reflection of parent, a monster, nothing, an abstraction, a container on a journey toward life-preserving self-awareness, self-love. The self changes, becomes other, becomes aware. Don Snyder describes feeling "as if I were standing away from myself." William Styron experiences "the sense of being accompanied by a second self—a wraithlike observer."

If what is called the self can be reinvented, conscious, and multipart, then can it also not disintegrate? If we always hope for reinvention, for transformation, then should we not also fear the slippage of what we feel to be our truest selves? Laura Benedict represents a changing self with compelling coldness in "The Second Divorce," a confession of guilt and penance for adultery. How can this self's actions be accounted for? How much of a self is idea, or image, and what of it persists? Alan Shapiro's final vision of his sister implies that identity is partly the spangled show we put on for the world. What lies beyond the show? Christina Middlebrook's italicized *I* emphasizes an essential entity, "the me of me" that separated from her body during the ordeal of a bone marrow transplant. She describes how visitors, "sympathetic witnesses," helped keep the *I* in the room, "held my identity for me when I dared not."

Part of the task of the memoirist is to present the "I"—the persistent, changeful self—as wholly and forcefully as possible. For the writer, constructing an "I" is part of restoring life to wholeness, creating, as Middlebrook desires, "a continuum from then to now." Constructing an "I" is part of surviving—to take a narrative stance at all, to adopt a point of view, is to step away from the experience. As much as writers evoke and reenter life through writing, they also stand apart from it. Christopher Davis says that writing was the "way to transform pain back into love." Maxine Scates says, "Writing is one long story of how I remember." Allende comments that "my life is created as I narrate, and my memory grows stronger with writing."

Memoir is, literally, the story of a mind. The crisis memoir is often the story of a crisis of meaning, chronicling revelation if not resolution. In "Healing Powers," a catalog of opinions about the causes and cures of chronic fatigue syndrome becomes an ironic litany, as Floyd Skloot sifts through theory and experience to find a viable approach to an utterly changed life. Arguing that the illness is poorly named, he comments that "calling it chronic fatigue syndrome is like calling Parkinson's disease chronic shaking syndrome or emphysema chronic coughing syndrome." Lauren Slater examines the prevailing view of obsessive compulsive disorder as biochemical in origin, a view she finds dehumanizing and suggestive that "illness lacks any creative possibilities." Reynolds Price ends his book with the instructive chapter included here about how one can reinvent the self after one's life has been overturned; furthermore, he asserts, his new life is better than the old one. As an unemployed teacher forced into construction work to support his family, Don Snyder writes of a disillusioned middle class: "I'd always believed there would be a slot for me somewhere near the top, a long way from guys with mud on their faces who couldn't earn a living." Lucy Grealy addresses our belief in one's face as reflective of one's soul, as well as societal emphasis on female beauty. She describes hearing sexual taunts from men "not because I was disfigured but because I was a disfigured *woman.*" Hoping that surgery could correct the facial damage caused by Ewing's sarcoma, she waits for the day when she would therefore be "whole, content, loved."

Mental confrontation is a dominant quality of a crisis memoir; the biblical nature of the individual faced with larger powers of culture and belief is part of what makes these stories so compelling. Suddenly the individual stands not comfortably within a marriage, a family, an idea of oneself, but outside, looking in. Maybe the individual is, as if standing outside the house of one's life, simply looking in the window at what used to be normal. Jamaica Kincaid, fully aware and enraged at the poverty of her place in racist Antigua, writes with near disbelief of her seven-year-old self, "I once stood in hot sun for hours so I could see a putty-faced Princess from England disappear behind these walls." Alan Shapiro writes, "I lived, we all lived, with a doubled, dreamlike consciousness of what we all were going through, bewildered most by what remained familiar, like anthropologists discovering that the never before encountered culture they're observing is their own." Where am I? the writer must ask. And what's it like here?

Contemporary American memoirs tend toward personal, private subjects. Frances Mayes comments on a Polish friend, a World War II survivor, whose "early years played out against the large backdrop of history." Her story can't claim the global theater: "No, nothing here but my family's closet-drama group." We have no war here, no shelling, no mass graves or internment camps. Much of American memoir writing is private, is from the home, rather than reflective of public life.

Perhaps there is a corollary site, an office or funeral parlor or hospital, but the root in terms of character and place and action is often domestic. How common the experiences are, and yet how closely held. So that articulating them is a different exercise from collective grief or mourning; it may be a step toward such collective feeling by bringing outside what was inside the house. Sometimes I feel as if writers are putting their stories in the front yard, and for the first time everyone can see that the stuff set out on the lawns and sidewalks is the same. One's body, one's family, and one's place in society—these map the territory of much American memoir now. The single voice of the memoirist speaks to the individual reader, preserving, as Rita Dove has said of poetry, "the quality of intimacy" while addressing the soul's innermost subjects.

Is there anything shameful about memoirists' material? Is it shameful to write of adultery, illness, unemployment, or death? I'm thinking about the issue of memoirs, privacy, and shame, because critics do. Crisis memoirs have taken various forms throughout history, in North America certainly from the 1500s with the European explorers' accounts of the New World, and in slave narratives, pioneers' writings, and illness narratives. In the late twentieth century, critics take an easy pleasure lumping crisis memoirs with the talk-show culture and recovery movement, as if memoirs were bits of exotica held up for viewer consumption, or word problems meant to be solved in twelve steps. The crisis memoir serves as an instrument of discovery rather than as a document of exposure or complaint, its writers often explicitly disclaiming victim status. Natalie Kusz, disfigured after being attacked by dogs as a child, writes that crisis "bred in me understandings I would not relinquish now." When people feel sorry for Jane Bernstein, she thinks, "Good days and bad days, same as for you." In purpose, method, and effect, crisis memoirs do not resemble an exploitative talk show or a support group. The memoirists I read, like all good writers, dwell in complexity and irresolution, transforming what happened into language to create an account that approaches wholeness. The crisis memoir reflects the truth that there is no ending, while simultaneously presenting a crafted story that allows both writer and reader to feel a sense of resolution. If the choice of subject seems somehow unseemly, perhaps this reflects a flaw in our notion of art rather than with the art itself. As a goal of her work, Nancy Mairs is after "reclaiming human experience . . . from the morass of secrecy and shame into which Christian and pre-Christian taboos have plunged it." Her essay "Here: Grace" shows even in the construction of its title her belief that grace exists in, is equivalent to, our daily existence.

Though memoirs of crisis tell extraordinary stories, the experience of crisis is universal, being a moment of decision or upheaval that changes the course of a life. It is likely that such moments and their consequences are highly personal, which only contributes to the difficulty of writing well about them.

The memoirs collected here represent, for me, excellent contemporary American writing about crisis. I chose them not for any specific content but for their ability to express the experience. These memoirs seek to articulate—and, in articulating, create—the bridge between one part of a life and another. What is the bridge? Writing is a process of discovery—through writing, the bridge is revealed. I wondered, for whom is the memoir form an actual bridge to the next part of one's life? Who needed to write about a particular crisis before they could think about anything else, before their mental, creative life could continue? For whom was the memoir *that essential?*

William Loizeaux asks, "Should I keep looking at what, in the end, is so unbearable? I'm not sure. But is there really an alternative?"

Of necessity, then, these memoirs were not solicited as original works. Writers wouldn't be doing this work as a freelance assignment. I wanted memoirs that people were writing because they had to, not because they were asked. I was lucky to catch writers who were in the midst of projects and would complete a chapter or an essay in time for this book. Other memoirs I found in literary magazines, and some are excerpted from books.

Reynolds Price comments in his memoir about spinal cancer that after his first radiation treatments, he searched for books that would serve as "companions more than prayers or potions that had worked for another." He was hardly alone in his desire for books as company. As a writer, he was asked by people to add his recollections of illness "to the very slim row of sane printed matter which comes from the far side of catastrophe." I hope this anthology will also be a worthy addition to the shelf.

Demonology

They came in twos and threes, dressed in the fashionable *Disney* costumes of the year—Lion King, Pocahontas, Beauty and the Beast—or in the costumes of televised superheroes, Protean, shape-shifting, thus arrayed, in twos and threes, complaining it was too hot with the mask on, *Hey, I'm really hot!,* lugging those orange plastic buckets, bartering, haggling with one another, *Gimme your Smarties, please?* as their parents tarried behind, grown-ups following after, bantering about the schools, or about movies, about local sports, about their marriages, about the difficulties of long marriages, kids sprinting up the next driveway, kids decked out as demons or superheroes or dinosaurs or as advertisements for our multinational entertainment-providers, beating back the restless souls of the dead, in search of sweets.

. . .

They came in bursts of fertility, my sister's kids, when the bar drinking, or home-grown dope-smoking, or bed-hopping had lost its luster; they came with shrill cries and demands—little gavels, she said, instead of fists—*Feed me! Change me! Pay attention to me!* Now it was Halloween and the mothers in town, my sister among them, trailed after their kids, warned them away from items not fully wrapped, *Just give me that, you don't even like apples,* laughing at the kids hobbling in their bulky costumes—my nephew dressed as a shark, dragging a mildewed gray shark's tail behind him. But what kind of shark? A great white? A blue? A tiger shark? A hammerhead? A nurse shark?

She took pictures of costumed urchins, my sister, as she always took pictures, e.g., my nephew on his first birthday (six years prior), blackfaced with cake and ice cream, a dozen relatives attempting in turn to read to him from a brand-new rubberized book about a tugboat. *Toot toot!* His desperate, needy expression, in the photo, all out of phase with our excitement. The first nephew! The first grandchild! He was trying to get the cake in his mouth. Or: a later photo of my niece (his younger sister) attempting to push my nephew out of the shot—against a backdrop of autumn foliage; or: a photo of my brother wearing my dad's yellow double-knit paisley trousers (with a bit of flair in the cuffs), twenty-five years after the heyday of such stylings; or my father and stepmother on their powerboat, peaceful and happy, the riotous wake behind them; or my sister's virtuosic photos of *dogs*—Mom's irrepressible golden retriever chasing a tennis ball across an overgrown lawn, or my dad's setter on the beach with a perspiring Löwenbräu leaning against his snout. Fifteen or twenty photo albums on the shelves in my sister's living room, a whole range of leathers and faux-leathers, no particular order, and just as many more photos loose, floating around the basement in cartons, castoffs, files of negatives in their plastic wrappers.

.   .   .

She drank *the demon rum,* and she taught me
how to do it, too, when we were kids; she taught me how to drink. We
stole drinks, or we got people to steal them for us; we got reprobates of
age to venture into the pristine suburban liquor stores. Later, I drank
bourbon. My brother drank beer. My father drank single malt scotches.
My grandmother drank half-gallons and then fell ill. My grandfather
drank the finest collectibles. My sister's ex-husband drank more rea-
sonably priced facsimiles. My brother drank until a woman lured him
out of my mother's house. I drank until I was afraid to go outside. My
uncle drank until the last year of his life. And I carried my sister in a
blackout from a bar once—she was mumbling to herself, humming
melodies, mostly unconscious. I took her arms; Peter Hunter took her
legs. She slept the whole next day. On Halloween, my sister had a
single gin and tonic before going out with the kids, before ambling
around the condos of Kensington Court, circling from multifamily unit
to multifamily unit, until my nephew's shark tail was grass-stained
from the freshly mown lawns of the common areas. Then she drove
her children across town to her ex-husband's house, released them into
his supervision, and there they walked along empty lots, beside a
brook, under the stars.

When they arrived home, these monsters,
disgorged from their dad's Jeep, there was a fracas between girl and
boy about which was superior (in the Aristotelian hierarchies), Milky
Way, Whoppers, Slim Jim, Mike 'n Ikes, Sweet Tarts, or Pez—this
bounty counted, weighed, and inventoried (on my niece's bed). Which
was the Pez dispenser of greatest value, a Disney Pez dispenser or a
Hanna-Barbera Pez dispenser? Or, say, a demonic *totem pole Pez
dispenser?* And after this fracas, which my sister refereed wearily
(Look, if he wants to save the Smarties, you can't make him trade!), they
slept, that family, and this part is routine, my sister was tired as hell;
she slept the sleep of the besieged, of the overworked, she fell pre-
cipitously into whorls of unconsciousness, of which no snapshot
can be taken. Somewhere there is a dream book, though, a catalog

of those narratives, with its repetitions and displacements and abbreviations.

In one photograph my sister is wearing a Superman outfit. This from a prior Halloween. I think it was a *Supermom* outfit, actually, because she always kind of liked these bad jokes, degraded jokes, things other people would find ridiculous. (She'd take a joke and repeat it until it was leaden, until it was funny only in its awfulness.) Jokes with the fillip of sentimentality. Anyway, in this picture, her blond hair—brightened a couple of shades with the current technologies—cascades around her shoulders, disordered and impulsive. *Supermom*. And her expression is skeptical, as if she assumes the mantle of Supermom—raise the kids, accept wage-slavery, grow old and contented—and thinks it's dopey at the same time.

Never any good without coffee. Never any good in the morning. Never any good until the second cup. Never any good without freshly ground Joe, because of my dad's insistence, despite advantages of class and style, on *instant coffee*. No way. Not for my sister. At my dad's house, where she stayed in summer, she used to grumble derisively, while staring out the kitchen windows, out the expanse of windows that gave onto the meadow there, *instant coffee!* There would be horses in the meadow and the ocean just over the trees, the sound of the surf, and *instant coffee!* Thus the morning after Halloween, with my nephew the shark (who took this opportunity to remind her, in fact—by way of expositional dialogue—that last year he saved his Halloween candy *all the way till Easter, Mommy)* and my niece, the Little Mermaid, orbiting around her like a fine dream. My sister was making this coffee with the automatic grinder and the automatic drip device, and the dishes were piled in the sink behind her, and the wall calendar was staring her in the face, with its hundred urgent appointments, such as *jury duty* (for the following Monday) and *R&A to pediatrician;* the kids whirled around the kitchen, demanding to know who got the last of the Lucky Charms, who had to settle for the Kix. My sister's eyes were barely open.

. . .

Now this portrait of her cat, Pointdexter, twelve years old—he slept on my face when I stayed at her place in 1984—Pointdexter with the brain tumor, Pointdexter with the pheno-barbital habit. That morning—All Saint's Day—he stood entirely motionless before his empty dish. His need was clear. His dignity was immense. Well, except for the seizures. Pointdexter had these seizures. He was possessed. He was a demon. He would bounce off the walls, he would get up *a head of steam*, mouth frothing, and run straight at the wall, smack into it, shake off the ghosts, and start again. His screeches were unearthly. Phenobarbital was prescribed. My sister medicated him preemptively, before any other chore, before any diplomatic initiatives on matters of cereal allocation. *Hold on, you guys, I'll be with you in a second*. Drugging the cat, slipping him the Mickey Finn in the Science Diet, feeding the kids, then getting out the door, pecking her boyfriend on the cheek on the way (he was stumbling sleepily down the stairs).

She printed snapshots. At this photo lab. She'd sold cameras (mnemonic devices) for years, and then she'd been kicked upstairs to the lab. Once she sold a camera to Pete Townshend, the musician. She told him—in her way both casual and rebellious— that she didn't really like the Who. Later, from her job at the lab, she used to bring home *other people's pictures*, e.g., an envelope of photographs of the Pope. Had she been out to Giants Stadium to use her telephoto lens to photograph John Paul II? No, she'd just printed up an extra batch of, say, Agnes Venditi's or Joey Mueller's photos. *Caveat emptor*. Who knew what else she'd swiped? Those Jerry Garcia pix from the show right before he died? Garcia's eyes squeezed tightly shut as he sang in that heartbroken, exhausted voice of his? Or: somebody's trip to the Caribbean or to the Liberty Bell in Philly? Or: her neighbor's private documentations of love? Who knew? She'd get on the phone at work and gab, call up her friends, call up my family, printing pictures while gabbing, sheet after sheet of negatives, of memories. Oh, and circa Halloween, she was working in the lab with some new, exotic chemicals. She had a wicked headache.

All Saints' Day. My sister didn't pay much attention to the church calendar. Too busy. Too busy to concentrate on theologies, too busy to go to the doctor, too busy to deal with her finances, her credit card debt, etc. Too busy. (And maybe afraid too.) She was unclear on this day set aside for God's awesome tabernacle, unclear on the feast for the departed faithful, didn't know about the church of the Middle Ages, didn't know about the particulars of the druidic ritual of Halloween—it was a Hallmark thing, a marketing event—or how All Saints' Day emerged as an alternative to Halloween. She was not much preoccupied with, nor attendant to articulations of loss nor interested in how this feast in the church calendar was hewn into two separate holy days, one for the saints, *that great cloud of witnesses*, one for the dearly departed, the regular old believers. She didn't know of any attachments that bound together these constituencies, didn't know, e.g., that God would *wipe away all tears from our eyes and there would be no more death*, according to the evening's reading from the Book of Revelation. All this academic stuff was lost on her, though she sang in the church choir, and though on All Saints' Day, a guy from the church choir happened to come into the camera store, just to say hi, a sort of an angel (let's say), and she said, *Hey Bob, you know, I never asked you what you do.*

To which Bob replied, *I'm a designer.*
My sister: *What do you design?*
Bob: *Steel wool.*
She believed him.

My sister was really small. She barely held down her clothes. Five feet tall. Tiny hands and feet. Here's a photo from my brother's wedding (two weeks before Halloween): we were dancing on the dance floor, she and I. She liked *to pogo* sometimes. It was the dance we preferred when dancing together. We created mayhem on the dance floor. Scared people off. We were demons for dance, for noise and excitement. So at my brother's wedding reception I hoisted her up onto my shoulder, and she was so light, just as I remembered from years before, twenty years of dances, still tiny, and I wanted to crowd-surf her across the reception, pass her across upraised hands, I wanted to impose her on older couples, gentlemen in their cummerbunds, old guys with tennis elbow or arthritis, with red faces and gin blossoms; they would smile, passing my sister hither, to the microphone, where the wedding band was playing, where she would suddenly burst into song, into some sort of reconciliatory song, backed by the wedding band, and there would be stills of this moment, flash-bulbs popping, a spotlight on her face, a tiny bit of reverb on her microphone; she would smile and concentrate and sing. Unfortunately, the situation around us, on the dance floor, was more complicated than this. Her boyfriend was about to have back surgery. He wasn't going to do any heavy lifting. And my nephew was too little to hold her up. And my brother was preoccupied with his duties as groom. So instead I twirled her once and put her down. We were laughing, out of breath.

On All Saints' Day she had lunch with Bob the angelic designer of steel wool (maybe he had a crush on her) or with the younger guys from the lab (because she was a middle-aged free spirit), and then she printed more photos of Columbus Day parades across Jersey, or photos of other people's kids dressed as Pocahontas or as the Lion King, and then at five-thirty she started home, a commute of forty-five minutes, Morristown to Hackettstown, on two-laners. She knew every turn. Here's the local news photo that never was: my sister slumped over the wheel of her Plymouth Saturn after having run smack into a local deer. All along those roads the deer were upended, disemboweled, set upon by crows and hawks, and my sister on the way back from work, or on the way home from a bar, must have grazed an entire herd of them at one time or another, missed them narrowly, frozen in the headlights of her car, on the shoulders of the meandering back roads, pulverized. Venison.

Her boy lives on air. Disdains food. My niece, meanwhile, will eat only candy. By dinnertime, they had probably made a dent in the orange plastic bucket with the Three Musketeers, the Cadburys, Hot Tamales, Kit Kats, Jujyfruits, Baby Ruths, Bubble Yum—at least my niece had. They had also insisted on bringing a sampling of this booty to school and from there to their after-school play group. Neither of them wanted to eat anything; they complained about the whole idea of supper, and thus my sister offered, instead, to take them to the *McDonaldLand play area* on the main drag in Hackettstown, where she would buy them a Happy Meal, or equivalent, a hamburger topped with *American processed cheese food,* and, as an afterthought, she would insist on their each trying a little bit of a salad from the brand-new McDonald's salad bar. She had to make a deal to get the kids to accept the salad. She suggested six mouthfuls of lettuce each and drew a hard line there, but then she allowed herself to be talked down to two mouthfuls each. They ate indoors at first, the three of them, and then went out to the playground, where there were slides and jungle gyms in the reds and yellows of Ray Kroc's empire. My sister made the usual conversation, *How did the other kids make out on Halloween? What happened at school?* and she thought of her boyfriend, fresh from spinal surgery, who had limped downstairs in the morning to give her a kiss, and then she thought about *bills, bills, bills* as she caught my niece at the foot of a slide. It was time to go sing. Home by nine.

My sister as she played the guitar in the late sixties with her hair in braids; she played it before anyone else in my family, wandering around the chords, "House of the Rising Sun" or "Blackbird," on classical guitar, sticking to the open chords of guitar tablature. It never occurred to me to wonder about which instruments were used on those AM songs of the period (the Beatles with their sitars and cornets, Brian Wilson with his theremin), not until my sister started to play the guitar. (All of us sang—we used to sing and dance in the living room when my parents were married, especially to *Abbey Road* and *Bridge over Troubled Water.)* And when she got divorced she started hanging around this bar where they had live music, this Jersey bar, and then she started hanging around at a local record label, an indy operation, and then she started *managing a band* (on top of everything else), and then she started to sing again. She joined the choir at St. James Church of Hackettstown and she started to sing, and after singing she started to pray—prayer and song being, I guess, styles of the same beseechment.

I don't know what songs they rehearsed (at choir rehearsal), but Bob was there, as were others, Donna, Frank, Eileen, and Tim (I'm making the names up), and I know that the choir was warm and friendly, though perhaps a little bit out of tune. It was one of those Charles Ives small-town choruses that slips in and out of pitch, that misses exits and entrances. But they had a good time rehearsing, with the kids monkeying around in the pews, the kids climbing sacrilegiously over that furniture, dashing up the aisle to the altar and back, as somebody kept half an eye on them (five of the whelps in all) and after the last notes ricocheted around the choir loft, my sister offered her summation of the proceedings, *Totally cool! Totally cool!,* and now the intolerable part of this story begins—with joy and excitement and a church interior. My sister and her kids drove from St. James to her house, her condo, there was this picturesque drive home, Hackettstown as if lifted from picture postcards of autumn, the park with its streams and ponds and lighted walkways, leaves in the streetlamps, in the headlights, leaves three or four days past their peak, the sound of leaves in the breeze, the construction crane by her place (they were digging up the road), the crane swaying above a fork in the road, a left turn after the fast food depots, and then into her parking spot in front of the condo. The porch by the front door with the Halloween pumpkins, a cat's face complete with whiskers, a clown, a jack-o'-lantern. My sister closed the front door of her house behind her. Bolted it. Her daughter reminded her to light the pumpkins. Just inside the front door, Pointdexter, on the top step, waiting.

Her keys on the kitchen table. Her coat in the closet. She sent the kids upstairs to get into their pajamas. She called up to her boyfriend, who was in bed reading a textbook, *What are you doing in bed, you total slug!,* and then, after checking the messages on the answering machine, looking at the mail, she trudged up to my niece's room to kiss her good night. Endearments passed between them. My sister loved her kids, above all, and in spite of all the work and the hardships, in spite of my niece's reputation as a firecracker, in spite of my nephew's sometimes diabolical smarts. She loved them. There were endearments, therefore, lengthy and repetitive, as there would have been with my nephew too. And my sister kissed her daughter multiply, because my niece is a little impish redhead, and it's hard *not* to kiss her. *Look, it's late, so I can't read to you tonight, okay?* My niece protested temporarily, and then my sister arranged the stuffed animals around her daughter (for the sake of arranging), and plumped a feather pillow, and switched off the bedside lamp on the bedside table, and she made sure the night-light underneath the table (a plug-in shaped like a ghost) was illumined, and then on the way out the door she stopped for a second. And looked back. The tableau of domesticity, of family, was what she last contemplated. Or maybe she was composing endearments for my nephew. Or maybe she wasn't looking back at my niece at all. Maybe she was already lost in this next tempest.

Out of nowhere. All of a sudden. All at once. In an instant. Without warning. In no time. Helter-skelter. *In the twinkling of an eye.* My sister's legs gave out, and she fell over toward my niece's desk, by the door, dislodging a pile of toys and dolls (a Barbie in evening wear, a posable Tinker Bell doll), colliding with the desk, sweeping its contents off with her, toppling onto the floor, falling heavily, head by the door. My niece, startled, rose up from under covers.

More photos: my sister, my brother, and I, *back in our single digits*, dressed in matching, or nearly matching outfits (there was a naval flavor to our look), playing with my aunt's basset hound—my sister grinning mischievously; or: my sister, my father, my brother and I, in my dad's Karmann Ghia, just before she totaled it on the straightaway on Fishers Island (she skidded, she said, *on some antifreeze or something slippery)*; or: my sister, with her newborn daughter in her lap, sitting on the floor of her living room—mother and daughter with the same bemused impatience.

My sister started to seize.

The report of her fall was, of course, loud enough to stir her boyfriend from the next room. He was out of bed fast. (Despite the physical pain associated with his recent surgery.) I imagine there was a second in which other possibilities occurred to him—hoax, argument, accident, anything—but quickly the worst of these seemed most likely. You know these things somewhere. You know immediately the theme of all middle-of-the-night telephone calls. He was out of bed. And my niece called out to her brother, to my nephew, next door. She called my nephew's name, once, plaintively, like it was a question.

My sister's hands balled up. Her heels drumming on the carpeting. Her muscles all like nautical lines, pulling tight against cleats in some storm. Her jaw clenched. Her heart rattling desperately. Fibrillating. If it was a conventional seizure, she was unconscious for this part—maybe even unconscious throughout—because of reduced blood flow to the brain, because of the fibrillation, because of her heart condition; which is to say that my sister's *mitral valve prolapse*—technical feature of her *broken heart*—was here engendering this arrythmia, and now, if not already, she began to hemorrhage internally. Her son stood in the doorway, in his pajamas, shifting from one foot to the other (there was a draft in the hall). Her daughter knelt at the foot of the bed, staring, and my sister's boyfriend watched as my poor sister shook, and he held her head, and then changed his mind and bolted for the phone.

After the seizure she went slack. (Meredith's heart stopped. And her breathing. She was still.) For a second she was alone in the room, with her children, silent. After he dialed 911, Jimmy appeared again, to try to restart her breathing. Here's how: he pressed his lips against hers. Unlike televised versions of this desperate measure, he didn't have time to say, *Come on, breathe dammit,* or to make similar imprecations, although he did manage to shout at the kids, *Get the hell out of here, please! Go downstairs!* (It was advice they followed only for a minute.) At last my sister took a breath. Took a deep breath, a sigh, and there were two more of these. Deep resigned sighs. Five or ten seconds between each. For a few moments more, instants, she looked at Jimmy as he pounded on her chest with his fists, thoughtless about anything but results, stopping occasionally to press his ear between her breasts. Her eyes were sad and frightened, even in the company of the people she most loved. But she was probably unconscious. The kids sat cross-legged on the floor in the hall, by the top of the stairs, watching. Lots of stuff was left to be accomplished in these last seconds, even if it wasn't anything unusual, people and relationships and small kindnesses, the best way to fry pumpkin seeds, what to pack for Thanksgiving, whether to make turnips or not, snapshots to be culled and arranged, photos to be taken—these possibilities spun out of my sister's grasp, torrential futures, my beloved sister, solitary with pictures taken and untaken, gone.

EMS technicians arrived and carried her body down to the living room, where they tried to start her pulse with expensive engines and devices. Her body jumped, of course, while they shocked her—and she was a revenant in some corridor of simultane-

ities, some cyberspace of flindering neurons—but her heart wouldn't
start, and then they put her body on the stretcher. To carry her away.
Now the moment arrives when they bear her out the front door of her
house and she leaves it to us, leaves to us the house and her things and
her friends and her memories and the involuntary assemblage of these
into language. Grief. The sound of the ambulance is pretty much how
they always sound, and the road is mostly clear on the way to the
hospital; my sister's route is clear.

I should fictionalize it more, I should conceal
myself, I should consider the responsibilities of characterization, I
should conflate her two children into one, or reverse their genders, or
otherwise alter them, I should make her boyfriend a husband, I should
explicate all the tributaries of my extended family (its remarriages, its
internecine politics), I should novelize the whole thing, I should make
it multigenerational, I should somehow work in my forefathers (stone-
masons and newspapermen), I should let artifice create an elegant
surface, I should make the events orderly, I should wait and write
about it later, I should wait until I'm not angry, I shouldn't clutter a
narrative with fragments, with mere recollections of good times, or
with regrets, I should make Meredith's death shapely and persuasive,
not blunt and disjunctive, I shouldn't have to think the unthinkable, I
shouldn't have to suffer, I should address her here directly *(these are
the ways I miss you)*, I should write only of affection, I should make
our travels in this earthly landscape safe and secure, I should have a
better ending, I shouldn't say her life was short and often sad, I
shouldn't say she had her demons, as I do too.

from *A Small Place*

JAMAICA KINCAID

The Antigua that I knew, the Antigua in which I grew up, is not the Antigua you, a tourist, would see now. That Antigua no longer exists. That Antigua no longer exists partly for the usual reason, the passing of time, and partly because the bad-minded people who used to rule over it, the English, no longer do so. (But the English have become such a pitiful lot these days, with hardly any idea what to do with themselves now that they no longer have one quarter of the earth's human population bowing and scraping before them. They don't seem to know that this empire business was all wrong and they should, at least, be wearing sackcloth and ashes in token penance of the wrongs committed, the irrevocableness of their bad deeds, for no natural disaster imaginable could equal the harm they did. Actual death might have been better. And so all this fuss over empire—what went wrong here, what went wrong there—always makes me quite crazy, for I can say to them what went wrong: they should never have left their home, their precious England, a place they loved so much, a place they had to leave but could never forget. And so everywhere they went they turned it into England; and everybody they met they turned English. But no place could ever really be England, and nobody who did not look exactly like them would ever be English, so you can imagine the destruction of people and land that came from that. The English hate each other and they hate England, and the reason they are so miserable now is that they have no place else to go and nobody else to feel better than.) But let me show you the Antigua that I used to know.

In the Antigua that I knew, we lived on a street named after an English maritime criminal, Horatio Nelson, and all the other streets around us were named after some other English maritime criminals. There was Rodney Street, there was Hood Street, there was Hawkins Street, and there was Drake Street. There were flamboyant trees and mahogany trees lining East Street. Government House, the place where the Governor, the person standing in for the Queen, lived, was on East Street. Government House was surrounded by a high white wall—and to show how cowed we must have been, no one ever wrote bad things on it; it remained clean and white and high. (I once stood in hot sun for hours so that I could see a putty-faced Princess from England disappear behind these walls. I was seven years old at the time, and I thought, She has a putty face.) There was the library on lower High Street, above the Department of the Treasury, and it was in that part of High Street that all colonial government business took place. In that part of High Street, you could cash a check at the Treasury, read a book in the library, post a letter at the post office, appear before a magistrate in court. (Since we were ruled by the English, we also had their laws. There was a law against using abusive language. Can you imagine such a law among people for whom making a spectacle of yourself through speech is everything? When West Indians went to England, the police there had to get a glossary of bad West Indian words so they could understand whether they were hearing abusive language or not.) It was in that same part of High Street that you could get a passport in another government office. In the middle of High Street was the Barclays Bank. The Barclay brothers, who started Barclays Bank, were slave traders. That is how they made their money. When the English outlawed the slave trade, the Barclay brothers went into banking. It made them even richer. It's possible that when they saw how rich banking made them, they gave themselves a good beating for opposing an end to slave trading (for surely they would have opposed that), but then again, they may have been visionaries and agitated for an end to slavery, for look at how rich they became with their banks borrowing from (through their savings) the descendants of the slaves and then lending back to them. But people just a little older than I am can recite the name of and the day the first black person was hired as a cashier at this very same Barclays Bank in Antigua. Do you ever wonder why some people blow things up? I can imagine that if my life had taken a certain turn, there would be the Barclays Bank, and there I would be, both of us in ashes. Do you ever try to understand why people like me cannot get over the past, cannot forgive and cannot forget? There is the Barclays Bank. The Barclay brothers are dead. The human beings they traded, the human beings who to them were only commodities, are dead. It should not have been that they came to the same end, and heaven is not enough of a reward for one or hell enough of a punishment for the other. People who think about these things believe that every bad deed, even every bad thought, carries with it its own retribution. So do you see the queer thing about people like me? Sometimes we hold your retribution.

And then there was another place, called the Mill Reef Club. It was built by some people from North America who wanted to live in Antigua and spend their holidays in Antigua but who seemed not to like Antiguans (black people) at all, for the Mill Reef Club declared itself completely private, and the only Antiguans (black people) allowed to go there were servants. People can recite the name of the first Antiguan (black person) to eat a sandwich at the clubhouse and the day on which it happened; people can recite the name of the first Antiguan (black person) to play golf on the golf course and the day on which the event took place. In those days, we Antiguans thought that the people at the Mill Reef Club had such bad manners, like pigs; they were

behaving in a bad way, like pigs. There they were, strangers in someone else's home, and then they refused to talk to their hosts or have
anything human, anything intimate, to do with them. I believe they
gave scholarships to one or two bright people each year so they could
go overseas and study; I believe they gave money to children's chari-
ties; these things must have made them seem to themselves very big
and good, but to us there they were, pigs living in that sty (the Mill
Reef Club). And what were these people from North America, these
people from England, these people from Europe, with their bad behavior, doing on this little island? For they so enjoyed behaving badly, as
if there was pleasure immeasurable to be had from not acting like a
human being. Let me tell you about a man; trained as a dentist, he took
it on himself to say he was a doctor, specializing in treating children's
illnesses. No one objected—certainly not us. He came to Antigua as a
refugee (running away from Hitler) from Czechoslovakia. This man
hated us so much that he would send his wife to inspect us before we
were admitted into his presence, and she would make sure that we
didn't smell, that we didn't have dirt under our fingernails, and that
nothing else about us—apart from the color of our skin—would of-
fend the doctor. (I can remember once, when I had whooping cough
and I took a turn for the worse, that my mother, before bundling me
up and taking me off to see this man, examined me carefully to see that
I had no bad smells or dirt in the crease of my neck, behind my ears, or
anywhere else. Every horrible thing that a housefly could do was
known by heart to my mother, and in her innocence she thought that
she and the doctor shared the same crazy obsession—germs.) Then
there was a headmistress of a girls' school, hired through the colonial
office in England and sent to Antigua to run this school which only in
my lifetime began to accept girls who were born outside a marriage; in
Antigua it had never dawned on anyone that this was a way of keeping
black children out of this school. This woman was twenty-six years
old, not too long out of university, from Northern Ireland, and she
told these girls over and over again to stop behaving as if they were
monkeys just out of trees. No one ever dreamed that the word for any
of this was racism. We thought these people were ill-mannered and we

were so surprised by this, for they were far away from their home, and we believed that the farther away you were from your home the better you should behave. (This is because if your bad behavior gets you in trouble you have your family not too far off to help defend you.) We thought they were un-Christianlike; we thought they were small-minded; we thought they were like animals, a bit below human standards as we understood those standards to be. We felt superior to all these people; we thought that perhaps the English among them who behaved this way weren't English at all, for the English were supposed to be civilized, and this behavior was so much like that of an animal, the thing we were before the English rescued us, that maybe they weren't from the real England at all but from another England, one we were not familiar with, not at all from the England we were told about, not at all from the England we could never be from, the England that was so far away, the England that not even a boat could take us to, the England that, no matter what we did, we could never be of. We felt superior, for we were so much better behaved and we were full of grace, and these people were so badly behaved and they were so completely empty of grace. (Of course, I now see that good behavior is the proper posture of the weak, of children.) We were taught the names of the Kings of England. In Antigua, the twenty-fourth of May was a holiday—Queen Victoria's official birthday. We didn't say to ourselves, Hasn't this extremely unappealing person been dead for years and years? Instead, we were glad for a holiday. Once, at dinner (this happened in my present life), I was sitting across from an Englishman, one of those smart people who know how to run things that England still turns out but who now, since the demise of the empire, have nothing to do; they look so sad, sitting on the rubbish heap of history. I was reciting my usual litany of things I hold against England and the English, and to round things off I said, "And do you know that we had to celebrate Queen Victoria's birthday?" So he said that every year, at the school he attended in England, they marked the day she died. I said, "Well, apart from the fact that she belonged to you and so anything you did about her was proper, at least you knew she died." So that was England to us—Queen Victoria and the glorious day of her coming into the world, a beautiful place, a blessed place, a living and blessed thing, not the ugly, piggish individuals we met. I cannot tell you how angry it makes me to hear people from North America tell me how much they love England, how beautiful England is, with its traditions. All they see is some frumpy, wrinkled-up person passing by in a carriage waving at a crowd. But what I see is the millions of people, of whom I am just one, made orphans: no motherland, no fatherland, no gods, no mounds of earth for holy ground, no excess of love which might lead to the things that an excess of love sometimes brings, and worst and most painful of all, no tongue. (For isn't it odd that the only language I have in which to speak of this crime is the language of the criminal who committed the crime? And what can that really mean? For the language of the criminal can contain only the goodness of the criminal's deed. The language of the criminal can explain and express the deed only from the criminal's point of view. It cannot contain the horror of the deed, the injustice of the deed, the agony, the humiliation inflicted on me. When I say to the criminal, "This is wrong, this is wrong, this is wrong," or, "This deed is bad, and this other deed is bad, and this one is also very, very bad," the criminal understands the word "wrong" in this way: it is wrong when "he" doesn't get his fair share of profits from the crime just committed; he understands the word "bad" in this way: a fellow criminal betrayed a trust. That must be why, when I say, "I am filled with rage," the criminal says, "But why?" And when I blow things up and make life generally unlivable for the criminal (is my life not unlivable, too?) the criminal is shocked, surprised. But nothing can erase my rage—not an apology, not a large sum of money, not the death of the criminal—for this wrong can never be made right, and only the impossible can make me still: can a way be found to make what happened not have happened? And so look at this prolonged visit to the bile duct that I am making, look at how bitter, how dyspeptic just to sit and think about these things makes me. I attended a school named after a Princess of England. Years and years later, I read somewhere that this Princess made her tour of the West Indies (which included Antigua, and on that tour she dedicated my school) because she had fallen in love with a married man, and since she was not allowed to marry a divorced man she was sent to visit us to get over her affair with him. How well I remember that all of Antigua turned out to see this Princess person, how every building that she would enter was repaired and painted so that it looked brand-new, how every beach she would sun herself on had to look as if no one had ever sunned there before (I wonder now what they did about the poor sea? I mean, can a sea be made to look brand-new?), and how everybody she met was the best Antiguan body to meet, and no one told us that this person we were putting ourselves out for on such a big scale, this person we were getting worked up about as if she were God Himself, was in our midst because of something so common, so everyday: her life was not working out the way she had hoped, her life was one big mess. Have I given you the impression that the Antigua I grew up in revolved almost completely around England? Well, that was so. I met the world through England, and if the world wanted to meet me it would have to do so through England.

Are you saying to yourself, "Can't she get beyond all that, everything happened so long ago, and how does she know that if things had been the other way around her ancestors wouldn't have behaved just as badly, because, after all, doesn't everybody behave badly given the opportunity?"

Our perception of this Antigua—the perception we had of this place ruled by these bad-minded people—was not a political perception. The English were ill-mannered, not racists; the school headmistress was especially ill-mannered, not a racist; the doctor was crazy—he didn't even speak English properly, and he came from a strangely named place, he also was not a racist; the people at the Mill Reef Club were puzzling (why go and live in a place populated mostly by people you cannot stand), not racists.

Have you every wondered to yourself why it is that all people like me seem to have learned from you is how to imprison and murder each other, how to govern badly, and how to take the wealth of our country and place it in Swiss bank accounts? Have you ever wondered why it is that all we seem to have learned from you is how to corrupt our societies and how to be tyrants? You will have to accept that this is mostly your fault. Let me just show you how you looked to us. You came. You took things that were not yours, and you did not even, for appearances' sake, ask first. You could have said, "May I have this, please?" and even though it would have been clear to everybody that a yes or no from us would have been of no consequence you might have looked so much better. Believe me, it would have gone a long way. I would have had to admit that at least you were polite. You murdered people. You imprisoned people. You robbed people. You opened your own banks and you put our money in them. The accounts were in your name. The banks were in your name. There must have been some good people among you, but they stayed home. And that is the point. That is why they are good. They stayed home. But still, when you think about it, you must be a little sad. The people like me, finally, after years and years of agitation, made deeply moving and eloquent speeches against the wrongness of your domination over us, and then finally, after the mutilated bodies of you, your wife, and your children were found in your beautiful and spacious bungalow at the edge of your rubber plantation—found by one of your many house servants (none of it was ever yours; it was never, ever yours)—you say to me, "Well, I wash my hands of all of you, I am leaving now," and you leave, and from afar you watch as we do to ourselves the very things you used to do to us. And you might feel that there was more to you than that, you might feel that you had understood the meaning of the Age of Enlightenment (though, as far as I can see, it had done you very little good); you loved knowledge, and wherever you went you made sure to build a school, a library (yes, and in both of these places you distorted or erased my history and glorified your own). But then again, perhaps as you observe the debacle in which I now exist, the utter ruin that I say is my life, perhaps you are remembering that you had always felt people like me cannot run things, people like me will never grasp the idea of Gross National Product, people like me will never be able to take command of the thing the most simpleminded among you can master, people like me will never understand the notion of rule by law, people like me cannot really think in abstractions, people like me cannot be objective, we make everything so personal. You will forget your part in the whole setup, that bureaucracy is one of your inventions, that Gross National Product is one of your inventions, and all the laws that you know mysteriously favor you. Do you know why people like me are shy about being capitalists? Well, it's because we, for as long as we have known you, *were* capital, like bales of cotton and sacks of sugar, and you were the commanding, cruel capitalists, and the memory of this is so strong, the experience so recent, that we can't quite bring ourselves to embrace this idea that you think so much of. As for what we were like before we met you, I no longer care. No periods of time over which my ancestors held sway, no documentation of complex civilizations, is any comfort to me. Even if I really came from people who were living like monkeys in trees, it was better to be that than what happened to me, what I became after I met you.

Vital Signs

Natalie Kusz

I. In Hospital

I was always waking up, in those days, to the smell of gauze soaked with mucus and needing to be changed. Even when I cannot recall what parts of me were bandaged then, I remember vividly that smell, a sort of fecund, salty, warm one like something shut up and kept alive too long in a dead space. Most of the details I remember from that time are smells, and the chancest whiff from the folds of surgical greens or the faint scent of ether on cold fingers can still drag me, reflexively, back to that life, to flux so familiar as to be a constant in itself. Years after Children's Hospital, when I took my own daughter in for stitches in her forehead, and two men unfolded surgical napkins directly under my nose, I embarrassed us all by growing too weak to stand, and had to sit aside by myself until all the work was over.

It seems odd that these smells have power to bring back such horror, when my memories of that time are not, on the whole, dark ones. Certainly I suffered pain, and I knew early a debilitating fear of surgery itself, but the life I measured as months inside and months outside the walls was a good one, and bred in me understandings that I would not relinquish now.

There was a playroom in the children's wing, a wide room full of light, with colored walls and furniture, and carpets on the floor. A wooden kitchen held the corner alongside our infirmary, and my friends and I passed many hours as families, cooking pudding for our dolls before they were due in therapy. Most of the dolls had amputated arms and legs, or had lost their hair to chemotherapy, and when we put on our doctors' clothes we taught them to walk with prostheses, changing their dressings with sterile gloves.

We had school tables, and many books, and an ant farm by the window so we could care for something alive. And overseeing us all was Janine, a pink woman, young even to seven-year-old eyes, with yellow, cloudy hair that I touched when I could. She kept it long, parted in the middle, or pulled back in a ponytail like mine before the accident. My hair had been blond then, and I felt sensitive now about the coarse brown stubble under my bandages. Once, on a thinking day, I told Janine that if I had hair like hers I would braid it and loop the pigtails around my ears. She wore it like that the next day, and every day after for a month.

Within Janine's playroom, we were some of us handicapped, but none disabled, and in time we were each taught to prove this for ourselves. While I poured the flour for new Play-Doh, Janine asked me about my kindergarten teacher: what she had looked like with an eye patch, and if she was missing my same eye. What were the hard parts, Janine said, for a teacher like that? Did I think it was sad for her to miss school sometimes, and did she talk about the hospital? What color was her hair, what sort was her eye patch, and did I remember if she was pretty? What would I be, Janine asked, when I was that age and these surgeries were past? Over the wet salt smell of green dough, I wished to be a doctor with one blue eye, who could talk like this to the sick, who could tell them they were still real. And with her feel for when to stop talking, Janine turned and left me, searching out volunteers to stir up new clay.

She asked a lot of questions, Janine did, and we answered her as we would have answered ourselves, slowly and with purpose. When called to, Janine would even reverse her words, teaching opposite lessons to clear the mist in between; this happened for Thomas and Nick in their wheelchairs, and I grew as much older from watching as they did from being taught. Both boys were eleven, and though I've forgotten their histories, I do remember their natures, the differences that drew them together.

They were roommates and best friends, and their dispositions reverberated within one another, the self-reliant and the needy. Thomas was the small one, the white one, with blue veins in his forehead and pale hair falling forward on one side. He sat always leaning on his elbows, both shoulders pressing up around his ears, and he rested his head to the side when he talked. He depended on Nick, who was tight-shouldered and long, to take charge for him, and he asked for help with his eyes half open, breathing out words through his mouth. And Nick reached the far shelves and brought Thomas books, and proved he could do for them both, never glancing for help at those who stood upright. His skin was darker than Thomas's, and his eyes much lighter, the blue from their centers washing out into the white.

When they played together, those boys, Thomas was the small center of things, the thin planet sunken into his wheelchair, pulling his friend after him. It must not have seemed to Nick that he was being pulled, because he always went immediately to Thomas's aid, never expecting anyone else to notice. Janine, of course, did. When Thomas wanted the television switched, and Nick struggled up to do it, she said, "Nick, would you like me to do that?"

"I can do it," he said.

"But so can I," Janine said, and she strode easily to the television and turned the knob to *Sesame Street*. "Sometimes," she said to Nick, "you have to let your friends be kind; it makes them feel good." She went back to sit beside Thomas, and she handed him the Erector set. How would he turn the channel, she said, if no one else was here? What could he do by himself? And as the TV went unnoticed, Thomas imagined a machine with gears and little wheels, and Janine said she thought it could work. After that, Thomas was always building, though he still asked for help, and he still got it. Nick never did ask, as long as I knew him, but in time he managed to accept what was offered, and even, in the end, to say thanks.

               In this way and in others, Janine encouraged us to change. When we had new ideas, they were outstanding ones, and we could count almost always on her blessing. We planned wheel-chair races, and she donated the trophy—bubble-gum ice cream all around. When she caught us blowing up surgical gloves we had found in the trash, she swiped a whole case of them, conjuring a helium bottle besides; that afternoon the playroom smelled of synthetic, powdery rubber, and we fought at the tables over colored markers, racing to decorate the brightest balloon. Janine's was the best—a cigar-smoking man with a four-spiked mohawk—and she handed it down the table to someone's father.

     She always welcomed our parents in, so long as they never inter-fered, and they respected the rule, and acted always unsurprised. When Sheldon's mother arrived one day, she found her son—a four-year-old born with no hands—up to his elbows in orange finger paints. She stood for a moment watching, then offered calmly to mix up a new color.

     We children enjoyed many moments like these, granted us by adults like Janine and our parents, and these instants of contentment were luxuries we savored, but on which, by necessity, we did not count. I've heard my father, and other immigrant survivors of World War II, speak of behavior peculiar to people under siege, of how they live in terms not of years but of moments, and this was certainly true of our lives. That time was fragmentary, allowing me to remember it now only as a series of flashes, with the most lyrical event likely at any moment to be interrupted. We children were each at the hospital for critical reasons, and a game we planned for one day was likely to be missing one or two players the next, because Charlie hemorrhaged in the night, Sarah was in emergency surgery, or Candice's tubes had pulled out. I myself missed many outings on the lawn because my bone grafts rejected or because my eye grew so infected that I had to be quarantined. At these times, I would watch the others out the closed window, waiting for them to come stand beyond the sterile curtain and shout to me a summary of the afternoon.

In the same way that the future seemed—because it might never arrive—generally less important than did the present, so too was the past less significant. Although each of us children could have recited his own case history by heart, it was rare that any of us required more than a faint sketch of another child's past; we found it both interesting and difficult enough to keep a current daily record of who had been examined, tested, or operated on, and whether it had hurt, and if so, whether they had cried. This last question was always of interest to us, and tears we looked on as marks not of cowards but of heroes, playmates who had endured torture and lived to testify. The older a child was, the greater our reverence when her roommate reported back after an exam; we derived some perverse comfort from the fact that even twelve-year-olds cracked under pressure.

Those of us who did choose to abide vigorously in each instant were able to offer ourselves, during the day, to one another, to uphold that child or parent who began to weaken. If her need was to laugh, we laughed together; if to talk, we listened, and once, I remember, I stood a whole morning by the chair of a fifteen-year-old friend, combing her hair with my fingers, handing her Kleenex and lemon drops, saying nothing. At night, then, we withdrew, became quietly separate, spoke unguardedly with our families. We spent these evening hours regrouping, placing the days into perspective, each of us using our own methods of self-healing. My mother would read to me from the Book of Job, about that faithful and guiltless man who said, "The thing that I so greatly feared has come upon me," and she would grieve, as I learned later, for me and for us all. Or she would sit with me and write letters to our scattered family—my father at work in Alaska, my younger brother and sister with an aunt in Oregon. Of the letters that still exist from that time, all are full of sustenance, of words like "courage" and "honor." It should have sounded ludicrous to hear a seven-year-old speaking such words, but I uttered them without embarrassment, and my parents did not laugh.

For most of us, as people of crisis, it became clear that horror can last only a little while, and then it becomes commonplace. When one cannot be sure that there are many days left, each single day becomes as important as a year, and one does not waste an hour in wishing that that hour were longer, but simply fills it, like a smaller cup, as high as it will go without spilling over. Each moment, to the very ill, seems somehow slowed down and more dense with importance, in the same way that a poem is more compressed than a page of prose, each word carrying more weight than a sentence. And though it is true I learned gentleness, and the spareness of time, this was not the case for everyone there, and in fact there were some who never embraced their mortality.

I first saw Darcy by a window, looking down into her lap, fingering glass beads the same leafy yellow as her skin. She was wearing blue, and her dress shifted under her chin as she looked up, asking me was I a boy, and why was my hair so short. Behind us, our mothers started talking, exchanging histories, imagining a future, and Darcy and I listened, both grown accustomed by now to all this talk of ourselves. Darcy was ten, and she was here for her second attempted kidney transplant, this time with her father as donor. The first try had failed through fault, her mother said, of the surgeons, and Washington State's best lawyer would handle the suit if anything went wrong this time. This threat was spoken loudly and often as long as I knew Darcy, and it was many years before I realized that her parents were afraid, and that they displayed their fear in anger and those thousand sideways glances at their daughter.

As a playmate, Darcy was pleasant, and she and I made ourselves jewelry from glitter and paste, and dressed up as movie stars or as rich women in France. We played out the future as children do, as if it were sure to come and as if, when it did, we would be there. It was a game we all played on the ward, even those sure to die, and it was some time before I knew that to Darcy it was not a game, that she believed it all. We were holding school, and Nick was the teacher, and Darcy was answering that when she grew up she would own a plane, and would give us free rides on the weekends.

"What if," Nick said to her, "what if you die before then?"

Darcy breathed in and out once, hard, and then she said, "I'm telling my mother you said that." Then she stood and left the playroom, and did not come back that day. Later, her father complained to Nick's, called him foolish and uncaring, and demanded that such a thing not happen again.

After that, Darcy came to play less often, and when she did, her parents looked on, even on days when Janine took us outside to look at the bay. Darcy grew fretful, and cried a good deal, and took to feeling superior, even saying that my father didn't love me or he wouldn't be in Alaska. When I forgave her, it was too late to say so, because I was gone by then and didn't know how to tell her.

Darcy's absence was a loss, not just to her but to us other children as well. Just as we had no chance to comfort her, to offer our hands when she was weak, we could not count on her during our worst times, for she and her family suffered in that peculiar way that admits no fellowship. I don't remember, if I ever knew, what became of Darcy, because I came down with chicken pox and was discharged so as not to jeopardize her transplant. I like to think she must have lived, it was so important to her, and as I think this, I hope she did survive, and that one day she grew, as we all did in some way, to be thankful.

One of my smallest teachers during this time was a leukemia patient, just three years old, who lived down the hall. Because of his treatments, Samuel had very little hair, and what he did have was too blond to see. There were always, as I remember, deep moons under his eyes, but somehow, even to us other children, he was quite beautiful. His teeth were very tiny in his mouth, and he chuckled rather than laughed out loud; when he cried, he only hummed, drawing air in and out his nose, with his eyes squeezed shut and tears forming in the cracks where there should have been lashes. Most children's wards have a few favorite patients, and Samuel was certainly among ours. Those few afternoons when his parents left the hospital together, they spent twenty minutes, on their return, visiting every room to find who had taken off with their son. More often than not, he was strapped to a lap in a wheelchair, his IV bottle dangling overhead like an antenna, getting motocross rides from an amputee.

Samuel possessed, even for his age, and in spite of the fact that he was so vulnerable, an implicit feeling of security, and it was partly this sense of trust that lent him that dignity I have found in few grown people. His mother, I remember, was usually the one to draw him away from our games when it was time for treatments, and, although he knew what was coming, he never ran from it; when he asked his mother, "Do I have to?" it was not a protest but a question, and when she replied that yes, this was necessary, he would accept her hand and leave the playroom on his feet.

I have heard debate over whether terminally ill children know they are going to die, and I can't, even after knowing Samuel, answer this question. We all, to some extent, knew what death was, simply because each of us had been friends with someone who was gone, and we realized that at some point many of us were likely to die; this likelihood was enough certainty for us, and made the question of time and date too insignificant to ask. I remember the last day I spent with Samuel, how we all invited him for a picnic on the lawn, though he could not eat much. He had had treatments that morning, which made him weak, made his smile very tired, but this was the same vulnerability we had always found charming, and I can't recall anything about that after-noon that seemed unusual. The rest of us could not know that Samuel would die before we woke up next morning, and certainly some things might have been different if we had; but I tend to think we would still have had the picnic, would still have rubbed dandelion petals into our skin, would still have taught Samuel to play slapjack. And, for his part, Samuel would, as he did every day, have bent down to my wrist and traced the moon-shaped scar behind my hand.

I I .   A t t a c k

Our nearest neighbors through the trees were the Turners, two cabins of cousins whose sons went to my school. Both families had

moved here, as we had, from California, escaping the city and everything frightening that lived there. One of the women, Ginny, had a
grown son who was comatose now since he was hit on the freeway,
and she had come to Alaska to get well from her own mental breakdown, and to keep herself as far away as she could from automobiles.

Brian and Jeff Turner were my best friends then, and we played
with our dogs in the cousins' houses or in the wide, snowy yard in
between. On weekends or days off from school, my parents took us
sledding and to the gravel pit with our skates. Sometimes, if the day
was long enough, Brian and Jeff and I followed rabbit tracks through
the woods, mapping all the new trails we could find, and my mother
gave me orders about when to be home. Bears, she said, and we
laughed, and said didn't she know they were asleep, and we could all
climb trees anyway. We were not afraid, either, when Mom warned of
dog packs. Dogs got cabin fever, too, she said, especially in the cold.
They ran through the woods, whole crowds of them, looking for
someone to gang up on.

That's okay, I told her. We carried pepper in our pockets in case of
dogs: sprinkle it on their noses, we thought, and the whole pack would
run away.

In December, the day before my birthday, when the light was dim
and the days shorter than we had known before, Dad got a break at the
union hall, a job at Prudhoe Bay that would save us just in time, before
the stove oil ran out and groceries were gone. Mom convinced us
children that he was off on a great adventure, that he would see foxes
and icebergs, that we could write letters for Christmas and for New
Year's, and afford new coats with feathers inside. In this last I was not
much interested, because I had my favorite already—a red wool coat
that reversed to fake leopard—but I would be glad if this meant we
could get back from the pawnshop Dad's concertina, and his second
violin, and mine, the half-size with a short bow, and the guitar and
mandolin and rifles and pistol that had gone that way one by one.
Whether I played each instrument or not, it had been good to have
them around, smelling still of campfires and of songfests in the summer.

It was cold after Dad left, cold outside and cold in our house. Ice on the trailer windows grew thick and shaggy, and my sister and I melted handprints in it and licked off our palms. There had been no insulation when the add-on went up, so frost crawled the walls there, too, and Mom had us wear long johns and shoes unless we were in our beds. Brian and Jeff came for my birthday, helped me wish over seven candles, gave me a comb and a mirror. They were good kids, my mother said, polite and with good sense, and she told me that if I came in from school and she was not home, I should take Hobo with me and walk to their house. You're a worrywart, Mommy, I said. I'm not a baby, you know.

On January 10, only Hobo met me at the bus stop. In the glare from the school bus headlights his blue eye shone brighter than his brown, and he watched until I took the last step to the ground before tackling me in the snow. Most days, Hobo hid in the shadow of the spruce until Mom took my book bag, then he erupted from the dark to charge up behind me, run through my legs and on out the front. It was his favorite trick. I usually lost my balance and ended up sitting in the road with my feet thrown wide out front and steaming dog tongue all over my face.

Hobo ran ahead, then back, brushing snow crystals and fur against my leg. I put a hand on my skin to warm it and dragged nylon ski pants over the road behind me. Mom said to have them along in case the bus broke down, but she knew I would not wear them, could not bear the plastic sounds they made between my thighs.

No light was on in our house.

If Mom had been home, squares of yellow would have shown through the spruce and lit the fog of my breath, turning it bright as I passed through. What light there was now came from the whiteness of snow and from the occasional embers drifting up from our stovepipe. I laid my lunchbox on the top step and pulled at the padlock, slapping a palm on the door and shouting. Hobo jumped away from the noise and ran off, losing himself in darkness and in the faint keening dog sounds going up from over near the Turners' house. I called, "Hobo. Come back here, boy," and took to the path toward Brian's, tossing my ski pants to the storage tent as I passed.

At the property line, Hobo caught up with me and growled, and I fingered his ear, looking where he pointed, seeing nothing ahead there but the high curve and long sides of a Quonset hut, the work shed the Turners used also as a fence for one side of their yard. In the fall, Brian and Jeff and I had walked to the back of it, climbing over boxes and tools and parts of old furniture, and we had found in the corner a lemming's nest made from chewed bits of cardboard and paper, packed under the curve of the wall so that shadows hid it from plain sight. We all bent close to hear the scratching, and while Brian held a flashlight, I took two sticks and parted the rubbish until we saw the black eyes of a mother lemming and pink naked bodies of five babies. The mother dashed deeper into the pile and we scooped the nesting back, careful not to touch the sucklings for fear that their mama would eat them if they carried scent from our fingers.

The dogs were loud now beyond the Quonset, fierce in their howls and sounding many more than just three. Hobo crowded against my legs, and as I walked he hunched in front of me, making me stumble into a drift that filled my boots with snow. I called him a coward and said to quit it, but I held his neck against my thigh, turning the corner into the boys' yard and stopping on the edge. Brian's house was lit in all its windows, Jeff's was dark, and in the yard between them were dogs, new ones I had not seen before, each with its own house and tether. The dogs and their crying filled the yard, and when they saw me they grew wilder, hurling themselves to the ends of their chains, pulling their lips off their teeth. Hobo cowered and ran and I called him with my mouth, but my eyes did not move from in front of me.

There were seven. I knew they were huskies and meant to pull dogsleds, because earlier that winter Brian's grandfather had put on his glasses and shown us a book full of pictures. He had turned the pages with a wet thumb, speaking of trappers and racing people and the ways they taught these dogs to run. They don't feed them much, he said, or they get slow and lose their drive. This was how men traveled before they invented snowmobiles or gasoline.

There was no way to walk around the dogs to the lighted house.

The snow had drifted and been piled around the yard in heaps taller than I was, and whatever aisle was left along the sides was narrow and pitted with chain marks where the animals had wandered, dragging their tethers behind. No, I thought, Jeff's house was closest and out of biting range, and someone could, after all, be sitting home in the dark.

My legs were cold. The snow in my boots had packed itself around my ankles and begun to melt, soaking my socks and the felt liners under my heels. I turned toward Jeff's house, chafing my thighs together hard to warm them, and I called cheerfully at the dogs to shut up. Oscar said that if you met a wild animal, even a bear, you had to remember it was more scared than you were. Don't act afraid, he said, because they can smell fear. Just be loud—stomp your feet, wave your hands—and it will run away without even turning around. I yelled "Shut up" again as I climbed the steps to Jeff's front door, but even I could barely hear myself over the wailing. At the sides of my eyes, the huskies were pieces of smoke tumbling over one another in the dark.

The wood of the door was solid with cold, and even through deerskin mittens it bruised my hands like concrete. I cupped a hand to the window and looked in, but saw only black—black, and the reflection of a lamp in the other cabin behind me. I turned and took the three steps back to the ground; seven more and I was in the aisle between doghouses, stretching my chin far up above the frenzy, thinking hard on other things. This was how we walked in summertime, the boys and I, escaping from bad guys over logs thrown across ditches: step lightly and fast, steady on the hard parts of your soles, arms extended outward, palms down and toward the sound. That ditch, this aisle, was a river, a torrent full of silt that would fill your clothes and pull you down if you missed and fell in. I was halfway across. I pointed my chin toward the house and didn't look down.

On either side, dogs on chains hurled themselves upward, choking themselves to reach me, until their tethers jerked their throats back to earth. I'm not afraid of you, I whispered; this is dumb.

I stepped toward the end of the row and my arms began to drop slowly closer to my body. Inside the mittens, my thumbs were cold, as cold as my thighs, and I curled them in and out again. I was walking past the last dog and I felt brave, and I forgave him and bent to lay my mitten on his head. He surged forward on a chain much longer than I thought, leaping at my face, catching my hair in his mouth, shaking it in his teeth until the skin gave way with a jagged sound. My feet were too slow in my boots, and as I blundered backward, they tangled in the chain, burning my legs on metal. I called out at Brian's window, expecting rescue, angry that it did not come, and I beat my arms in front of me, and the dog was back again, pulling me down.

A hole was worn into the snow, and I fit into it, arms and legs drawn up in front of me. The dog snatched and pulled at my mouth, eyes, hair; his breath clouded the air around us, but I did not feel its heat, or smell the blood sinking down between hairs of his muzzle. I watched my mitten come off in his teeth and sail upward, and it seemed unfair then and very sad that one hand should freeze all alone; I lifted the second mitten off and threw it away, then turned my face back again, overtaken suddenly by loneliness. A loud river ran in my ears, dragging me under.

My mother was singing. *Lu-lee, lu-lay, thou little tiny child*, the song to the Christ child, the words she had sung, smoothing my hair, all my life before bed. Over a noise like rushing water I called to her and heard her answer back, Don't worry, just sleep, the ambulance is on its way. I drifted back out and couldn't know then what she prayed, that I would sleep on without waking, that I would die before morning.

She had counted her minutes carefully that afternoon, sure that she would get to town and back, hauling water and mail, with ten minutes to spare before my bus came. But she had forgotten to count one leg of the trip, had skidded up the drive fifteen minutes late, pounding a fist on the horn, calling me home. On the steps, my lunchbox had grown cold enough to burn her hands. She got the water, the groceries, and my brother and sisters inside, gave orders that no one touch the wood stove or open the door, and she left down the trail to Brian's, whistling Hobo in from the trees.

I know from her journal that Mom had been edgy all week about the crazed dog sounds next door. Now the new huskies leaped at her and Hobo rumbled warning from his chest. Through her sunglasses, the dogs were just shapes, indistinct in window light. She tried the dark cabin first, knocking hard on the windows, then turned and moved down the path between doghouses, feeling her way with her feet, kicking out at open mouths. Dark lenses frosted over from her breath, and she moved toward the house and the lights on inside.

"She's not here." Brian's mother held the door open and air clouded inward in waves. Mom stammered out thoughts of bears, wolves, dogs. Ginny grabbed on her coat. She had heard a noise out back earlier—they should check there and then the woods.

No luck behind the cabin and no signs under the trees. Wearing sunglasses and without any flashlight, Mom barely saw even the snow. She circled back and met Ginny under the window light. Mom looked that way and asked about the dogs. "They seem so hungry," she said.

Ginny said, "No. Brian's folks just got them last week, but the boys play with them all the time." All the same, she and Mom scanned their eyes over the kennels, looking through and then over their glasses. Nothing seemed different. "Are you sure she isn't home?" Ginny said. "Maybe she took a different trail."

Maybe. Running back with Ginny behind her, Mom called my name until her lungs frosted inside and every breath was a cough. The three younger children were still the only ones at home, and Mom handed them their treasure chests, telling them to play on the bed until she found Natalie. Don't go outside, she said. I'll be back right soon.

Back at the Turners', Ginny walked one way around the Quonset and Mom the other. Mom sucked air through a mitten, warming her lungs. While Ginny climbed over deeper snow, she approached the sled dogs from a new angle. In the shadow of one, a splash of red—the lining of my coat thrown open. "I've found her," she shouted, and thought as she ran, Oh, thank God. Thank, thank God.

The husky stopped its howling as Mom bent to drag me out from the hole. Ginny caught up and seemed to choke. "Is she alive?" she said.

Mom said, "I think so, but I don't know how." She saw one side of my face gone, one red cavity with nerves hanging out, scraps of dead leaves stuck on to the mess. The other eye might be gone, too; it was hard to tell. Scalp had been torn away from my skull on that side, and the gashes reached to my forehead, my lips, had left my nose ripped wide at the nostrils. She tugged my body around her chest and carried me inside.

III. Vital Signs

I had little knowledge of my mother's experience of the accident until many months afterward, and even then I heard her story only after I had told mine, after I had shown how clearly I remembered the dogs, and their chains, and my own blood on the snow—and had proven how little it bothered me to recall them. When I said I had heard her voice, and named for her the songs she had sung to me then, my mother searched my face, looking into me hard, saying, "I can't believe you remember." She had protected me all along, she said, from her point of view, not thinking that I might have kept my own, and that mine must be harder to bear. But after she knew all this, Mom felt she owed me a history, and she told it to me then, simply and often, in words that I would draw on long after she was gone.

She said that inside the Turners' cabin, she laid me on Ginny's couch, careful not to jar the bleeding parts of me, expecting me to wake in an instant and scream. But when I did become conscious, it was only for moments, and I was not aware then of my wounds, or of the cabin's warmth, or even of pressure from the fingers of Brian's grandfather, who sat up close and stroked the frozen skin of my hands.

Ginny ordered Brian and Jeff to their room, telling them to stay there until she called them, and then she stood at Mom's shoulder, staring down and swaying on her legs.

Mom looked up through her glasses and said, "Is there a phone to call an ambulance?"

Ginny was shaking. "Only in the front house, kid, and it's

locked," she said. "Kathy should be home in a minute, but I'll try to break in." She tugged at the door twice before it opened, and then she went out, leaving my mother to sing German lullabies beside my ear. *When morning comes,* the words ran, *if God wills it, you will wake up once more.* My mother sang the words and breathed on me, hoping I would dream again of summertime, all those bright nights when the music played on outside, when she drew the curtains and sang us to sleep in the trailer. Long years after the accident, when she felt healed again and stronger, Mom described her thoughts to me, and when she did she closed her eyes and sat back, saying, "You can't know how it was to keep singing, to watch air bubble up where a nose should have been, and to pray that each of those breaths was the last one." Many times that night she thought of Job, who also had lived in a spacious, golden land, who had prospered in that place, yet had cried in the end, "The thing that I so greatly feared has come upon me." The words became a chant inside her, filling her head and bringing on black time.

The wait for the ambulance was a long one, and my mother filled the time with her voice, sitting on her heels and singing. She fingered my hair and patted my hands and spoke low words when I called out. Brian's grandfather wept and warmed my fingers in his, and Mom wondered where were my mittens, and how were her other children back home.

Ginny came back and collapsed on a chair, and Kathy, her sister-in-law, hurried in through the door. Ginny began to choke, rocking forward over her knees, telling Kathy the story. Her voice stretched into a wail that rose and fell like music. "It's happening again," she said. "No matter where you go, it's always there."

Kathy brought out aspirin, then turned and touched my mother's arm. She said that as soon as Ginny was quiet, she would leave her here and fetch my siblings from the trailer.

"Thank you," Mom told her. "I'll send someone for them as soon as I can." She looked at Ginny then, wishing she had something to give her, some way to make her know that she was not to blame here; but for now Mom felt that Ginny had spoken truth when she said that sorrow followed us everywhere, and there was little else she could add.

The ambulance came, and then everything was movement. I drifted awake for a moment as I was lifted to a stretcher and carried toward the door. I felt myself swaying in air, back and forth and back again. Brian's whisper carried over the other voices in the room, as if blown my way by strong wind. "Natalie's dying," he said; then his words were lost among other sounds, and I faded out again. A month later, when our first-grade class sent me a box full of valentines, Brian's was smaller than the rest, a thick white heart folded in two. Inside it read, "I love you, Nataly. Pleas dont die." When I saw him again, his eyes seemed very big, and I don't remember that he ever spoke to me anymore.

It was dark inside the ambulance, and seemed even darker to my mother, squinting through fog on her sunglasses. She badgered the medic, begging him to give me a shot for pain. Any minute I would wake up, she said, and I would start to scream. The man kept working, taking my pulse, writing it down, and while he did, he soothed my mother in low tones, explaining to her about physical shock, about the way the mind estranges itself from the body and stands, unblinking and detached, on the outside. "If she does wake up," he said, "she'll feel nothing. She won't even feel afraid." When Mom wrote this in her journal, her voice was filled with wonder, and she asked what greater gift there could be.

At the hospital there were phone calls to be made, and Mom placed them from outside the emergency room. First she called Dick and Esther Conger, two of the only summertime friends who had stayed here over winter. We had met this family on the way up the Alcan, had been attracted to their made-over school bus with its sign, DESTINATION: ADVENTURE, and to the Alaskan license plates bolted to each bumper. Sometime during the drive up, or during the summer when we shared the same campfires, the children of our families had become interchangeable; Toni and Barry were in the same age group as we were, and discipline and praise were shared equally among us all. It was never shocking to wake up in the morning and find Toni and Barry in one of our beds; we just assumed that the person who belonged there was over sleeping in their bus. Now, as my mother explained the accident to Dick, our friend began to cry, saying, "Oh, Verna. Oh, no," and Esther's voice in the background asked, "What's happened? Let me talk to her." Mom asked the Congers to drive out for my brother and sisters, to watch them until my father came.

Leaning her head to the wall, Mom telephoned a message to the North Slope. She spoke to Dad's boss there, explaining only that "our daughter has been hurt." Just now, she thought, she couldn't tell the whole story again, and besides, the worst "hurt" my father would imagine could not be this bad. The crew boss said a big snowstorm was coming in, but they would try to fly my father out beforehand; if not, they would get him to the radio phone and have him call down. A nurse walked up then and touched Mom's shoulder, saying, "Your daughter is awake, and she's asking for you." A moment before, Mom had been crying, pressing a fist to her teeth, but now she closed up her eyes like a faucet and walked after the nurse, pulling up her chin and breathing deeply in her chest. She had trembled so that she could hardly wipe her glasses, but when she moved through the door and saw the white lights and me lying flat on a table, she was suddenly calm, and the skin grew warmer on her face.

Mom positioned herself in front of my one eye, hoping as she stood there that she wasn't shaking visibly, that her face was not obviously tense. She need not have bothered; as I lay staring right to where my eye veered off, the room was smoky gray, and I was conscious only of a vicious thirst that roughened the edges of my tongue, made them stick to my teeth. I was allowed no water, had become fretful, and when my mother spoke to me, I complained that the rag in my mouth had not been damp enough, and that these people meant to cut my favorite coat off me. I have to think now that my mother acted courageously, keeping her face smooth, listening to me chatter about school, about the message I had brought from my teacher, that they would skip me to the second grade on Monday. Mom's answers were light, almost vague, and before she left the pre-op room, she told me to listen to the nurses, to let them do all they needed to; they were trying to help me, she said. A little later, after I was wheeled into surgery, a nurse handed her the things they had saved: my black boots and the Alice in Wonderland watch Mom had given me for Christmas.

My mother made more phone calls, to churches in town and to ones in California that we'd left behind, telling the story over again, asking these people to pray. Old friends took on her grief, asking did she need money, telling her to call again when she knew more. These people knew, as my mother did, that money was not so much the question now, but it was something they could offer, and so they did. And for months and years after this they would send cards and letters and candy and flowers and toys, making themselves as present with us as they could. For now, on this first night, they grieved with my mother, and they said to go lie down if she could, they would take over the phones. And each of these people made another call, and another, until, as my mother walked back to the waiting room, she knew she was lifted up by every friend we had ever made.

The Turners had arrived, and for a little while they all sat along the waiting room walls, stuffing fists into their pockets and closing their eyes. None of them wanted to talk about the accident, or to wonder about the progress in surgery, and when my mother said to Kathy, "I just talked to some people in California who would never *believe* the way we live here," her words seemed terribly funny, and started the whole room laughing. It wasn't so much, she said later, that they were forgetting why they were there; in fact, they remembered very well— so well that, compared to that fact, everything else was hilarious. And they could not possibly have continued for as long as they had been, she said, pressing their backs to the walls and waiting. So for hours after Mom's joke, and far into the night, the adults invented names for our kind—"the outhouse set," "the bush league"—and they contributed stories about life in Alaska that would shock most of the people Outside. They joked about Styrofoam outhouse seats—the only kind that did not promote frostbite—about catalogs that no one could afford to buy from, but whose pages served a greater purpose, about the tremendous hardship of washing dishes from melted snow and then tossing the gray water out the door. From time to time, Ginny got up from her seat to walk alone in the hall, but when she came back in she was ready again to laugh.

My father arrived about midnight, dressed in a week's growth of beard and in an army surplus parka and flight pants. Mom met him in the hall and stood looking up; Dad dropped his satchel to the floor, panting, and he watched my mother's face, the eyes behind her glasses. He spoke first, said his was the last plane out in a heavy snowstorm. Then: "How did it happen," he said. "Did she fall out the door?"

My mother waited a beat and looked at him. "It wasn't a car accident, Julius," she said. She started telling the story again, and my father looked down then at the blood crusted on her sweater, and he closed his eyes and leaned into the wall. My mother told him, "You can't appreciate how I feel, because you haven't seen her face. But I wish that when you pray you'd ask for her to die soon."

Dad opened his eyes. "That must seem like the best thing to ask," he said. "But we don't make decisions like that on our own. We never have, and we can't start now."

Sometime after two A.M., my three surgeons stepped in. My mother said later that had they not still worn their surgical greens, she would not have recognized them; during the night she had forgotten their faces.

The men sagged inside their clothes, three sets of shoulders slumped forward under cloth. I was still alive, they said, but only barely, and probably not for long. I had sustained over one hundred lacerations from the shoulders up, and had lost my left cheekbone along with my eye. They'd saved what tissue they could, filling the bulk of the cavity with packings, and what bone fragments they found were now wired together on the chance that some of them might live.

My father groped for a positive word. "At least she doesn't have brain damage. I heard she was lucid before surgery."

Dr. Butler brushed the surgical cap from his head and held it, twisting it in his hands. His eyes were red as he looked up, explaining as kindly as it seemed he could. A dog's mouth, he said, was filthy, filthier than sewage, and all of that impurity had passed into my body. They had spent four hours just cleaning out the wounds, pulling out dirt and old berry leaves and dog feces. Even with heavy antibiotics, I would likely have massive infections, and they would probably spread into my brain. His voice turned hoarse and he looked across at Dr. Earp, asking the man to continue.

Dr. Earp rubbed hard at the back of his head and spoke softly, working his neck. For now, Dr. Earp said, they had been able to reconstruct the eyelids; that would make the biggest visible difference.

On my parents' first hourly visit to intensive care, Mom stopped at the door and put her hand to my father's chest. "No matter how she looks," she said, "don't react. She'll be able to tell what you're thinking."

The nurse at the desk sat under a shaded lamp, the only real light in the room. She stood and whispered that mine was the first bed to the left. "She wakes up for a minute or so at a time," she said. "She's been asking for you."

"First one on the left," my father said after her, a little too loud for that place, and from somewhere inside a great rushing river I heard him and called out. At my bed, Mom watched him as he stood looking down, and when the lines in his face became deeper, she turned from him, pinching his sleeve with her fingers. She walked closer to me and held the bedrail.

I V .   T h e   F e a r

It had to happen eventually, that I found a mirror and looked in. For the first days after my accident, I had stayed mostly in bed, leaning my bandages back on the pillow and peeling frostbite blisters from my hands. The new skin was pink, and much thinner than the old, as sensitive to touch as the nail beds I uncovered by chewing down to them. I had taken to running two fingers over stitches standing up like razor stubble on my face, then over the cotton that covered the right side and the rest of my head. The whole surgical team came in daily to lift me into a chair and unwind the gauze, releasing into the room a smell like old caves full of bones. And all this time I had never seen myself, never asked what was under there, in the place where my eye belonged.

I had asked my mother once if I would again see out of that eye. It was an hour after my dressings had been changed, and the smell of hot ooze still hovered in my room. Mom stood up and adjusted my bedrail. "Do you want your feet a little higher?" she said. "I can crank them up if you like."

I said, "Mommy, my eye. Will I be able to see from it?"

"Hang on," she said. "I need to use the little girls' room." She started to the door and I screamed after her, "Mommy, you're not answering me." But she was gone, and after that I did not ask.

Later, when the light was out, I lay back and looked far right, then left, concentrating hard, trying to feel the bandaged eye move. I thought I could feel it, rolling up and then down, ceiling to floor, matching its moves with my other eye. Even after I was grown, I could swear that I felt it blink when I pressed my two lids together.

Men from down the hall visited me during the day, rolling in on wheelchairs or walking beside their IV racks. They all wore two sets of pajamas, one wrong way forward so their backsides were covered. The hospital floor was old, its tiles starting to bubble, and the wheels on my friends' IV racks made rumbling sounds as they passed over. If a nurse passed by the door and looked in, the men waved her away, saying, "It's all right, dear. I'm visiting my granddaughter." For a kiss they gave me a sucker and a story about bears, or they carried me to a wheelchair and took me around to visit. In this way, I passed from room to room, brushing at the green curtains between beds, pouring water into plastic glasses, gathering hugs and learning to shake hands in the "cool" way. I signed plaster casts in big red letters, and I visited the baby room, pressing my chin to the glass.

On a day when I felt at my smallest and was in my bed still sleeping, one of my favorite men friends checked out, leaving on my nightstand a gift and a note that said he would miss me. The gift was a music box in pink satin, with a ballerina inside who pirouetted on her toes when I wound the key. And behind her inside the lid, a triangular-looking glass not much bigger than she was.

My mother came in behind me as I was staring into the mirror, holding it first from one angle, then from another, and she stood by the bed for a moment, saying nothing. When I turned, she was looking at me with her shoulders forward, and she seemed to be waiting.

"My eye is gone, isn't it?" I said.

She kept looking at me. She said, "Yes it is."

I turned again and lifted the box to my face. "I thought so," I said. "Those dogs were pretty mean."

I didn't understand, or was too small to know, what my mother thought she was protecting me from. It must be something very bad, I thought, for her to avoid every question I asked her. "Mommy," I said once, "I don't *feel* like I'm going to die."

She looked up from her book and the light shone off her glasses. She said, "Oh, no. You're certainly not going to do anything like that."

"Then will I be blind?"

"Well," she said. "You can see now, can't you?" And when I pressed her with more questions, she looked toward the door and said, "Shh. Here comes your lunch tray."

It all made me wonder if my wounds were much worse than everyone said—and of course they were, but there were long years of surgery still ahead, and no one wanted me to feel afraid. I was angry, too—as angry as a seven-year-old can be—that Mom patted my cheek with her palm and said she'd be taking my malemute to the pound before I came home. I stared at her then with my head up and sputtered out a peevish tirade, telling her I didn't hate all dogs, or even most dogs, but just the ones who bit me. It didn't occur to me until my own daughter was seven, the same age I was when I was hurt, that Mom might have been sending my dog away for her own sake.

V . Small Purchase

I have bought a one-eyed fish. As he drifts around the tank near my desk, his skin ripples silver like well-pressed silk, and he moves under the light and hovers with his one bronze eye turned toward me, waiting to be fed. His body is smooth and flat, like a silver dollar but twice the size, and his fins are mottled gold. He is a relative of the piranha, a meat eater with a bold round mouth, but even when the smaller fish challenge him, swishing their tails at his eye, he leaves them alone and swims off. He has not eaten one of them.

I call him Max, because my sister said I should. She did not remind me, when I brought him home, that I had wanted no pets, nothing with a life span shorter than my own, nothing that would die or have to be butchered as soon as I had given it a name. She just looked up with her face very serious as if she knew well how one could become attached to a fish, and she said to me, Max. Yes, that should be his name.

I had told us both, when I bought the aquarium, that fish were low-maintenance animals, without personalities and incapable of friendliness, and if one of them died you just flushed it away and got another. And besides, I said, I needed a fish tank. I had begun to feel stale, inert. I needed the sounds of moving water in my house, and I needed, too, something alive and interesting to stare at when I stopped typing to think of a new sentence.

Last summer, when I was tired and the writing was going badly, I got superstitious about the sea and thought that the lurch and pull of waves would freshen my ears and bring on clean thoughts. So I packed some books and a portable typewriter, drove to Homer on the coast, and rented a cabin near the beach. Something about the place, or its fishy air, or my aloneness in the middle of it worked somehow, and I breathed bigger there in my chest and wrote more clearly on the page.

I had forgotten about tides and about the kelp and dried crabs that came in with them, and every morning I shivered into a sweater, put combs in my hair, and walked out to wade and to fill my pockets with what I found. I liked it best when the wind was blowing and the sky was gray, and the sounds of sea gulls and my own breathing were carried out with the water.

Kelp pods washed up around my feet, and I stomped on them with tennis shoes to find what was inside. I collected driftwood, and urchins, and tiny pink clamshells dropped by gulls, thin enough to see through and smaller than a thumbnail. When the tide had gone far out, I climbed the bluff back to my cabin and sat writing in front of the window, eating cheese on bread and drinking orange spritzers or tea. The walls and windows there had space in between, and they let in shreds of wind and the arguing of birds and the metal smell of seaweed drying out on the beach. When the tide started back in, I took pen and notebook and sat on a great barnacled rock, letting water creep up and surround me, then jumping to shore just in time. An hour later, the rock would be covered, three feet or more under the gray, and I would know where it lay only because of the froth and swirl of whirlpools just above it.

When I came home I threw my bags on the bed and unfastened them, and a thousand aromas opened up then into my face, drifting out from the folds of my clothes, the seams in my shoes, the pages of my notebook. I had carried them back with me, the smells of wet sand and fish fins, of eagle feathers floating in surf, of candle wax burned at midnight and filled with the empty bodies of moths. I had grieved on the drive home for that place I was leaving, and for the cold wind of that beach, and I had decided that somehow water should move in my house, should rush and bubble in my ears, should bring in the sound of the sea, and the wind and dark currents that move it.

So I bought an aquarium, and fish to go in it, and a water pump strong enough to tumble the surface as it worked. I bought plants for the tank, and waved their smell into the room, and when I thought I was finished I made one more trip to a pet store, just to see what they had.

The shop was a small one, in an old wooden building with low ceilings, and the fish room in back was dark and smelled submarine— humid and slippery and full of live things. All light in the place came from the fish tanks themselves, and the plants inside them absorbed the glow and turned it green, casting it outward to move in shadowed patterns on my skin. When I closed my eyes, the sound was of rivers running out to the coast to be carried away mixed with salt. And the fish inside waved their fins and wandered between the rocks, opening and closing their mouths.

I glanced, but didn't look hard at the larger fish, because I had found already that they were always very expensive. I browsed instead through tetras and guppies, gouramis and cichlids, trying to be satisfied with the small ones, because after all, it was just the water and its motion that I really wanted. So when I saw the wide silver fish and a sign that said $10, I assumed it was a mistake but decided to ask about it while I ordered some neons dipped out. With my neck bent forward, I watched as fifty neons swam fast away from the net that would always catch them anyway. Was that big fish back there really only ten? I said.

The clerk said, "You mean the Matinnis with one eye. He's such a mellow guy."

I swung my head to look at her. One eye?

The woman stared at my face for a moment and opened her mouth. Her cheeks grew pinker, but when she answered me, her voice stayed even. She said, "Yes, his former owners thought he was a piranha and put him in the tank with some. They ate out one eye before anyone could get him back up."

"They go for the eyes so their lunch will quit looking at them," I said. I told the woman I would take the Matinnis. I thought we were a match, I said.

And I was right. As absurd as I felt about my affinity with a one-eyed fish, I found myself watching him for the ways he was like me, and I did find many. Max had already learned, by the time I got him, to hold his body in the water so that whatever he was interested in lay always on the same side of him as his eye. In the same way that I situate myself in movie theaters so that my best friend sits on my right side, Max turns his eye toward the wall of his tank, watching for my arm to move toward the food box. When I drop a worm cube down to him, he shifts his eye up to look at it and then swims at it from the side so he never loses it from vision. If the smaller fish fight, or behave defiantly around him, he turns his dead eye against them and flicks himself away to a far corner of the tank.

I don't know if it is normal to befriend a fish. I think probably not. I do know that as I sit by Max's tank and write, I stop sometimes and look up, and I think then that he looks terribly dashing, swimming around with his bad eye outward, unafraid that something might attack him from his blind side. I buy him special shrimp pellets, and I feed them to him one at a time, careful always to drop them past his good eye. My friends like to feed him, too, and I teach them how, warning them to drop his food where he can see it. Now one of my friends wants to introduce me to his neighbor's one-eyed dog, and another wishes she still had her one-eyed zebra finch so she could give it to me.

That's just what I need, I think—a houseful of blind-sided pets. We could sit around together and play wink-um, wondering was that a wink or just a lid shut down over a dry eyeball. We could fight about who got to sit on whose good side, or we could make jokes about how it takes two of us to look both ways before crossing the street. I laugh, but still I intend to meet the one-eyed dog, to see if he reminds me of Max—or of me. I wonder if he holds himself differently from other dogs, if when he hears a voice he turns his whole body to look.

And I wonder about myself, about what has changed in the world. At first, I wanted fish only for the water they lived in, for the movement it would bring to my house, the dust it would sweep from my brain. I thought of fish as "safe" pets, too boring to demand much attention, soulless by nature and indistinguishable from their peers. Maybe this is true for most of them. But I know that when the smaller fish chase after Max, or push him away from the food, I find myself fiercely angry. I take a vicious pleasure in dropping down shrimp pellets too big and too hard for the small ones to eat, and I find pleasure, too, in the way Max gobbles the food, working it to bits in his mouth. When he is finished, he turns a dead eye to the others and swims away, seeking things more interesting to look at.

Winter Work
Diary of a Day Laborer
DON J. SNYDER

Though winter was nearly a month away, the mornings were cold, and I would go to the beach and fill a canvas bag with wood to build a big fire in the living room so that when my four kids got up there would be one warm place where they could get dressed for school. This was better than turning on the furnace. I had lost my college teaching job eighteen months earlier. We were down to our last $200 the morning I saw what I thought at first was just a mirage that you sometimes see when the tide is out and the sunlight shimmers off the mud flats like ribbons of heat off a highway. It looked like hundreds and hundreds of wooden ladders standing on the ledges half a mile away. I kept walking until I got close enough to see clearly the enormous wooden frame of a structure that looked much too large to be a house.

We were living in one of the most beautiful places on earth, in a summer colony in Maine called Prouts Neck, a place made famous in

Winslow Homer's watercolors. On Labor Day, we had arrived ten minutes too soon, with everything we owned jammed into our rusted station wagon. Somehow a frying pan fell out of the rear window, startling the man who was putting suitcases into the trunk of his Mercedes. Soon workmen boarded up the other houses after their owners left for the great cities of the East, and we had the place to ourselves. We had picnics at the private beach club and rode bicycles over the boardwalk that ran through the bird sanctuary. It was like stumbling upon some wonderful set left behind by a summer stock theater. My five-year-old son and I trespassed at the golf course, stole balls from the rough, and sold them at the end of the road for a dollar apiece. On the clay tennis courts, I taught one daughter how to hit a decent serve.

I kept thinking I would find another teaching job, but eventually we reached the point where my wife, Colleen, stood in line for food stamps and I stood in line for work at the Maine employment office in Portland. In front of me a thin man in a ripped windbreaker with SPORTSMAN'S LOUNGE lettered across the back was yelling at the woman behind the counter, "I have my tools, I can do that job!" She held her ground, and the Vietnamese man behind me whispered sadly, "No address, no job." I had brought along *Herzog* by Saul Bellow and I pretended to be reading it, hoping to look careless. When it got to be my turn, the lady handed me a brochure that the city published with forty-seven helpful hints for the unemployed: "Have the cable disconnected from your television set. Look for coupons in the newspapers."

I waited for my interview and began writing out another budget in Bellow's novel. I'd written these budgets in neat columns of numbers in the margins of every book I'd read since I was fired, dividing the next year into monthly payments, subtracting it right out of existence. For rent, food, heat, electricity, telephone, and gas, $1,535 a month—a sum that should not be terrifying to a forty-four-year-old man.

I got home just after noon and was wiping the kitchen table, when Colleen came in carrying our three-year-old daughter, Cara, who was crying at the top of her lungs. "I slammed the door on her finger," Colleen said sorrowfully as she set Cara down on the counter and took off her blue mitten. Then I heard her scream. "Her finger came off! The top of her finger came off, Don!"

It was more than the bills for the emergency room and the hand surgeon that carried me back to the house to ask for a job. It was the memory of me just standing there in the kitchen inside my fears, taking all that time to feel sorry for myself while Colleen zipped Cara inside her down coat and ran outside into a snowstorm, heading for the hospital seven miles away.

I walked back to the house the next morning, very early, I guess to show whoever was in charge that he could count on me not to be late for work. A hard wind had kicked up big waves in the cove. I gazed across the rocks. The wood frame rose three stories from the foundation, each story twelve or fourteen feet high. I guessed the structure to be eighty feet by forty feet, with a roofline that was fifty feet from the ground. There were four carpenters climbing and descending like acrobats through the wooden frame and trailing long hoses behind them that supplied the air for their pneumatic hammers, which went off like gunshots in the stillness.

Before I walked out into view, I took off my woolen hat and scarf and stuffed them in my coat pockets to try and look like a guy who wasn't bothered by the weather.

Larry, the contractor, was working with a vibrating saw that he held like a machine gunner. He dropped the saw with disdain when he spotted me and swung down through the frame, jumping the final four feet. He looked happy and fit enough to build the place by himself, but I'd chosen the right day to hit him up for work. We stood talking in the midst of an equation that even his ferocious energy couldn't change: there was a mountain of a house left to build and a stretch of blistering cold days ahead in which to build it.

It would be outside work, all winter: there was the rest of the plywood sheathing, then the whole structure had to be wrapped, then the windows and doors, roof, trim, decks, and porches. He went through it all as if it would fall into place like it had a thousand times in his head. "Maybe a month and a half of shingling alone," he said. "Have you put on cedar shingles before?"

I lied to him for the first time. "It's a big house," I said, looking up to the roof.

"It's a dream," he said. He told me it was almost 13,000 square feet and that it might end up costing a million dollars to finish.

I liked him instantly and felt bad that I was going to have to hide from him the crushed disk in my back and everything that I didn't know about carpentry.

"We start at seven. Ten-hour days. I'll pay you fifteen dollars an hour," he said.

"I'll start tomorrow morning," I said.

"Just bring your carpenter's belt," he said as he jumped back onto the framed wall and began climbing. He was above my head when he called out, "You have a carpenter's belt?"

I lied to him again.

I hadn't earned a penny in eighteen months, but by the time I reached the electronic gate at the end of Winslow Homer Road, I was dreaming of buying Colleen a new dress and taking her out to dinner.

Later that day I took all four kids with me to Wal-Mart to buy a carpenter's belt. I tried it on for them and showed them the leather pockets for a tape measure and knife, the pouches for nails, and the clip that would hold my hammer. We gave Cara a ride on the mechanical horse. I'd spent a year trying to convince them that we weren't poor, just broke, and now I wanted them to see me spend some money.

When I got up the next morning, I turned the heat on and listened to the furnace kick in. One hundred and fifty bucks before the day was over. Seven hundred and fifty when the week was done. Three thousand by Christmas.

At six I made a thermos of tea and two peanut butter and jelly sandwiches, then put on all the warm clothes I had. It took me about as long to dress as it had to put on my goalie equipment when I used to play ice hockey. On top I wore the heavy quilted greatcoat that my father-in-law had found in his attic from the nights he worked the docks in South Portland.

At six-thirty I left the house with the empty carpenter's belt hanging from my waist. The sand along the shore was frozen as hard as cement. I wore the only boots I owned, a pair of Wellingtons, and I could feel my toes going numb by the time I reached the main road. Across the cove the islands were swimming in plum-colored light, and a small parade of fishing boats reached to the horizon.

I stepped inside the house through an opening in the studs where a chimney was going up. It was like standing within the ruins of a great cathedral with vaulted ceilings and high walls and long, wide floors. Waves pounded the rocks, and the freezing sky was falling through the open roof. It seemed a struggle was taking place. The house itself looked as much like it was being torn down as being built.

Larry arrived just as I finished rubbing my new carpenter's belt in sawdust to try to make it look old. He got out of his truck with a pot of coffee in one hand and a canvas attaché case in the other. Under one arm he had a roll of blueprints. He yelled good morning, asked me if I didn't own any better boots, and gestured with the coffeepot to follow him.

"We've got to get this beam up," he said, setting everything down on the plywood floor. I took a look at it. Thirty feet. Three hundred pounds. My wife's mother, a nurse, had lectured me about stretching exercises since I had crushed a disk in my back dragging a rowboat the spring before, but I was of the unenlightened old school of athletes: I believed that stretching was for the self-righteous joggers who crept along the side of the road or the guys on bicycles dressed like court jesters.

Larry wanted to lift the beam over our heads together, one end at a time. He paused and eyed the beam with relish. When we were getting into place he told me about a children's book he read to his girls every night. "It's all about these lumberjacks in the Maine woods, you know?" We stood side by side, bent down together, and on the count of three raised the beam, first to our waist, then to our shoulders. *"Push!* How they used to move logs down the rivers, and how they'd strip them. It's great." Slowly we climbed the ladder with the beam. *"Easy, easy.* Every night I say, 'Okay, what book do you want me to read to you tonight, girls?' And before they can answer, I pull out the lumberjack book—'How about this one, girls?' *Okay, on the count of three, then. You ready? One, two, three!"* We got the end just above the top of the wall where it was going to be nailed into place to hold the floor above it. "Drive a couple spikes in it before it kills us," Larry groaned. He was above me one step on the ladder, with his shoulder and his head pressed against the beam. I couldn't help him. Finally he looked at me. *"You got nails?"* he asked.

"I didn't bring any tools," I said. He gave me a curious look and then saw my empty carpenter's belt. "I thought you just wanted me to bring my belt," I said.

I looked down at it, empty and useless as a prop I'd picked up on my way from central casting. It was the sort of moment you hope you can redeem yourself from someday.

"Okay, let's start over," Larry said after he issued me a tape measure, hammer, two chisels, a knife, and a pencil. I filled the leather pouches with nails and wore the belt low on one hip like a gunslinger's holster the way the rest of the crew wore theirs. At the end of the day, rather than hang it up, I kept mine on under my overcoat and walked home. Everyone was having supper when I came into the kitchen. I dropped my coat on a chair and unhitched the belt as casually as if I'd been wearing it my whole working life.

On my first dump run I told the men who were waiting in line, smoking cigarettes and leaning against their pick-ups, that I was working on the mansion at Prouts Neck.

"It's a huge sucker, ain't it?" said a man with paint all over his jacket. "I heard from a plumber that the place has got ten bathrooms." He chuckled and rolled a wooden kitchen match between his teeth. "Well, these rich buggers are full of shit anyway."

. . .

For three days I worked with Billy, Larry's partner, wrapping the back end of the house with some polyester material that has replaced the more modest tar paper and that felt to me exactly like a pair of bell-bottom pants I once owned. A full roll weighed fifty pounds, and Billy and I worked on two ladders, passing the roll back and forth and leapfrogging each other as we went along tacking it to the plywood with heavy-duty staplers that made a thunking sound Billy imitated the whole time rather than talk to me. I took his silence to mean that he wasn't sure I was worth the money. I had heard from a guy at the dump that Billy was from out of state and had grown up summering down the shore near Kennebunk, where he met and married President Bush's daughter.

Billy coached the Scarborough High School ice hockey team and had to leave work on Friday afternoons for practice. Before he climbed down from his ladder, he told me to nail the last sheet of plywood in place on the east wall before I finished up.

I tried three times to climb the ladder with the sheet of plywood, but my arms went numb before I reached the top and I had to drop the thing and start again. It took me so long that when I finally made it up the ladder and onto the scaffolding, everyone else had gone home and it was nearly dark. I was about forty feet above the granite ledges where the waves were breaking hard and throwing a salt spray against the house that had iced the plank of wood beneath my feet. When I raised the plywood above my head, a gust yanked it and spun me around. I caught an iron bar of the scaffold with my left elbow and held on. I was thinking, *How in God's name would Billy or any other real carpenter have done this?* It was a strange moment. The blood ran out of my arms and there was a pain in my back like a cold spark. Then I began to feel very calm about letting go of the scaffolding. I heard the waves crashing on the rocks, and I felt the wind wash over me and a lightness fill my lungs. I had the sense that if I just leaned back slightly onto my heels, the wind would do the rest.

.   .   .

There were six of us working on the crew, but the house was so large that we seldom saw one another. Larry insisted that we all take our fifteen-minute coffee break and our half-hour lunch together whenever possible. We were his crew, and he wanted us to appreciate one another. Once I walked right by a man in my haste to get back to a second-story deck where I had been tearing down staging. Larry saw this, and he climbed down from the third story to set me straight. "You can't just walk by people," he said. "It's going to be a long winter."

We took our breaks in the basement, in a makeshift room stuffed with fiberglass insulation and covered with clear plastic. Two four-foot lengths of electric baseboard heating had been hooked up along the cement floor, as well as a single lightbulb that swung from the ceiling. We stripped off our clothing the second we entered the room so that we wouldn't sweat and so we'd feel the warmth when we went back out. Sometimes we sat there as silent as monks, heads bowed, each one of us too cold to speak.

I thought of the place as a locker room, the kind of male sanctuary where we would have been less surprised to hear gunfire than a female voice. In this room I got to know the other men, listening carefully while they consulted one another about whatever problem they faced on the job, drawing pencil diagrams on the cement floor to explain themselves or gathering around the blueprints. These few minutes in the locker room was the only downtime in the crew's ten-hour workday, but each man seemed to know intuitively how enormous the job was and how no time could be wasted if it was going to be completed on schedule.

I was the rookie, and in the locker room I took some ribbing for being a professor. Mostly they teased me about my boots. Riding boots, they called them. "Where'd you leave your horse today, Professor? . . . I bet you need a good pair of high boots like that to teach in."

My boots were the first thing Cal had noticed the day I met him. "You won't survive the winter in boots like that," he said. I was carrying lumber, and he was taking one of his long walks around the neck. We got into it quickly that first day, and after that he told me how he had grown up on his father's farm in Maine and how he had never brushed his teeth in any bathroom except his father's until he went into the army. He fought in the Philippines as an infantryman for two years, and then he worked thirty-five years at the shipyard in Kittery, Maine, and when he retired from that job, he and his wife traveled cross-country on a motorcycle, and then he started another career working summers on the golf course. He was seventy-three now and still working.

One day in the locker room Luke, whose knowledge of construction had earned him the only title in the crew, that of project manager, said to me, "Once you start shingling this place, we'll have to scrape the ice off you before you come in for coffee."

I laughed along with them and didn't dare tell them how I was looking forward to that job. After three weeks I had revealed all my inadequacies, and most days now I spent sweeping scrap lumber into piles, loading the piles into trash cans, lugging the trash cans to Larry's truck, and then driving to the dump. No matter how many times Larry told me how good a job I was doing and how important it was to keep the job site clean because it reflected on the company, I knew I was a $15-an-hour trash man who occasionally got to carry lumber or take nails out of boards, and though I was just as cold as anyone else and my clothes were just as dirty, when I came into the locker room for coffee break, I didn't feel like I'd earned it. I always looked at Billy and figured he wasn't speaking to me because he was *building a house* and he hadn't figured out yet what the hell I was doing.

It was like standing outside reading a book in a freezing cold wind, on a busy street with traffic roaring by, reading page after page and trying to grab hold of the meaning of the pages amid the noise and the cold, but the paragraphs just turn into more paragraphs and no story ever begins. I kept looking for the narrative in my work, something that was moving forward and would add up to a house. Instead, I worked for hours cutting boards I didn't nail into place and stacking lumber in piles that vanished by the end of the day. I was so far out of the logic of the operation that I didn't realize we were actually building two houses. I had asked Guy, the French-Canadian carpenter, one day about the handsome place under construction at the top of the driveway just off the lane, thinking it was a neighbor's house. It had been framed and sheathed, and it seemed to be finished except for doors, windows, and siding. *"There?"* Guy asked, trying to get over his disbelief. "That's the carriage house. You know, the garage."

           The trouble was, whenever I was given a real job, I made mistakes. For four days I worked in the basement blocking the floor joists. The joists were one-by-twelve pieces of lumber that ran the length of the house every fourteen inches, and they had to be held in place by fourteen-inch blocks of wood. I kept cutting them too long or too short.

    But the house was being built—the proof was right there in front of my eyes—and I was there every day for ten hours, working without stopping in order to finish the jobs Larry assigned to me. Yet I was waiting for the kind of purpose and satisfaction I imagined the Italian masons took home each night. There were three of them, and I loved watching them build the stone wall that was covering the foundation. They arrived each morning in one truck with the youngest man behind the wheel. The old man got out first and walked straight to the large pile of stones, where he stood for a while by himself until the other two men came up behind him. Then, as if he had been dreaming the stones into their shapes in his sleep, he peered down at the pile and pointed slowly to those he believed would fit together to make the section of the wall they were going to work on that day. In the first strokes of sunlight I saw their St. Christopher medallions glistening as the men leaned over their trowels.

. . .

I had no idea why the excavation crew had dug the enormous hole, six feet deep and eight feet wide, that ran the entire eighty feet of the foundation wall along the front of the house. But every night the hole filled with water from the swamp, and one of my jobs was to go down into the hole and turn on the pump as soon as I got to work. One morning I slid down one bank, broke through the ice, and landed in water up to my neck. I started the pump and then headed home for some dry clothes, cutting through the golf course so that I wouldn't be seen by the rest of the crew coming to work. I had just walked across a green, when someone yelled at me: "This is a private golf course!" I couldn't believe anyone was playing golf in the middle of December, and when I turned I saw a big, broad-shouldered woman glaring at me. I was thinking maybe I would tell her that I was a professor of literature on sabbatical. "You walked right across the green," she said.

"I'm sorry," I told her.

"You're not one of those workers building that dreadful house, are you?"

My whole life I'd feared women like this one, suspecting them to be the people behind the scenes deciding how the world should work.

"No," I told her. "I'm an astronaut. I'm on vacation with my family. We're renting a place across the road."

She seemed relieved, and I felt grateful and asked her how the fairways were playing.

"The course is in awful shape," she said. "You know I was playing golf in Turkey two weeks ago—have you ever been to Turkey?"

I almost said, *Only once*. "Turkey? No."

"The fairways are so lush that the ball boys go barefoot so they can find your ball."

For three days I had a good job building temporary windows and doors we needed until the custom-made windows and doors arrived from Minnesota. When I nailed the last one in place, the house was closed in, and this meant we could begin running propane heaters. That night I fell asleep thinking about working the next day where it was warm.

When I arrived, Larry was already there, standing in the hole along the front of the house. He had blueprints spread out on the ground above his head, and he had hooked up two pumps, one electric and one with a gas motor that made it hard to hear what he was saying.

He climbed out of the hole, we knelt down in the frozen dirt, and I tried to follow him as he explained how we were going to build concrete footings the entire length of the hole and then a perimeter retaining wall on top of the footings. He traced his finger along the blueprint. "You can follow it here," he said. "It goes in for twenty-two feet, then it cuts out six feet to grab the front of the porch, then it winds back. See?"

I said I did.

"Let's get going," he said, rolling up the blueprints. "Five days and we'll have it done."

We got right into it. Luke lined up the cement truck for two o'clock that afternoon, and then he put on his boots and got down in the hole with Larry and me. We measured for the forms, cut the wood, and built them right in the hole, and then we surveyed them to make sure they were level. All the while the pumps were sucking out the water that ran in from the marsh. It was mostly pick-and-shovel work, and we got soaked and the water froze our clothing. We worked against the clock, cutting the steel rods to reinforce the concrete and laying them in grids in the mud on the bed of the forms. The first day everything went smoothly. I was fastening the last pieces of steel, when the cement truck pulled in at the top of the driveway. We stood in the hole, pushing the cement through the forms with our shovels while it ran down the chute. Then we smoothed out the surface and climbed out of the hole just as it was getting dark.

The next morning we started in again, only this time I was left on my own while Larry and Luke had a breakfast meeting with the architects. It was my first real chance, and I studied the blueprints before I began building the forms. Right from the start, though, nothing looked right. I built one form and then ripped it apart and started again. Then a third time. The blueprints fell into the water and were unreadable, and I began to think maybe that would be my excuse. By noon, when Larry and Luke returned, there wasn't enough time left to finish before the cement arrived. "I'll call and try and stop the truck," Luke said.

Larry jumped down into the hole. "Let them come," he yelled above the pump.

For a while I tried to keep up with him and be of some help. But then I just stood there. I remembered a moment at the university when pipes had burst in one wall in the conference room of the English department. It was an ancient granite wall, and all through the afternoon the room was filled with workmen tearing the place apart with jackhammers and chisels, trying to get to the pipe. Water was running down the hallway, and as a precaution all the utilities had been shut off in the building. The room was dark, and the men were shouting and gesturing to one another while the water gushed through the ceiling. It was like a scene from a catastrophe film, maybe a submarine sinking, and I was standing there, watching, when one of the professors from the classics department wandered in with a batch of term papers in one hand and said very loudly, "Excuse me, but there's a terrible chill in my office and I wonder what the prospects are that heat will be restored this afternoon?" All of a sudden the workmen stopped and turned and stared at him with that universal and timeless expression that men who work hard reserve for men who do not.

The next day Larry let me cut the steel myself. "Just read the prints carefully," he said. I did, but I still cut twenty pieces two inches short. "Do them again," he said.

At fifteen below zero, each time we bent over in the icy water it felt like my bones were grinding in their sockets. At one point I had to climb out of the hole to piss. I walked around to the back of the house, and when I took out my penis it was covered in wet blood the color of raspberries. I bent over and looked through the open fly. There was blood everywhere. It had soaked my long underwear and my boxer shorts and was half frozen, thick and sticky like jam. It scared me, and I began jumping out of my clothes until I found where a blood vessel had broken.

I had been back in the hole just a few minutes, when I looked up and saw a woman standing there smiling at me. "Will you give me a grand tour?" she asked pleasantly. At first I thought I hadn't heard her correctly. I knew she was a Prouts Neck woman because she had one of those highly bred collies with sawed-off legs. "I've known Larry since he was a boy," she said just as pleasantly. "He won't mind if you give me the Cook's tour."

As soon as I showed her inside, her mood changed. "You could build places like this at the turn of the century," she snarled at me. "But today they just scream one word: *pretentious*! Look at that London stairway," she exclaimed.

I thought I heard her dog growl at me on the way out.

The house was a curiosity, and when the owners of the summer houses returned for long weekends, they often wandered by. "Excuse me," Larry called from the roof when two women emerged from the house. "Who are you?"

They told him that a certain man from Prouts Neck, one of the largest landowners, had given them permission to take a tour. A few minutes later this man appeared, dressed in a brand-new camouflage jump suit.

"Hey," Larry called, "I'm trying to run a business here. I don't go walking around your office, do I?"

"I'm so sorry," he said unctuously. "The last thing I want to do is upset you. What tool is that you're using there?"

"A hammer," Larry called back.

One day I moved boulders in a sleet storm. There were nearly a hundred of them and they were too heavy to lift, so I had to stay down on my knees the whole day, pushing them an inch or two at a time. When I got home there was another rejection letter from a college I'd applied to for work.

. . .

The subcontractors arrived one morning and began unloading the forms we needed to start the retaining wall. The foreman was a goofy-looking guy who stood in one place, eating doughnuts while he yelled orders at his crew. I figured he was the son who had inherited the business. It was barely above zero and the wind was vicious, and he kept telling his men to set things down one place and then changing his mind and telling them to move them someplace else.

He was back again the next morning, shouting more orders. The electric pump had gone off for some reason, and I was down on my knees in the water, checking to see if it was clogged. I unplugged it and was about to plug it in again, when he yelled at me: "Somebody got electrocuted doing the same thing last week. You better smarten up."

I turned and looked at him. All four of his workers had stopped and were looking at him too. And then they turned to me. It was just a moment, but it was worth something to me for some reason. I raised the electric cord so he could see it. I held up the plug from the pump so he could see that too. Then I plugged it in and held it in my hands until he turned away.

At dinner I tried to explain to Colleen. "I guess I just wanted to shut him up," I said.

"Well, that was pretty stupid," she said.

I went outside into the garage with two more rejection letters. So far there were thirty-seven of them, and I had begun tacking them to the wall above some beach chairs and the kids' plastic swimming pool.

The next day when I got to work Cal was standing there holding a paper bag. "How you doing?" he asked.

"Digging ditches," I said.

"You'll be strong by spring," he said, handing me the bag. It was a beautiful pair of work boots. Leather with felt liners.

"I can't take them," I said.

"You have to," he said.

.   .   .

It was the premium due on the car insurance that broke us the next week. We sent the check off on the last possible day and then had nothing left for groceries. Two days later, the day our son Jack turned six, our first food stamps arrived in the mail. We were going to have a nice birthday dinner, and I went to the Shop 'n Save with our seven-year-old daughter, Nell, to get a few things. There was a young man in a beautiful camel's-hair overcoat standing behind us in the checkout aisle. The woman on his arm was wearing a cocktail dress slit up one thigh. As soon as I started to pay for the shrimp with food stamps, I heard the man groan. I was nervous, afraid the cashier might ask me for some kind of identification that I didn't have. I don't know what the man said to the woman, but when she sighed, I told myself to hit him first and say whatever came to mind later. Instead, I turned and faced them. "Nell," I said to my daughter, "you know why this man is groaning? If we were buying boxes of macaroni and cheese with our food stamps, it would be all right with him. But he's groaning because we're buying the kind of food he eats." He turned and walked toward the next aisle. The woman looked back at me with disgust.

I was thinking about that when I climbed the ladder the next day to paint a coat of primer on the trim at the roofline. It was a long way up, fifty or sixty feet. I was holding on with one hand, carrying a gallon of paint in the other, and thinking about how angry I was. I was angry because I didn't have any skills and because I was being paid good money and wasn't earning it. And because I'd always believed there would be a slot for me somewhere near the top, a long way from guys with mud on their faces who couldn't earn a living. At the top of the ladder I stepped onto the plank that hung from wall brackets just below the roof. I started painting, inching my way along the plank and telling myself that there were too many people waiting at every good slot today, the competition was maddening. Somehow when I took a half-step back I missed the plank. I felt my heel in the air, and a cold emptiness suddenly rushed through me. I stood there thinking how nice it would be to just drop down to my knees slowly and then to lie flat on the plank and wrap my arms around it.

It was Rob, another carpenter, who came outside and talked to me until I finally climbed down.

Just before Christmas I was telling an old friend about my last day in the hole. Somehow it had fallen to me to prepare the section of earth where the main sewer pipe ran out from the basement wall of the house and through the hole before it was filled in with six feet of gravel and concrete. Everyone else had gone on to do other things, so I cut some shims of wood to place under the pipe so that it ran downhill slightly, away from the house. Then I covered the pipe with straw. It took maybe twenty minutes, but it hit me that I had in my hands, the one job that could sabotage a rich man's house. All I had to do was turn the little shims so that the pipe ran back toward the house. My little secret would have been buried beneath gravel and concrete, and no one would have found out until the toilets had been flushed about forty times and the stuff started backing up toward the walls of the house. "I almost turned it backward," I said to my friend. "I don't know why. I think I just wanted to take something."

He listened patiently, a good-hearted, hardworking lawyer who had already paid off the mortgage on his house and set aside enough money for his three kids' college education. He told me how glad he was that I'd found work.

"It doesn't matter what kind of work we do," he said. "All work has value."

I told him he was full of shit. "My grandfather never finished eighth grade," I said. "He was a laborer all his life, but he could live on his low wages. Today he'd be a beggar."

My friend let me go on and on.

After New Year's we heard that the owner of the house was arriving in two days. My job was to clean not just the place again but all the property that surrounded it.

I wanted everything to be perfect. I climbed the owner's tree to get a plastic sandwich bag that had blown into the branches. I crawled through the thickets of the marsh and got one of my boots sucked off trying to reach a Styrofoam coffee cup.

I didn't see the owner arrive. I was in the basement painting trim boards for Luke. I had one bare foot propped up on a roll of insulation next to a propane heater, trying to thaw it out, when two women appeared in fur coats and a cloud of perfume. "Have you got anything warm to drink?" I heard one of them ask. The other woman was carrying a Gucci bag stuffed with material samples. "If you put fiberglass showers in the bathrooms, the whole house will be ruined," she exclaimed.

At the end of the second week of January the shingles arrived. Hundreds of boxes of cedar shingles that I stacked in the garage, thinking of all the work and of the weeks and weeks of paychecks they represented.

Larry started me on the back of the carriage house, the one place that would never be seen. He showed me how he wanted it done, how to run a chalk line and then nail a board along the line to use as a guide, setting each shingle on the edge of the board and moving along, one at a time. Right from the first shingle, I loved the order and the slow momentum of it and how it steadily amounted to something that looked finished. I loved the solid sound of the hammer in the cold air.

But I was terribly slow. Part of my trouble was the brutal cold. It was below zero when I began each morning and barely above through most of the day. I dropped five nails for every one I managed to get into place, and some days there would still be three hours left to go when I'd look at my watch and think I couldn't take the cold another fifteen minutes.

Working up the gabled end of the carriage house was even slower, because I had to cut the shingles at the ends of each row to follow the slant of the roof and to fit tightly against the trim that had already been nailed on. I used a knife to cut them and a block plane to finish them. By eleven o'clock one morning, all the subcontractors had gone home and we were waiting to get hit by the first big storm of the winter. The ocean was buried beneath sea smoke, the temperature with the windchill was thirty-seven below. I was high up on a ladder, putting the last few shingles in the peak of the gabled end, when Larry came around the corner. I saw him standing there. It had just begun to snow. He took the hammer out of his belt, and I watched him use the claws to pry up the piece of trim at the end of my rows.

"I cut them all along the angle," I said hopefully.

"Yeah," he said, "but I wanted them to slide under the trim. You see, like this? That's the only way to make it watertight."

He started peeling off the shingles with the hammer. It made a horrible noise, the creaking nails and the ripping sound as the shingles snapped and split into pieces that fell into the snow. "You'll have to start over on this end," he said. "Don't worry about it."

I went back on Saturday, when I hoped no one would be there to see, or hear, me ripping off all those shingles.

Monday I came into the locker room for lunch, and I heard Billy saying something to Larry about the labor costs. They stopped talking as soon as I came in, but for the rest of the day I felt it coming, and when Larry told me he was going to lay me off because the doors and windows were late and they had to go in before we could really shingle the place, I didn't believe him.

I stayed in bed for four days, feeling sorry about everything. My son kept coming to my room, standing outside the locked door, tapping it with his fingertips. "It's me. Jack," he would say. Each time I heard him outside my door I had the same feeling I'd had at the supermarket, as if I were standing away from myself.

Every morning when my family was asleep I looked down the shore at the house to make sure that the doors and windows weren't in and that no shingles had gone on. Then I went back to bed. "That's the difference between fathers and mothers," Colleen said. "A mother can't just give up and stay in bed."

It came down to needing one day's work to put together enough money for our February rent, and when I called Larry to ask him if he needed me to do anything, he told me to come in the next morning. I got dressed, then stopped to say good-bye to Colleen. "Wipe off your lips," she said. "You've got Maalox on them."

I spent the whole ten hours on my knees, picking up every stick of wood inside and outside the house and the carriage house. I was picking up wood shavings and telling myself that all work had dignity if it paid you enough to make your rent. The guy driving the bulldozer jumped down and came up to me. "That guy who used to stop here?" he said. "Cal?"

"Yeah?"

"He died," he said. "I guess he was full of cancer."

By now I knew the men waiting in line at the dump: the one with the handlebar mustache, the one with the Playboy bunny hanging from his rearview mirror, the ones who did cocaine drops on the weekend because they couldn't pay their bills on eight bucks an hour. They were killing time, smoking and talking, and I stayed with them a little while and began picturing them as the boys I had walked past on autumn afternoons toward dusk when I was seventeen and headed toward a full college scholarship for playing football and then a fellowship for graduate school. On those afternoons we always came out of the football locker room into the cold light and crossed the parking lot in our spiked shoes like a small army, helmets on or cocked under our arms. On our way to the practice field we passed the hoods sitting on the steps out behind the wood shop, hunched over their cigarettes, watching us with bored, superior expressions. Though I never spoke with any of them, their names still were real to me almost thirty years later: Percy Sergeant. Wayne Lavasseur. Paul Gaudette. They had nothing but disdain for us in our uniforms, taking orders, believing things that they already knew were not true. I looked down on them with their go-to-hell sunglasses and their shitkicker boots. But there at the dump, I now saw them as survivors of some kind of night journey that I had never believed was out there for me. Watching them, I saw how desperately I had always wanted to dance with America and how I always wanted to believe that I could hear the band starting up in the distance for me, and how those boys outside the wood shop had already taken America by the hand and disappeared with her down Flamingo Lane. We had all come of age in the midst of a magician's trick when he could still pull the rabbit out of the hat, and lately, of course, he had slowed down a bit, and you could see the little trapdoors and hinges in his act and in my own act as well. Maybe this was why disillusionment was spreading into the middle class, not because disillusionment was rising but because the middle class was falling.

It was snowing when I walked home. I took the long way, hoping the kids would be asleep when I came in, but the three oldest ones were right there telling me that they had driven by with mommy and seen me at work. "What were you doing crawling in the woods?" Erin asked.

Larry called me back to work the day the windows and doors arrived. We had to get all one hundred and seven of them in in advance of a northeaster that was blowing up the coast and due to dump heavy snow. The sky was black when I walked down the shore. Out at sea there were ships heading into the cove, their running lights like low-hanging stars. We worked without a break, and I was on the south end of the house when the Italians finished the chimney just as the snow began to blow across the marsh. It was a beautiful stone chimney, and they stood there for a moment looking up at it, blocking the snow out of their eyes. I told the old man that it was something, and I stood there next to him, waiting for him to mark the moment in some way. He took one last look and said, "There it is." Then he turned and picked up his lunchbox and walked to his truck.

Eleven hours after we arrived that morning we finished the last window. Larry had cut his face on a nail, and there was dried blood on his cheek. He was happy. "Let it snow," he said. "Another month and this place will be close. Real close."

My last job that day was to climb up onto all the scaffolding and turn the planks on their edges so that they wouldn't get buried under the snow, and then to bring all the ladders down off the sides of the house. I got all but one plank. It was fifty feet above my head, and I could barely see it in the blowing snow.

The waves were breaking over the seawall when I began walking home. I was sure the wind was blowing better than sixty miles an hour. It took me almost an hour to walk home. Colleen had taken the kids to her mother's, and I got a fire going and then fell asleep in a chair and dreamed about the snow piling up on that last plank that I hadn't moved. The weight of the snow would snap the plank in half, and both pieces would go sailing through the beautiful triple windows.

I put all my clothes on and started back down the beach.

Overnight the storm passed, and I was the first one at work in the morning. The living room—a ninety-six-foot-long great hall with three Rumford fireplaces, wide triple windows, and seventeen doors, each eight feet tall, with twelve one-foot-square panes of glass—was drenched in sunlight. It was more than just the light; the windows and doors made it seem like music had been turned on in the house, and I found myself walking from one window to the next, just looking at the view and imagining people living in this light, pulling a chair up to one window early some morning to watch the ships at sea.

In the last days, Larry put me on the front of the main house, the first part of the house the owner would see when he returned, and I worked at it until the weather got warm, wanting it to be perfect for him and for reasons that had nothing to do with things I'd thought much about before. The last time I climbed down the scaffolding and looked up, the house was bathed in moonlight.

Larry came up behind me. "It's amazing," he said. "Someone draws a picture of a place, and then suddenly there it is, exactly like the picture." He had lived with this place for almost a year, always un-whole, broken into small pieces. He had made a hundred decisions a day about the pieces, and lay awake at night wondering if he'd made the right decisions and if he'd overlooked something. But standing there, looking back at the house, it was whole; all the pieces had come together.

If I had known Larry better, I would have admitted that throughout the winter I had resented the man who owned this house. Though I knew nothing about him, I had thought of him as a luckier man than I was, a man with proof that his life was adding up to something. But maybe he wasn't lucky at all, or even if he *had* been handed everything, still, somewhere along the line, he must have risked something or worked hard or made the right decision or just kept his mouth shut, so that tomorrow he wasn't going to have to start looking again for a job. We said good-bye. Larry was hurrying to finish a toy stove he was building for a daughter's birthday party. I thanked him for the work. "Hey," he said, shaking my hand, "thanks for all your help."

Black Swans

LAUREN SLATER

There is something satisfying and scary about making an angel, lowering your bulky body into the drowning fluff, stray flakes landing on your face. I am seven or eight and the sky looms above me, gray and dead. I move my arms and legs—expanding, contracting—sculpting snow before it can swallow me up. I feel the cold filter into my head, seep through the wool of my mittens. I swish wider, faster, then roll out of my mold to inspect its form. There is the imprint of my head, my arms which have swelled into white wings. I step back, step forward, pause, and peer. Am I dead or alive down there? Is this a picture of heaven or hell? I am worried about where I will go when I die, that each time I swallow, an invisible stone will get caught in my throat. I worry that when I eat a plum, a tree will grow in my belly, its branches twining around my bones, choking. When I walk through a door I must tap the frame three times. Between each nighttime prayer to Yahweh I close my eyes and count to ten and a half.

And now I look down at myself sketched in the snow. A familiar anxiety chews at the edges of my heart, even while I notice the beauty of the white fur on all the trees, the reverent silence of this season. I register a mistake on my angel, what looks like a thumbprint on its left wing. I reach down to erase it, but unable to smooth the snow perfectly, I start again on another angel, lowering myself, swishing and sweeping, rolling over—no. Yet another mistake, this time the symmetry in the wingspan wrong. A compulsion comes over me. I do it again, and again. In my memory, hours go by. My fingers inside my mittens get wrinkled and raw. My breath comes heavily and the snow begins to blue. A moon rises, a perfect crescent pearl whose precise shape I will never be able to re-create. I ache for something I cannot name. Someone calls me, a mother or a father. *Come in now. Come in now.* Very early the next morning I awaken, look out my bedroom window, and see the yard covered with my frantic forms—hundreds of angels, none of them quite right. The forms twist and strain, the wings seeming to struggle up in the winter sun, as if each angel were longing for escape, for a free flight that might crack the crystal and ice of her still, stiff world.

Looking back on it now, I think maybe those moments in the snow were when my OCD began, although it didn't come to me full-fledged until my mid-twenties. OCD stands for obsessive compulsive disorder, and some studies say over three million Americans suffer from it. The "it" is not the commonplace rituals that weave throughout so many of our lives—the woman who checks the stove a few times before she leaves for work, or the man who combs his bangs back, and then again, seeking symmetry. Obsessive compulsive disorder is pervasive and extreme, inundating the person's life to the point where normal functioning becomes difficult, maybe even impossible.

For a long time my life was difficult but not impossible. Both in my childhood and my adulthood I'd suffered from various psychiatric ailments—depressions especially—but none of these were as surreal and absurd as the obsessive compulsive disorder that one day presented itself. Until I was twenty-five or so, I don't think I could have been really diagnosed with OCD, although my memory of the angels indicates I had tendencies in that direction. I was a child at once nervous and bold, a child who loved trees that trickled sap, the Vermont fields where grass grew the color of deep-throated rust. I was a child who gathered earthworms, the surprising pulse of pink on my fingers, and yet these same fingers, later in the evening, came to prayer points, searching for safety in the folds of my sheets, in the quick counting rituals.

Some mental health professionals claim that the onset of obsession is a response to an underlying fear, a recent trauma, say, or a loss. I don't believe that is always true, because no matter how hard I think about it, I remember nothing unusual or disorienting before my first attack, three years out of college. I don't know exactly why at two o'clock one Saturday afternoon what felt like a seizure shook me. I recall lying in my apartment in Cambridge. The floors were painted blue, the curtains a sleepy white. They bellied in and out with the breezes. I was immersed in a book, *The Seven Storey Mountain*, walking my way through the tale's church, dabbing holy water on my forehead. A priest was crooning. A monk moaned. And suddenly this: A thought careening across my cortex. I CAN'T CONCENTRATE. Of course the thought disturbed my concentration, and the monk's moan turned into a whisper, disappeared.

I blinked, looked up. I was back in Cambridge on a blue floor. The blue floor suddenly frightened me; between the planks I could see lines of dark dirt, and the sway of a spider crawling. Let me get back, I thought, into the world of the book. I lowered my eyes to the page, but instead of being able to see the print, there was the thought blocking out all else: I CAN'T CONCENTRATE.

Now I started to panic. Each time I tried to get back to the book, the words crumbled, lost their sensible shapes. I said to myself, *I must not allow that thought about concentration to come into my mind anymore,* but, of course, the more I tried to suppress it, the louder it jangled. I looked at my hand. I ached for its familiar skin, the paleness of its palm and the three threaded lines that had been with me since birth, but as I held it out before my eyes, the phrase I CAN'T CONCENTRATE ON MY HAND blocked out my hand, so all I saw was a blur of flesh giving way to the bones beneath, and inside the bones the grimy marrow, and in the grimy marrow the individual cells, all disconnected. Shattered skin.

My throat closed up with terror. For surely if I'd lost the book, lost language, lost flesh, I was well on my way to losing the rest of the world. And all because of a tiny phrase that forced me into a searing self-consciousness that plucked me from the moment into the meta-moment so I was doomed to think about thinking instead of thinking other thoughts. My mind devouring my mind.

I tried to force my brain onto other topics, but with each mental dodge I became aware that I was dodging, and each time I itched I became aware that I was itching, and with each inhalation I became aware that I was inhaling, and I thought, *If I think too much about breathing, will I forget how to breathe?*

I ran into the bathroom. There was a strange pounding in my head, and then a sensation I can describe only as a hiccup of the brain. My brain seemed to be seizing as the phrase about concentration jerked across it. I delved into the medicine cabinet, found a bottle of aspirin, took three, stood by the sink for five minutes. No go. Delved again, pulled out another bottle—Ativan—a Valium-like medication belonging to my housemate, Adam. Another five minutes, my brain still squirting. One more Ativan, a tiny white triangle that would put me to sleep. I would sleep this strange spell off, wake up me again, sane again. I went back to my bed. The day darkened. The Ativan spread through my system. Lights in a neighboring window seemed lonely and sweet. I saw the shadow of a bird in a tree, and it had angel wings, and it soared me someplace else, its call a pure cry.

"What's wrong with you?" he said, shaking my shoulder. My housemate, Adam, stood over me, his face a blur. Through cracked eyelids I saw a wavering world, none of its outlines resolved: the latticed shadow of a tree on a white wall, my friend's face a streak of pink. I am okay, I thought, for this was what waking up was always like, the gentle resurfacing. I sat up, looked around.

"You've been sleeping for hours and hours," he said. "You slept from yesterday afternoon until now."

I reached up, gently touched a temple. I felt the faraway nip of my pulse. My pulse was there. I was here.

"Weird day yesterday," I said. I spoke slowly, listening to my words, testing them on my tongue. So far so good.

I stood up. "You look weird," he said, "unsteady."

"I'm okay," I said, and then, in that instant, a surge of anxiety. I had lied. I had not been okay. *Say God I'm sorry fourteen times*, I ordered myself. *This is crazy*, I said to myself. *Fifteen times*, a voice from somewhere else seemed to command. "You really all right?" Adam asked. I closed my eyes, counted, blinked back open.

"Okay," I said. "I'm going to shower."

But it wasn't okay. As soon as I was awake, obsessive thoughts returned. What before had been inconsequential behaviors like counting to three before I went through a doorway or checking the stove several times before bed, now became imperatives. There were a thousand and one of them to follow: rules about how to step, what it meant to touch my mouth, a hot, consuming urge to fix the crooked angles of the universe. It was constant, a cruel nattering. *There, that tilted picture on the wall. Scratch your head with your left hand only.* It was noise, the beak of a woodpecker in the soft bark of my brain. But the worst, by far, were the dread thoughts about concentrating. I picked up a book but couldn't read, so aware was I of myself reading, and the fear of that awareness, for it meant a cold disconnection from this world.

I began to avoid written language because of the anxiety associated with words. I stopped reading. Every sentence I wrote came out only half coherent. I became afraid of pens and paper, the red felt tip bleeding into white, a wound. What was it? What was I? I could not recognize myself spending hours counting, checking, avoiding. Gods seemed to hover in their air, inhabit me, blowing me full of their strange stellar breaths. I wanted my body back. Instead, I pulsed and stuttered and sparked with a glow not my own.

I spent the next several weeks mostly in my bedroom, door closed, shades drawn. I didn't want to go out because any movement might set off a cycle of obsessions. I sat hunched and lost weight. My friend Adam, who had some anxiety problems of his own and was a real pooh-pooher of "talk therapy," found me a behaviorist at McClean.

"These sorts of conditions," the behavioral psychologist, Dr. Lipman, told me as I sat one day in his office, "are associated with people who have depressive temperaments, but, unlike depression, they do not yield particularly well to more traditional modes of psychotherapy. We have, however, had some real success with cognitive/behavioral treatments."

Outside it was a shining summer day. His office was dim though, his blinds adjusted so only tiny gold chinks of light sprinkled through, illuminating him in patches. He was older, maybe fifty, and pudgy, and had tufts of hair in all the wrong places, in the whorls of his ears and his nostrils. I had a bad feeling about him.

Nevertheless, he was all I had right now. "What is this sort of condition exactly?" I asked. My voice, whenever I spoke these days, seemed slowed, stuck, words caught in my throat. I had to keep touching my throat, four times, five times, six times, or I would be punished by losing the power of speech altogether.

"Obsessive compulsive disorder," he announced. "Only you," he said, and lifted his chin a little proudly, "have an especially difficult case of it."

This, of course, was not what I wanted to hear. "What's so especially difficult about my case?" I asked.

He tapped his chin with the eraser end of his pencil. He sat back in his leather seat. When the wind outside blew, the gold chinks scattered across his face and desk. Suddenly, the world cleared a bit. The papers on his desk seemed animated, rustling, sheaves full of wings, books full of birds. I felt creepy, despondent, and excited all at once. Maybe he could help me. Maybe he had some special knowledge.

He then went on to explain to me how most people with obsessive thoughts—*my hands are filthy*—for instance, always follow those thoughts with a compulsive behavior, like handwashing. And while I did have some compulsive behaviors, Dr. Lipman explained, I also reported that my most distressing obsession had to do with concentration, and that the concentration obsession had no clear-cut compulsion following in its wake.

"Therefore," he said. His eyes sparkled as he spoke. He seemed excited by my case. He seemed so sure of himself that for a moment I was back with language again, only this time it was his language, his words forming me.

"Therefore you are what we call a primary ruminator!"

A cow, I thought, chewing and chewing on the floppy scum of its cud. I lowered my head.

He went on to tell me about treatment obstacles. Supposedly "primary ruminators" are especially challenging because, while you can train people to cease compulsive behaviors, you can't train them nearly as easily to tether their thoughts. His method, he told me, would be to use a certain instrument to desensitize me to the obsessive thought, to teach me not to be afraid of it, so, when it entered my mind, I wouldn't panic and thereby set off a whole cycle of anxiety and its partner, avoidance.

"How will we do it?" I asked.

And that is when he pulled "the instrument" from his desk drawer, a Walkman with a tiny tape in it. He told me he'd used it with people who were similar to me. He told me I was to record my voice saying "I can't concentrate I can't concentrate" and then wear the Walkman playing my own voice back to me for at least two hours a day. Soon, he said, I'd become so used to the thought, it would no longer bother me.

He looked over at the clock. About half the session had gone by. "We still have twenty more minutes," he said, pressing the red recorder button, holding the miniature microphone up to my mouth. "Why don't you start speaking now."

I paid Dr. Lipman for the session, borrowed the Walkman and the tape, and then left, stepping into the summer light. McClean is a huge, stately hospital, buildings with pillars, yawning lawns. The world out-side looked lazy in the sweet heat of June. Tulips in the garden lapped at the pollen-rich air with black tongues. A squirrel chirped high in the tuft of a tree. For a moment the world seemed lovely. Then, from far across the lawn, I saw a shadow in a window. Drawn for a reason I could not articulate, I stepped closer, and closer still. The shadow resolved itself into lines—two dark brows, a nose. A girl, pressed against glass on a top-floor ward. Her hands were fisted on either side of her face, her curls in a ratty tangle. Her mouth was open, and though I could not hear her, I saw the red splash of her scream.

Behavior therapy is in some ways the antithe-sis of psychoanalysis. Psychoanalysis focuses on cause, behavior ther-apy on consequence. Although I've always been a critic of old-style psychoanalysis with its fetish for the past, I don't completely discount the importance of origins. And I have always believed in the mind as an entity that at once subsumes the body and radiates beyond it, and therefore in need of interventions surpassing the mere technical; inter-ventions that whisper to mystery, stroke the soul.

The Walkman, however, was a completely technical intervention. It had little red studs for buttons. The tape whirred efficiently in its center like a slick, dark heart. My own voice echoed back to me, all blips and snaky static. I wondered what the obsession with concentra-tion meant. Surely it had some significance beyond the quirks in my own neuronal wiring. Surely the neuron itself—that tiny pulse of life embedded in the brain's lush banks—was a God-given charge. When I was a girl, I had seen stalks of wheat filled with a strange red light. When I was a girl, I once peeled back the corn's green clasps to find yellow pearls. With the Walkman on, I closed my eyes, saw again the prongs of corn, the wide world, and myself floating out of that world, in a place above all planets, severed even from my own mind. And I knew the obsession had something to do with deep disconnection and too much awe.

"There may be no real reasons," Dr. Lipman repeated to me

during my next visit. "OCD could well be the result of a nervous system that's too sensitive. If the right medication is ever developed, we would use that."

Because the right medication had not yet been found, I wore the Walkman. The earphones felt spongy. Sometimes I wore it to bed, listening to my own voice repeat the obsessive fear. When I took the earphones off, the silence was complete. My sheets were damp from sweat. I waited. Shadows whirled around. Planets sent down their lights, laying them across the blue floor. Blue. Silver. Space. *I can't concentrate.*

I did very little for the next year. Dr. Lipman kept insisting I wear the Walkman, turning up the volume, keeping it on for three, now four hours at a time. Fear and grief prevented me from eating much. When I was too terrified to get out of bed, Dr. Lipman checked me into the local hospital, where I lay amid IV drips, bags of blood, murmuring heart machines that let me know someone somewhere near was still alive.

It was in the hospital that I was first introduced to psychiatric medications, which the doctors tried me on to no avail. The medications had poetic names and frequently rhymed with one another—nortriptyline, desipramine, amitriptyline. Nurses brought me capsules in miniature paper cups, or oblong shapes of white that left a salty tingle on my tongue. None of them worked, except to make me drowsy and dull.

And then one day Dr. Lipman said to me, "There's a new medication called Prozac, still in its trial period, but it's seventy percent effective with OCD. I want to send you to a Dr. Vuckovic, here at McClean. He's one of the physicians doing trial runs."

I shrugged, willing to try. I'd tried so much, surely this couldn't hurt. I didn't expect much though. I certainly didn't expect what I finally got.

In my memory, Vuckovic is the Prozac Doctor. He has an office high in the eaves of McClean. His desk gleams.

His children smile out from frames lined up behind him. In the corner is a computer with a screen saver of hypnotic swirling stars. I watch the stars die and swell. I watch the simple gold band on Vuckovic's hand. For a moment I think that maybe in here I'll finally be able to escape the infected repetitions of my own mind. And then I hear a clock tick-tick-ticking. The sound begins to bother me; I cannot tune it out. "The clock is ruining my concentration," I think, and turn toward it. The numbers on its face are not numbers but tiny painted pills, green and white. A chime hangs down, with another capsule, probably a plastic replica, swinging from the end of it. Back. Forth. Back. Back.

The pads of paper on Vuckovic's desk are all edged in green and white, with the word "Prozac" scripted across the bottom. The pen has "Prozac" embossed in tiny letters. He asks me about my symptoms for a few minutes, and then uses the Prozac pen to write out a prescription.

"What about side effects?" I ask.

"Very few," the Prozac Doctor answers. He smiles. "Maybe some queasiness. A headache in the beginning. Some short-term insomnia. All in all, it's a very good medication. The safest we have."

"Behavior therapy hasn't helped," I say. I feel I'm speaking slowly, for the sound of that clock is consuming me. I put my hands over my ears.

"What is it?" he asks.

"Your—clock."

He looks toward it.

"Would you mind putting it away?"

"Then I would be colluding with your disease," he says. "If I put the clock away, you'll just fixate on something else."

"Disease," I repeat. "I have a disease."

"Without doubt," he says. "OCD can be a crippling disease, but now, for the first time, we have the drugs to combat it."

I take the prescription and leave. I will see him in one month for a follow-up. Disease. Combat. Collusions. My mind, it seems, is my enemy, my illness an absurdity that has to be exterminated. I believe this. The treatment I'm receiving, with its insistence upon cure—which means the abolition of hurt instead of its transformation—helps me to believe this. I have, indeed, been invaded by a virus, a germ I need to rid myself of. Looking back on it now, I see this belief only added to my panic, shrunk my world still smaller.

On the first day of Prozac I felt nothing, on the second and third nausea, and then for the rest of that week headaches so intense, I wanted to groan and lower my face into a bowl of crushed ice. I had never had migraines before. In their own way they are beautiful, all pulsing suns and squeezing colors. When I closed my eyes, pink shapes flapped and angels' halos spun. I was a girl again, lying in the snow. Slowly, one by one, the frozen forms lifted toward the light.

And then there really was an angel over me, pressing a cool cloth to my forehead. He held two snowy tablets out to me, and in a haze of pain I took them.

"You'll be all right," Adam said to me. When I cried, it was a creek coming from my eyes.

I rubbed my eyes. The headache ebbed.

"How are you?" he asked.

"Okay," I said. And waited for a command. *Touch your nose, blink twelve times, try not to think about think about concentrating.*

The imperatives came—I could hear them—but from far far away, like birds beyond a mountain, a sound nearly silent and easy to ignore.

"I'm . . . okay," I repeated. I went out into the kitchen. The clock on the stove ticked. I pressed my ear against it and heard, this time, a steady, almost soothing pulse.

Most things, I think, diminish over time, rock and mountain, glacier and bone. But this wasn't the nature of Prozac, or me on Prozac. One day I was ill, cramped up with fears, and the next day the ghosts were gone. Imagine having for years a raging fever, and then one day someone hands you a new kind of pill, and within a matter of hours sweat dries, the scarlet swellings go down, your eyes no longer burn.

The grass appears green again, the sky a gentle blue. *Hello hello.*
Remember me? the planet whispers.

But to say I returned to the world is even a bit misleading, for all
my life the world has seemed off kilter. On Prozac, not only did the
acute obsessions dissolve; so, too, did the blander depression that had
been with me since my earliest memories. A sense of immense calm
flooded me. Colors came out, yellow leaping from the light where it
had long lain trapped, greens unwinding from the grass, dusk letting
loose its lavender.

By the fourth day I still felt so shockingly fine that I called the
Prozac Doctor. I pictured him in his office, high in the eaves of Mc-
Clean. I believed he had saved me. He loomed large.

"I'm well," I told him.

"Not yet. It takes at least a month to build up a therapeutic blood
level."

"No," I said. "It doesn't." I felt a rushing joy. "The medicine you
gave me has made me well. I've—I've actually never felt better."

A pause on the line. "I suppose it could be possible."

"Yes," I said. "It's happened."

I became a "happening" kind of person. Peter
Kramer, author of *Listening to Prozac,* has written extensively on the
drug's ability to galvanize personality change as well as to soothe fears
or elevate mood. Kramer calls Prozac a cosmetic medication, for it
seems to reshape the psyche, lift the face of the soul.

One night, soon after the medication had "kicked in," I sat at the
kitchen table with Adam. He was stuck in the muck of his master's
thesis, fearful of failure.

"It's easy," I said. "Break the project down into bits. A page a day.
Six days, one chapter. Twelve days, two. One month, presto." I
snapped my fingers. "You're finished."

Adam looked at me, said nothing. The kitchen grew quiet, a deliberate sort of silence he seemed to be purposefully manufacturing so I
could hear the echo of my own voice. Bugs thumped on the screen. I

heard the high, happy pitch of a cheerleader, the sensible voice of a vocational counselor. In a matter of moments I had gone from a fumbling, unsure person to this—all pragmatism, all sure solutions. For the first time on Prozac I felt afraid.

I lay in bed that night. From the next room I heard the patter of Adam's typewriter keys. He was stuck in the mire, inching forward and falling back. Where was I; who was I? I lifted my hand to my face, the same motion as before, when the full force of obsession had struck me. The hand was still unfamiliar, but wonderfully so now, the three threaded lines seams of silver, the lights from passing cars rotating on my walls like the swish of a spaceship softly landing.

In space I was then, wondering. How could a drug change my mind so abruptly? How could it bring forth buried or new parts of my personality? The oldest questions, I know. My brain wasn't wet clay and paste, as all good brains should be, but a glinting thing crossed with wires. I wasn't human but machine. No, I wasn't machine, but animal, linked to my electrified biology more completely than I could have imagined. We have come to think, lately, of machines and animals, of machines and nature, as occupying opposite sides of the spectrum—there is IBM and then there's the lake—but really they are so similar. A computer goes on when you push its button. A gazelle goes on when it sees a lynx. Only humans are supposedly different, above the pure cause and effect of the hard-wired, primitive world. Free will and all.

But no, maybe not. For I had swallowed a pill designed through technology, and in doing so, I was discovering myself embedded in an animal world. I was a purely chemical being, mood and personality seeping through serotonin. We are all taught to believe it's true, but how strange to feel that supposed truth bubbling right in your own tweaked brainpan. Who was I, all skin and worm; all herd? For the next few weeks, amid feelings of joy and deep relief, these thoughts accompanied me, these slow, simmering misgivings. In dreams, beasts roamed the rafters of my bones, and my bones were twined with wire, teeth tiny silicone chips.

I went to Drumlin Farm one afternoon to see the animals. A goose ate grass in an imperturbable rhythm. Sheep brayed robotically, their noses pointing toward the sky. I reached out to touch their fur. Simmering misgivings, yes, but my fingers alive, feeling clumps of cream, of wool.

Every noon I took my pill. Instead of just placing it on my tongue and swallowing with water, I unscrewed the capsule. White powder poured into my hands. I tossed the plastic husk away, cradled the healing talc. I tasted it, a burst of bitterness, a gagging. I took it that way every day, the silky slide of Prozac powder, the harshness in my mouth.

Mornings now, I got up early to jog, showered efficiently, then strode off to the library. I was able to go back to work, cutting deli part-time at Formaggio's while I prepared myself for divinity school the next year by reading. I read with an appetite, hungry from all the time I'd lost to illness. The pages of the book seemed very white; the words were easy, black beads shining, ebony in my quieted mind.

I found a book in the library's medical section about obsessive compulsive disorder. I sat in a corner, on a corduroy cushion, to read it. And there, surrounded by pages and pages on the nature of God and mystery, on Job, who cried out at his unfathomable pain, I read about my disorder from a medical perspective, followed the charts and graphs and correlation coefficients. The author proposed that OCD was solely physical in origin, and had the same neurological etiology as Tourette's. Obsessive symptoms, the author suggested, are atavistic responses left over from primitive grooming behaviors. We still have the ape in us; a bird flies in our blood. The obsessive person, linked to her reptilian roots, her mammalian ancestors, cannot stop picking parasites off her brother's back, combing her hair with her tongue, or doing the human equivalent of nest building, picking up stick after stick, leaf after leaf, until her bloated home sits ridiculously unstable in the crotch of an old oak tree.

Keel keel, the crow in me cries. The pig grunts. The screen of myself blinks on. Blinks off. Darkens.

Still, I was mostly peaceful, wonderfully organized. My mind felt lubed, thoughts slipping through so easily, words bursting into bloom. I was reminded of being a girl, on the island of Barbados, where we once vacationed. My father took me to a banquet beneath a tropical Basian sky. Greased black men slithered under low poles, their liquid bodies bending to meet the world. Torches flared, and on a long table before me steamed food of every variety. *A feast,* my father said, *all the good things in life.* Yes, that was what Prozac was first like for me— all the good things in life—roasted ham, delicate grilled fish, lemon halves wrapped in yellow waxed paper, fat plums floating in jars.

I could, I thought, do anything in this state of mind. I put my misgivings aside (how fast they would soon come back; how hard they would hit) and ate into my days, a long banquet. I did things I'd never done before, swimming at dawn in Walden Pond, writing poetry I knew was bad, and loving it anyway.

I applied for and was awarded a three-month grant to go to Appalachia, where I wanted to collect oral histories of mountain women. I could swagger anywhere on the Zack, on Vitamin P. Never mind that even before I'd ever come down with OCD I'd been the anxious, tentative sort. Never mind that unnamed trepidations, for all of my life, had prevented me from taking a trip to New Hampshire for more than a few days. Now that I'd taken the cure, I really could go anywhere, even off to the rippling blue mountains of poverty, far from a phone or a friend.

A gun hung over the door. In the oven I saw a roasted bird covered with flies. In the bathroom, a fat girl stooped over herself without bothering to shut the door, and pulled a red rag from between her legs.

Her name was Kim, her sister's name was Bridget, and their mother and father were Kat and Lonny. All the females were huge and doughy, while Lonny stood, a single strand of muscle tanned to the color of tobacco. He said very little while the mother and daughters chattered on, offering me Cokes and Cheerios, showing me to my room, where I sat on a lumpy mattress and stared at the white walls.

And then a moon rose. A storm of hurricane force plowed through fields and sky. I didn't feel myself here. The sound of the storm, battering just above my head, seemed far, far away. There was a whispering in my mind, a noise like silk being split. Next to me, on the night table, my sturdy bottle of Prozac. I was fine. So long as I had that, I would be fine.

I pretended I was fine for the next couple of days, racing around with manic intensity. I sat heavy Kat in one of her oversized chairs and insisted she tell me everything about her life in the Blue Ridge Mountains, scribbling madly as she talked. *I am happy happy happy* I sang to myself. I tried to ignore the strange sounds building in my brain, kindling that crackles, a flame getting hot.

And then I was taking a break out in the sandy yard. It was near one hundred degrees. The sun was tiny in a bleary sky. Chickens screamed and pecked.

In one swift and seamless move, Lonny reached down to grab a bird. His fist closed in on its throat while all the crows cawed and the beasts in my bones brayed away. He laid the chicken down on a stump, raised an ax, and cut. The body did its dance. I watched the severing, how swiftly connections melt, how deep and black is space. Blood spilled.

I ran inside. I was far from a phone or a friend. Maybe I was reminded of some preverbal terror: the surgeon's knife, the violet umbilical cord. Or maybe the mountain altitudes had thrown my chemistry off. I don't really know why, or how. But as though I'd never swallowed a Prozac pill, my mind seized and clamped and the obsessions were back.

I took a step forward and then said to myself *don't take another step until you count to twenty-five*. After I'd satisfied that imperative, I had to count to twenty-five again, and then halve twenty-five, and then quarter it, before I felt safe enough to walk out the door. By the end of the day, each step took over ten minutes to complete. I stopped taking steps. I sat on my bed.

"What's wrong with you?" Kat said. "Come out here and talk with us."

I tried, but I got stuck in the doorway. There was a point above the doorway I just had to see, and then see again, and inside of me something screamed *back again back again* and the grief was very large.

For I had experienced the world free and taken in colors and tasted grilled fish and moon. I had left one illness like a too-tight snakeskin, and here I was, thrust back. What's worse than illness is to think you're cured—partake of cure in almost complete belief—and then with no warning to be dashed on a dock, moored.

Here's what they don't tell you about Prozac. The drug, for many obsessives who take it, is known to have wonderfully powerful effects in the first few months, when it's new to the body. When I called the Prozac Doctor from Kentucky that evening, he explained to me how the drug, when used to treat OCD as opposed to depression, "peaks" at about six months, and then loses some of its oomph. "Someday we'll develop a more robust pill," Dr. Vuckovic said. "In the meantime, up your dose."

I upped my dose. No relief. Why not? Please. Over the months I had come to need Prozac in a complicated way, had come to see it as my savior, half hating it, half loving it. I unscrewed the capsules and poured their contents over my fingers. Healing talc, gone. Dead sand. I fingered the empty husks.

"You'll feel better if you come to church with us," Kat said to me that Sunday morning. She peered into my face, which must have been white and drawn. "Are you suffering from some city sickness?"

I shrugged. My eyes hurt from crying. I couldn't read or write; I could only add, subtract, divide, divide again.

"Come to church," Kat said. "We can ask the preacher to pray for you."

But I didn't believe in prayers where my illness was concerned. I had come to think, through my reading and the words of doctors, and especially through my brain's rapid response to a drug, that whatever was wrong with me had a simplistic chemical cause. Such a belief can be devastating to sick people, for on top of their illness they must struggle with the sense that illness lacks any creative possibilities.

I think these beliefs, so common in today's high-tech biomedical era, where the focus is relentlessly reductionistic, rob illness of its potential dignity. Illness can be dignified; we can conceive of pain as a kind of complex answer from an elegant system, an arrow pointing inward, a message from soil or sky.

Not so for me. I wouldn't go to church or temple. I wouldn't talk or ask or wonder, for these are distinctly human activities and I'd come to view myself as less than human.

An anger rose up in me then, a rage. I woke late one night, hands fisted. It took me an hour to get out of bed, so many numbers I had to do, but I was determined.

And then I was walking, outside, pushing past the need to count before every step. The night air was muggy, and insects raised a chorus.

I passed midnight fields, a single shack with lighted windows. Cows slept in a pasture.

I rounded the pasture, walked up a hill. And then, before me, spreading out in moonglow, a lake. I stood by its lip. My mind was buzzing and jerking. I don't know at what point the swans appeared— white swans, they must have been, but in silhouette they looked black—that seemed to materialize straight out of the slumbering water. They rose to the surface of the water as memories rise to the surface of consciousness. Hundreds of black swans suddenly, floating absolutely silent, and as I stood there, the counting ceased, my mind became silent, and I watched. The swans drifted until it seemed, for a few moments, that they were inside me, seven dark, silent birds, fourteen princesses, a single self swimming in a tepid sea.

I don't know how long I stood there, or when, exactly, I left. The swans disappeared eventually. The counting ticking talking of my mind resumed.

Still, even in chattering illness I had been quieted for a bit; doors in me had opened; elegance had entered.

This thought calmed me. I was not completely claimed by illness, nor a prisoner of Prozac, entirely dependent on the medication to function. Part of me was still free, a private space not absolutely permeated by pain. A space I could learn to cultivate.

Over the next few days I noticed that even in the thicket of obsessions my mind sometimes swam into the world, if only for brief forays. There, while I struggled to take a step, was the sun on a green plate. *Remember that,* I said to myself. And here, while I stood fixated in a doorway, was a beetle with a purplish shell like eggplants growing in wet soil. *Appreciate this,* I told myself, and I can say I did, those slivers of seconds when I returned to the world. I loved the beetle, ached for the eggplant, paddled in a lake with black swans.

And so a part of me began to learn about living outside the disease, cultivating appreciation for a few free moments. It was nothing I would have wished for myself, nothing to noisily celebrate. But it was something, and I could choose it, even while mourning the paralyzed parts of me, the pill that had failed me.

A long time ago, Freud coined the term "superego." A direct translation from German means "over I." Maybe what Freud meant, or should have meant, was not a punitive voice but the angel in the self who rises above an ego under siege, or a medicated mind, to experience the world from a narrow but occasionally gratifying ledge.

I am thirty-one now, and I know that ledge well. It is a smaller space than I would have wished for myself—I who would like to possess a mind free and flexible. I don't. Even after I raised my dose, the Prozac never worked as well as it once had, and years later I am sometimes sad about that, other times strangely relieved, even though my brain is hounded. I must check my keys, the stove; I must pause many times while I write this and do a ritual count to thirty. It's distracting to say the least, but still I write this. I can walk and talk and play. I've come to live my life in those brief stretches of silence that arrive throughout the day, working at what I know is an admirable speed, accomplishing all I can in clear pauses, knowing those pauses may be short-lived. I am learning something about the single moment, how rife with potential it is, how truly loud its tick. I have heard clocks and clocks. Time shines, sad and good.

And what of the unclear, mind-cluttered stretches? These, as well, I have bent to. I read books now, even when my brain has real difficulties taking in words. Half a word, or a word blurred by static, is better than nothing at all. There is also a kind of stance I've developed, detaching my mind from my mind, letting the static sizzle on while I walk, talk, read, while the obsessive cycles continue and I, stepping aside, try to link my life to something else. It is a meditative exercise of a high order, and one I'm getting better at. Compensations can be gritty gifts.

Is this adaptation a spiritual thing? When I'm living in moments of clarity, have I transcended disease or has disease transformed me, taught me how to live in secret niches? I don't know.

A few nights ago, a man at a party, a Christian psychologist, talked about the brain. "The amazing thing," he said, "is that if you cut the corpus callosum of small children, they learn without the aid of medication or reparative surgery how to transfer information from the left to the right hemisphere. And because we know cerebral neurons never rejuvenate, that's evidence," he said, "for a mind that lives beyond the brain, a mind outside our biologies."

Perhaps. Or perhaps our biologies are broader than we ever thought. Perhaps the brain, because of its wound, has been forced into some kink of creativity we can neither see nor explain. This is what the doctors didn't tell me about illness; that an answer to illness is not necessarily cure, but an ambivalent compensation. Disease, for sure, is disorganization, but cure is not necessarily the synthetic pill-swallowing righting of the mess. To believe this is to rigidly define brain function in terms of "normal" and "abnormal," a devastating definition for many. And to believe this, especially where the psyche is concerned, may also mean dependence on psychotropic drugs, and the risk of grave disappointment if the drugs stop working.

I think of those children, their heads on white sheets, their corpus callosums exposed and cut. I wonder who did that to them, and why. I'm sure there is some compelling medical explanation—racking seizures that need to be stopped—but still, the image disturbs me. I think more, though, of the children's brains once sewn back inside the bony pockets of skull. There, in the secret dark, between wrenched hemispheres, I imagine tiny tendrils growing, so small and so deep, not even the strongest machines can see them. They are real but not real, biological but spiritual. They wind in and out, joining left to right, building webbed wings and rickety bridges, sending out messengers with critical information, like the earliest angels who descended from the sky with news and challenge, wrestling with us in nighttime deserts, straining our thighs, stretching our bodies in pain, no doubt, until our skin took on new shapes.

Heading North

WILLIAM VAN WERT

I think of my mother in Canada somehow. My dead and disembodied mother. In Canada now. She was French-Canadian and she had a feel for cold breezes that come over lakes in late autumn, but she never went back there. She was deathly afraid of water, the result of a childhood fear of drowning and bad eyesight as an adult, but I always put her near water when I think of her: a thousand lakes in Canada, loons in lackadaisical flight over finger lakes, bass breaking water as though for bragging rights, and stunted pine trees everywhere. In every direction, this sanctuary. How could something so wild be synonymous with safety? Here the quiet teems and overflows with noise: crickets, whistling, thumping, snapping, cackling, the quick shuttle of Canada geese, always flying, forever afraid. I put my mother there, in the pause before everything scatters.

But she died in Florida, in a hospital too pretty for Hallmark cards, a room too ripe with olive colors, a bed so near the beach she could feel the tides changing without ever looking out. She died of cancer, her disease somehow a metaphor for the heat of late March, the harbor near Naples too hot to walk with bare feet, the highways cluttered with cars trying to go north, the smells of lime and coconuts, fan palms and bougainvillea all permeated with exhaust fumes, oil stains, construction tar, mowed lawns, pesticides, and the rush of rank odor from shellfish or chowder at every other restaurant. She died in Florida, where she never wanted to be, and I was there, holding her wet, shorn head when she went, feeling so alive that I was humbled with joy, so much so that it took weeks to miss her.

My father still loved my mother, but he could not bear to speak of dying. And so they spared each other: he spared her his tears and despair, she spared him her agony and death. My wife still lived with me then, but she could not stand to see me go to my mother. There are great divides to every death. My father's cheer, my marriage, neither survived my mother's death.

And yet I never mourned those things. The clarity of her dying made me cold to things I could not control. It is easy to think after a death that such things might be inevitable, the way people live with new priorities who come through a plane crash or avalanche, hurricane, or world war. I was sobered into final manhood by her death, but I was also lightened up for life. I could never again not laugh at little things. I was filled with little ragtag adages, like unmatched socks, left by my mother: "Some people are so petty, they could play handball against the curb." Back in the big cities of the Northeast and stuck in senseless traffic jams, I would look for the curb and laugh. Curbs and laughter. And I realized that we can only truly mourn what we refuse to accept, what we think we could have changed.

Long after a death ceases to be real, mourning has the feel of something childlike in our memories.

"I want to go out," my mother says. "Who's game?"

"You should rest," my father says.

"I'll take you," I say, seeing that she means it.

She who has hidden for a year and a half wants to be shown. She's sick and tired of going out only to be radiated in Fort Myers or take massive doses of cytoxin in Naples. She puts a bonnet on to cover her bald head, and she says she's ready. She looks Amish, her body more brittle and camelbacked than ever her sense of humor would have allowed.

"I look pretty sexy, huh?"

I don't know what to say. I wonder if she tries these lines on my father. Questions like taunts. My father, always so dignified, goes gray with grace. He is Dutch and silent, appropriate and dull. My mother cracks her chewing gum with the irreverence of a teenager. She is nervous, moody, easily bred, hard to hold, quick to cry.

"You don't have to take me so seriously," she says, slapping my accelerator knee and causing us to go momentarily faster.

"Hey," she says, mock-horrified, "I've had better rides in an ambulance."

We go to Naples, to Hudson's, the best clothing store. She heads immediately for the muumuus and Hawaiian wear.

"I've got thirty of these already," she says. "What am I doing?"

"Going for thirty-one," I say. "My treat."

"Nix that," she says. "I'm loaded. Your father gave me three grand to buy a piano."

She waits for me to ask why we aren't buying a piano.

"Because he'd be stuck with it after I'm gone."

As usual, she doesn't wait long enough for me to ask.

"I have a joke for you," she says, three muumuus wrapped over her arm, leading me to the cashier, "but you have to ask me two questions. First, 'What is your occupation?' and then, 'What is the secret of your success?' "

"Okay," I say, "what is your occupation?"

"World's greatest Polish comedian."

"And what is the sec—"

"Timing."

She shouts the word, and the cashier has only heard a customer with three muumuus scream "timing." She laughs anyway, and her polite laughter only makes me laugh even harder. I am in Florida to cheer up my dying mother, and instead she is telling me jokes.

I look outside while I wait for my mother to pay. I feel like such a stranger to this state. Florida is a rain forest, Florida is a desert, the two truths ten minutes apart, as the sun reacts to the insult of wetness. There are sudden storms, purple east-west torrents that make a mockery of umbrellas, followed by piercing heat, as though the two were inextricably tied to some primitive worship ritual. Boys of summer play baseball in March, even as the retirees go back to the Midwest to wait out the summer, descending again about the time the World Series is over in October.

My mother is caught in this unbearable heat, shipwrecked on land and restricted by her treatments and her fragile body from going back to Michigan, where she left all her roots and memories.

In the parking lot she is depressed.

"Three more things I can't give away."

"Why not?"

"Because your father would think I'd given up the fight if I gave anything away. You know, there was a pleasure in buying them, but now they make me sad. When you opened the trunk, I thought of a casket . . ."

"Let's take them back."

"We can't do that."

"Then let's give them away."

"How?"

We went back into Hudson's and we looked for someone the same size as my mother. The other customers were either too old or too fat or too fancy for muumuus. Then I noticed that our cashier was about the same height and build as my mother.

"Why are you doing this?" she asked, reluctantly taking her gift along with the sales slip.

"Because you laughed at her joke," I lied.

My mother is still not convinced. Outside in the parking lot she grabs my arm and asks.

"What did we do that for?"

"I don't know. How do you feel?"

"Great. And a little guilty at the same time."

"Can you live with the guilt?" I ask.

"Not for long." She smiles.

I think of my mother at the piano at the cottage in Michigan and how she loved to play when it was raining outside, as though the rain on the lake, the wind through the birch trees, and the muffled staccato of plunking on the closed windows made her playing even better. I think of her as someone who always played for others at parties, and so one night I played for her, and I played her songs: "You Were Meant for Me" and "Since I Don't Have You" and "Memories" and "On Moonlight Bay." Her era, her tempo, her fingering, I played them as close to my memory of her playing them as I could, and when my father, watching TV in the other room, said, "You ought to be resting," I knew I was playing them well. And my mother, her knees propped up under her muumuu in the red rocker, sometimes sang, sometimes hummed, once whistled, and once talked about the man she might have married if she hadn't married my father, because "You Were Meant for Me" was their song.

"But then I wouldn't have had you," she said, cracking her gum and getting up, asking me if I wanted a midnight snack of brownies and ice cream.

I declined and kept on playing, while she fed my father the brownies and vanilla ice cream, because, when I put my mother in that music, I knew she was safe.

We're at Bonita Beach at my insistence, and my mother will not leave the Bonneville.

"You're really pressing your luck," she says. "Go take your swim."

She stays in the car, the blue scarf wrapped like a turban around her head. My parents have been in Florida for ten years, and, except for the occasional group outing to Sanibel or Marcos Islands, they have not been to the ocean. On purpose I stayed away from Fort Myers Beach, too crowded with other retirees, and Vanderbilt Beach, where the elite meet to go topless and bury their feet in the admission-only sand. Here at Bonita Beach there is only the occasional tourist from the condominiums and the Cubans who live in town. My mother is in remission, and still she refuses to leave the hot car.

I go to change in the woods. I hide my clothes in a cluster of hunchbacked pines that have settled at a forty-five-degree angle to the waves. It is high tide, late afternoon, and the water is aqua, moving to a velvety green the color of Astroturf in the slanting rays of the sun. I urinate in the pine needles before I put on my bathing suit. My urine crackles, fizzes, and bubbles up in the pine straw, as though I had put hydrogen peroxide on a dirty wound. I have goose bumps all over my body, because I am suddenly naked. I have a chill, even though I am sweating.

There is a profound pleasure to my running full-tilt into the water, knee-high and kicking, until I lose my balance and fall headlong into the surf. I am thinking about making love as I come up and taste the salt on my tongue, feel my pores opening up, smell the vast irregular ocean as a sweaty woman underneath me, full of taut muscles and moaning with joy. I accelerate my swimming, because I know my mother is waiting in the car, and still I indulge in my sexual fantasies, my respite from her cancer like a sacrilege, a sudden surge of animal bad manners. I can feel my erection, and, the more inappropriate it feels, the more ecstatic I become. This is what it means to have a body that sings, and because my mother, the last buffer between me and my own aging, disease, and dying, doesn't have one, I revel in my own, as though I were doing a fox trot instead of swimming.

I run to the woods and dress in a hurry. I try unsuccessfully to get my legs into my underpants without depositing beach sand in my pants. My damp shirt and shorts stick to me as I run to the car.

I stop short when I see my mother asleep at the wheel. She is, I think I see, in the pose that death will take her, her head cocked back, her jaws stretched, her mouth open like some prehistoric skull. Her snoring sounds like the mild blowing of a nose.

I feel like a voyeur as I tiptoe toward the front of the car to get a better look at her face. There are perspiration beads on her forehead. She who has never sweated and hates the feel and smell of sweat is sweating now.

She jumps when I open the passenger door. She clears her throat, adjusts her glasses, leans forward, and turns on the ignition to my father's big Bonneville, all in one motion, and then she turns to look at me.

"You peed in the bushes over there, didn't you?"

"Could you see?"

"No, but I could tell."

I put my seat belt around my waist and wait for the lecture that doesn't come.

"I never did that," she says, a lilt in her voice, her eyes bloodshot and dreamy-bashful.

I look at my mother as though for the first time.

I think of my mother as a vessel for birth, forever child-rearing, even children, the children of their children, a sea horse that spit children. I think of her as sacrifice, her ego suppressed, years of formal authority, common sense, a problem-solving propriety. Cancer stripped her of her dignity, until one day, Florida or not, self-doubt and bald desires broke through her skin like a rash.

Her name was Dolores, which means "sorrows," and she seemed born for sacrifice, more a fact in our growing up than a tragedy. We never stopped to wonder about the worth of such a person.

I think of my mother sweating as her moment of most human frailty, and I put her up north, at first in Canada and then in big cities by the lakes—Milwaukee, Chicago, Cleveland—cities of severe winters to exhilarate her, cities of windblown summers to soothe her, because the thing I wanted least in the world was responsibility for her sweat, her self-awareness, her stink.

My father and I are at the driving range across the road from his retirement park in Bonita Spring. I am either looking at his back or he is looking at mine. Either way, the symbolism does not escape me. I have no need to hit a ball three hundred yards, and so I hit for the sound, the pure solid whack, and pay no attention to distance or direction. My father takes longer to swing, and his stroke is shorter, more compact than mine. He wants a straight ball, a line drive, low to the ground and hissing. No pop-ups, hooks, or slices.

I catch him feeling under his arm. My father is the invisible victim, looking for lumps when no one else is looking.

"I want to thank you for coming down," he says, hitting his ball like he hates it, "and for all you've done for your mother."

He acts renegade in saying this, as though half the thanks were an accusation that I have somehow usurped his place.

He cannot help himself. Model father, gentle man, he cannot refrain from complaining just a little bit about my mother.

"She won't eat, you know. I've never cooked a thing in my whole life, and, finally, when I have to learn and she's shouting directions from the head and I think I've made a good meal, she won't eat it. And the golf. I don't even play nine anymore. Whole year's dues and cart privileges, shot to hell. I get over here to the driving range, it's the only time I get away from her. She doesn't understand, though. She pouts and pretends she's asleep when I come back. And then I try to cheer her up. I tell her we'll travel when she gets better."

"She doesn't want to travel, Dad."

"Well, she doesn't want to stay here, that's for sure."

"I don't think she wants to hear about when she gets better either."

"I don't know what, then. She turns her face away and doesn't want to talk at all. Forty-two years we've been married, we've always been able to talk."

"Talk to her about dying."

"Are you crazy?"

"Then let her talk to you about how it feels to be dying."

"I can't do that."

"Why not?"

"It scares the shit out of me."

My father who has never sworn in my presence now curses.

"It isn't fair," he whines, out of control and hurling his number one wood to the ground. "You work a lifetime for this, a little quiet and companionship, and then you get this nightmare instead. What's it all mean anyway?"

I don't have a pocket axiom for him. I have been asking myself that question a lot, the repetition in asking for lack of an answer.

"Your mother tells me you are wise. So, wise man, what should I do?"

"What you're able."

I say this to be kind, to forgive him for not being able to cure her cancer, for not being able to take it on himself, but the words sound hollow to me as soon as I say them. They sound like the advice of a Little League coach: stay within yourself, check your velocity and location, stick to basics, watch your mechanics, know the score, and do what you're able to do.

One Sunday my mother and I are supposedly going to church. She has been bedridden for two weeks, so this is a shock to my father, who has already gone to the early Mass and is outdoors, spraying his lime trees. He looks at me oddly, as though I had worked a miracle. But, once outside the park, my mother tells me she is still too angry with God to go to church.

We go to the Sunday brunch at a restaurant called the Clock in Bonita Springs. She lights up a cigarette.

"I thought you quit."

"I did."

"But?"

"I started again."

"Why?"

"Doctors' orders. They said smoking wouldn't help, wouldn't hurt, at least in my case. They said, 'Live it up,' so here I am."

"I thought they made you nauseous."

"Everything makes me nauseous. Besides, I like the way they make me dizzy. Takes my mind off things."

I stare at the red ring of lipstick smear round the white filter of her Salem. I get eggs, sausage, and honeydew melon from the buffet. When I come back to the table, she is ordering liver and onions from the supper menu.

"I'll have to check, hon," the waitress says.

"Tell them it's the only thing I can keep down," my mother says.

The waitress looks at my mother, at the tight scarf, the black bags under the eyes, the sandpapered cheek. Awareness sets in.

"We'll make an exception," she says, winking at my mother.

"Can't beat the preferential treatment," my mother whispers to me. "You threaten to throw up, they'll cook you anything you want."

I know this time is precious, but I can't think of how to make it special. I'm not very good at talking about dying over breakfast. I feel lazy, lethargic, overweight somehow. I have this panic suddenly that I haven't felt since my first dates as a teenager, the panic of having absolutely nothing to say.

She saves me.

"There's trouble in your marriage, isn't there?"

"Why? Because I've been coming down here?"

"No, because you never talk about Jane. You used to quote her all the time when you first got married."

"I don't find her very quotable these days. I think there's been trouble, as you put it, for quite some time."

"How long?"

"Since Teddy's birth. Jane loved being pregnant. Seemed like she was born to it. But she wasn't cut out for raising kids. Took us three babies to find that out. We fight all the time now. Little things. Stupid things. Petty things."

"Handball against the curb, huh?"

"Something like that."

"What does she think about you being down here?"

"She doesn't like it. She thinks you're acting out some sort of elaborate game to get your sons back."

"Acting, huh? Well, after all this, I sure hope I get the part."

She laughs and chokes a little on her smoke.

"Anyway, it can't be helped," I say, trying to change the topic.

"Don't be too hard on her, okay?"

"What do you mean?"

"I think there may be some truth in what she says. Jane's unhappy with three little guys around the house. I'm unhappy because my seven have all grown up and gone. All those years raising you kids, I was never sick a day in my life. Now I'm dying. Some women go one way, some go another, and you can't judge them for the way they go. It's just the way it is."

The way it is feels flat, false, like saying "do what you're able."

"What do your kids say?"

"I was packing to come down here and Teddy came up and hugged my leg. And he told me, 'Daddy, everything you say and do is right and true.' It felt like prophecy or Scripture somehow. It even came out rhymed."

My mother smiles with love awash on her face, and I'm not sure whether it's for me or for Teddy.

"Do you see what's happening?" she asks, lighting another cigarette and ignoring her liver and onions. "You're quoting your son now instead of your wife."

"So?"

"Don't get defensive. I do that too."

"I didn't know you had a wife."

"Smartypants," she snorts, blowing smoke in my face.

"So, how's your marriage?"

"Never been better."

This was the joy my father could bring and nobody but my mother could see. He suppressed his fear in front of her. He allowed no talk of dying in her presence. He pretended life as usual and talked tentatively of moving to Texas or Arizona, there sun belts, distant dreams. But he backed up his suffocating cheer with a calm self-confidence, a control my mother could always rely on, a caretaking unusual in older men, gentle hands, loving looks. It was his gift, this tenderness.

He believed her inability to get to church to be physical. My parents were both "cradle Catholics," and my father could not bear to think that my mother was angry with God, suffering from spiritual dread. My mother faked her bad back and nausea on Sunday mornings. My father began to prepare himself to be a lay deacon, so that one day he could bring the eucharist home to her.

I went to church with my father. I took communion in my cupped hands instead of on my tongue. I held the wafer in between my folded hands and put it in my shirt pocket when I got back to my pew. Later, when my father went out to water the lime trees, I gave the host to my mother.

"What are you doing?" she asked, incredulous.

"Bringing the mountain to Mohammed."

"That's the wrong religion." She laughed.

"I figured you could use it more than I could."

"Since when have you gotten so holy?"

"It's not that. On the other hand, I'm not the one who's mad at God."

"How'd you know?"

"No crystal ball. It would be a little abnormal if you weren't angry."

"Yes, but what do I do with it?"

"Get it out?"

"I can't."

"You think your anger is so ferocious that God can't take it? You're pissed with God. You're furious. Admit it. That anger is the best prayer you've got right now. Tell God to go to hell."

"That's an impossibility."

"You know what I mean."

"Do you really think I could?" she asks, the look of hazy redemption in the corner of her eye.

"If you get the anger out, you'll feel the love again. You know how this cancer feels. Close your eyes and imagine giving it over to God."

"What if she won't take it?"

I never knew my mother to be such a feminist.

"God will take whatever you've got to give. That's the way religion works, isn't it?"

She likes it. My mother smiles and takes the wafer into her mouth.

"Could you leave us alone for a while?" she asks.

I was so caught off guard by her modesty, I almost said "Who?"

I coax my father into a game of catch. I didn't used to have to coax. When he was in his thirties and I was growing up, baseball was a ritual between us. It was his time to father us before supper. We all had our own autographed gloves, Detroit Tiger signatures: Al Kaline, Harvey Kuenn, Ray Boone, Ferris Fain, Frank Lary, Dick McAuliffe. We dreamed the dream he seeded as we made up imaginary players and swung for homers against the birch trees. But now he is almost seventy, I am almost forty, and that dream is clearly over for both of us.

He has arthritis and cannot swing his leg for a follow-through when he throws. I am overweight and have trouble bending for some of his low throws. Still, I bring two gloves and a ball, because it is fast, physical, and not far away. We play tired catch, and still I take pleasure in this tossing and taking, perhaps because there is absolutely no sense to it.

People come and go from the park, mostly wide-hipped women with coiled gray hair, too much lipstick, too much perfume, bringing desserts: cakes of all sorts and sizes, lemon meringue pies, cheese danish, apple fritters, sticky buns, and cinnamon rolls. My father is gracious and offers a drink, which they take or refuse. In either case, they stare at my mother, they talk about her instead of to her, they pat her on the head or hand when they leave. Cancer is the leprosy.

Sometimes my mother reacts with jealousy. She thinks they have come to put out their smell for my father. She calls them "the hens, waiting to get at the rooster." Sometimes it is less personal. Then she is simply reacting to their cowardice by leaving the room to go lie down, leaving these women to drink with my father. Most of the desserts go out in the next morning's trash.

Some people do not come at all. They send cards instead: holy cards with Masses to be said; lame cards with rhymed lines, more expensive than thoughtful; cards with poems by Rod McKuen or Kahlil Gibran; cards with Snoopy on top of his dog house, a thermometer in his mouth.

"I don't know how to answer them," she tells me, showing me a stack of more than fifty.

"What do you want to say?"

"Oh, I don't know. Something between skip it and shove it."

The cards become a night's diversion. In Florida, the land of *Miami Vice*, marijuana is legalized for advanced-stage cancer patients. My mother and I eat laced brownies one night, and I get so stoned that I decide to answer her cards for her.

"Dear Mrs. Lammoreaux:

Thank you for the poem by Burl Ives.

May you get hives."

And:

"Dear Paul and Alma:

Your sunshine smile made me want to say:

May your teeth fall out from tooth decay."

And:

"Dear Marge and Charley:

Thank you for the packaged fruit;

it spoiled en route."

After each one is written, I show it to my mother, who howls with delight. She is high, unused to feeling no pain and, for the time being, beyond good etiquette. She has tears in her eyes from so much laughing.

"I like your sense of revenge," she says.

"It's hereditary."

My father gets up, complaining that he can't sleep because of all the noise we're making.

"Eat a cookie, you old coot," my mother says, serving him laced brownies and black coffee.

"That stuff doesn't have any effect on me," he says.

"You want sticky buns from Mrs. Savage instead?"

"No, I'd rather have a brownie."

My mother reads him some of my cards. He doesn't think they're funny. I don't know any longer if they're funny or not, because everything is funny to me now, even my father's lack of laughing.

My mother shuffles to the refrigerator and opens the vegetable bin.

"What if these," she starts to say, holding an enormous green pepper in her hand, "tasted like spearmint gum?"

She begins to clean out the refrigerator at three in the morning. My father does not try to stop her. He still appears to be logical.

"I'll defrost the top," he says, "when you're done with the bottom."

I go to the hideaway bed in the Havana room. I look out the window before I sleep. Strange for Florida, the night is full-moon cold, like November nights over vacant cornfields in the Midwest. There is a faint smell of leaves burning.

When I get up the next morning, my mother is still in her bed and my father is still at the kitchen table. He has paid all his bills and rewritten all the thank-you notes, apparently unaware that he has stayed up all night, hyper on brownies. He never listens to the radio, except for baseball games, but here he is, listening to Bob Dylan's "Lily, Rosemary and the Jack of Hearts." The program is a potpourri of Dylan's longest songs: "Like a Rolling Stone," "Desolation Row," "With God on Our Side," and "Sad-Eyed Lady of the Lowlands." I wonder who the target audience is for these Dylan songs. "Ballads for salads," the deejay calls them, and it reminds me of my mother, holding a ball of iceberg lettuce and saying, "Do with me what thou wilt."

We are at supper suddenly. My father and I have collaborated on a pot roast, and my mother, who has been in bed all day, gets up at our insistence. She says she won't eat, just watch. My father, who has always said the blessing for as long as I can remember, is ready to do so again, when I interrupt.

"What if we let Mom say the blessing tonight?"

She blushes.

"I wouldn't know what to say."

She has never once said the blessing in forty-two years of marriage. She seems flattered and flustered, both at once.

"Say anything," my father says, "the food's getting cold."

"Okay. God bless Papa Bear, and God bless Baby Bear, and may the porridge be just right tonight. Amen."

I spent four separate weeks with my parents during the two years of my mother's dying. I remember every moment of that time. I remember almost nothing of the other twenty-three months I was in Philadelphia with Jane and the kids.

The last time I went to Florida to see my mother, she was in Naples Hospital and not coming out again. I sat down next to her bed and my father left the room. I took my mother's hand in mine and looked straight into those blue-glossy eyes.

"So, you're going to do it this time."

"Yup," she said as though she were holding a thermometer in her mouth.

"Any regrets?"

"Only that I can't take you all with me. I saw it all in a dream the other day. It was lovely. Like all the pretty parks you've ever seen, rolled into one. Not trees exactly, but the color and smell of trees. And water, but not flowing. And people all over the place, but not rooted to any ground. Dancing on air, flying, somersaults, things like that. I tried to tell your father, but he said he couldn't listen. He thought my Brompton dosage must be too strong."

"Maybe it is."

"You know what the doctor told me? He said I had so much morphine in me that I would be a junkie if I ever got better."

"More encouragement from the medical profession."

"He's okay. At least, he has a sense of humor."

"You know, Mom, all this time I've been more like a friend to you than like your son. Just this once I wanted to be your son and let you know how much I've loved you and how much I'm going to miss you."

"Just for that, I'm going to write you a really nasty thank-you note."

She died three days later. It was Saturday night, ten minutes shy of midnight, and she died in my arms a half hour after my father had gone home to wait for my call. When she shot through her body, it healed for twenty minutes, until rigor began to set in. Color came back to her face, her bloodshot eyes cleared, the ash circles went away. I stayed with her for an hour before I went out to tell the nurses and fill out the forms.

The next morning my father became a lay deacon at the twelve o'clock Mass. I couldn't bear to watch it. I went out back, behind the church, and lit a cigarette. Suddenly, I felt wrapped-around, as though encased in pillow feathers. At first I was afraid. This hug had no humor, no bones, no personal touch at all. It was vast and impersonal. I felt crowded inside, too much other-peopled and private, as though naked. I was small in this embrace and completely safe. It put my pride away, so that I could go back to church in a neutral way, no presence in my presence, no prejudice at all.

My mother wanted to be cremated. But when she died, my father shipped her home and showed her: her thin hair done up in a wasp's-nest way she never would have worn; her lips sewn shut and covered with lipstick, to look like a roaring twenties pout; her cheeks and hands, their marble sheen, cold as bruises. An open casket, a High Mass with homilies, a gig burial.

I felt no judgment at all. Who knows? If my father had died first, she might have done him the same way.

I put her back in Canada after the funeral. And I reflected, not so much on the dying itself, but on the small graces of her going. I am still embarrassed, six years later, to feel so much love, a son for his mother. It offends my Dutch control, my macho sense of mind over matter, my fear of Freud. To feel so stupidly devotional toward this woman who put me into the world and whom I befriended only at the very end, it makes me feel shy to tell it. My father is changed, my brothers and sisters are changed, and I am changed, more by the two years it took her to die than by all the years of raising.

I believe in the in-between moments now. I look forward to certain sorts of loneliness, little forays into the empty nest when Teddy and his brothers will have grown up and left me. I take pleasure in the way my sons' shoes look when they are asleep and not wearing shoes. I play catch with myself late at night when everyone else is asleep, throwing pop-ups into the darkness, not knowing whether they'll land in my glove or on my head. I dance with myself before and after every shower. Slowly, I am overcoming all my embarrassments.

There is this crazy notion in the culture that we should all be affluent enough to age gracefully, retire in the sun belts of the South and die without pain in our sleep. Me, I am more inclined to head north, to go where the cold sorts out all extraneous thoughts and where the nights are so long that you grow cat's eyes and the sudden blinding piebald days look like a park where nothing grows and everything flies.

Talking Back

FRANCES MAYES

On the frontispiece of childhood, a white goat pulls a painted cart. A long-haired goat brushed to shine, with a garland of violets around its ears. True red cart with wooden wheels. I am standing up in it wearing a sundress: a little charioteer of Delphi, only this is down in Georgia, where the flat pine country begins to go swampy. That was my desire, the goat I would name my own secret name, Nicole. I liked looking into the eyes of a goat, that black bar for a pupil. Did it see in blocks, like looking through a crack in the wall? Silky hair to comb and braid, the hard knobs that slowly would turn into curving horns.

But I had no training in getting what was unavailable to the imaginations of parents who thought of dolls as presents, and so I did not obtain my goat to prance me through the streets of Fitzgerald. With logic of their own, they gave me a green parakeet named Tweedle. They thought my fear of birds was silly and I should get over it. When my mother put her finger in the cage and said, "Pretty boy, pretty boy," the bird went crazy, all wings, and flew against the bars, turning over the water and lid of seed.

I wanted to be a child. "Successfully disguised to myself as a child," James Agee wrote. To myself, I was not disguised, only to others. I knew from stories and friends the concept of childhood. Magic and fairies and castles and the family going on family trips in the car over the river and through the woods. Picnics at the beach and family reunions and holding hands around the dinner table for silent prayers. I wanted to be a read-to child with a bedtime and warm milk and snow days. Instead, my parents let me run wild. The lavish events of reality constantly undercut the power of Oz dreams and animals that talked at midnight in tiny books. My parents, powerful, slapdash, sick of children, led unexamined lives. The brakes simply were gone. Calm days: my father at work, my mother playing bridge. Violent nights: nothing to do except face each other. Southern Comfort, recriminations, and if-onlys. Therefore, childhood, that time I knew I was entitled to, was impossible.

This can't be momentous. A Polish friend never hears about my past. He was found after World War II, when he was seven, eating beet peels in garbage bins. His parents, snuffed out when he was four. His early years played out against the large backdrop of history. No, nothing here but my family's closet-drama group. But the performances were first rate and convincing.

          In the bubble bath I still make low-cut dresses with foamy boas. Sometimes I sleep with the light on. Look under the bed when I come home late. In early afternoon the shadow growing away from my feet is the same one I cast as a child. When the last politeness is exhausted, I let the anger fly out where it will. I can still fall off the chair laughing, still suppress the desire to pinch hard when meanness in me wants to be resolved. Holdovers. As much as childhood existed then, it does now. The grown-up woman I am, I also was then: a palindrome. I've kept a vulgar streak, as my mother called it.

And no wonder, no wonder. How they howled when Ina's father told the Jehovah's Witness he was sorry it took him so long to get to the door but he'd been out back fucking a sheep, and the Witness ran off screaming. Extremes kept topping out over the limits of childhood. I observed. If I ever have a child, I'd say to myself, I'll give her a normal life.

Other families were happy. "The Greeks" were happy even though their daughter, Calliope, had polio and had to walk with crutches and go to Warm Springs and lie in an iron lung, that awful water heater turned on its side, a shape as terrifying then as the nuclear fires are now. The Lanes were happy even though the father drove a potato chip truck and they were common. My best friend was the only child in the perfect family.

She was doted on, prettily plump, their house had French doors that opened onto a long porch with a swing, beds with dips in the middle like nests. Happy mother and daddy who called her by a nickname leftover from baby talk. I could not be there enough. There was no chink. Ribbon candy always filled the same dish on the sideboard. We licked peach ice cream off the wooden beater, loved pouring the rock salt slush out of the churn. They were all admiring, told jokes, hugged, their garden fish pool had a statue of a naked boy, clean water coming out of his thing, landing on the old goldfish in the murk. There was a baby grand piano. My friend plunked out, "Song of the Volga Boatman," and "Blessed Be the Tie That Binds." Church not only Sunday morning but the evening service too. (I drew the line at that.)

At my house, in place of living we had commotion. Dingbat fights beginning with the whereabouts of keys and bills. A five-year-old could sense the idiocy. A seven-year-old could figure out that misery was entertainment. At bedrock, I sensed that my parents loved each other. I still feel that was true, still never have broken their code of relentless destructiveness, the determination to stay in the motion they were in. Some principle of thermodynamics in action. Or spiders, continuing to spin out the same weak, tenacious thread.

The house was short on closets. Mine was in the hall. My row of shirts and dresses, pile of shoes, squeezed in with the linen, my father's hunting guns, a shelf of medicines (I loved the deep blue Milk of Magnesia bottle), boxes of Mother's old love letters up top, and, on a hook, the rag bag sewn from a navy bedspread my uncle brought home from war. I hid. Closed the closet door, pulled open the drawstring of the rag bag, and crawled in. I settled in the corner and turned on my flashlight to read while my parents in the kitchen laughed those HA! false laughs, broke glasses, and shouted. At some hour, one of them would weep. At his worst, my father ripped open his white shirt, buttons popping off, carried his loaded rifle through the house, aiming at us or lamps and complaining that no one appreciated him. He was getting a sloping belly. His scar, an exploded star from when he was shot, shone on his side, front and back. A bullet, meant for my grandfather, had gone straight through his body and hit the wall and he'd lived. Even so, he was in the hospital a long time and had to be carried on a stretcher to the trial. I was in the back of the courtroom on the colored side with our cook, Willie. He rose up on his elbow, pointed his finger at Willis Barnes. My father was a hero. He'd jumped in front of my grandfather when a mill worker came to their office waving a pistol and shouting he get that bastard. He referred to Daddy Jack, "the cap'n," the big boss, my grandfather, whom my father saved. Joe Peacock and another man I don't remember were killed in the outer office. Everyone left the trial excited, saying Barnes would fry. My father: bullet in the gut from three feet. Later we dig it out of the wall with the ice pick and it sits upright on his desk. First memory: a man at the back door is saying, *I have real bad news*, sweat is dripping off his face, *Garbert's shot*, noise from my mother, I run to her room behind her, I'm jumping on the tester bed while she cries, she's pulling out drawers looking for a handkerchief, *now he's all right*, the man says, *they think*, patting her shoulder, I'm jumping higher, I'm not allowed, *they think he saved old man Mayes*, the bed slats dislodge and the mattress collapses. My mother lunges for me. The imprint of chaos.

From the blue light of the rag bag, if I heard him in the hall or banging the toilet lid in the bathroom, I clicked off my flashlight, crouched still on the worn-out towels and torn sheets until he wandered away, my toes curled against the butt of his smooth, polished gun.

Years later my plump friend wrote me, "I would not have you believe that we were not happy." She's still puzzling out the day she came home from cheerleading and her mother in the kitchen had shot herself in the mouth with a rifle. Gingerbread on the counter and her teeth stuck in the ceiling. I'm stuck on that image, and the barbed notion that years of perfection got mocked by that act. For me, present acts constantly rearrange the past, that sliding scale. What did all that gentleness mean? Why did we churn all that ice cream? Mystery. The seven veils, the fifteen losses, the ten thousand things. Even the perfect childhood replays itself in a different key, or in silence.

Every morning I exercise to rock music, a record of my daughter's with a thudding, monotonous beat. I lift the plastic five-pound weights so that I may someday carry my suitcase without my arms pulling out of their sockets. Strap two-and-a-half-pound weights onto my ankles, ride a bicycle and do splits in the air, preparing to ride one all day along the river in the delta. Close my eyes and row, row my machine boat, pretending I glide across the Coca-Cola bottle green waters of Lake Rabun in North Georgia. From an oak table, the two young faces of my parents watch these strange motions. Often, I stare back. *Like that,* I say, I'd like to have met you *like that.*

Restless and bored, we went at least once a month to the beach at Fernandina when I was a child. We could stay at the Seaside Inn anytime because my father gave them the drapery material (Tung Shan, which he invented) for the whole hotel.

Whatever else they were, my parents would give anyone anything. At Fernandina they behaved better: smoldered rather than blazed. I heard them as a drone through the wall while I sat cross-legged on my bed reading Nancy Drew mysteries and eating oyster crackers softened by sea air. A hot day; I open their door to say I'm going down to the beach. My parents are sleeping on twin beds. My mother's gown twists around her legs, the spongy pouf of her stomach rising and falling, the tiny scar on her nose. A soured towel smell, the frosty gin bottles. My father in his boxer shorts is frowning, his eyes roving back and forth under the pale lids veined blue like a film of oil over water. His arm is flung out toward my mother's and hers is also, but they are not touching. I run down the hall and out. I can't wait to roll down the dunes, chase sandpipers, run after fluffs of foam. On the beach something in me stretches out. If I went out early I sometimes found a sea turtle making her way back to the water after laying eggs. I stepped up on the barnacled back, my arms out for balance. At edge of the waves, I jumped off, gave her a push from behind, and watched her slowly move toward deep water. Sometimes I'd look back at the hotel and see one of my parents at the window. Why are they awake so early? I wave but my mother must be looking farther out to sea, my father must have his eye on the sunrise. They're vague shapes behind rusting screened windows a long time ago.

But the faces that watch me exercise are legendary. She's in the sequined dress her father bought for her when her mother said no. Her round, pampered shoulders and perfect twenties mouth, those heaven eyes that say nothing is ever enough. My mother in sparkling white met my father at a dance at the Lee Grant Hotel. She was down from Georgia State College for Women, ready to dazzle. Already she had a boyfriend, Max, who flew low over the campus scattering red roses for her. Those are his letters on the closet shelf, him, who went out rabbit hunting when he heard she'd married, and shot himself in the heart. On this night my parents met, my father was just up from a mysterious year in a wheelchair when he did

nothing but raise white doves. When he was expelled from high school
for pushing a teacher downstairs, he was sent to Riverside, a military
academy. Things didn't go well there either.

He'd come home sick to stare for a year at the sky and to train
birds to come back to him. Now he drives up in a cream-colored
convertible with a horn that plays a tune. Hair black as a wing and the
eyes I've seen in the photographs of snow leopards. The orchestra is
playing "The Darktown Strutters' Ball," and he asks Harvey Jay,
"Who's the new girl in white?" They dance, her hand is light on his
neck, they walk out on the long porch facing Central Avenue lined
with magnolias and the legend ends there, fades out into the heavy
fragrance and darkness. I've never heard a record of "The Darktown
Strutters' Ball," only one of my parents humming it in odd moments, a
deep groove in my memory. *I'll be down to get you in a taxi honey;* and
in such a small town no taxi ever was.

My daughter is a rider. She knows how to
ride behind the motion of the chestnut, to adapt to the loose and easy
leaping. A pliant movement. To jump, you must relax. Balance alone
will carry you through stony fields. Nothing to strike out against. Such
wisdom: training her horse, she is training herself. But the stable is an
intense microcosm. I'm striking wet matches if I think I'm in charge of
her childhood. Fealty to the dark will be extracted. The riding instructor dies of kidney failure and her ashes are scattered in the ring where
my child rides every day; the hooves toss up china bits of bone. The
favorite school horse, Winkie, is hauled off to the glue factory. The
stable owner dies fast of a heart attack. The girl who owns Krill is
flattened by a truck as she jumps on her bike to follow my daughter
into the road. An older girl flips in her sports car and is gone.

The girls huddle together at the funeral. It's muggy, crowded, and
my daughter passes out, wakes alone on a cot. Where's protection?
Too many deaths circle over this idyllic stable where the fortunate
suburban girls are indulged in their passion for horses. Blind in one
eye, Heartbreak looks normal from one side; from the other the empty

eye socket is black and hollow as a nest. I watch from the side of the covered ring as my daughter, up on her gelding Chelsea, approaches the five-foot jump and there's no stopping her. I've seen this skittish horse shy at the last instant, crash the fence, have seen her body loop in the air, the confusion of his legs and her head, the slow fall to the sawdust. That time-stopped moment before she stirs, once again unbroken. I know, too, the elegance of her straight back bending into the jump. Then, to go over seems smooth and inevitable, a pure conception. Relentless, the practice of the gambado; that low leap of a horse in which all four feet are evenly off the ground.

Time sputters. And as Auden's refrain goes, time tells us nothing but I told you so. I thought, with luck, the Gypsies would steal me and I would disappear *without a trace*. My parents, those stars, proclaimed a daily misery to the heavens and the rains, a face-to-face, hand-to-hand combat. Border wars. Territorial disputes. Manifest destiny. Why were they wild? Why did my mother court trouble? Why did my father carouse? I found the pink pop-apart pearls on the floor of his Oldsmobile. What was most amazing was that they were tacky. When I answered the telephone, a woman laughed and hung up. She didn't sound like anyone we would know. I said many things to myself by the age of seven. *If I ever get out of here, I will never select unhappiness*. When the plate of unhappiness is passed around and more and more are offered, I say no thank you, no. But they wanted seconds, thirds. Maybe they got frantic when they felt the first slow sliding toward the grave, the controlled fall downward. My father got something awful. His hair came out in clumps, and he was taken to Atlanta. When he came home I didn't recognize him and he cried. My mother practiced her filibustering on all our real and imagined faults.

This semester I'm teaching undergraduate poetry writing. A woman named Evelyn enrolled under the Golden Age program for older people who want to take a class or two. I was asking her a few questions today about one of her poems I couldn't get the gist of. "Well, you see," she says, "it's about my family. My parents separated when I was seven and this is about the family getting back together again and it being the way it was supposed to be." She is perhaps in her early seventies. The poem, I learned, takes place in heaven. I felt the connection stun my face. Both parents had other families, lived long lives, decades and decades passed, and this child of theirs takes up the pen to write about the heavenly reunion when childhood will be set right.

At grammar school I could fall, mostly, into being a child. Impossible now to distinguish actual education from the fatigue of the teacher's gabardine suit. Now and then a fact sticks: the capital of Afghanistan, vitamin C prevents scurvy, slavery was "a good idea" at the time, times change. My country was represented in the corner by the mended flag, there is only one way to fold it, like a note you throw across the room, and only one way to raise it and Bill Daniels was chosen. For the rest, chalk sounds on the board gave the teacher the creeps, and she crossed her legs in support stockings and ugly shoes, and told dull stories of her vacation to Vero Beach when she left her bag in the car and came back four hours later and no one had touched it: *people are basically decent*. The desk with initials cut deep. Cards with holes and numbers turn to faces when sewn right with yarn. At recess, I love taking out the coil of rope. Double time, red pepper, hot stitches, and: "Mother, Mother, I feel sick, call for the doctor, quick quick quick, Mother Mother will I die, Yes my child but do not cry, How many cars will be at my funeral? One, two, three . . ."

Negro houses surround the playground on three sides. Wash-women scrubbing pots of clothes under the pecan trees, folding sheets on the sloping porches. In one of the leaning houses a fortune-teller lives and big cars pull up and white women go in. Maybe one is the voice on the telephone. *Why don't Negro children have to go to school? Because they don't need to know. You do.* Grade to grade, I worked my way around the playground. Hopscotch, jump rope, red rover, jungle gym: the cardinal points. Outside I was a whole-hearted child, under

the watchful playground duty of Miss Pope, Miss Hattaway, Mrs. Gur-
ganus, Mrs. Bailey, and Miss McCall, who'd been, once, to Mexico and
wore for the seven years of grammar school, a red felt jacket embroi-
dered with sombrero, cactus. It always caught my eye. *Lamentable*, my
mother said.

Because my family was overwhelming, the small self-conscious
pains of ordinary childhood never bothered me. I learned to juggle
three then four oranges right in front of the class. I could take the
hooked stick and fish for the window shade ring in the hot classroom
with everyone staring while I aimed and missed and let the shade fly up
and hit the ceiling until everyone laughed and Miss Hattaway got
furious. The fury of teachers never impressed me much. I envied Jane
Floyd's total blush when she was embarrassed. I rarely was. I felt bad
for Joan Appleton's face while she had a *fainting fit* with her tongue
out. The teacher got a spoon out of her desk drawer. I held down
Joan's arms, skinnier than mine, and saw her fascinated face in its
privacy and twisting. It seemed she let some anger out, anger I might
have too, then she was limp. She wet her pants too, but never cried
when she woke up, just let herself be led to the nurse's room. I
pretended to be simple because it was easier. At the fair, picked up,
swung by the farmer square dancing, I was not a smiling rag doll, but
stiff as wire, face pressed under his arm and him hahooing, moonshine
breath. I thought of kicking and did not, rode it out, only made a face
when he put me down. The more I rubbed it out, the more I rubbed it
in. *Ain't she cute?* I made my calculation on every model. My English
was only as far as a lisp of bad words said to the mirror.

Yesterday in the chic Third Hand Rose store,
I saw a jacket like Miss McCall's felt one. This one was green but had
the same overstitching in thick yarn, the Mexican sleeping against a
cactus. I didn't buy it at ninety dollars, but I tried it on and remembered Hill C. Griffin saying to her: *You look like a bulldog*, and she
said, *Would you say that again*, and he didn't have the sense to shut up,
we were all thrilled, and he said straight up, *You look like a bulldog*, and

she told him to get out of her class and she started to cry and said we'd have to excuse her, she wasn't used to putting up with white trash. (Lesson 999 in class action.)

She hoped none of us ever would be rude, crude, and socially unacceptable like that. Her jacket is trendy now. The possibility of open rebellion. Truth. Hill C., like a horse running into fire.

In summer, the transfer to Laughing Camp, an interruption to the sound and fury of 711 South, where the horizon note was violence. Camp was tall pines and good girls, willow-twig armchairs and wisteria. We bathed in cold water, rubbed archery blisters with balm, learned to post. The girls shared a family inheritance, a litany of running off at the mouth, screaming giggles. I'm in a skit. I'm a planter with nothing to do for months of winter. "Accompany me to Paris," I say in French. Madame says it is important to open your mouth and speak up, curl your tongue around the vowels. I've escaped. My new friend from Marietta has a golden retriever at home and her father is a pediatrician and I don't know what that is. She plays voluntaries on the cello and says the word should have an apostrophe in front of it but people are too ignorant to know that. She wants an English saddle, will get one. I hide notes in boxes in the woods: *If you ever find this please write to me.* I see an opening I've seen only in books. I'm out of the mess and rattling of home. My father turning over the table during a game of penny ante, pulling down the chintz draperies. My mother rising the next morning to her All Clear. On the final night of camp, with candlelight and the girls with arms linked singing, "Thy sunshine is fairest, my summer-time home," I'm suddenly homesick for somewhere, not there, but somewhere. Four hundred girls in pressed white shirts and shorts, everyone waiting for Mrs. Sykes to give out the achievement awards. Everyone anticipating. I arrange the blank on my face. High dive. Beauty queen. Progress. Equitation. Archery. Best camper . . . This is weeks after I arrived and the counselor jerked me aside after fifteen minutes, said I had the wrong attitude, was cheeky, a troublemaker, and I'd have to clean my plate whether I liked it or not. Now the girls, running up to the podium one after another claiming a bit of glory. Tennis. Crafts. And at the very end my name is called, a special award announced, *For Learning to Eat the Crust of Bread*.

I could not be a child. There were too many cooks who wished they did not have to tie my sash and jerked it tight, though not with cruelty. But wait, as their child, my parents regarded me as smart and beautiful. She's the cleverest little thing you've ever seen, they'd tell anyone. Praise was for the wrong things, often, but it was plentiful. I was showered throughout childhood with a feeling of immense (if inappropriate) possibilities. *You are going to grow up to be Miss America! You have a memory like an elephant! You can have anything in the world you want, just tell me what you want and you can have it! You could float down the Nile covered with flowers!* No one was strong on realism; inexplicably, the strong suit was family pride. *Never forget you're a Mayes.* Looking around, I could see no possible reason to do anything else but try my best to do exactly that. Sometimes, when my mother was crazed she'd say, "Marry a Hungarian peasant, the blood's all shot in this line." I felt bad for my new cousin when he was named the Fourth because his father, the Third, banged on our back door drunk and shouting at least once a week and his mother, who was Miss University of Georgia once, had sugar diabetes and speckled hands that trembled when she lit a cigarette. By day, the Third sat by the short-wave Stromberg-Carlson listening to static and foreign voices, staring at the cover which flipped up to show a map of the world time zones and frequency bands. He twitched in his leather wing chair and said when I walked by, "Well you think you're something don't you Miss Priss. Well *I* am a graduate of Georgia Tech." Adults could do anything. Anything.

My ally was Willie Bell. It was not a cozy, member-of-the-family, Aunt-Jemima thing. She and I simply knew we were in it together. She for her twenty dollars a week and I for the duration of childhood. "Just run out and play, try not to pay them any mind, they all crazy," she'd say, not looking up from the stove. She offered me not sympathy, but a steady point of view. One sass at the table and out I had to go to pick my switch in the yard. As I stalked through the kitchen, Willie shook her head. "When are you going to learn," she said quietly, "just don't talk back." My mother switched until my legs bled, frowning and working her lips. My father read the paper, looking bored. If I cried he'd say, "Cry and I'll give you something to cry about," or "Cry louder! Can't you cry louder? I can hardly hear you."

Usually they were too busy between themselves to notice what I did. I began to drive the car at nine and they never knew. Once, when I punished them for something that even now I could not write about, I ran away. I stayed in a culvert all night. When I went home blank and tired the next morning, I felt grimly triumphant. I expected the state patrol, my mother properly distraught, my father taking vows never to lift a finger again. No one had noticed that I was missing. Consequences are random.

                          I was unguided, rebellious, solitary, a prankster, at war. No side to take. I taught myself the bull's eye with arrows. I had a hideout in a vacant lot. I could disappear in the tops of trees. I walked home every day past the restaurant, through the Blue and Gray Park, past poorhouses, sidewalk graffiti (only one word, relentlessly repeated), cottages, flowers, up the trail. Lonely, rowdy. I knew everything and pretended to know nothing. I reported to the empty streets, level in view, as through a telescope. I passed Mrs. Drummond every day, her huge bulk in the rocker behind the coffee cans of geraniums lining her porch. Her daughter, Emma Sue, worked at the Spotted Pig and brought home leftover chicken-fried minute steak. I know because Judy Pike and I combed the alleys and pulled things out of trash cans. We held up bloody Kotex, rubbers, bills demanding payment, the tinfoil and remains of the old steaks from the Pig. As I walked home every day, I smiled a sweet six-year-old smile at Mrs. Drummond, who said, "How you today little missy." Like policemen are said to understand crime and are trained to respond with a shot, they're closer to crime, in their fastest blood, so was I to innocence. A girl in a sundress skipping home. The apple of her family's eye. Mrs. Drummond has a brass vase made out of a bomb her son brought home from Germany. *In bad taste.* She weighed at least three hundred pounds, all steak. Her false teeth were whiter than paint chips. One day, on my way home, a spot of warm blood blown by the wind landed on my blouse. From where? An angel with a halo, a bird, a body going to heaven? I could not be sure.

from *Anna:*
A Daughter's Life
WILLIAM LOIZEAUX

August 21, 1989
Hyattsville, Maryland

On January 21, 1989, our first child, a daughter, Anna, was born. Five months and thirteen days later, on the morning of July 4, she died. During that time a small life was lived. And during that time my wife, Beth, and I were more alive than we ever have been—more alive with pain, sadness, fear, joy, hope, and despair.

Now it is seven weeks since the Fourth of July, and it is the day when Anna would have been seven months old. We have visited our families in Minnesota and New Jersey. We have hiked in the clean, clear air of the Adirondacks, swum in cold water where you can see straight to the sandy bottom. But today we are home in our asbestos-sided 1930s bungalow, where my study is still half painted, where the water still drips in the sink upstairs, where cicadas churr in the oaks outside, where it has just rained, the air sweltering, air conditioners buzzing—another summer in metro D.C.—and where Anna's things are still scattered about: the four-legged Swyngomatic, a basket of toys in the dining room, the Wiggleworm, and on the floors, if you look closely, here and there her grainy splashes of dried spit-up. We haven't had the heart, yet, to change a thing. It all looks the same.

Though if you were to walk through these rooms, you would sense in the air that something has happened here, something with such a residue of silence, sadness, and remembered joy. You would sense that nothing here is as it should have been.

So we walk through these rooms with aimless questions. Where is she now? Why? What reason? Why can't we hold her? Why isn't she asleep in the crib upstairs? When will she return? (another stay in the hospital?)—though of course there is the small blue box of ashes, a cup's worth, heavy, like a strange paperweight, on my bedroom bureau.

How can this be? How can any of this have really happened? And now I wonder, Should I write about this? Should I sit in the mornings and try to remember her, bring it all back, every detail: her long thumbs, her crazy hair, and the way she lay in a hospital crib for her last week—transformed, unconscious, though still alive, still her, still hearing our voices through the sedation, and squeezing our fingers, hard? Should I go over and over what shouldn't have been? Should I keep looking at what, in the end, is so unbearable?

I'm not sure. But is there really an alternative? For here was a life. Anna. A pure thing in a bare hand. To write her name is a painful comfort. It holds close what I can't let go, and what I can't forget.

There is nothing in this life without a marker.

August 22

When I came downstairs this morning to let out the dog, I saw that Beth had clipped a picture of Anna on our refrigerator door, alongside the grocery list and postcards there. In the photo, taken on the morning of June 27, the day she was admitted to the hospital for her heart surgery, Anna is looking straight into the camera—or straight at me right now as I look at an identical photograph on my desk before me. Anna's eyes are huge, dark, the flash of the camera in the points of her pupils. Her eyebrows are light brown, her lashes long. Her nose is small and rounded, her mouth slightly open, not exactly smiling, but she seems to be surprised by the flash, on the edge of delight, or on the edge of one of her bubbling sounds. Cooing. She was at that stage. In the mornings she would babble for a half hour at a time, sometimes even before we were out of bed. We'd just lie there and listen, and she'd go on and on in her room around the corner, as if the whole world were nothing but sunlight in a dormer window. As if nothing in the world could change any of this.

How can I explain what it feels like for a sound to be gone? When each morning comes with birds and light and rustling traffic. When the newspaper thuds on the front porch step. When we get up without hearing, and go downstairs.

August 23

I was describing the photo. And I have said nothing about Anna's hair, which was simply wild, strands of it going this way and that, hanging over her ears, over one eyebrow or another. In the mornings it looked as if she had spent the night in a swirling windstorm, a child brought in from outdoors, all sleeked and tangled with oil or rain or dew or sweat. Her hair was turning brownish-blond at the time, a little darker than mine. When she was born it was jet black, and it was the first thing I saw as the doctor gracefully lifted Anna from the incision in Beth's stomach, turning her toward me with his hand behind her neck.

And there was all that hair. Black as a mink's, slick and gleaming beneath the big domed light. "She is beautiful," I remember saying to Beth, whose face was behind the blood-speckled screen. "She is beautiful." And after they had clipped the cord, suctioned her throat and lungs, and finished a quick exam, I remember the nurse laying Anna on the pillow beside Beth's shoulder. I remember Beth touching her carefully; Anna's bright red skin, her small fists clenched and toes curled in. I remember seeing their heads together, their hair identically black, identically messed, matted, wild—Beth and Anna—as if they had been out in the wind together.

That was on January 21, at 2:20 P.M. I have no idea what the weather was like or if anything else happened in the world that day. Anna was six pounds two ounces. She had black hair and huge eyes. She was all alive, all there, though, as we would soon find out, she was not altogether well.

A u g u s t   2 4

I have been reading Rilke's *Letters to a Young Poet*, and last night I came upon that passage where he writes, "We know little, but that we must hold to what is difficult . . . that something is difficult must be a reason the more for us to do it."

Now, I am not exactly young, nor a poet, but reading this fills me with strange hope. Loss is difficult. Sadness is difficult. To remember is difficult. I hope from all of this that something can come, something maybe not whole or expressible, but true.

One of the sad things about losing Anna is that we will never be able to tell her (it would have been at some appropriate time) how strange, hard, and even humorous it was to conceive her. I don't remember the exact day it happened—it must have been about mid-May—but that doesn't matter. What I do have firmly in mind is a general sense of that period of our lives, which, since Anna's death, has become familiar to us once again. Beth was thirty-seven. I was thirty-five. There were books on bureaus about "primelife pregnancy," the basal body temperature graph beside the bed, the morning thermometer, our monthly visits to our ob/gyn. Then later, for Beth, there were prescriptions for Clomid, progesterone, a cervical mucus test. And once, for me, a singularly unclimactic semen analysis: me alone in a pure white hospital bathroom, with a Dixie cup in my hand, a plastic pouch in the cup, my manhood on the line, and the whole room in a swirling cold sweat until I fled, careening out the door, my cup empty, fainting flat out on the waiting room floor.

Anna, maybe when you were older, maybe when you were a mother yourself, we might have laughed about this.

Or this: that every time Beth's temperature went up, we seemed to be visiting my parents or hers, their doors open all night, the walls thin. It was like being in high school all over again, on a ratty sofa in a basement den, with your folks "up talking" in the kitchen above. At least once while we were camping with Beth's parents in the Adirondacks, right there in the very midst of what might have become Anna, I remember a cheery camper's call from outside our tent. It was Beth's mom, Betsy, and a whiff of bacon: "Yoo-hoo. Time for breakfast!"

A u g u s t   2 6

There are acorns falling from the oak trees these days, hundreds of them, banging down on the tin roof over our back porch. When the wind blows, it sounds like a hailstorm, and if you walk in the yard, you can feel them crunching under your feet. Our next-door neighbor, who has lived in the area all her life, says that the acorns are particularly heavy this year. It means that we will have a "hard winter," she says, and I wonder what exactly she means.

When Anna was born, there were no leaves or acorns on the oaks, and I wasn't thinking very much about trees. Some months later, though, I was. Back at the end of March, five weeks after we brought Anna home from the hospital for the first time, some friends of ours gave us a pink dogwood decorated with ribbons, a sapling, no higher than your waist, which we planted in our backyard. We were doing a lot of gardening then. During the warmest parts of the afternoons we'd have Anna out there in the carriage, bundled up, the dog (have I mentioned her name? Jessie, a manic unpurebred retriever) rolling in the sun, and Beth and I up to our elbows in dirt and peat moss, until Anna started fussing. Anyway, the dogwood, in our vocabulary, became "Anna's tree," and I recall having to work around some thick oak roots when I was digging the hole to plant it. I couldn't get the tree exactly where we wanted it, but soon that didn't seem to matter. In May it blossomed, those delicate light pink flowers. It grew thick with leaves, and by mid-June it was as high as my chest.

Then, in a matter of days, it died. The leaves on the lowest branch shriveled. I called the nursery and pruned off the diseased branch, but two mornings later, a Friday, June 16, the leaves on the entire tree had gone pale and wilted. I dug it up, and we all took it back to the nursery, where a salesman cut into the bark with his penknife and said it was already gone, hit by a fungus that "was going around." Beth, who had Anna over her shoulder, told me she thought this meant something, and I told her not to be silly, superstitious. Then the man wrote out a credit slip: $34.95 for "1 dogwood; middle died; dogwood blight." Since then we've kept the slip in an old cigar box where we have our unpaid bills and mortgage stubs. Now I have it right here in my hand. And in a few weeks, when their new stock comes in, we will take this slip back to the nursery, get another dogwood, bring it home, and plant it.

August 28

The nursery. How that word rings in my brain. A place to buy dogwoods. A dormer bedroom with a spool crib and impatiens in the window boxes. Or a long room at Georgetown Hospital, fluorescent lit, monitors, alarms, plastic boxes with babies inside, "isolettes," portals for your hands, for your heart, for your whole being to pour through—to touch and hold.

Anna was born with a rare association of physical problems called VATER syndrome. Moments after her birth, one of our doctors told me she had an imperforate anus, her throat ended in a blind pouch, and—this was immediately life-threatening—the lower part of her esophagus was connected to her bronchi, already filling her lungs with gastric juices. There would be other tests and other problems that we would learn of later, but this had to be dealt with now.

I remember pushing Anna down the hall from the delivery room to the intermediate nursery (Nursery D), still in my blue scrubs, with something like a shower cap on my head. I was so proud and tired, hyped-up and scared. Beth had been through five hours of labor; Anna had flipped back into a breech position. I had eaten three boxes of raisins so I wouldn't faint through the C-section, and now I was literally running between Nursery D, where they began prepping Anna for surgery, and the maternity wing, where Beth was lying, woozy with morphine.

"Where is she?" Beth kept asking.

"Around the corner. She'll be all right."

Then I wheeled Beth down to see Anna again. She remembers none of this now; it is all a fog. But I will not forget her holding Anna, really holding her, tight, for the first time. I will not forget holding her myself, and putting her, all warm and wriggling, in one of those portable isolettes with wheels, wires, monitors. Then, with the nurse showing the way, I pushed Anna down to the elevator. We rode to the bottom floor—Surgery—with Anna's silent crying behind the plastic, and a loud beeping sound that was the beat of her heart. She was less than an hour old.

"Do you want a priest? Baptism?" the nurse had asked before we took Anna down. I think I just shook my head. For how, in the circumstances, could I explain that I wasn't Catholic, that I wasn't really anything, that I only truly believed in the necessity of human love and human effort; that I found it hard to believe in a God that might discriminate between a child baptized and a child not? I still find that hard to believe, even harder now. Or to tell you the truth, I find it impossible.

. . .

The next time I saw Anna, a few hours later, she was in the intensive care nursery (the ICN) in another isolette that would be her home for nearly the first month of her life. An emergency gastrostomy had been successfully performed to drain her stomach, and another tube had been put through her nose to suction her throat. She was fed with an IV in her hand. Her heart rate, breathing, and oxygen saturation were monitored on digital machines. She was all wires, tubes, and gauze, but she was so beautiful. I was there when she first opened her eyes after the operation. Just as Beth and I were there when she closed them for the very last time. That was precisely two months ago, early in the morning of June 28, when Anna was sedated for her heart surgery. We were in a tiled room on the bottom floor with X rays on the walls and surgical equipment. We were holding Anna in our arms as they shot in the syringe. She was happy, unafraid, and we were there. I say this not so much out of pride, but out of something inside me that fights my own reproach. Something was happening that was wrong and unimaginable. Something was happening that we couldn't stop. Something was happening, but we didn't turn away.

August 29

In the last week, we have been painting the room in the front of our house that is to serve as a study for me and a sort of extension of our tiny living room. It's been a year-long project: first my homemade built-in bookshelves that aren't exactly plumb or square; then the demolition work—myself and a few friends, mostly spindly academics, but on that day like mighty woodsmen, chopping out lath and plaster, opening a doorway, a great swath of light to our living room. Next came the framing, building a header, and hanging the French doors. That was done over the Thanksgiving holiday last year, with the help of Beth's father and younger brother. Beth herself was seven months pregnant with Anna at the time, and in one of our albums we have a photo of her standing sideways between the open two-by-four studs.

She is a slender, delicate woman, but with Anna on board, she was all full and globed; she could hardly fit between the studs. Now those studs are covered with wallboard, the joints plastered and sanded. Beth is again slender, almost a swimmer's body, and we have rolled a light gray over the walls and painted the woodwork pure white. Somehow it feels good to be doing this, to draw clean paint over an old surface. It doesn't change anything essential here. It is still hard to look at these floors, these walls, to go into a room without any sound. Yet this is the place where we must live. No one is moving. I can't imagine being anywhere else.

August 30

Just what does it mean for the trees to be gone, with those slivers of light between the leaves? What does it mean to hear a voice, to squeeze a hand, to sense something familiar, then let it go?

August 31

The night before last, Beth dreamed about Anna for the first time. She dreamed that Anna was being cared for in the apartment above ours in the house where we rented a few years ago. Evidently we had worked out a baby-sitting arrangement with the woman who was still living there, and soon we would be driving over to pick Anna up.

So far I have not dreamed at all about Anna, or at least I don't remember my dreaming. In fact, I don't remember any dreams since Anna has died, though I do get up in the middle of the night with things in my head too vivid for dreams. I see a small hospital room all cleared of machines. There are no sounds, no monitors, respirators, or heat lamps. The nurses are gone, the doctors gone. The door is closed behind us. In the window the sun has risen above the trees, traffic is light—it's a holiday morning—and a weary jogger circles a playing field.

Anna lies alone on the freshly made bed. She is different than when we knew her, but once again she is simply herself—no wires, tubes, nothing but her. It is the last time we will hold her. She is swaddled in pink, and her eyes are closed.

September 1

Two days ago, in the afternoon, we went back to the hospital for a meeting with our "genetics counselor." It was odd driving there along the same roads that we traveled so often during Anna's life. There were all the familiar landmarks: the domed cathedral at Catholic University, the winos and drug dealers at Fourteenth and Harvard, the posh shops on Wisconsin Avenue, and the crush of traffic turning into the hospital. During all of Anna's life, the city had been reconstructing a bridge on Michigan Avenue. For a half a year, as we drove back and forth to Georgetown Hospital, we watched this process: the big trucks hauling off rubble, then masons building the stone pillars, the giant girders craned into place, and concrete poured on a mesh of steel. There were detour signs that we always followed, and yesterday, though the signs were gone, the bridge finished, we automatically drove our usual way, squirreling through unlikely side streets.

On our return trip, we still didn't go across that bridge, though at a stoplight, I could see the cars whizzing up over the new smooth surface, heading crosstown, making time. It is an attractive bridge; it speeds traffic; and sometime soon I'm sure I'll drive over it. But not just yet. It doesn't seem right. It's as if this stretch of the road is too simple now, too easy. As if a corner has been cut, or some difficulty skirted by, unacknowledged.

September 2

We are trying to get another baby going—I should say that straightaway. Thus, our meeting with the genetics counselor who has reviewed our family trees and what literature there is on Anna's VATER syndrome. So far, it is unexplained, just as the cause of Anna's death itself is still unexplained, a mystery. These things happen "sporadically" in the population at large. VATER syndrome is unpredictable, undetectable. Something happens, or doesn't happen, about the sixth week of pregnancy. Organs in a line down the middle of a baby's body form abnormally: the heart, trachea, esophagus, ureters, kidneys, and lower GI tract. It is no one's fault. There is no preventing it. It is unlikely to recur in a family, but it is impossible to rule anything out.

So where is the sense in all this? The reason? A child is born with terrible difficulties. She is heroically mended. Loved. She grows, is happy. She dies months later from unknown complications after successful heart surgery, after doctors and nurses have worked for days, around the clock, to save her. Why is there so much devastation in this life? Why take an innocent, joyful child away? I have been told that this could be "all for the best," that she has been "spared much pain," that she is "in the hands of God," or "in a better place."

What extraordinary presumption. Or what blind hope in the face of randomness. Don't tell me there is some beneficent force or being who has everything under control. Don't tell me "he works in mysterious ways." For I cannot understand such ways, and I am not about to give up my own understanding—the only thing I have—for a wisp called faith.

September 4

Labor Day. Another holiday, another anniversary. It is two months since Anna's death. This afternoon we will have hot dogs and barbecued chicken with a group of friends, and that will be good. For it is with friends who knew Anna that we feel most comfortable, people who held her and know what that means, people who have children of their own, or babies they allow—actually want—us to hold.

What I want most is to be reminded of her, and to say what has happened. Without these friends it would all be so much harder—their long listening over cups of coffee, their clear eyes rimming with red. This isn't easy for anyone, but they hear it all and look straight back at us. This, too, I must never forget.

September 5

Anna's first days were a matter of recovering from the surgery (the gastrostomy) performed on the day of her birth. She lived in that plastic isolette in the intensive care nursery. She was cared for around the clock by at least one nurse, often two; and even now, seven months later, I remember their faces and names. Jodie, Angela, Susan, Terri. Their hands in the portals, changing IVs, diapers, electrical leads. Or adjusting her blankets, making her comfortable, and making us all as comfortable as possible.

That night after Anna was born, I slept on a rollaway bed in Beth's room, and the next day I pushed Beth in a wheelchair down to the ICN, where for a short time the nurses took Anna out of her box and we could hold her, tubes and all, while they watched the monitors. Beth herself had an IV in her arm, and there was a tangle of cords and wires whenever we moved. Mostly Anna slept, but when she awoke, her eyes were wide. She wasn't in pain. On that day her hair seemed to sweep up from both sides, like two giant waves, and crest near the middle. When later, on the phone, a friend asked what she looked like, the only thing I could think of was Elvis, the young Elvis: that waved black hair and big eyes, a little bewildered by all the attention.

September 6

Yesterday afternoon the preliminary autopsy report arrived in the mail. The report is a simple page-long printout, a list of nine visual observations. There is nothing surprising. It is still unknown exactly what happened to cause Anna's death, but maybe later, when the final histological examination is complete, we will have some better idea.

Until then, we have this, a list of medical observations, as dry as a sales report. They describe various conditions or parts of Anna's body, parts that we knew all along did not work very well.

But this is only the machinery of her, or some of her machinery. There is nothing here about her hair, her pixie smile, or the way, when we took her into a dark room, her eyes would open even wider.

Although I am not a religious man, I think that the spirit of a person continues in the memories of others. I know that Anna fought very hard to live. I know that at some infant level she meant to persevere, to hold tight to those who loved her; I felt that in the squeeze of her hand, and I feel that now.

And while it is true that she died of her ailments—this stark list of medical conditions—it is also true that for a time she lived in spite of them. She surprised the experts. She was home, a normal kid, for four months. During her last stormy week, twice we were told that Anna was about to die, and twice, as we talked to her and she held our fingers, twice she didn't die. She lived, as though by the force of her own will, something beyond medical explanation, something that in my own mind dwarfs this list of conditions that somehow killed her.

If Anna had survived, someday, when she was a teenager perhaps, I would have taken an odd pleasure in reminding her of what she had come through. I would have told her that if she could come through all that, she could see her way through just about anything.

Then I would have tried to remind myself of the same.

September 7

A friend called last night to say that he and his wife were thinking of us. They have a son who was born about three months after Anna, and I remember Beth and me taking Anna over to Holy Cross Hospital to see their new child sleeping behind a glass window in the nursery. Now our friend says that when he holds his son, he often thinks of Anna and he finds himself crying. I wish that he didn't have to cry, and yet I am terribly grateful for his tears. I want him to cry over this, and to bring my own tears once again to my eyes.

Never before did I understand how important it was, this sharing of grief. It disperses and intensifies it, widens and deepens it. I can't imagine what it would be like without Beth or our friends.

Yet I know that it could be worse. This grief is sharp and deep, but it feels pure and uncomplicated. At five months old, Anna was nothing but innocent. Her needs could be bothersome, tiring, but she was never old enough to do anything that would anger us, that would give us cause for regret.

There is a woman we know in Minnesota whose teenage daughter was hit by a truck and killed in front of their house. Theirs was a normal, healthy, hectic mother-daughter relationship. Yet even now, twenty years later, what this woman remembers most is an argument with her daughter that morning, their harsh words as the girl, Sally, stormed out the kitchen door.

September 8

Because it was clear from the start that Anna wouldn't be nursing for some time (her esophagus ended in a blind pouch), Beth began pumping her breasts and storing her milk in small plastic vials that were stacked in the ICN freezer. The idea was that eventually, if Anna's throat could be repaired, we could feed her mother's milk through a tube, then a bottle, and then, if all went well, she could breast-feed like any other baby. So, long before Beth could get out of her hospital bed, she had the electric pump going on the tray-table, that rhythmic whirring sound for fifteen minutes, then I'd label the vials (Loizeaux, Anna, baby girl), date them, and take them, still warm in my hands, down the hall to the freezer.

It would be six days after Anna's birth before Beth left the hospital, and for much of that time, I slept on that rollaway bed. It was a difficult week for both of us, especially for Beth. There is great pain after a cesarean; there are the usual hormonal changes; and on top of this, our child lay in a plastic box, down a hall, past the nurses' station, and through a set of swinging doors that read "Hospital Personnel," a world away from Beth's arms.

Moreover, it was during these first days that we learned, bit by bit, of the extent and severity of Anna's problems. Each day there were more tests, X rays, ultrasounds, or echocardiograms. Though she looked perfect on the outside, things were scrambled within. I have already mentioned her imperforate anus and disconnected esophagus. Her kidneys functioned but were oddly shaped (bilateral hydronephrosis), her ureters wide and meandering. Her bladder, vagina, and rectum came together in a common chamber (persistent cloaca). Then lastly, she had an association of heart defects called Tetralogy of Fallot: abnormal openings between her atria and between her ventricles; her aorta emerged from both ventricles instead of one; her right ventricle was enlarged; and there was a narrowing of her pulmonary artery, a condition that, over time, would get worse.

September 11

I mention all this not to appall, but to lay out the medical facts of Anna's life as we learned of them that week. It was frightening. The doctors came to Beth's room and drew us diagrams with explanations and labels. When they shut the door, I would turn to Beth and see in her eyes my own confusion and fear. On the windowsill there were cheery flowers and cards. Kids played soccer on the frosted field across the road. We cried for what seemed to be hours. And then there came a strange feeling—as there still comes to me now—that if I looked at these medical facts hard enough, if I took them all in, learned their names, the language of Anna's frailties, if I watched the echocardiograms, saw the blood leaking through the holes in her heart, if I stood there and didn't turn my eyes, then I could somehow stare it all down, push it cowering into a corner.

Even during Anna's last hours, I believed at some level that if we kept holding her, kept talking, we could keep her alive.

And perhaps we did, for a very short time. But the final fact is that Anna did die. She is ashes. She is dead now—incredibly—even as I keep on talking.

September 12

Yesterday evening, before dinner, I planted another dogwood in the place in our backyard where Anna's tree had stood. I can see it now through the window where I am working in Beth's study. It is a beautiful tree, about five feet tall. Its leaves are green, lush, and ribbed with veins. When you touch them, they are smooth on the bottom and slightly napped, like felt, on top.

We went back to the nursery last Saturday, and the new trees were in, all lined up in black plastic tubs. There were plenty of pink dogwoods, the kind we originally had, but we decided this time on a different variety, a Chinese dogwood, that is more resistant to fungal diseases. The woman at the cash register accepted our credit slip, and we brought the tree home, crammed in the backseat of the car. On Sunday, it stood regally in the wheelbarrow on our cracked concrete driveway, then yesterday I pushed it across the yard and dug the hole.

It was easy digging, as the earth was still soft and loamy from the last time I had dug there just three months ago. I dug out the same dirt and peat moss that I had shoveled in twice before. I dug up the same shredded pine bark that I had mulched with. And here and there, I even found in the dark dirt the tiny fibrils, like splayed hands: perhaps the most deep and fragile roots of Anna's tree.

Is it smart to be doing this? Or healthy? This planting where something before has died? As I dug deeper my shovel rang against the oak root, thick as your arm, that I had encountered early last spring when daffodils were out and Anna lay bundled up in the carriage. This dogwood, too, I have planted beside that root, in the same ground, with the same hope—though fiercer now, as the last acorns rattle on the roof, and the leaves of the pin oaks turn at the tips.

September 13

About a month after Anna's death, a friend of ours sent us a letter with a poem of May Sarton's enclosed. This morning I read the poem, "An Observation," again.

> True gardeners cannot bear a glove
> Between the sure touch and the tender root,
> Must let their hands grow knotted as they move
> With a rough sensitivity about
> Under the earth, between the rock and shoot,
> Never to bruise or wound the hidden fruit.
> And so I watched my mother's hands grow scarred,
> She who could heal the wounded plant or friend
> With the same vulnerable yet rigorous love;
> I minded once to see her beauty gnarled,
> But now her truth is given me to live,
> As I learn for myself we must be hard
> To move among the tender with an open hand,
> And to stay sensitive up to the end
> Pay with some toughness for a gentle world.

I wish, at some time, I could have read this poem to Anna; or perhaps she would have found it on her own. I wish that I could have meant to her what the mother in this poem meant to the poet. I wish that despite the inevitable arguments, the slamming doors, the walkings out, and reluctant returns—I wish that I could have given Anna a truth to live: "To move among the tender with an open hand," to "Pay with some toughness for a gentle world."

Instead, she has given it to me.

September 14

Over that first week of Anna's life, she got a little better each day, and each day we could take her out of her box a little longer. I suppose that in holding her, we felt very much as any other parents feel in holding a newborn: proud, a little awkward—her strange otherness; already she seemed to have a will of her own, preferring the crook of my left arm to my right, and letting me know it. I remember a profound sense (which I would have for all her life) of her fragility and her toughness, this little six-pound bug with all the hair, who had already been through surgery with only a local anesthetic, and who would be through so much more. As for the wires, tubes, and monitors, it is amazing how quickly we accepted them. We learned what each of them did, and in days they took on an almost comforting familiarity. This small, rectangular machine pumped lipids at a prescribed rate into her IV. This vial collected the juices from her stomach, and that one saliva from her throat. An infrared sensor caught her heartbeat. Two leads, attached to her chest, measured her breathing. And there on the screen you could see it graphically: the rolling hills of her breath, and the quick, jagged blips of her heart.

It was reassuring, in fact; and once all these monitors probably saved her. Small newborns, especially premature ones or ones under stress, sometimes have brady spells, times when they simply forget to breathe. One day this happened to Anna. An alarm went off on one of her machines. The nurse—it was Angela—opened the front of the box, shook her, and pumped oxygen into her mouth. Anna breathed again, and the flat line on the screen resumed its rolling geography, those hills that remind me of the Adirondacks, a place we would have liked to take Anna, to show her those rounded mountains, like old men's shoulders.

September 15

About two weeks after Anna died, Beth and I drove up to the Adirondacks, to a place on Piseco Lake, where seven years ago we were married. Never before had it been so hard for us to leave home. The previous night we had packed the car with our clothes and camping equipment. We had canceled the newspaper and put timers on the lights. But on that morning, it seemed impossible to go out our front door, to turn the key and walk down the porch stairs with so much left behind. There was a powerful, almost physical, sense of ripping ourselves away. Like some kind of abandonment—the blue box of ashes on top of my bureau, Anna's toys all over, the smell of her still in her unwashed clothing.

I started the car and turned it off. We talked for a while until I could start it again. Then I pulled out of the driveway and onto the road.

A week from today, we will again pack our gear in the car, close the front door, and drive up to the Adirondacks for a weekend visit. I'm sure it will be different this time, though not without pain. In the mountains, the maples should be turning red and orange. The grasses and alders in the vleis will be tan and brown and crackle in the wind. At night there could be frost, and lying in our tent, in the place where Anna was conceived, we will pull our sleeping bags over our shoulders.

September 18

I think it was on Monday or Tuesday, January 23 or 24, that I came home for the night for the first time since Anna's birth. Beth was gaining strength and Anna was stable. I remember coming in the door and greeting Jessie, who had been tended by our friends for the past few days. There was a pile of mail on the dining room table, and dog hair, like tumbleweed, on the floor. Upstairs in the bathroom, towels lay about, still heavy and wet with amniotic fluid. Beth's side of the bed was still soaked, and it struck me that this couldn't have happened just a few nights before: Beth sitting up rigid in bed, then running for the bathroom; and me trying to be cool, calm, calling the doctor, shaking like a leaf, forgetting my wallet, keys, remembering to turn down the thermostat.

I collected the wet linen, took it downstairs, and started a wash. It was almost midnight, but I was wildly exhausted. I vacuumed the house and scoured the sinks and tubs. Then I went out for a jog around our neighborhood, my usual route, past the rows of squat bungalows on our street, the porch swings still, the dogs curled and quiet behind chain-link fences. I ran up around the old Masonic lodge and the Independent Order of Oddfellows. Coming down our own street again, I passed our house, taking it in as a stranger might see it: another sleepy bungalow with scraggly yews as high as the porch railing, a concrete walk, milky in the moonlight, a three-window dormer behind a bare pin oak overhanging the street.

How many times have I jogged by our house and seen in its clean, spare lines no hint of trouble? In the spring and summer, we have white flower boxes on the railings and below each dormer window. When Anna was home, I would see in those three windows the glow of her night-light beyond the flowers, and often I would see the top of Beth's head, slowly moving, and I would know she was rocking in the chair beside the crib, nursing Anna.

But on that night, as on these mild September nights, there was no light in the window, and I remember trying to imagine what it would be like if this child were to die.

What is surprising, and perhaps frightening, is that I *could* almost imagine it. I could almost feel its sheer weight and exhaustion. The aimless anger. I even saw Beth and myself going away to a clear, clean place. I saw myself at home doing small, achievable jobs.

Could I have known then that I was steeling myself for this? Could I, in just imagining, have somehow brought all this about?

No, I don't believe that, though sometimes I wonder.

September 19

What I couldn't imagine that night as I ran past our house was what Anna's death might be like for her. In the end, my imagination then and now is terribly limited or selfish, a kind of envisioning of my own survival, not an imagining of her death itself. To do so, I suppose, would be awfully close to imagining my own death—not just that vague sense that, as certain as taxes, we will all die, but I mean the real dying part of it, the time when you know that yes, this is it, and it is there right in front of you.

What did Anna sense of this? And what will my own sense of it be? Was it like a spiraling down? Or a fading away? Or a rising, like mist on a glassy lake? Or was it more sudden, fierce, the pull of a waterfall, a tearing away, that last beat of her heart—not a giving-in, but a clench?

There are times when I am involved with something else that I almost forget Anna. There are other times when I want to remember her, but she seems so far away. And then there are times, unexpected and unprepared for, when she comes to me so vividly that she is almost there.

Yesterday evening I was arranging my desk in my study, which we have finished painting and I will soon move into. I was putting some old letters in a drawer, when I thought I could feel Anna over my shoulder, her arms hanging loose, relaxed, that damp, drooly spot near my collarbone. I have held a good number of kids, and they all feel different. Anna was long and light and limber. Except for when she was crying, she would mold to your shoulder and chest. I had a way of carrying her with one arm, my left. It made me feel cocky, a father. She would have her head on my shoulder, and I would have my forearm beneath her rump and my hand around her right leg, just above her ankle. I remember the narrow fold of flesh that was there, and the curl and splay of her toes. I could even show you exactly the size of her leg where I held it, if you could just see the circle I make when I touch my thumb and index finger.

Someday, I have read, the sudden presence of a lost and loved one will be consoling. And yes, I want these moments to happen, this strange sense of her proximity, the smell of her skin in the air. But this is not consoling. There is no peace in this. When I feel her presence, I feel her loss. I feel it right here in my hands.

Healing Powers

Floyd Skloot

I have now been sick for two thousand one hundred and eleven straight days. Ayurvedic medicine says I am sick because my body and spirit are not in harmony. The word Ayurveda means "life knowledge," and the Ayurvedic system—a 5,000-year-old science of healthy living and longevity founded in India—is based on the principle that consciousness, not matter, is primary. What is truly wrong with me is wrong at the level of awareness. I have lost focus and therefore my "quantum mechanical body" cannot keep itself healthy. Chinese medicine says that I am sick because the balance within my body—my *yin* and *yang*—or the balance between my body and environment, is disrupted. My vital energy, my *qi*, which connects me with the vital energy of the universe, is no longer in balance with my blood. Tibetan medicine says that all of us are sick; my disease just happens to be manifest. One of three negative states of mind—desire, hatred, or obscuration—has combined with my ignorance of how things exist and what they mean, leading to the present condition of illness. Chiropractic medicine says I am sick because subluxation of the spine has thrown my body into chaos. As a result, I lack normal nerve function. Homeopathic medicine says my disease represents the body's own fight for health. My array of symptoms is merely the wisdom of the body in action, fighting to regain equilibrium, and instead of trying to suppress those symptoms, I should stimulate my body to push them even further. New Age thinking suggests that I am sick because I have forgotten who I am. This caused me to live an unhealthy lifestyle, which in turn made me ill. My illness is a kind of lesson, specifically designed to lead me back to myself. The Bible says that if I am sick, I must have violated stipulations of the covenant with God. Deuteronomy 28 is clear about the source of illness: "If you are not careful to do all the words of this law which are written in this book," the Lord will bring on "extraordinary afflictions, afflictions severe and lasting, and sicknesses grievous and lasting." A corollary biblical explanation holds that my illness is part of undisclosed divine plans. This is something Job came to understand, realizing that "Of a truth, God will not do wickedly." A support group I once attended maintained that we all were sick because we were damaged by our parents or our bosses or environment. We had wounds that festered and finally erupted into illness. A vocal subgroup clarified that we all had similar disease-prone personalities and developed our particular disease because it fit our personality type. My medical doctor says I am sick because on December 7, 1988, a virus targeted my brain and triggered an immune system cascade that my brain cannot turn off. Tests not only trace this path, they confirm the ongoing devastation.

"All our knowledge brings us nearer to our ignorance," T. S. Eliot says in *Choruses* from *The Rock*. Indeed, I have spent nearly seven years reading about illness, learning how the immune and central nervous systems work, understanding how viruses and bacteria and parasites challenge the body, researching drugs and herbs and vitamins, experimenting with the connections between healing and the mind. For all that I have come to know, it seems to me now that the mysteries only grow deeper.

Even without that medley of explanations about the nature of illness to sort through, it is very confusing to be chronically ill. The machine of my body is broken; a delicate poise between body and spirit is disturbed. I have been cut off from my past as an athlete, as a member of the workforce, as a vital human being. Family relationships and friendships have altered. Whether I have sinned or lived wrong, expended too much or held too much in, deserved my virus or was stricken arbitrarily, my life has been changed utterly. This is difficult to grasp, even now.

And the messages about how to get well are far more confusing than the messages about what illness is. Let me tell you, sick as long as I have been, you are tempted to try anything.

I did not used to say I put the milk in the *shower* instead of in the *refrigerator*. I could distinguish between the *excerpts* of Portland and the *outskirts* of Portland. I would never have said we had a *garlic* driveway when I meant a *gravel* driveway. I did not *Xerox* my coffee, I *microwaved* it.

When I saw a wall, I walked past it rather than smack into it. I could drive. On a typical day, I ran ten miles in less than fifty-five minutes, worked eight hours, cooked dinner for my kids, wrote for several hours, and then read. I could do math and spell reliably, could stand with my eyes closed and not topple, could remember your name after being introduced.

But I have chronic fatigue syndrome, a poorly named and poorly understood illness that throws the body's intricately balanced, complex systems in disarray. Nothing works as expected anymore. Without the help of orange ribbons looped around tree limbs, I cannot find my way along a familiar trail through the woods where my wife Beverly and I live. I cannot eat in a restaurant unless I sit facing a wall. I peel a cucumber and dispose of its flesh instead of its rind. Viruses my body's defenses conquered decades ago suddenly erupt again; my eyes have dried out, and although my body temperature seldom rises over 97.2 degrees, I am always hot.

This is not a disease of fatigue, though that is one of its principal symptoms. Calling it chronic fatigue syndrome is like calling Parkinson's disease chronic shaking syndrome or emphysema chronic coughing syndrome. Since the viral attack on my brain, my immune system has been in overdrive, endlessly and futilely combating a virus that may no longer even be there. Meanwhile, my system teems with long-dormant viruses, but I seldom catch colds or flu. I have either too much or too little of nearly everything doctors like to test for, such as activated memory T-cells and suppressor cells, interleukin receptors, sedimentation rates or protein in the spinal fluid. Balance, memory, abstract reasoning, concentration, coordination, stamina, are damaged. In conversation and when I try to write, I often cannot locate—or thoroughly misuse—words that are in my vocabulary.

In *The Sorcerer's Apprentice,* her brilliant book about medical miracles and life in hospitals, Sallie Tisdale notes that "certain diseases become metaphors, such as cancer or leprosy. They wreak a kind of devastation on the body that seems more than simple-minded cell growth, more than misfortune. They seem to be symbolic of the larger condition, of humanity's changing states." Of course, as Susan Sontag argued in *Illness as Metaphor,* "illness is *not* a metaphor," nor are illnesses "tropes for new attitudes toward the self." She asserts that "nothing is more punitive than to give a disease a meaning" but also realizes that the tendency to do so is "always an index of how much is not understood about the physical terrain of a disease."

Surely both Tisdale and Sontag are right. While my brain is scarred so that lesions are visible on magnetic resonance imaging tests and the damage to my immune system is readily apparent from laboratory tests, it remains tempting to see chronic fatigue syndrome as somehow symbolic: our world at the millennium is exhausting. Or it is a hostile place that defeats one's defenses. Or the weak fold; this illness is a perfect example of natural selection at work. Or pushing as hard as most Americans do, we court collapse.

Ultimately, the key issue remains how to balance the quest for understanding my illness with the quest to lead a rich life despite my illnesses' inexorable presence. Keeping up with the literature, evaluating options, experimenting, but yet not becoming obsessed with treatments and cures, not allowing the stress of such uncertainty to exacerbate symptoms. It is enough to make a person sick.

Try as I might, the temptation to seek strange remedies, to court the healing powers both within and without my body, is often irresistible. In certain moods, I cannot help but see healing as transformation or feel that I must somehow reinvent myself in order to get well. When the brain is scarred, when blood flow to it is diminished and functions that were quite literally unconscious suddenly go haywire—like regulating body temperature or remembering to breathe while asleep—a person can grow desperate to get back in balance. When you can neither sit nor lie without pain, nor walk without a cane, nor sleep through six years of nights, you will consider even the most bizarre remedies.

There is a simple prescription for treating one of the newer things that has gone wrong with me. In his book *Treatment of Disease with Acupuncture*, Dr. James Tin Yau So provides the recipe for a drink that will fix me right up. First, I should obtain a live frog. Next I fill its mouth with whole peppercorns, bind its mouth and legs with thread, wrap it in soft wet clay, and put it on a charcoal stove, where it chars until the clay dries and there is no smoke. After the frog cools, I should grind it into a fine powder and place $^1/_7$ ounce of it into one or two tablespoons of wine. Then I must drink it once daily until the symptoms are gone.

I no longer laugh at such suggestions. In fact, I am trying to choose between the frog that lives loudly in our small pond among the water lilies and hyacinths or the one summering in the heel of Beverly's right Wellington boot on the front porch.

For another set of ongoing problems, there are teas to drink. A mixture of bogbean, black cohosh, celery seed, meadowsweet, and yarrow three times a day; then just before bed, a cup of Jamaican dogwood, valerian, and passion flower. In addition, I would benefit from wearing topaz and, from time to time, pearl. Aromatherapy with pennyroyal or peppermint would be very good, as would the use of blue blankets or red T-shirts. Crushed radish juice mixed with a little camphor and taken as nose drops would also help, to say nothing of reviewing the ways I may have violated the Lord's covenant.

I have lain on a table and could have been mistaken for a prickly pear, with erect acupuncture needles covering nearly every inch of my body. I have visualized a team of frogmen swimming through my bloodstream to retrain my sluggish natural killer cells in wetwork, and little men in white coveralls scrubbing the lesions from my brain. Every morning I consume a cornucopia of eleven and a quarter different tablets. And, of course, I am often tempted to do nothing at all.

That is sometimes offered to me as the soundest advice. Do nothing. Surrender to your illness in order to defeat it. Stop searching for a cure and be healed. Oddly enough, because medical science does not yet know how to treat my illness, it is the traditional western medical doctor who often recommends doing nothing other than rest and taking drugs to alleviate symptoms. A problem with an approach focused on symptoms is the exaggerated impact and side effects drugs have on people with chronic fatigue syndrome. Medications are often taken in minuscule doses, by shaving an eighth of a tablet or opening a capsule to separate its contents into portions the size of a cracker crumb. Still the response might be a complete shutting down of the digestive system, or the sleep of the dead. Another problem is addiction; using drugs for relief of constant pain, sleep disturbance, or breathing difficulty carries significant risk while offering little hope of genuine future gain.

So what is a person to do?

In *The Body at War: The Miracle of the Immune System*, Australian immunologist John M. Dwyer devotes an entire chapter to chronic fatigue syndrome in which he berates fellow physicians for their insensitivity and arrogance in handling the disease's mysteries. Failing to get beyond "high technology investigation," they do not consider "medical science's ignorance of so much of the body's ordered and disordered function" and thus do not offer the support their patients need. They dismiss them, ignore them, accuse them of malingering, advise mental health treatment. This has "driven patients with chronic fatigue syndrome and indeed all incurable and poorly understood diseases into the somewhat dangerous world of alternative medicine." With sorrow, Dwyer cites cases of patients who "have flocked to New Zealand to a man who claims to cure chronic fatigue syndrome by exposing one to a specific sequence of colors. Others have been fed massive amounts of vitamin C, tryptophan, lecithin, macrobiotics, cod liver oil, etc. One American healer claims that chronic fatigue syndrome can be cured by tapping repeatedly over the thymus gland and summoning, with all one's mental energy, the T cells that lurk within." Finally, and in a tone of deep despair, Dwyer talks about patients who "go to detoxification units to be purified by enemas, vitamins, and exercise."

Well, I tried every one of the remedies on Dwyer's list except thymus tapping. And in June 1994, Beverly and I drove to Vancouver, British Columbia, to give detoxification therapy a whirl. It made a kind of sense. Even my physician had compared chronic fatigue syndrome to an internal toxic spill, with the immune system dumping its poisons into my bloodstream regularly, so why not clean it up?

The first step in the detoxification program known as Panchakarma was to be done at home a week before actual treatments began. It was called *sneehana* and involved the consumption of various oils intended to "put out the digestive fire." Beverly cooked up a batch of clarified butter, or *ghee*, which we were to drink in increasing amounts all week, followed by a glass of hot water, till we finished with eight teaspoons on Friday. She said she enjoyed watching it bubble, like a fire flickering, and I was struck by the frenetic sizzling sound, as though the process of purifying butter—and by extension, purifying my body—required a level of intensity and a magic beyond anything I had been working with. For someone with my genetic cholesterol problems, drinking butter was akin to asking a heart-attack patient to run a four-minute mile to strengthen the damaged muscle. It seemed ironic, if not self-destructive, that my detoxification should begin with ingesting something like butter, which I had avoided for the last decade as toxic, but I kept repeating to myself, mantralike, that this was *clarified* butter.

Each day's increased dosage of *ghee* was a little more difficult to get down, and was followed by slight nausea, but it certainly did diminish my appetite. Beverly, who was going to undergo the same treatments as a preventive rather than curative measure, felt herself being calmed and slowed down.

On the third day, the Panchakarma clinic's director called, just to check on how we were doing and answer any questions we might have. I could not recall my various medical doctors having done that, even after a spinal tap one of them performed on me led to "a neurological event" that left me bedridden for nineteen days.

On the next-to-last day, I found myself deeply fatigued and depressed. Beverly said that the clinic director predicted *ghee* would release old emotions; it was all right, a good sign. That evening, the climax of our preparations, we took hot baths and then consumed six teaspoons of castor oil in a half cup of hot water and the juice of an orange. We held our noses while we drank, then ate a segment of orange to cleanse our palates. I will mention the gurgling in my stomach at bedtime, but not what happened the next morning. Be assured that my digestive tract was cleansed.

Beverly and I had decided to undergo Panchakarma therapy far more circuitously than we make most decisions. After a period of relative equilibrium in the management of my symptoms, the first half of 1994 had seen me worsen notably. My doctor, an infectious disease specialist in whom I have full confidence, had been talking lately about new therapies that were being tried elsewhere—nitroglycerin patches to reverse the restriction of blood flow to the brain, injections of a pig's liver extract, intravenous magnesium—and I found myself hesitant to try another round of experiments. In the past, the experiments had not only failed to help, they often set me back further.

I had been seeing Beverly's naturopathic physician and supplementing my medical doctor's regimen of vitamins, enzymes, and supplements with the naturopath's remedies. He gave me tiny white pellets to be taken three times a day without touching them by hand, which is quite a trick for someone with chronic fatigue syndrome. In the quiet evenings here, where we live in the middle of twenty hilly, wooded acres outside a town of 1,100, Beverly and I had been talking about how far I was willing to venture into the medically unknown in order to stop the latest decline.

"Somewhere new," I said.

"What about this?" she asked, handing over the issue of *Yoga Journal*. It was open to an article about Panchakarma, an Ayurvedic practice that she had heard about before. I thought it sounded like a Mexican curry dish, myself.

Panchakarma is aimed at dislodging toxins from cells and flushing them out of the body. It was based on the premise that disease follows from the accumulation of such toxins and getting rid of them restores the body's proper balance. Every avenue of egress from the body is used, but it is supposed to be a gentle, soothing process. After being cleansed, a person goes home to work on the forces that allowed the toxins to build up in the first place—behaviors, particularly dietary, which are antithetical to the particular body type a person is born with.

I read the article, then the chapter on Panchakarma in Deepak Chopra's *Perfect Health*, and we sent away for brochures from a half dozen clinics offering the treatment. The world of Ayurvedic medicine is as alien to me as space/time travel, but I thought the literature sounded convincing enough to give it a try, despite the scoffing in Dr. Dwyer's book. Although the settings, accommodations, and trappings varied widely, the actual detoxification routines were fairly similar. So instead of paying $2,850 plus air fare to Iowa for a week-long residential package, or about $1,600 for a five-day sojourn in New Mexico, or driving all the way to the Santa Cruz area, we opted for Vancouver, a six-hour drive from home, a city we both enjoy visiting.

The clinic occupied the upstairs unit of a town house in a quiet residential neighborhood on Vancouver's south side. I was glad the area seemed clean and friendly, because with no sign on the street or the door, it felt less like visiting a clinic than a bookie. Inside, the furnishings were spare—two bedrooms used as treatment rooms and containing only a padded table for the patient, in the living room a futon that faced a long table where only a telephone sat, a bathroom, a kitchen where the various oils and herbal potions were concocted, and behind a folding Japanese screen in the dining area, a computer and fax machine hummed.

Our first visit was for a Sunday-evening conference with the clinic's director and medical doctor. The doctor would briefly examine us and outline our specific treatment plans. She had a separate, "regular" practice in family medicine and was working with the Panchakarma clinic out of her personal belief in the value of Ayurveda. After a lengthy round of questions about my health, my diet, and my lifestyle, and a three-minute reading of my pulse, she asked whether I was a person who meditated.

"I haven't had much luck with that," I said.

She looked at the clinic director and frowned. "I can't work with people who don't meditate. I just can't relate to them."

She prescribed a series of treatments for me over the next five afternoons, involving oil rubs, the dripping of warm oil onto the center of my forehead, herbalized steam treatments, a kind of full-body oil bath, daily enemas, inhalation of various oil and herbal mixtures, and music. Despite my preparatory reading, I was beginning to feel strongly as though I were trapped inside a film by Federico Fellini. The best surreal art is rooted in recognizable reality, and this was a real room, the staff looked as conservative as the merchants I had seen downtown, everyone was smiling encouragingly, but I was having trouble seeing this plan as something to heal and rejuvenate rather than punish me.

We were staying at an isolated bed and breakfast overlooking English Bay, a good ten miles from the city's hurlyburly, so that we could spend leisurely mornings and evenings resting between treatments. Our room, whose wallwide window crept up to serve also as half a roof, gave a remarkable view of woods, sea, and sky. Basic, elemental stuff as we lay there gazing at the stars, purifying ourselves, and yet by Tuesday night I was miserable. The mixture of summery heat and gallons of hot oil conspired with my body's inability to regulate its temperature, making me horribly uncomfortable. I could not tolerate the herbal steam treatment at its target heat level, which meant that I received a sort of luke-steam session. My eyes, already preternaturally dry, were ready to be reduced to powder if I had to put my face over a bowl of medicated vapors. The enemas seemed to trigger some deep, unacknowledged phobia, leaving me so stressed that I could barely sleep. I was not enjoying wearing a diaper all night either. Everything that bothered me was proclaimed to be a good sign by the clinic director, indications that the treatment was working. Beverly, meanwhile, felt wonderful and could not wait for the next day's treatment. Clearly, as she quietly reminded me, I needed to make a choice: quit or surrender to the program. "A massage and an enema," she said. "What's the big deal?"

I was a classic case of mind and body working at cross purposes in the healing process. Here they were trying to unleash my body's own healing powers and I was hindering them by using symptom warfare. Did I not trust them or the process enough? Did I want to stay sick? Well, no. It felt as though the treatment was worse than the illness, and would end up worsening it. I vowed to practice discipline the next day, to turn my body over to them and take my mind elsewhere. That was the day the enema tube, on being withdrawn, scratched my insides badly enough to make further enemas impossible, which was not a good sign.

Nevertheless, at the end of a week I had undergone most of the prescribed treatments, at nearly the prescribed levels of intensity and for close to the recommended amounts of time. I left Vancouver having experienced a simplified Panchakarma, a sort of Cliff's Notes version, and returned to Oregon with a recommended program of home care and diet, anxious to see what effect the experience would have. We were warned that it might take one to three months before we could fully assess the benefits.

I suppose if I were Forrest Gump, I might approach the end of this essay by saying "healing is as healing does." Because healing seems to me to be a phenomenon that involves action, however passive that action may appear to be. It is possible to rest aggressively. It is possible to empty oneself of thought, especially negative thought, or to train the mind away from its experience of pain, and thereby experience a lessening of symptoms. The very act of doing something perceived as potentially beneficial has certain healing consequences, whether or not the thing done is of any demonstrable value—this is referred to as the placebo effect, which my own doctor once said could amount to as much as a thirty percent improvement in symptoms.

Through all the years of my illness, through the many traditional and nontraditional efforts I have made to get better, I have developed deep respect for the paradoxes and possibilities of the body's healing powers, even if I have not been able to marshal them all on my own behalf. My symptoms wax and wane, sometimes, it seems, as a result of my efforts and sometimes despite them. Nevertheless, there will be times when I am able to function with a nearly clear mind for hours at a time or run a few steps up to the mailbox to see whether something I have written has found favor with an editor. I danced with Beverly at our wedding sixteen months ago, and though I am not sure if the enzyme supplement CoQ 10 I was taking had anything to do with it, I am still taking the stuff.

It is now September 1994, and I must say that a number of strange changes have developed over the three months since my experience with Panchakarma. Almost immediately, I began to sleep through the night for the first time since the winter of 1988. Did Panchakarma do this for me? I had a brief period of slightly more stamina, during which I was able to walk for a half hour at a time and write for as much as three hours during the day. My cholesterol went down twenty points, but there has been no change in the profile of my overactive immune system.

However, my joint and muscle pain have increased enormously. The first signs of arthritis manifested themselves in my feet and hands, and headaches have put a stop to all activity for days at a time. I developed asthma. I developed a case of pityriasis rosea, an inflammatory skin disease common among young adults that left me covered in scaly lesions from thighs to chest for two months and for which my doctors have no explanation. They think it may have been a reactivation of an infection I caught and defended myself from in childhood, but which my damaged immune system could no longer subdue. Could Panchakarma have had anything to do with these new problems? Do I have to go back and try it again to find out?

I have neither lost my respect for the paradoxes and possibilities of the body's healing powers nor figured them out well enough to make use of them. I have not yet worked out a master theory on why I got sick or a master plan on how to get well. But as the contradictions deepen, as what works and what does not work develops its own strange rhythm, I feel as though I have learned to approach the dance of hope and despair with high style. A maturing expert in the healing fandango, I have achieved a state of mind that allows me to accommodate its variations, to risk the odd step for the sake of the song. That alone seems like growth.

Taking Care

JANE BERNSTEIN

My uncle Ben is ninety years old—maybe. He isn't exactly sure anymore, and no one is left to argue that his real age is eighty-nine or ninety-one, or tell those in the next generation the actual date of his birthday. Both Ben and his brother took the Fourth of July as their birth dates when they came here from Russia or Romania—there's even disagreement about the name of the country they emigrated from, since the borders in that region have changed so often.

Forgetting his age is the least of Ben's problems. He remembers his two daughters, but not necessarily his sister or brother, or his first wife, though they had been married for forty-three years when she died. On a more practical level, he cannot remember where he put his toothpaste, or his shirts. He cannot remember why he has been separated from his second wife, Rose. Every day, dozens of times a day he asks, "Where's Rose?"

His daughter says, "Rose is in Florida, Dad."

Why can't he see her?

Ben's younger daughter, a patient, soft-spoken woman, says, "Rose is sick, Dad," and once again explains why Rose is in Florida and he is thousands of miles away. Ben nods in understanding, and minutes later asks, "Where's Rose?"

Rose is the one person Ben never forgets—not for a moment it seems. Wife and companion for the last sixteen years, it's as if her presence, her importance, has expanded to fill the void. The world of both the past and present has become treacherous and unfamiliar, and the image of Rose has become gigantic. He is obsessed.

Why isn't he in Florida with Rose? Because Ben drove her crazy. Literally, says the daughter who lives in Chicago. The daughter in a suburb of New York is dubious, or perhaps too enraged to care about the breakdown of this wife of sixteen years, no mother to her. Rose had been complaining a lot about Ben over the last few years, the way he hounded her with the same questions, over and over; how, whatever she told him, he forgot. In the summer of 1993, the calls started: Rose yelling over the line at Ben's daughters, increasingly agitated; the calls becoming more frequent. They better get their father. She couldn't live with him anymore. In October the big call came. She was kicking him out. They had to get him immediately or they'd find him on the street. This was absolutely it.

Remember the story that was picked up by every wire service and all the network news: Old-timer abandoned at an airport in his wheelchair, gaunt and unshaven. And to further tug on us and confuse us, the lap blanket tucked carefully over his knees, the adult diapers and teddy bear alongside him. My uncle Ben strolled off the plane, a fit, bantam-sized gent, with a smile that crinkles up his eyes. Arms around his daughter, happy to see her; getting his luggage, belting himself in the car. Hello, hello.

"Where's Rose?"

"Rose is in Florida."

Without time to plan for Ben's future, the sisters made hasty temporary arrangements: The New York son-in-law, who ran a business from his home, would look after Ben until they could think clearly about what was best for their father.

Imagine hearing this for a first time: A ninety-year-old man, thrown out of his house by his wife of sixteen years. Wandering in his daughter's house, a place that has become as unfamiliar as the rest of his landscape. Following whomever he sees. Down in the basement; barging into his granddaughter's room. Why were they keeping him here? Why wouldn't they let him go home and be with Rose?

I'm listening to this story from my kitchen in Pittsburgh. The image I have of Ben is from childhood, when he was one of two little look-alike uncles, Ben Tsion, who took the name Sidney, and Dov Baer, who became Ben, both busy taking pictures at family gatherings. One dour as he arranges people: Sit here, move left, bend your head closer, where's the smile, say cheese; the other edging through the crowd, big smile crinkling up his face, quietly snapping photos. The second one is Ben.

I am no stranger to taking care of people. In the foreground there's my retarded ten-year-old daughter with problems far more compli-cated than that single word suggests. In the background: a husband with chronic liver disease, and aging parents who left their home of forty years and moved to the city where I now live. Like Ben, they are in good physical shape, though my father complains with good reason that the marbles are rattling around in his head.

Even so, I am disgusted by Rose, utterly without sympathy. There are social services in Florida, local programs. Rose is no dummy; she is a woman of experience and education. All right, it's hard, but to kick him out? Why couldn't she have asked for help?

My Chicago cousin has no answers, but while scrambling for solu-tions, she has learned a number of things: In places like Florida, where there are so many elderly people, there's an abrupt loss of status when one's mate becomes senile. Instead of getting help or sympathy from friends, people are often dropped, left behind. Perhaps it's because old age, with all its attendant ailments, looms over everyone like a plague, and as in plague days, the healthy lock their doors to ward off contagion. Or maybe, instead of seeing their health as the luck of the genetic draw, people consider it a kind of superiority, albeit a fragile one that must be closely protected.

But to kick out her husband! What about commitment?

My cousin in Chicago tells me that her father's story isn't so uncommon. "Apparently the commitment isn't always as great in second marriages."

It's six-thirty on a December evening, and I'm on the phone to my Chicago cousin, getting an update on Uncle Ben. This is the only time I can make calls because I'm getting dinner ready and, therefore, not fully engaged.

Ben is miserable. They had tried letting him call Rose, but she screamed at him on the phone. So now he is writing her instead, long letters that are eloquent and clear. Love letters, filled with grief. *How could you do this to me? We were in love.* My cousin has been looking for day programs for her father, but all he wants is to be with Rose.

Same as every night, my daughter Rachel trails beside me as I roam from counter to sink to stove. She is so close that often I bump or elbow her accidentally. Sometimes she is stunned, but neither words nor the memory of her bruises are strong enough to convince her to back up.

My cousin tells me: "When I explain that Rose is sick, he understands completely, but then ten minutes later he asks me why he can't be with her." Rachel murmurs when I murmur, speaks loudly when I raise my voice. My husband thinks she stands on top of us because she's visually impaired; in my opinion it's because, among other things, she lacks a sense of personal space.

Where's Rose?

My daughter says, "I'm hungry, can I have an apple?"

She's just finished an apple.

We were good together, I loved her. Where's Rose?

Can I have an apple? I'm hungry, can we have tortellini?

I clutch my daughter by the shoulders to steer her away from me, and, thinking of my own beloved father, say, "It must be awful. I don't know how you can take it."

I'm hungry, can I have an apple? Are we having tortellini?

The day programs were for people with Alzheimer's. When Uncle Ben saw all the people slumped in wheel-chairs, or pacing across the room, vacant looks on their faces, he said, "They're old!" Why did his daughter take him there? He turned away, puzzled and alarmed. These people suffered from the plague of physical disabilities, while Ben was a tough old bird, only, as my father says about himself, his marbles were rattling around.

How could Rose get rid of him, as if he were a vicious dog? How could she be so despicable?

For a long time, whenever I was asked to describe my daughter Rachel, I stressed her sweetness. How different she was from the boy who bit her twice at school, or the girl who pulled a hank of hair out of her head and had to wear a restraining device on the bus because she was, in the jargon of special education, physically disinhibited. No, I would say; my daughter is good-natured. Good-natured, and completely dependent upon us, from the moment she wakes—and she wakes early—until she is tucked in bed.

Total dependency means not merely that I must help her dress and get her meals, but that she is right beside one of us, most often me, whenever she is home. During the school week, this isn't so bad. In the morning she is at her most alert and able, cheerful with the routine: same cereal, medication, seat at the table; same toothbrush, jacket, backpack on the hook, yellow school bus outside at eight A.M., Flo in the driver's seat, tooting the horn. She is gone until six o'clock, when one of us picks her up at a child care center, notable for its inclusion of children like Rachel, and takes her home, where she chants about apples and tortellini, or whatever food she's locked into that week.

It's the weekends that are tough. If I am home, wherever I am, third floor to basement, she is an inch away from me, talking, talking, her language perseverative, painfully limited, reminding me of my silent entreaties when she was a baby—Please, oh, please, let her talk. Who knew my most fervent wish would be granted in such an exaggerated way—a daughter who talks ceaselessly, except when she's asleep? If I want to take a walk with my older daughter, go shopping with her, sit and have a cookie without Rachel's continual birdlike, in-your-face chatter, I have three choices: Pay for it; bargain with my husband; not do it. I don't know what other people's weekends are like, but ours most often begin with negotiating for time and freedom. If you take Rachel Saturday morning, I'll take her Sunday afternoon. . . . Like that.

And yet, when people, knowing my situation, regard me with mournful eyes, I think: Hey, it's my life, I'm used to it. I think: Good days and bad days, same as for you. And: There are worse kids, worse situations. The fatigue I sometimes feel is natural and cyclic. True, weekends are tough and school vacations tougher. True, she seems overwhelming at times. But so does the awesome responsibility of watching over my teenage daughter, and the pile of manuscripts on my desk.

Around the time when Rose evicted Ben, the voice that said "Hey, it's my life" began to be replaced by a whisper that said "How much longer can I . . ." It's not just the number of years I have already taken care of her—eleven—or the number of years before she becomes an adult—ten. It's that I've gotten tired; I have more people to take care of, and Rachel has become more difficult. My once-pleasant daughter has begun to shriek at me, apropos of nothing as far as I can tell. Sometimes she simply says, "I hate you!" and other times, "You have no right to talk to students that way!" I might be examining apples in a supermarket when she yells, "DON'T YOU DARE YELL AT ME." Or helping her down a flight of stairs, when suddenly, "You're not the boss!"

It took me a while to understand that the origin of the expressions is unimportant, as are the words themselves. The emotion underlying her yelling is what's real, an emotion caused by fatigue or frustration. I understand this and try not to take it personally, but try listening to someone—to a recording, a disembodied voice—say "I hate you!" several hundred times, and the diminishing effect of these words will become clearer.

As I trudge onward with my furious child, I am reminded that I cannot use hugs or sweet talk to jolly her out of her mood. Nor can I fall back on the usual (if regrettable) "if . . . then" statements that parents use as a last resort. In a world of things with the capacity to delight, nothing much delights her—not dolls or stuffed toys or the pictures I hang on the wall of a room decorated to please some child, but not her; not undershirts with hearts on them or trips to the zoo; not me. I cannot tempt her, threaten her, get her to remember simple things. Once I saw myself as the one who knew her best: protector, teacher, expert, but, because my efforts have not come to much, there are times when it feels ridiculous to keep struggling to fit her into our household. Her chatter is so incessant, my own marbles have begun to rattle too. May I have an apple? Didn't you just have an apple? Yes. May I have an apple?

Where's Rose?

How do we placate ourselves during hard times? Things will change. Isn't that what we say? I imagine my cousins thinking: We will help him. He will get used to it here. Things will get smoother.

As the weeks pass, Ben becomes more miserable at his daughter's house. More confused, more disoriented. The only program even vaguely appropriate for him meets two days a week until three o'clock. The rest of the time, he wanders through the house, barging into rooms, demanding to know why the hell he is there and Rose is not. He has become increasingly hostile. The house is a prison. They are feeding him shit. Where the hell is Rose?

I imagine my cousin switching off the bedside lights, wondering how much longer she can hold out. She loves her father. (I love my daughter.) I can imagine Ben's son-in-law, Richard, prime caregiver of Ben, afraid to even form that question. Richard, born and raised in Argentina, his own parents dead, burst into our extended family with a passionate need to be one of us, not just a relative by marriage. He is an emotional man, the staunchest defender of Ben, the one who is angriest at Rose. His sister-in-law has begun to say that Rose had a mental breakdown, and her anger has lessened, but to Richard, family and responsibility are holy words, and Rose cannot be excused for her actions.

I can imagine my cousin, awake at night, thinking: He is my father. She is my daughter.

If she really hates me? If my parenting is irrelevant, my place in her life unimportant?

This is what you do: You take care of your children and your parents.

At the expense of our emotional needs and our professional goals? Some would say yes, this is what you do.

At the expense of the others in the family? Some, fewer perhaps, would say: Caring for those who cannot care for themselves comes first.

At the expense of our physical and mental health?

Richard had a heart attack in January. In between trips to the hospital, his wife drove Ben to LaGuardia Airport, where he got on a flight to Chicago. He stepped off the plane at O'Hare, fit and grinning, and asking about Rose, his problems now in the hands of his older daughter.

For most caregivers, there is heartache, but no cardiac arrest, no clear physical manifestation that allows us to say "enough" and feel certain about our decisions. This is not to say that Richard staged his heart attack as a metaphor for the occasion. No, it was real, and it was clearly stress-related. And now Richard must struggle to prevent further damage to his weakened heart. But there was no question that his heart attack ended his three-month stint as caregiver.

My Chicago cousin found an apartment for her father in a development, where, for a fee, aides help him with whatever he cannot do, or, more often, what he cannot remember to do. Ben's room is spacious and cheerful, and he has a private bath. For a fee, he is escorted to his meals; for a fee, someone takes him for a walk. To save money, my cousin keeps a list of his activities on her desk at work. Although he is not interested in attending any of them, several times each day she stops work and calls her father to remind him to go downstairs. When I ask if he might make friends, she laughs ruefully: He cannot remember on Tuesday the person he met on Monday. It's a hard condition for friendship.

When my cousin started Ben's phone service, she got him speed dialing to her home, fifteen minutes away. He calls her twenty times, day and night, frustrated because he can't find his toothpaste, or toothbrush, or shirts. There is no phone service to Rose, which is a good thing. He is still enraged, still beginning every conversation with questions about Rose.

I am very far from making a decision about Rachel. The only change is that once I assumed that she would live with us until she was a young adult, and now the word "enough" slips into my head with alarming frequency.

Not long ago, a woman who chose to send her profoundly disabled son to an institution castigated me for short-changing my older daughter and my husband by keeping Rachel at home. As she spoke, I felt my heart seize with alarm and heard myself defend my lovely, defenseless daughter. Not yet! We can still handle things. But two days into a holiday, when she has been stuck to me like Velcro, chanting, chattering, so that I am reminded that I cannot hear my own voice—death to a writer!—I wonder how much longer I can hold out. (It is no accident that this essay took hold as I was driving to the airport to catch a plane to New York, and that at the gate, while all around me babies yowled and adults cursed and rumbled about the delays, I wrote in a frenzy, my head unusually clear.)

Of course, this is the issue that most polarizes parents of special-needs kids.

On one side are people like the woman who accused me of expending my energy in the wrong place, and on the other side the ones who say: Tough luck if your career suffers. This is a living, breathing child, your daughter, your responsibility. I ricochet between these sides, bounce off these walls so regularly that when students—young women struggling with relationships and careers, say in breathless awestricken tones: You teach! You write! You have a family! How do you do it? I hear myself answer: Badly. This is perceived as a joke, when in fact it's how I feel much of the time.

My mother says, "You moved us here!" because she has not seen me in a week.

Rachel hates me.

My husband says, "You're always running around."

My older daughter feels that because I worry more about Rachel, I love her more, a formula that is utterly untrue. Just when I feel as if I can explain this to her, and have her believe it, a friend who grew up with a retarded sister and moved oceans and continents away from her family tells me that Charlotte will grow up and never come home. It will be too painful for her to confront what she left behind.

That makes me cry. Even so, I'm not sure what will shake the bonds enough for me to say "enough." Sometimes I think it will be hearing Rachel say "I hate you" for the millionth time. Sometimes the knowledge that if I fell through a gaping hole, she wouldn't miss me much. Or perhaps circumstance will change things for me, the way it changed things in Ben's family. My husband is ill; my daughter is spreading her wings.

When Richard looks back to the time he took care of Ben, he says, "I don't know how Rose could stand it for so many years." A far cry from his rage at her abandonment. "In just three months, he gave me a heart attack!"

On that trip to New York, I tried to imagine a time when Rachel would be living away from home, tried to drum up a feeling of relief or pleasure, to shape a memory of reading a newspaper in peace. But I find myself imagining my years without her as a little fable:

Once upon a time there was a woman named Jane who took care of a lot of people. Many years passed, and soon, one by one, everyone was gone. So Jane lived all alone for the rest of her life. The end.

The Dreaming Back

MAXINE SCATES

"The act of writing becomes a settlement of memory, a recovery of self by dreaming back through nightmare."
—TERRENCE DES PRES

i. My Father's Body

          is indistinguishable from mine. My father's body is a body of redness. When I cry I bleed into my father's body. We are the pool of redness together. I hate myself. He is crying. He screams "I am dying." My father is drunk. My father is large. My father's arms are long and his hands are huge. My father has tattoos on his arms. One of them is scraped away, traces of blue etching drift under the scar tissue. My father's hands fling Christmas gifts, bowls of spaghetti sauce, and ashtrays at my mother. One hand holds the knife. My father's hands are swollen from gripping the wheel of the truck from punching the man at the hardware store from slamming his fist through the windshield of my brother's car. My father's body is full of shrapnel. He is still. My father is drunk. My father is on the couch and I am sitting on the other end of the couch. I am walking by the couch and my father's hands reach out. I am walking by the couch and my father says "You're getting titties." He touches my breasts. My mother is walking by the couch and my father is saying, "Baby you've got such beautiful legs." My father's shirt pulls out of his dirty pants, the crack in his ass is always showing. My father's belly is hanging over his belt. My father's body is unwashed. My father does not bathe, the smell of him is stomach-turning, a sweet rottenness. You know it if you've smelled it. My father has jungle rot on his feet, purple blotches eating them away. My father is drunk. His face is a smirking moon. His big head is in my mother's face shouting, *Cocksucker, cunt* . . . my mother's face is red in his face shouting, *Shut up* . . . *Lying sack of shit* . . . she slaps him . . . *Fucking Catholics* . . . she slaps him harder, *Shut up,* and harder until his glasses break on the bridge of his nose. My father is behind the bedroom door. My mother is there with him. My father is sitting smiling at the table. He says, *Your mother is crazy.* The glass my mother flings at his head has white figures on it. The blood and the orange juice are all mixed up. My mother is sleeping in my room now. My father is behind the bedroom door. Sometimes he is there for the whole weekend. I open the door. He is naked. He wakes, and he is sober, and he tells me never to open the door. I am standing by the couch punching my father's huge belly. I hit him down there. He winces. He says to never hit him down there. My mother is at work, and he is on the couch. We've taken a trip together. We share the bed in the motel. There is a stream outside the window. I know where to look for what I do not understand, for what I won't remember. Redness. Rising. At twenty I write "I don't know the stream flows/behind there is blood on your/bed I don't know what you've shot your veins with/I don't know about any of that . . ." I'll write this for years before I see it. We both want my mother. On the couch, we both want my mother. She passes out of the room. She goes to work. I see his body everywhere—in the fields, in copses of trees. I sink into him as if he were a marsh. I understand his redness, his blood on the kitchen floor, the individual hairs of his head on the edge of the porcelain pan where his head came to rest when the large mass of him fell. He is stumbling. He is stumbling drunk. I look into the pool of redness as if it were my future, the wound I will fall into. It was. The thick blood holds to its own circle. It is my future; this is the redness. I hurt. I harm. I am drunk. This is what makes it a circle. I rise from him as if he were a swamp of redness. I dress the redness in pants, a shirt. I hit it again and again. I tell it to stop. I'm about to fall in when she grabs me. I bury the shirt, the pants. I rise. I remember. This is the beginning. I am not my father.

ii. Exteriors

I sat on the neighbor's fence. It was six o'clock and the other kids had gone in for dinner. My mother and brother were at work and my father had come home from work. I did not want to go home, but I did when the fog finally rolled down the street. I left my brown jacket on the fence, and the next day it was gone, stolen by the fog. Now I stand on the opposite corner and take photographs of the house and the jets flying overhead. The playground of the school is behind me, and in the far corner, across the wide asphalt shimmering in iridescent waves of heat, is the same iron playground equipment that was there in the fifties. Wherever I sit or stand, I am happier outside.

My parents moved to their two-bedroom seven-hundred-square-foot home a mile south and east of L.A. International Airport in 1949, just months before I was born. Bounded by Arbor Vitae to the north, La Cienega to the east, Century Boulevard to the south, and Aviation Boulevard to the west, our neighborhood rested in a pocket between Inglewood, a city unto itself, from which the San Diego Freeway would eventually separate us, and a district of Los Angeles called Westchester, which was farther to the west and from which we were separated by railroad tracks and factories. The location would mean that although our neighborhood was working-class, eventually I would go to schools that were predominantly middle class and almost one hundred percent white. My parents had purchased the house for $8,000 on the GI loan. My brother, born before the war, was already ten years old. It had taken them years, but they had finally left behind the multiethnic neighborhoods of downtown L.A., where my mother had grown up and where, on and off, my parents had spent the first eleven years of their marriage.

I say on and off because those years, like the years that would follow, had been turbulent, though unlike the years that would follow, those years had been dominated by the upheaval of public events. Children of the Depression, my parents were married in 1938 when my father was twenty and my mother nineteen. My mother was a high school graduate, but my father had dropped out of school in the eighth grade, when his mother, then in her late fifties, had suffered a stroke. His parents had been divorced when he was seven; his father had moved back east and out of his life. My mother had lost her mother to the mental institution when she was twelve; my father's mother would die by the time he was fifteen. In the years after her stroke he lived with first an aunt and then a half sister in Colorado—at fourteen he'd ridden the freights to join her. The year his mother died he was working in the CCC in northern California, where he learned to "run cat, run graders, run shovels, and drive truck." He hitchhiked home for the funeral.

When my parents got married, my father was walking a picket line at *Sunset News*. He had been earning thirty-five cents an hour, but once he joined the union, he earned eighteen dollars a week for walking two hours a day. When my brother "started coming along," he quit the picket line (the strike would eventually last eighteen months) and went to work for a lumber company driving trucks. He killed a man on that job, and though that's not actually what happened, that's the way he phrased it throughout my childhood, one of the cries that would escape from him when he was drunk. "I killed a man. I killed lots of men and I didn't have to." That first death occurred in the lumberyard when a longtime employee apparently walked deliberately into the path of his truck; a coroner's inquest eventually ruled that the death was a suicide, exonerating my father of any blame. But the fact remained, my father had driven the truck that killed a man. My uncle Carl, my aunt Milly's husband, remembers him showing up at his apartment crying and drunk and scared. When I was a child, I didn't know the circumstances of that death. I felt as befuddled as he did about it, and I retained the sense that this death was a particularly cruel act of fate, one, that since he referred to it so often, had left him impossibly scarred.

When they were first married, my parents lived with my grandparents on Toluca Street. After my brother was born, they moved to their first apartment on Emerald Street, a short distance away. Though after the war and during my childhood, when she was again a practicing Catholic, my mother rarely took a drink, then my parents spent a lot of time drinking together. My uncle Carl, who had known my father in the CCC, says my father was always an alcoholic. He was also good-looking in those days and apparently had a reputation for playing around. He was twenty-four when the war began, and because by then he worked for Douglas Aircraft, he had a deferment. Between 1941 and 1943 the marriage disintegrated and finally my father filed for a Mexican divorce. At the time, my father was having a fling with Gloria DeHaven, then an MGM starlet doing publicity for war bonds at the defense plants. Eventually the two of them married. I learned this when I was seven or eight, and one night, while my mother was at work, my father rose from the couch swearing at the *Herald Examiner* in his hands, yelling that Gloria DeHaven had not been married three times but four since he had been the first. When my mother came home from work that night, I told her what my father had said. I remember how tired she looked, and I remember that unlike many of the questions that would go unanswered in the future, she did answer this question, perhaps because the newspaper had, oddly, offered a public corroboration even if it was only in the sense of its omission. Yes, she answered, my father and Gloria DeHaven had been married though the marriage was not legal because the divorce he had filed for was not yet final.

In 1943 my father enlisted in the navy, where he became a gunnery captain on a destroyer. He came home "eighteen months and twenty-one days later." His ship had been in the South Pacific, "always, never got out of it . . . always." When I ask him now how he thinks the war affected his life, he doesn't understand my question. I ask if he thinks it had a lot of impact, "No, not really except that I seen a lot of death I wish I hadn't seen, lost a lot of friends."

At the veterans' home where he has lived since 1982, my father is telling me about his life. In the years preceding his arrival there, I had communicated with him sporadically until finally I had stopped altogether. My mother had divorced him when I was thirteen, in 1963. Within two years, due to his alcoholism, he had lost his job driving trucks for the Department of Water and Power, a job he had held since the late forties. A brief stint as a security guard followed along with an equally brief marriage to a woman he claims stole all his pension money. Throughout the late sixties and all of the seventies, he lived in the residential pay-by-the-week hotels near skid row in downtown L.A. surviving on social security income and toward the end of that time, contributions from my brother and myself. Though they were due him because of war-related injuries, he had never applied for the disability benefits until his arrival at the veterans' home. I can't help but see his inability to do so as emblematic of his failure to integrate that experience into his life, a sad irony since it was in fact his experience of the war that has dominated his life since that time.

When I ask him questions about the war, I remind him that he used to cry when scenes of the Second World War appeared on television. "Who, me?" When I reply, "Yeah, you," he responds, "Well, I know if I watch a picture, it still bothers me. Every once in a while they show it on television, and I'm glad I got a remote control because I just turn it off because I'll never forget it." The words that follow are my father's as he recounts his war, the same war that swirled through my childhood, the redness that swept over us.

                              "You see, honey, we knew, we knew ahead of time. There was this big island, Okinawa. Okay, they had what they call radar pickets around it. Radar pickets were two destroyers on a picket. Every two weeks they moved a position. Every time two destroyers got to picket number one, they got sunk. So, it was just a matter of time. We knew when we was goin' there we was gonna get hit.

"You just sort of waited and knew?"

"Well, certainly we knew."

"How was that for morale?"

"Well, it didn't go over big, but we had to do it . . . Each two ships moved one position every two to three weeks. One that started at thirteen. He would be the last one to get around to one. He'd last maybe twenty-six weeks. Okay. Number-one picket was the main bombing run comin' from Japan, we were only a hundred and fifty miles from Japan. All right, so they come over and they come over and they come over. And this one that they got us on, it was the biggest attack of the war . . . in May, the war ended in August. And they just come out and I'm tellin' you they looked like mosquitoes, there was so many of them. Did you ever read that citation?"

"Yeah, I did."

"We got more ships, we got more planes than any ship our size ever got. In one hour and forty-five minutes we shot down twenty-one planes. In the meantime we took two thousand-pound bombs right through the middle. That's what screwed me up, that bomb. The second plane that hit right behind me—that's the one where I got all these burns . . . you never looked at my arms good, did you?"

"No, I know what they look like. They're all spotted."

"Yeah, both of them. And the only reason my face didn't get burned, I had a, I had a lot of hair then, not a lot, but I had hair and I had a full beard. Well, when that second plane hit, they hit just the same time that the bomb hit. It was just one big flash of fire. There's, four guys in the gun, five. I'm the gun captain. These two guys . . . there's two men on each gun. No, three men on each gun. One firin', one loadin', one unloadin'. Six men, me I'm the seventh man, that's why I'm deaf. They wear earplugs. I cannot wear earplugs. I'm wearing phones. Here's five-inch guns, right below me here, two five-inch guns and right above me here, two five-inch guns. They fire twenty-five-hundred rounds of five-inch ammunition. And then that explosion . . . well, anyway, it killed every man on the gun except me. It blew me out."

"When the explosion came, it killed everybody around you?"

"It killed everybody except me, they're strapped in . . . to their guns. I'm loose I'm walking around with the phones and the wires. See.

I'm hollering for ammunition. I'm calling . . . *(pauses)* I'm calling . . . planes coming in on portside, portside, portside, aim over there so you find a direction. I'm spotting . . . I'm spotting planes and directing my crew at the same time. Anyway, I land on the lower deck, didn't have a stitch of clothes on, bare-ass naked and great big blisters on both legs from here to here. When I got on the hospital ship they just took a knife and, fshht, about a gallon of water come out of 'em. It never hurt. But this is what hurt, see that *(pointing to his hand)* I was scarred for life there."

"You were in the water, the ship went down, right?"

"No, no, our sister ship right alongside of us went down. We listed over forty-five, and I was bleeding like hell out of this hand. And my buddy, a boilermaker, a guy by the name of Dave Earl, he wrapped a black silk handkerchief, you know like the neckties we used to wear, a black one. He got it stopped and we got a billy poke and we was fighting the fire. Well, anyway, finally our air cover come over. They was late. Man, they was flashin' them just like shooting fish out of a barrel. I was never so glad to see anything in my life. Anyway, that took the pressure off and then two APDs come alongside. That's the old-fashioned four-stackers that was used in World War One. They tied up alongside on both sides of us. They kept her afloat. They got a seagoing barge, tug. They towed her into Naha harbor, that's in Okinawa, we had the part of Okinawa secured.

"In the meantime they take me out and put me in a hospital ship. In the hospital ship they take me to Guam. From Guam they fly me to Hawaii and from Hawaii they fly me to the States. But anyway they put her into floating dry dock, and they put steel beams around her and weld her together and put seagoing tugs on her, and they were gonna tow her back to the States and they did. It took them sixty-three days. In the meantime, four days before they got into San Francisco, the war ended. They just pulled her into Mirror Island Naval Yard and put a torch to her and cut her to pieces."

"Well, when did you get back?"

"Well, I got back . . . I was back in the States . . . We got hit on the eleventh of May 1945. I was four days in a hospital ship, the

USS *Hope* it took me to Guam. I spent twenty-one days layin' in a stretcher in a muddy tent, mud about that deep. Then they flew me to Honolulu. I was there thirty days. Then they flew me to San Francisco. Then I went by rail to San Diego Naval Hospital. Then back up to San Francisco, then to Treasure Island Hospital. And then the most beautiful part of it all, forty-five days rehabilitation leave in Santa Cruz. They took the biggest hotel in town at this time. Big indoor swimming pool, two men to a room, rugs about that deep, got up at nine o'clock in the mornin', got up anytime you wanted to. You had to report, to what you call "doctor call" at nine o'clock. Then you could do anything you wanted to, go swimming, sit in the bar, do anything. Walk into the restaurant downstairs, big hotel restaurant, sit down, order what you wanted, they waited on you, oh, man, it was great for forty-five days there."

"Was any of it devoted to trying to talk about what had happened, or some of the trauma that had happened?"

"Well, they used to ask questions. I tell them, 'None of your business. You want to find out, go out there and find out for yourself.' "

"I just wondered, you know they'd be more conscious of something like that now . . ."

"You can't tell anybody what you went through. I can't even tell you. I'll tell you this much, I was scared to death, every minute, and there's nobody who come under the fire that we did that can't tell us that they weren't scared. I was. I'll admit it. But I had to keep going. I keep remembering what my dad told me, don't take any crap from nobody. So you might get whipped, but so what? That's what the American Navy won the war on. Guts."

"So then that forty-five days is over and then you go back to L.A.?"

"Yeah, I went back to L.A."

He flew to Long Beach from Santa Cruz on a navy transport plane, took a cab all the way to Toluca Street, where my mother, who had spent the war working in a defense plant, and my brother were again living.

"So, when you came home from the war, the war was over, it was just this experience that you had and that was it, life went on?"

"Well, yeah, sure. I could of laid around for three months, but I wanted to go to work. So I called up Douglas. 'Hey,' I says, 'I'm out. I want to come to work.' He says, 'How long you been out?' I says, 'Four days.' He says, 'Whaat? You don't want to come to work yet.' He says, 'Go ahead, take a while off.' I says, 'I want to go to work. I'm tired. I want to get back in the swing.' So, I went down to see the general manager down there. He says, 'Go on, take some more time off. Your job's here.' I says, 'Sir, I want to go back to work. That's what you guaranteed me and the country guaranteed me. The job is mine.' So, I went back to work."

I remember a photograph from that time which shows my parents, newly reunited, arms around each other, his hands bandaged from the shrapnel wounds, her wrists bandaged from torn ligaments suffered while she worked a punch press. Both had survived the war, albeit damaged. They remarried. My mother soon had her first white collar job working as a clerk for the L.A. Police Department, and my father, after quitting his job at Douglas, because there was no hope of advancement, went to work for the Department of Water and Power, driving trucks.

Four years later, my mother was pregnant, and they had finally found a home they could afford on 97th Street. My mother's brothers and sisters and their families had taken their GI loan money and all moved from downtown to Monterey Park, east of downtown L.A., but my mother wanted to be as close to the ocean as possible. We lived perhaps ten miles away. Just built, the tract where I would grow up was at first a kind of blankness, a monochrome of chain link, stucco, and no vegetation; in those days there were no jets, just the prop planes flying overhead though even then the window screens were grimy with the fuel the planes dumped as they approached the airport. My mother chose a house on a street in the center of the tract where she thought she would be between two flight paths. The war was over and they had a home and a second chance. My mother says that in those years everyone was filled with hope.

I grew up knowing nothing about my father. The few facts I've gleaned have come only during the last few years, during the conversations we've had at the veterans' home, where he finally seems to have reached some sort of peace—perhaps because he now lives in a community where he does not have to explain himself, where others have had experiences closer to his own. When I was growing up, he could explain nothing; usually drunk, he was incapable of telling any kind of story. When I ask him about his drinking now, he takes pride in saying that, though I remember differently, he never drank on the job. But when I press further, when I ask why he thinks that he drank so much, he says, "Ohh, I don't know, just for the hell of it, I guess . . ."

Still, I ask, "Weren't there times when you thought that you had a problem with it?"

"Not really, honey. I mean, ah, I think it was mostly out of boredom . . . Let's put it this way. Your mother never liked to go much. You should know this . . . She didn't. She wasn't much of a party hound, or anything like that. So, I'd sit there watchin' television or do somethin' like that. I used to drink because I was bored. I guess. And then it got to be worse and worse and worse. I saw that. I knew it got worse as it went along. Well, I know that as soon as I got off work I'd buy a bottle, head home."

"Well, it's very hard to get out of once you're in it. I mean, it's very hard to change that."

"Well, it's kind of a rut, you know."

When I was growing up, it was my mother who was the voice-over, who attempted coherence, who came up with a story she clung to, a story that stretched like a tightrope over the abyss where my father is caught in what he calls a "rut" but what I remember as that moment on the deck of the ship, that moment where he is still in the present tense: *I'm calling . . . I'm calling*, where he wakes up nights swinging wildly at the planes flying over the house, where he can't tell us, where he screams again and again *I am dying*.

iii. Interiors

Our houses were built in the bean fields and that is why we had field mice. As a child, I liked to think about the field. The mice would run out of the incinerator when I stuffed the trash in to burn it. I had a hoe and pretended that I was a farmer. Out there, by the incinerator, as far away from the house as I could get, my parents had planted rosebushes. My father had even laid out an irrigation system to water them. I dream the roses, a beautiful yellow that had Texas somewhere in its name, a large thorny white that stood in a row with three others by the fence. In the years when we still burned trash, my mother cultivated and fed the roses. Later the roses were overrun with weeds and dog shit. The neighbors who lived behind us had planted a peach tree which flourished. Each summer they picked the peaches on their side of the fence, though the peaches that fell from the branches that hung over the fence rotted where they landed. I was afraid of peaches. I could remember sitting in a high chair eating a peach and screaming when I bit to its porous, rutted core.

It's hard to go back into the house. I want to tell a story, but it has always been difficult to tell a story. When I first learned to read, I loved the way that stories had such a clear beginning, middle, and end. But the images that float in our house are unreferenced, unconnected to specific time. There was no beginning and for years, though we wished for an end, it did not come until my mother finally obtained permission from the Catholic Church to file for divorce. We lived in the middle:

A Small Death

One night my mother woke wondering why my father did not lie beside her in bed. Opening the bedroom door, she heard the engine of the car running. When she went outside to investigate, she found the garage door closed. Opening the door, she found my father unconscious inside the car. She turned off the motor and shook him back to consciousness. He awoke, more drunk than poisoned by carbon monoxide, and came inside and went to bed. In the morning they both got up and went to work—neither of them ever mentioned the incident again.

They did not speak to each other. They did not have conversations. If my father was sober, he was unapproachable, and if he was drunk, as he often was by the time he got home on weekday evenings, he was an incoherent mass on the couch. Weekends were the worst because they were the longest days that we spent together, the days when the drinking began early and continued on into the evening until he passed out. If we were lucky, he would pass out without incident. But on a typical Saturday in the first eight years of my life, when my brother still lived at home, my brother was often my father's target, literally having to fight his way out the door to work or a Saturday night date. After he'd go, the tirade against Catholics would begin as Sunday morning and my mother's church attendance loomed. But that's the telling from a distance, indeed, I never knew of that suicide attempt as a child, my mother told me of it only recently. Here's the kind of story I can tell.

The Black Pickup

I don't know how old I am, but I've come home because I see my father's black pickup in the driveway. Somewhere between the ages of seven and twelve, because the truck is a '57 Chevy which he destroyed in an accident when I was twelve; I'd say I'm closer to ten or eleven because I have a sense of my own height. It's the wrong time of day for him to be home. When I open the front door, no, that's the narrative, the opening-the-door part. I see the truck, so I must open the door to get into the living room. In the living room three people bob to the surface, my father and a woman and a neighbor who moved away years before; all of them are drunk. I know the woman from some other time but not in connection with my father and certainly not the neighbor. The brown paper bag is in the house. Usually it's in the garage. It's on the table. I understand the woman is with my father; they are laughing. They are raising and sharing the bottle. He has his arm around her, but if my mother were here, this woman would pay attention to me. If my mother were here, this woman and my father would not be paying attention to each other. The woman is my mother's friend. Then my father and the woman are no longer in the living room bobbing up and down out of place, and I am on the back porch where the dog sleeps though the dog is outside where I am trying to go but can't because the other man, the old neighbor, has pinned me up against the washing machine. He wants a kiss. I think I came into the house thinking they couldn't see me. I can only see them. But he has seen me. He tells me he remembers me when I was a little girl, and now he wants a kiss, but it's more than a kiss, it's him pressing me hard against the washing machine. It's him pushing and pushing and then saying, "That wasn't so bad, was it," and then I'm outside with my dog in the backyard

where years before I sat between this man and my father in a lawn swing in the man's yard next door. They have cans of beer and I am sitting between them, and they are talking about their wives. But they're really talking about June. This man's wife is named June. I love June. She holds me in the afternoons in the darkened interior of her house, and she is filled with a sadness that is not in my mother though I know it's a kind of sadness that comes when June, too, drinks. They are complaining about June. It's more than complaining. They hate her. They are calling her a bitch. My father says, "You just send that bitch over here." One of them says, "They all want it." I understand that I, too, am "they."

Sometime later my father opens the front door, where June stands on the porch, crying. He shouts, "Go home, bitch," slamming the door in her face just as my mother comes out of the kitchen, heading for the door, yelling, "What are you doing?" He shouts back, "I don't want the bitch in my house." My mother is furious, an argument follows. I know that I am responsible for all of this because I could have told June. I could have warned her. I heard them plotting against her, and I did nothing to save this woman that I love.

Maybe they are paying June back for what she did to help my mother. I think when they were sitting on the swing that her husband was saying it was June's fault, that it was June who had called the police when I ran to their door just as she had run to ours. I know that I am four. I don't know why I know this, but I do. I thought it was just my mother backed into the junction of kitchen counter and sink, but now I see my brother was there too. My father has a knife on them. I know this knife. I know that he brought it back from the war. I've seen it since, though I don't know if I'd seen it before. I remember a series of yellow stripes around its brown handle. I think my father is swearing. I know he is drunk. Everything is floating. I stand at the front door. I am very large, and I have one hand on the door. I am looking back into the kitchen, where my mother is very far away, the air between us fallen into pieces, the way light falls down at the end of the day.

My mother is screaming at me, telling me to run, but I'm frozen. A moment before, I think that I was scampering, frantic with them in the kitchen. I think there was that ominousness throughout the afternoon. It had been gathering; it felt more and more dangerous, a kind of heightening, all things enlarged, ominous and bright until he has taken that knife down from the rafters in the garage and brought it into the house, where the fat handle is in the grip of his heavy hands as he waves it in my mother's face. Pinned against the counter, she screams at me to run, and finally I do. I open the door and run down the two steps and across the driveway under the willow tree and up the steps to June's house.

It seems a long way though perhaps it is only thirty or forty feet. My feet are weighted as if in dream, though perhaps I dream this since that time. I knock on the door. Maybe I am crying. I don't remember, but I think it's dinnertime because soon I'm eating cake and June and her husband, the old neighbor, Bob, are arguing about what to do. He doesn't want her to call the police, but since the police do finally come, I assume now that she did call them. Before they come, my father has thrown the knife out into the yard. Now it's night and my brother has jumped over the fence to find it and my mother, too, has come across the grass to join us. It seems like a long time passes and then I watch the police talking to him out there under the streetlight. The police drive away, and my mother, brother, and I cross back under the willow into our house. My father must come too.

iv. What I Learned There

I think that was the only time that the police came and then, as now, I am struck by the fact that I was the one who told though it was June who picked up the phone to call and June who suffered for calling because I did not warn her of the retribution they plotted. This particular series of connections has never been more clear to me than it is now at this moment of writing though the images have surfaced before in fragments in my poetry. What is also very clear to me at this moment is the sense that I was the one who wanted to leave, and I am the one who has. Though, of course, I am still there in some sense, it is my parents who have never left. At my mother's urging, I was the one who opened the door and left though soon enough I learned that what I saw and heard and experienced there was not to be spoken of to others.

The Pope Is Dead

I must have been around eight the Saturday morning Pope Pius XII died and the orange juice glass came down on my father's head. He'd been taunting her, telling her how happy he was that the pope was dead though perhaps the pope had died the night before since I remember that all of this seems to have carried over to morning. But it's not the pope's death that causes the glass to come down, that's not working. Now he's talking about Nana. He says, "Your mother is crazy." I am sitting at the table with him, and she must be standing, because the glass comes from above, suddenly, deliberately, directly on top of his head. Blood and orange juice everywhere. He runs from the dining room table through the kitchen and onto the back porch, where he stands yelling for a towel. Somebody must give him one. Then he drives himself to the emergency room. I don't know if he was drunk when he left, but he certainly is by the time he gets back, looking wounded, satisfied with his head wrapped in gauze.

While he was gone, I ran next door to the house on the other side of us to lean into the screen door to tell Rosie, who took care of me after school while my mother worked, that my mother had just hit my father over the head with a glass. When I went back home, my mother was mopping up the trail of blood which led from the kitchen and out the back door, where he had stood on the porch. My mother asked me if I had told anyone. When I replied that I had, she told me that I should not, and, so, I promptly crossed the lawn again to Rosie's to tell her that my mother said I shouldn't tell her.

The narrative here is a trail of blood. My mother is mopping it. I do not know what it felt like to be my mother mopping the blood. I do not know what it felt like to fling the glass at his head. I do not know what it takes to do that. As for the child who was me, I had begun to treat such moments with a certain matter-of-factness until I could say them now, when I have come to a fuller understanding of what it meant to be that child. The blood was thick, viscous, and silver boats of glass floated in it. The blood was the circle I fell into. I remember. It has stayed with me forever. It has stayed with my mother forever, but I am the one who speaks: my mother does not.

My mother never spoke of such things to anyone. Indeed, she always prided herself, particularly during the first five years of my life, when she was not yet working again, on *not* gossiping over the back fence with her neighbors. Even her own sister, Milly, who says she could not ignore my father's alcoholism even as my mother denied it, did not know of the violence taking place within the house.

v .   M y   F a t h e r ' s   B o d y

He is the wave of his redness that sweeps over us. What will I leave out? I could not have known any of this had I not written it down, and I am still writing it down, still coming to know what I have hidden from myself, what I, the pair of eyes who seems to watch all of this, have not yet said because I couldn't yet see it. I have always thought that I am like him. Why? Temperamentally, perhaps, I am quick to anger and soon full of remorse. But I identify with my father. Sometimes I think that I see life from his position on the couch. He cries so much. He overwhelms our small house with emotion, emotion that we have to ride with, anticipate. I learn to watch, observe. Drunk, he is a slovenly pool. I do not respect him, but I do have an odd sort of empathy for him:

My brother is going out on a date, and my father quite ceremoniously has mixed him a cocktail, which is unusual because he always keeps his fifth in the garage. "Drink this," he says. "Drink this" as if it were a magic elixir that will change my brother's life. And my brother, he ignores him. He says, "Get out of my way." Maybe he pushes him, and this poor, slovenly mass stumbles and the drink falls on the floor and my father begins to cry. Somehow this is all he has to offer, this sadness which no one will accept. I believe in elixirs too. I, too, have a sadness which no one will listen to; I, too, would like change.

My father and I are the ones who have been left behind. My brother is already a teenager and on his way out of the house as I am growing up. He is gone altogether by the time I am eight. My mother goes back to work when I am five. She needs the money to buy shoes, groceries, because so much of his salary goes to alcohol. She needs the money for the down payment on a divorce it will take her eight years to obtain. I don't know this, all I know is that she is gone five days a week and sometimes nights. My father and I have been left. He hates it that she's gone back to work. He is shamed by it. Each morning she makes casseroles for dinner; each evening he refuses to put them into the oven. He refuses to pick her up from work and lets her take the bus home, turning a ride that would take ten minutes by car into a two-hour bus ride complete with transfers. We have an odd camaraderie. I am an interloper. I am not really, unlike my mother and brother, the object of his wrath.

When my mother is home, she is always moving, in the kitchen mostly because in the same room they fight. But I can sit and watch movies on TV with him on the weekends. I know how to gauge his moods, the degrees of his inebriation. I try to stay out of his reach, but I am unluckier there. He mauls me. He sucks me into him. I am often, since he cannot reach my mother, the object of his affection, his pawing. When he is drunk, time stops for him. He cries. He screams *I am dying* over and over. He remembers the man he killed in the lumberyard. He remembers the men who died around him on the ship. He remembers how he harmed me and he is sorry. He calls to me, "Honey, come here and give me a kiss."

He Lets Go of My Hand

I was eighteen months old and he stood in the front yard of his half sister's house in Monrovia, talking to his brother-in-law and let go of my hand. I ran into the street and into the back tire of a passing ice truck. My skull was fractured, but although my legs were twisted and bruised, they were unbroken. Was he drinking when he let go of my hand?

I didn't learn about this incident until I was six or seven, when a neighbor boy, remembering my two black eyes, teased me about the accident, and I went into the house to ask my parents if it had taken place. It was on one of the few occasions that I can remember when we had visitors. My father's stepmother was visiting and my parents sat in the living room together. I had a question to ask, and when I asked it, my father denied it. Yet it was clear that he wasn't telling the truth. I had an odd sense of my own power. A few years later my mother would tell me that the incident had, in fact, taken place. And, as the years passed, he would refer to it again and again, saying that he began to drink hard only when it happened. Now my mother agrees. She says he couldn't handle the bills, the house payments, and the responsibility of another child.

The Trip to Bishop

Once my father and I took a trip. It is one of the few times that I can remember being with him outside the house. It is the beginning of the sadness I referred to earlier, what I share with my father that cannot be shared with others, what I have hidden from myself, what I am still coming to know as if my body were a many-chambered vault that I unlock room by room. There I wander in the redness, a kind of webbed intaglio of shame, of confusion I have carried with me in my body which has prevented me from saying because I did not know what to say, which surfaces in dreams where I know I have not yet told though I don't know what it is that I have to tell. Now it seems so obvious that it has always been there, always been part of the legacy my father passed to me, what I can't tell you, what I have been trying to tell you. Though even as I say this, I wonder if, like the incidents that mark my father's story, I am simply looking for the incident that will mark the turning point in my own story? That doubt is there too, for there is no one else to corroborate this story but my father, and I know we have an understanding—it's in the sly rejoinder, the pat on the ass that ignites the fragments of memory I push out of consciousness as soon as they appear on its edge.

Now, with the help of a therapist I trust, I try to remember. Now I am ready to remember. It takes place outside so it has a frame unlike other incidents: My father was taking me with him to Bishop. He was hauling transformers to Bishop in northern California. The day began in the work yard of Water and Power. Memory cuts in in the cab of the truck: I am sitting on the brown leather seat, looking out, excited by the long trip that we are about to take. The truck is already moving when he tells me to duck down as we move through the yard and out of the exit gate. I duck. I am surprised because I thought that I was allowed to go on this trip. The truck is huge, a Peterbilt. Sometimes he drives it home and the length of it parked out in front by the curb is the width of our house.

We are driving in the Mojave Desert, bouncing along, the truck engine roaring. The books from the library where my mother works are beside me on the seat. It's hot and because of the roar of the engine we cannot speak. Out the window in the desert I see a huge silver boulder. I am excited because I think that I've seen something no one has seen. I think that there's treasure to be found out in the desert. But when I look up to tell him I see that, he hasn't seen the boulder. He is staring straight ahead, one hand on the gearshift, the truck roaring and bouncing, and I feel small on the seat with this hidden knowledge of the thing that I have seen. I know the boulder is magic. I know I have seen something that no one has seen.

When we arrive in Bishop, we get out of the truck and go into the office of the dispatcher. My father introduces me, and I am shy. The man sits behind a desk, and he offers me some peanuts from a bowl sitting on his desk. The peanuts are stale, but I eat them anyway. He asks me how old I am. I am seven. Then since it is summer, I am seven going on eight. We go outside and stand by what seems a dam, looking down at the roaring water, and I am terrified that I'll fall in.

We drive to the motel in a company pickup, a brown pickup. Is this when he takes the bottle out of the glove compartment? Or was he drinking from it during the trip? Clear liquid in a fifth bottle, not Jim Beam, then, but I still know this means trouble. We get out of the truck and approach the room. There is greenery, perhaps ivy, and a large window. When we go inside he closes the curtains. He says that we are going to take a nap. He must go to sleep. But I cross the street to the park I saw on the way in, and I feel self-important because I know I am too little to be out there by myself. I play with another girl, who tells me in some detail about the skin graft on her hip. She takes me back to the table where her family is having dinner. My father comes into the park calling me. He is drunk and I know I am different. Do I show him the stream then? When we go back to the motel before we go in, I ask him to show me the stream and we walk to the stream, and I am very excited by the fish swimming there. I think I stand on the stones, and he tells me to be careful, but I am excited and not paying much attention. I am conscious of him big and soft and drunk. And I am grateful that he has shown me the fish.

We go back inside the motel room. There is one double bed, did we rest together on the bed earlier before I went into the park? I sit on a chair next to the bed and he gives me a candy bar, a Snickers, my favorite. He tells me not to tell my mother. I remember that, and when I first remember, I think it is about the candy bars. I am climbing into the bed with my white socks on. Does he tell me that I don't have to sleep in my pajamas? I remember my underpants and my white socks. I am in the bed, next to the window, where the stream flows out back, and I am waiting for him to get into bed. He turns out the light, sits on the side of the bed, and pulls his pants off. He climbs into the bed, and I know that he doesn't have any underwear on, conscious of his genitals under the sheets, the blankets, remembering how once I saw him through the bedroom door. My body is curled up in the bed. I don't want to touch him because I am afraid to touch him. I think I have my back to him but I see him getting into bed. I don't remember.

Now it is night. It is dark where I am used to things happening that I can't explain, the comings and goings, the hands that emerge from under my bed at night pinning my stomach, immobilizing me, the prowler who I know appeared at the window when I was four or five, but who I can tell no one about because I was not supposed to be out of bed, not supposed to be at the window. He is moaning. I keep seeing myself with my back to him. I try not to touch him. I don't remember, but I do. This is what I see: the intaglio is pubic hair, the redness is somehow him, but not him. My back is not to him. I fell asleep and then something happened. I am fully in his embrace. His long arms have reached out and pulled me into him. I am nothing. I am a little wooden stick figure floating in a big sea, my body is nothing, the sea is the flashing redness of my father's body suffocating me. The intaglio is pubic hair, my father recedes in the distance, and I wander in this kind of forest of hair and rising redness tentacling memory. I am facedown in it. I don't remember. I know it must be my fault because somehow I touched him. He has told me never to awaken him by kissing him. I must have done that. It is my fault. I have kept this secret because I did not know how to say it. I have kept it because if I tell, you will hate me. If I tell, everything will fall apart.

vi. How I Remember

Other images from those years flash into mind. Nikita Khrushchev passes through Los Angeles in a motorcade. My brother and soon-to-be sister-in-law have taken me ice skating for my birthday, and we arrive at the skating rink just as the motorcade passes. I remember that. I don't have any trouble saying it. Even the incidents that I have recounted earlier in this essay have emerged with a kind of assuredness in the confluence of saying and writing. What I have just told you is the first telling, no, the second. The first time I tried to tell it, only the barest bones were evident. That first telling has existed for some years. The story ended when I climbed into the bed, the story has always ended when I crawled into bed. So, I am learning now to say what I see. After the second telling, I did not fall apart. I think that is always the feeling I have had connected to this incident, that telling it would simply make me fall away from whatever self I was hanging on to. And the *you*, who is the *you* I am talking to? Well, now it is you, the reader, but then, in the years after that trip, *you* was my mother, whom I could not tell.

In the second telling, I began to see a number of things, most prominent among them is the sense that by saying nothing happened to me, I control what did. I start to feel the depth of the fear I had of him. I begin to hear his voice, what his words told me about my body, my self, throughout childhood. I hear his voice in the truck that day. I go back to the first three pages of this essay and I think of his hands again. His huge hands. I wonder why his visit last summer was so important? What do I have to say about the frail old man who came then, who again asked if I remembered that trip to Bishop, who I understood had something to say about it though I would not allow him to say it because I was afraid of where his saying would take me, afraid even then that assenting that something did happen when he asked "Do you remember the trip we took to Bishop?" would allow him to tell me that it did not.

That's the surface. I see more of what I do not say. The body. His body. Late last spring he had almost died from a bleeding ulcer. As soon as school was out, I'd driven down to pay him a quick visit, and although he was still in the hospital and frail, he wanted to show me his new car. He said he was coming to Oregon. I said fine, never believing that he would, since he never had before. But he did come. He drove ten hours straight and was in town, in a motel, a day before he was supposed to arrive. He checked himself into the motel because he'd had an accident on the way up which he blamed on medication that he was taking. He had defecated all over himself and the driver's side of the car.

We went to pick him up at the motel the morning after he had arrived. I knocked on the door and he said it was open. He was sitting in the dark room, curtains pulled, in a cloud of cigarette smoke, sunglasses and baseball cap on. He looked like death and had difficulty standing up. I said I'd drive his car back to the house. When I opened the car door, the smell was awful though he seemed not to notice it. I was gagging all the way home. Later I would clean the car and wash his clothes, which he seemed enormously touched by. It was this exchange that led me to the next memory, my sense of disgust for the presence of his body, the sense of its corruption that I had even as a child, the unwashed smell of it, the fleshy sexualized presence of his then enormous weight that I am still trying to disentangle myself from. That memory occurred when I sat down to work on a poem and I saw, eyes open, what I could not, would not, see before:

I sit on the chair and he hands me the candy bar. He is sitting on the bed. I have never remembered where he sat before. He says "Don't tell your mother" when he gives me the candy bar, and then I see him sitting on the bed unzipping his pants, lifting his penis, which is huge, erect, red, out of his fly. He asks, "Do you want to kiss it?" But there is no time to reply, his hand has simply reached across the arm's length between us and slammed me into him—it's all one motion, large hand clamped to the back of my head and that's when I'm nothing, flopping like a fish, wrenching, bucking, and he falls back on the bed. I see myself standing there, looking at him, fly open, and I think he's dead, that I've killed him, but he's moaning. This is the first time, too, that I can see where the bathroom is in the room. It's at the far end and I think I go into the bathroom and get sick though as I write I know that gagging, vomiting, what I have felt in my stomach in the last two days since I have remembered this scene is the whole association I have with this scene. Does he stand up? Does he come after me? He knows I'm sick. Now he's sorry, telling me I'll be okay, sloppy, drunk, weepy the way he was when he was telling me about the blood while we rode in the truck—telling me how I was going to become a woman, how I was going to bleed, and how he couldn't bear that. He was sorry then, and he's sorry as soon as it's over. The whole trip is like a tunnel ending in this scene: I have been a fetish, a little object he's been getting off on and that's what made slamming me into him so easy. I was nothing.

I can't quite see the rest of the sequence. But I see myself on the bed with him. As if he'd said, come and lie down, because he is so sorry, and then he does fall asleep, and he's all over me. I can feel the weight of his body and that's when I disentangle myself. I think that's when I go out into the park. I know how sorry he is later when he comes to get me. I know that's why he shows me the stream . . . I remember nothing of the trip home except one image that appears in the last stanza of a poem that I wrote in 1972, my first formal attempt at describing the memory of that trip. It must be the next day: the two of us stand looking up at the roof of what must be the Bishop county or city jail:

> We stood beneath the building
> peering up into sun and trees,
> at the man holding roof,
> the fence wire fawned
> and curled over them
> rimming their sky,
> gray material bodies
> aimless, legless,
> we hid beneath the furtive trees
> should these thousand bodies
> decide to punish and plunge down at me.

. . .

Writing is one long story of how I remember. I will keep remembering. And each time that I do I will be confronted by: I cannot say this, and then I will write it and find I do not have to hide it from you though it has taken me a long time to know that. This one event, perhaps emblematic of many, has constrained so much of what I know about myself, so much of what I could know. In my early twenties images of what happened that night or day started to show up in poems such as the one I have quoted above, and in my journals, where I wrote only in fragments, where having written those fragments down I promptly forgot them until I was ready to know—now, over twenty years later when that shame eases, when I can begin to say the sense of contamination in myself that it has taken me this long to recognize.

When I look at those journals of twenty years ago, I see the incident itself encoded in images that, like those three people in the living room, bob into consciousness and out again. I suspect I wrote in fragments rather than sentences, because I still could not privately acknowledge let alone publicly say what had happened that day in Bishop. When I found them again, I was stunned that those images had existed so long ago, when it seemed to me that they had only recently appeared in my consciousness.

So, like my father, I could tell no one, but unlike my father, I found a way to make meaning out of what had happened. Each day my mother brought me books when she came home from work, and in the images those books provided I began to enter the world of the imagination, where I could explain myself, though, of course, I was not conscious of that then. Then years passed and we continued to live in the middle of that redness. By the time I was twelve, my mother believed that I would run away if she did not divorce my father. She also believed that one of them would kill the other. It was the latter argument that finally convinced a priest that a civil divorce was a reasonable solution. I don't remember thinking about running away, but I do remember that my hatred for him had reached a peak. I didn't want to be like him, but in many ways I already was. I could not see myself for the way that he crouched there in the swamp of consciousness.

vii. A Final View

He's come home from work and he's sober. He lifts the trash cans at the curb and carries them up the driveway. I am eleven, and my mother had saved the thirty-five dollars to send me to camp. Now, ten days later, I have come home, someone has dropped me off at the curb just ahead of him. I watch from the window. I have been in the mountains for the first time, fallen suddenly into deep sleep under the shade of a tree after hiking up a dusty hillside in the middle of the day. I have never been able to carry a tune, but I have learned to sing around the campfire at night. Everything has changed. For the rest of the summer, each night under the streetlight I will teach the neighbor kids the songs I have learned, but in this moment, as I look at my father in his smudged work clothes walking up the driveway with a trash can in each hand, I understand that for him nothing will change. It never has.

from *A Whole New Life*

REYNOLDS PRICE

Was it disaster—all that time from my slapped-down sandal in spring '84 through the four years till I reentered life as a new contraption, inside and out? Is it still disaster, these ten years later? Numerous mouths and pairs of eyes have been, and still are, ready to tell me Yes every week. Very often occasional acquaintances will corner me on campus or at a party, then lean to my ear and ask how I am. When I tell them truthfully "Fine," their faces will crouch in solemn concern; and they'll say "No, *really*. How *are* you?" I'll give them a skull-grin to cover my amusement at the common eagerness of so many otherwise decent souls to see a fellow creature buried.

My amusement flows also from their hint that they know I'm hoarding a tragic secret to which they have an intimate right. They plainly believe that any chink in the normal human armor is a road down which all the curious are free to stream. That brand of assault is especially common now in politically correct middle-class America, where the socially and physically gimped are crowned with a misplaced, thoroughly unwanted beatitude—the blessings of sainthood are mostly appalling, as they've always been.

Physicians, in their admirable Greek and Latin mode, speak of a "catastrophic" illness. The Greek word *catastrophe* means an *overturning,* an *upending*—a system disarranged past reassembly, all signals reversed. The list of common catastrophes that wait for a final chance at each of us is virtually endless; and it now receives unimagined additions almost by the week from a viral kingdom that begins to hint at the chance of its ultimate victory over us, through cunning and patience.

Birth disasters, unstoppable cancers, disorders of the blood and lymph, external wounds to flesh and bone, those devastations in which the body turns on itself and eats its own substance, the mind's estrangement, the still irreparable disconnection of electrical service to major parts—each of a throng of catastrophes is as common as influenza or migraine, and so far I've missed a great many blows aimed at me; but I took this big one.

So *disaster* then, yes, for me for a while—great chunks of four years. *Catastrophe* surely, a literally upended life with all parts strewn and some of the most urgent parts lost for good, within and without. But if I were called on to value honestly my present life beside my past—the years from 1933 till '84 against the years after—I'd have to say that, despite an enjoyable fifty-year start, these recent years since full catastrophe have gone still better. They've brought more in and sent more out—more love and care, more knowledge and patience, more work in less time.

How self-deluding, self-serving, is that? Why do physically damaged people so often meet the world with clear, bright eyes and what seem unjustified or lunatic smiles? Have some few layers of our minds burned off, leaving us dulled to the shocks of life, the actual state of our devastation? Or are we merely displaying a normal animal pleasure in being at least alive and breathing, not outward bound to the dark unknown or anxious for some illusory safety, some guarantee we know to be ludicrous?

Maybe I'd answer a partial Yes to all such questions. Though there's no "we" of course in the damaged world—the possible array of damage is too vast—I can risk a few observations at least that have proved true for me, through much of the time, and that may prove useful to someone else who's faced with a sudden blank wall in life and who may care to hear them, for companionship if nothing more.

I take the risk for one main reason that I've mentioned earlier— friends and strangers have asked me to add my recollections to the very slim row of sane printed matter which comes from the far side of catastrophe, the dim other side of that high wall that effectively shuts disaster off from the unfazed world. I've known what they mean. I shared their frustration for some fellow-words to consume in those weeks after radiation in '84 when I finally recovered the will to read and searched around me for any book, essay, or sentence that might speak directly to the hole I was in—anything more useful than crack-pot guides to healing or death, impossibly complex starvation diets, alfalfa pills, and karmic tune-ups. In that deep trough I needed companions more than prayers or potions that had worked for another. But nothing turned up in my own library, apart from short stretches of the Bible, or in all the would-be helpful books that friends sent to me on every subject from crystals and macrobiotic cooking through cheerful wheelchair tours of Europe and the rules for a last will and testament.

Most of the books were either telling me why I had cancer—the utterly unproved claim again that I'd somehow brought it home in self-loathing—or they blithely prescribed in minute detail how to cure any tumor with moon-rock dust and beetle-wing ointment. Or they cheerfully told me what kind of deal I should offer God in hopes of the maximum chance at salvage—*I give you two good legs, the power of feeling from the soles of my feet on up to my nipples, control of numerous internal organs, and acceptance of pain like an acid bath with no letup. For that, you'll kindly permit me to crawl in and gorge my face by the television for however many minutes or years you can spare from your big store of eternity.*

I needed to read some story that paralleled, at whatever distance, my unfolding bafflement—some honest report from a similar war, with a final list of hard facts learned and offered unvarnished—but again I never found it. Admitted, there are richly useful methods, like the twelve-step program of Alcoholics Anonymous, for reversing long years of self-abuse. And the scathing self-disciplines of some religious sects have turned weak souls into flaming martyrs singing in the yawning teeth of Hell. But nobody known to me in America, or on the shady backside of Pluto, is presently offering useful instruction in how to absorb the staggering but not-quite-lethal blow of a fist that ends your former life and offers you nothing by way of a new life that you can begin to think of wanting, though you clearly have to go on feeding your gimped-up body and roofing the space above your bed.

So after ten years at what seems a job that means to last me till death at least, I'll offer a few suggestions from my own slow and blundering course. I make no claim for their wisdom or even their usefulness. Whether they'll prove merely private to me or available to a handful of others as ground for thought, I'd likely be the last to know; but at least I can try to keep them honest. Here then are the minimal facts that eventually worked for me, at least part of the time, and are working still. In all that follows, the pronoun *You* is aimed at me as much as any reader. I need steady coaching; I'm never home free. And when I refer to physical paralysis, I often suspect that other kinds of mind and body paralysis bring similar troubles with similar remedies.

Fairly late in the catastrophic phase of my illness, I began to understand three facts I'd known in theory since early childhood but had barely plumbed the reality of. They're things familiar to most adults who've bothered to watch the visible world and have sorted their findings with normal intelligence, but abstract knowledge tends to vanish in a crisis. And from where I've been, the three facts stand at the head of any advice I'd risk conveying to a friend confronted with grave illness or other physical and psychic trauma.

1. You're in your present calamity alone, far as this life goes. If you want a way out, then dig it yourself, if there turns out to be any trace of a way. Nobody—least of all a doctor—can rescue you

now, not from the deeps of your own mind, not once they've stitched your gaping wound.

2. Generous people—true practical saints, some of them boring as root canals—are waiting to give you everything on Earth but your main want, which is simply *the person you used to be*.

3. But you're not that person now. Who'll you be tomorrow? And who do you propose to be from here to the grave, which may be hours or decades down the road?

The first two facts take care of themselves; if you haven't already known them in spades and obeyed their demands, they'll blow you nearly down till you concede their force. Harder though, and even more urgent, admit the third fact as soon as you can. No child of the doomed Romanov czar, awaiting rescue or brutal death in 1917, was more firmly banished from a former life than you are now. Grieve for a decent limited time over whatever parts of your old self you know you'll miss.

That person is dead as any teen-aged Marine drilled through the forehead in an Asian jungle; any Navy Seal with his legs blown off, halved for the rest of the time he gets; any woman mangled in her tenderest parts, unwived, unmothered, unlovered and shorn. Have one hard cry, if the tears will come. Then stanch the grief, by whatever legal means. Next find your way to be somebody else, the next viable you—a stripped-down whole other clear-eyed person, realistic as a sawed-off shotgun and thankful for air, not to speak of the human kindness you'll meet if you get normal luck.

Your mate, your children, your friends at work—anyone who knew or loved you in your old life—will be hard at work in the fierce endeavor to revive your old self, the self they recall with love or respect. Their motives are frequently admirable, and at times that effort counts for a lot—they prove that you're valued and wanted at least—but again their care is often a brake on the way you must go. At the crucial juncture, when you turn toward the future, they'll likely have little help to offer; and it's no fault of theirs (they were trained like you, in inertia).

More likely they'll stall you in the effort to learn who you need to be now and how to be him or her by tomorrow or Monday at the latest. Yet if you don't discover that next appropriate incarnation of who you must be, and then *become* that person at a stiff trot, you'll be no good whatever again to the ruins of your old self nor to any friend or mate who's standing beside you in hopes of a hint that you're feeling better this instant and are glad of company.

The kindest thing anyone could have done for me, once I'd finished five weeks' radiation, would have been to look me square in the eye and say this clearly, "Reynolds Price is dead. Who will you be now? Who *can* you be and how can you get there, double time?" Cruel and unusable as it might have sounded in the wake of trauma, I think its truth would have snagged deep in me and won my attention eventually, far sooner than I managed to find it myself. Yet to this day, with all the kindnesses done for me, no one has so much as hinted that news in my direction; and I've yet to meet another dazed person who's heard it when it was needed most—*Come back to life, whoever you'll be. Only you can do it.*

How you'll manage that huge transformation is your problem, though, and nobody else's. Are there known techniques for surviving a literal hairpin turn in the midst of a life span—or early or late— without forgetting the better parts of who you were? What are the thoughts and acts required to turn your dead self inside out into something new and durably practical that, however strange, is the creature demanded by whatever hard facts confront you now? So far as I've heard, nobody else knows—or knows in a way they can transfer to others. If they know, I haven't encountered their method. I'll go on sketching my own course, then.

I've made it clear that the first strong props beneath my own collapse were prayer, a single vision that offered me healing, the one word *More* when I asked "What now?" and a frail continuing sense of purpose, though my hungry self often worked to drown any voice that might otherwise have reached me from the mind of God or plain common sense. But I well understand how that kind of help is all but incommunicable to anyone else not so inclined from childhood. If belief in an ultimately benign creator who notices his creatures is available to you, you may want to try at first to focus your will on the absolute first ground-level question to ask him, her, or faceless it. Again, that's not "Why me?" but "What next?"

In general the human race has believed that a God exists who is at least partly good. Recent polls have shown that a huge majority of Americans pray in some form daily; even many self-defined atheists pray apparently. And thousands of years of testimony from sane men and women is serious evidence, if not full proof, that God may consult you in unannounced moments. If he does so at all, it will likely mean that you've taken prior pains to know him. He'll almost surely lurk beyond you in heavy drapery with face concealed. He's likewise announced, in most major creeds, his availability for foxhole conversions. Yet foxhole occupants are often faced with his baffling slowness to answer calls, or they reach a perpetual busy signal or a cold-dead line. Again, the answer to most prayers is *No*.

My own luck here was long prepared, from early childhood; but as with all sorts of invisible luck, there have been forced treks these past ten years when I all but quit and begged to die. Even then though I'd try to recall a passage of daunting eloquence in the thirtieth chapter of the Book of Deuteronomy where the baffling God of Jews and Christians says

> I call Heaven and Earth to witness against you today that I have set life and death in front of you, blessing and curse. Therefore choose life so that you and your seed may last to love the Lord your God. . . .

Clear as the offered choice is, such a reach for life is another tall order, especially for a human in agonized straits. But even if you omit the last phrase from God's proposition (that you last to love him, even if you're a confirmed disbeliever), you're still confronted with another iron fact. The visible laws of physical nature are willing you to last as long as you can. Down at the core, you almost certainly want to survive.

You're of course quite free to balk that wish, by killing yourself and ending your physical will to endure; but amazingly few pained people choose death by suicide. And fewer still consider the strangeness of their endless moaning when death is so easy. To be sure, either God or the laws of nature will eventually force you to fall and die. But that event can tend to itself, with slim help from you. Meanwhile whether you see yourself as the temporary home of a deathless soul or as the short-term compound of skin and bone called *Homo sapiens*, your known orders are simply to *Live*. Never give death a serious hearing till its ripeness forces your final attention and dignified nod. It will of course take you screaming if it must, if you insist.

And keep control of the air around you. Many well-meaning mates, lovers, and friends will stand by, observing that you're in the throes of blind denial—*Give up. Let go*. Get them out of your sight and your hearing with red-hot haste; use whatever force or fury it takes. Then try to choose life. Then see who you can live with now.

In my case, life has meant steady work, work sent by God but borne on my own back and on the wide shoulders of friends who want me to go on living and have helped me with a minimum of tears and no sign of pity. My work admittedly has been of the sort that, when it's available, permits deep absorption. It's also brought me sufficient money to guarantee time for further work and appropriate space in which to do it. Since childhood I've been subject to frequent sixteen-hour days, chained to an easel or desk in my home and glad to be grounded. Some other home workers have similar luck—gardening, woodcraft, pottery, sewing, cooking, the ceaseless daily needs of a family. Even the man or woman who works in an office or mill, even at the dullest repetitive task, has a ready-made routine for muting painful cries from the self.

The killing dead-ends are strewn all around you in the idle or physically weak aftermath of calamity itself, the stunned hours of blank wall-gazing that eagerly await you. Find any legal way to avoid my first mistake, which was sitting still in cooperation with the cancer's will to finish me fast. Play cutthroat card games, leave the house when you can, go sit in the park near children at play, read to children in a cancer ward, go donate whatever strength you've got to feeding the hungry or tending the millions worse off than you. I wish to God I had—any legal acts to break the inward gaze at my withering self.

As soon as I could walk after my first surgery, Allan Friedman urged me to make immediate plans to return to campus—put a cot in my office, go there daily, deal with the mail, and at least see my colleagues for lunch and small talk, feel free to call on him anytime he kept clinic hours or to phone whenever. What he failed to know as a busy surgeon was, I'd never written ten words in my campus office and couldn't think of trying—I'd merely be alone in a different building. Since it was summer, most of my colleagues had fled their offices, unlike physicians, who work all seasons; and Duke Hospital, as a place to visit, felt like sure death.

But now I know Friedman was more than half right. Professors were not my only colleagues; in the long years of my life at Duke, I'd built a sizable village of friends—members of the post-office staff, workers in the dining rooms, bookstores, librarians, campus cops. Any trip to campus would have involved my meeting their usual hard-headed cheer; I'd have heard their own tales of good and bad luck. (Not at all incidentally, one of my friends on the postal staff phoned me one Sunday, a few weeks into the ordeal, and said that the members of his church had just agreed—they'd bring me all my meals, five days a week. I was amazed and thanked them firmly but declined the offer, at least for then.)

Surely I should have forced myself to move outward from the menacing house far sooner than I did. Though I couldn't drive, and was years away from thinking of an appropriate car, I might at least have ridden with my friend Betsy Cox to her regular stints at a home-less shelter in downtown Durham. I could have made bologna sandwiches as fast as she and listened to stories harder than mine; and if I wet my pants in the process, well, who the hell hasn't? Couldn't I have gone out and learned some useful degree of proportion, setting my woes in the midst of the world, yet still have kept my silent hours for learning how much damage I'd taken and how to build on it?

Anyone for whom such recommendations seem overly rosy should not miss the point. Your chance of rescue from any despair lies, if it lies anywhere, in your eventual decision to abandon the deathwatch by the corpse of your old self and to search out a new inhabitable body. The old *Theologica Germanica* knew that "nothing burns in Hell but the self"—above all, the old self broiling in the fat of its endless self-pity.

By very slow inches, as I've said, the decision to change my life forced itself on me; and I moved ahead as if a path was actually there and would stretch on a while. As truly as I could manage here in an intimate memoir, without exposing the private gifts of men and women who never asked to perform in my books, I've tried to map the lines of that change and the ways I traveled toward the reinvention and reassembly of a life that bears some relations with a now-dead life but is radically altered, trimmed for a whole new wind and route. A different life and—till now at least, as again I've said—a markedly better way to live, for me and for my response to most of the people whom my life touches.

I've tested that word *better* for the stench of sentimentality, narcissism, blind optimism, or lunacy. What kind of twisted fool, what megalomaniac bucking for canonization, would give his strong legs and control of a body that gave him fifty-one years' good service with enormous amounts of sensory pleasure (a body that played a sizable part in winning him steady love from others) and would then surrender normal control of a vigorous life in an ample house and far beyond it in exchange for what?—two legs that serve no purpose but ballast to a numb torso and the rest of a body that acts as a magnet to no one living, all soaked in corrosive constant pain?

I know that this new life is better for me, and for most of my friends and students as well, in two measurable ways. First, paraplegia with its maddening limitations has forced a degree of patience and consequent watchfulness on me, though as a writer I'd always been watchful. Shortly after my own paralysis, I heard two of Franklin Roosevelt's sons say that the primary change in their father, after polio struck him in midlife and grounded him firmly, was an increased patience and a willingness to listen. If you doubt that patience must follow paralysis, try imagining that you can't escape whoever manages to cross your doorsill.

Forced to sit, denied the easy flight that legs provide, you either learn patience or you cut your throat, or you take up a bludgeon and silence whoever's in reach at the moment. As I survived the black frustration of so many new forms of powerlessness, I partly learned to sit and attend, to watch and taste whatever or whomever seemed likely or needy, far more closely than I had in five decades. The pool of human evidence that lies beneath my writing and teaching, if nothing more, has grown in the wake of that big change.

Then the slow migration of a sleepless and welcome sexuality from the center of my life to the cooler edge has contributed hugely to the increased speed and volume of my work, not to speak of the gradual resolution of hungers that—however precious to mind and body—had seemed past feeding. It's the sex that's moved, in fact, not the eros. The sense of some others as radiant and magnetic bodies, bodies that promise pleasure and good, is if anything larger in my life than before.

And especially now that my remaining senses are free from the heavy damper of methadone, all other pain drugs, and the muscle relaxant baclofen that stunned me for seven years, specific desire does come again and find expression in new ways that match the rewards of the old. But the fact that, in ten years since the tumor was found, I've completed thirteen books—I'd published a first twelve in the previous twenty-two years—would seem at least another demonstration that human energy, without grave loss, may flow from one form into another and win the same consoling gains. (The question of why and how I was able to increase my rate is unanswerable, by me anyhow—a race with death and silence, a massive rerouting of sexual energy would be the easy answers. But if I was racing, I never felt chased; panic came elsewhere but never in my work. On the contrary, I sense strongly that the illness itself either unleashed a creature within me that had been restrained and let him run at his own hungry will; or it planted a whole new creature in place of the old.)

There've been other, maybe more private, gains. Once the hand wringers and ambulance chasers disperse from your side, you begin to feel and eventually savor the keener attentions of old friends who feel a complicated new duty to stand in closer. It's a duty that you have the duty to lighten, as Simone Weil said in her haunting law of friend-ship—

> Our friends owe us what we think they will give us.
> We must forgive them this debt.

In a country as addicted to calamitous news as America now, word of your illness or imminent death will likely draw not just a ring of crows—not all of whom are eager to feed—but likewise a flock of serious watchers. Both halves of my written work, the books from 1962 to '84 and those thereafter, have benefited from new readers summoned by word of an ordeal survived, however briefly. When I traveled across the states in the spring of '92, following the publication of *Blue Calhoun*—twenty-three readings in fourteen cities—I caught for the first time in the eyes of strangers a certain intense eagerness of response that I doubt was won by my gray hair alone. A certified gimp, in working order, is often accorded an unearned awe which he may be forgiven for enjoying a moment till he rolls on past the nearest mirror and adjusts his vision for colder reality.

I'm left today, as I write this page, with an odd conclusion that's risky to state. But since it's not only thoroughly true but may well prove of use to another, I'll state it baldly—*I've led a mainly happy life*. I can safely push further. *I've yet to watch another life that seems to have brought more pleasure to its owner than mine has to me*. And that claim covers all my years except for the actual eye of the storm I've charted, from the spring of 1984 till fall '88.

I'm the son of brave, magnanimous parents who'd have offered both legs in hostage for mine, if they'd been living when mine were required. I'm the brother of a laughing, openhanded man with whom I've never exchanged an angry adult word nor wanted to. I'm the cousin of a woman who, with her husband, offered to see me through to the grave. I'm the neighbor of a couple who offered to share my life, however long I lasted. I'm the ward of a line of responsible assistants who've moved into my home and life at twelve-month intervals, taken charge of both the house and me and ensured a safe and favorable atmosphere for ongoing work. I'm the friend of many more spacious and lively souls than I've earned. I've had, and still have, more love—in body and mind—than I dreamed of in my lone boyhood.

Doctors of superb craft and technical judgment, whatever their faults of attention and sympathy, ousted a lethal thing from my spine. Other resourceful attendants nursed me through pitch-black nights of roaring pain. An annual lot of intelligent students throws down a welcome gauntlet to me—*Give us all you've got, no discount for pain*. The unseen hand of the source of all has never felt absent as long as a week, and I share the sense of the holiday painter as she finishes her canvas at the end of Virginia Woolf's *To the Lighthouse*—"I have had my vision." Mine was a vision of healing that's remained in force for a decade full, at the least, of work.

So though I travel for work and pleasure, here I sit most weeks at work toward the end of ten years rocked with threats and hairbreadth rescues. Though I make no forecast beyond today, annual scans have gone on showing my spine clear of cancer—clear of visible growing cells at least (few cancer veterans will boast of a "cure"). When Allan Friedman's physician-wife heard the story of my continuing recovery at my sixtieth birthday party, she said to Allan, "But that's miraculous." Allan faced her, grinned, and said, "You could say that."

I've long since weaned myself from all drugs but a small dose of antidepressant, an aspirin to thin my blood, an occasional scotch or a good red wine, and a simple acid to brace my bladder against infection.

I write six days a week, long days that often run till bedtime; and the books are different from what came before in more ways than age. I sleep long nights with few hard dreams, and now I've outlived both my parents. Even my handwriting looks very little like the script of the man I was in June of '84. Cranky as it is, it's taller, more legible, with more air and stride. It comes down the arm of a grateful man.

Here: Grace

NANCY MAIRS

"You will love me?" my husband asks, and at *something in* his tone my consciousness rouses like a startled cat, ears pricked, pupils round and onyx-black.

Never voluble, he has been unusually subdued this evening. Thinking him depressed about the mysterious symptoms that have plagued him for months and that we know in our heart of hearts signal a recurrence of cancer, although the tests won't confirm it for several more days, I pressed up against him on the couch and whispered against his neck, "This may be the most troublesome time of our lives, but I'm so happy." This awareness of joy, though it's been growing for several years now, has recently expanded in response to my own failing health. A few weeks ago, pondering the possibility that I might die at any time, I posed myself a new question: *If I died at this very moment, would I die happy?* And the answer burst out without hesitation: *Yes!* Since then, in spite of my fears, I've felt a new contentment. What more could I ever ask than to give an unequivocal response to such a question?

His silence persisted. "Scared?" I asked him after a few moments, thinking of the doctor's appointment that morning, the CAT scan scheduled for later in the week. Head resting on the back of the couch, eyes closed, he nodded. More silence. Finally I said, "George, you know how I love words. I need words!"

And now, words: "You will love me?" Behind his glasses, his eyes have the startled look I associate, incongruously, with the moment of orgasm.

"Yes," I tell him, alert, icy all over. "I can safely promise you that. I will always love you."

"You asked the other day whether my illness could be AIDS," he says unevenly. "I'm pretty sure it isn't, because I had the test for HIV some time ago, after I had an affair for a couple of years with another woman."

The sensation is absolutely nonverbal, but everybody knows it even without words: the stunned breathlessness that follows a jab to the solar plexus. What will astonish me in the days to come is that this sensation can sustain itself long after one would expect to be dead of asphyxiation. I have often wished myself dead. If it were possible to die of grief, I would die at this moment. But it's not, and I don't.

A couple of years. *A couple of years.* This was no fit of passion, no passing fancy, but a sustained commitment. He loved her, loves her still: Their relationship, until he broke it off—for reasons having little to do with me—was a kind of marriage, he says. Time after time after time he went to her, deliberately, telling whatever lies he needed to free himself from me and the children, and later from his mother, when she came for a protracted visit after his father's death, throughout at least a couple of years.

More. He'd fallen in love with her six years earlier, I could sense at that time, and they'd had a prolonged flirtation. She was a bitter, brittle woman, and something about her rage inflamed him. Their paths had parted, however, and I had no way of knowing of their later chance encounter, courtship, years-long "marriage." And after that ended—

here, in this room, which will ever hereafter be haunted by her tears—
four years of silence: too late to tell me, he says, and then too later, and
then too later still. Twelve of our twenty-seven years of marriage
suddenly called, one way or another, into question. I recall my
brother's description of his framing shop after the San Francisco earth-
quake, how miraculously nothing in it was broken, not even the sheets
of glass for covering pictures, but it looked as though some giant
gremlin had come in and slid everything a few feet to one side. My past
feels similarly shoved out of whack, not shattered but strangely recon-
figured, and out of its shadows steps a man I have never seen before:
Sandra's lover.

If I were that proverbial virtuous woman, the
one whose price is far above rubies, perhaps I would have the right to
order George out of my sight, out of my house, out of my life. But I'm
not that woman. I'm the other one, the one whose accusers dropped
their stones and skulked away. I've desired other men, slept with them,
even loved them, although I've never felt married to one. I guess I took
my girlhood vow literally: I have always thought of marriage as something one did once and forever. All the same, in brief passionate bursts
I've transgressed the sexual taboos that give definition to Christian
marriage.

I'm not a virtuous woman, but I am a candid one. Many years ago,
George and I pledged that we would not again lie to anyone about
anything. I haven't been strictly faithful to the spirit of this promise,
either, because I've deliberately withheld information on occasion (although not, according to my mother, often enough, having an unfortu-
nate propensity for spilling the family beans in print); but I have not,
when directly challenged, lied. This commitment can have maddening
consequences: One night I listened for half an hour or longer to the
outpourings of a total stranger in response to an essay in one of my
books because I couldn't tell her that I had a pot on the stove about to
boil over when I actually didn't. Had Daddy and I meant that vow for
everybody, my daughter asked after I hung up the telephone, not just

for each other? Not even, I can see now, for each other: especially not for each other.

"How can you ever believe me again after this?" George asks, and I shrug: "I've believed you all this time. I'm in the habit of it. Why should I stop now?" And so I go on believing him, but a subtle difference will emerge over time: belief becomes a matter of faith, no longer logically connected to the "truth" of its object, which remains unknowable except insofar as it chooses to reveal itself. I suppose I could hire a private detective to corroborate George's tales, but I'm not going to because George's whereabouts are no less his own business now than they ever were. I can envision some practical difficulties in my being unable to locate him at any given time, but no moral ones, whereas I perceive a serious problem in seeking information that would curb his freedom to lie, a freedom without which he can't freely tell me the truth. I don't want to come by my belief through extortion. Once, I believed George because it never occurred to me not to believe him; now I believe him because I prefer belief, which affirms his goodness, to doubt, which sneers and sniggers at it. No longer a habitual response, belief becomes an act of love.

It does not thereby absolve George of responsibility for the choices he has freely made, however. The years while he was slipping away to sleep with Sandra were among the most wretched of my not conspicuously cheerful life; and by lying to me, he permitted—no, really encouraged—me to believe that my unhappiness was, as always, my own fault, even though, thanks to the wonders of psychopharmacology, I was at last no longer clinically depressed. I remember lying awake, night after night, while he stayed up late grading papers and then dropped into bed, and instantly into sleep, without a word or a touch; as he twitched and snored, I'd prowl through the dark house, sip milk or wine, smoke cigarettes, write in my journal until, shuddering with cold and loneliness, I'd be forced to creep back into bed. Past forty, he must have been conserving his sexual energies, I realize now, but when I expressed concern and sadness, he blamed our chilling relationship on me: I was distracted, too bitchy, not affectionate enough. . . . Ah, he knew my self-doubts thoroughly.

Breakdowns in our relationship, especially sexual ones, had habitually been ascribed to me. "I'm very tired," I wrote in my journal early in this period of misery, twenty years into our marriage, "of his putting me down all the time—telling me that I'm too involved with Anne, that I don't handle Matthew well, that I'm not affectionate (the only signs of affection he recognizes are physical, which I suppose makes sense, since he doesn't communicate verbally). In short, that I'm a bad mother and wife. I just don't know how to feel much affection for someone I feel sorry for, for being married to me." Tired of disparagement I may already have been, but I took over two years more to recognize myself as a collaborator in it: "He survives—thrives—on my culpability. Without it, where would he be today? We've *both* built our lives on it, and if I remove it, our relationship will no longer have any foundation."

This awareness of complicity precipitated out of a homely crisis (the form of most of my crises), in the winter of 1985, involving the proper setting of the thermostat, which George persistently left at sixty degrees even though I couldn't bear the temperature below sixty-five (and, as came out in the course of the dispute, neither could he). When I told him that the coldness of the house represented my growing feelings of neglect and abandonment, he countered that he had to go elsewhere (leaving the thermostat set at sixty) in order to get the touching and affection he needed. It was, I noted, "the same old ploy, trying to trigger my guilt for not being a physically affectionate wife. Only this time I could feel myself not quite biting. Because he wants the physical part to continue regardless of the pain I'm in, even if he causes the pain, and he blames me if I won't put out, come across, what have you. And I'm sick unto death of bearing the blame." He could, I suddenly understood, turn up the heat himself. He chose not to.

Or rather, he chose to turn it up in some other woman's house. In spite of the sexual stresses underlying this controversy, he gave no hint that his longing for "warmth and light" was taking him from the crumbling converted Chinese grocery where the children and I lived to a spacious, immaculate, perfectly appointed home in a tranquil neighborhood miles away; and I didn't guess. Just as he knew how to exploit my self-doubts, he knew how to escape me. Teaching in two programs, he was out of the house from at least eight-thirty in the morning until eight-thirty at night; he devoted his spare time to good works like cooking at Casa María soup kitchen, observing the federal trial of the people who had arranged sanctuary for refugees from El Salvador, and editing *¡Presente!*, the local Catholics for Peace and Justice newsletter. With such a schedule, of course he'd have little enough energy left for sex, or even a leisurely family dinner. Another woman (his lover, for instance) might have judged his devotion to illiterate, poor, and oppressed people sanctimonious, even morbid, but I found it natural and necessary.

As a result, he put me in a conscientious bind: I felt abandoned, and I believed that George was neglecting our troubled teenaged son dangerously, but I couldn't make our needs weigh heavily enough against those of five hundred empty bellies at the kitchen door or a Salvadoran woman who'd fled her village in terror when the last of her sons disappeared. Still, I wondered uneasily why the spiritual growth he said he was seeking necessitated his setting out on what appeared to be "a quest—Galahad and the Holy Grail—noble and high-minded and above all out there, beyond the muck and mire of daily living in a decaying house with a crippled wife and a rebellious adolescent son." Forced to let him go, I did so with a bitter blessing: "Feed the poor, my dear. Shelter the refugees. Forget the impoverishment you leave in your wake. It's only Nancy and Matthew and Anne, after all—nothing spiritual there, nothing uplifting, no real needs, just niggling demands that drag at you, cling to you, slow your lofty ascent into the light and life of Christ."

Our approaches to ministry were hopelessly at odds: "I think that the life of Christ is only this life, which one must enter further and further. And I hate the entering. I'd give anything to escape. . . . There's no glamour here, no glory. Only the endless grading of papers. The being present for two difficult children. The making of another meal. The dragging around of an increasingly crippled body, forcing it to one end of the house and back again, out the door, into the classroom, home again, up from the bed, up from the toilet, up from the couch. The extent of my lofty ascent. I want only to do what I must with as much grace as I can." That George, finding these conditions squalid and limiting, sought to minister elsewhere embittered but hardly surprised me. And so, whenever he wanted Sandra, he had only to murmur "Soup. Sanctuary. *¡Presente!*" in order to be as free of them as he liked.

I have been, it appears, a bit of a fool. "Where did I think you'd gone?" I ask George. "What lies did I believe?" He claims not to remember. He will always claim not to remember such details, which is his prerogative, but the writer in me obsessively scribbles in all the blanks he leaves. I imagine the two of them sitting half-naked beside her pool, sipping cold Coronas and laughing at my naïveté, and then I have to laugh myself: I would have been the last thing on their minds. This sense of my own extinction will prove the most tenacious and terrifying of my responses, the one that keeps me flat on my back in the night, staring into the dark, gasping for breath, as though I've been buried alive. For almost thirty years, except during a couple of severe disintegrative episodes, my presence to George has kept me present to myself. Now, at just the moment when cancer threatens to remove that reassurance of my own reality from my future, it's yanked from my past as well. Throughout his sweet stolen hours with Sandra, George lived where I was not.

"Are you all right?" my daughter asks on the day following George's revelation when she stumbles upon me huddled in my studio, rocking and shivering. I shake my head. "Shall I cut class and stay here with you?"

"No, go to class," I say. "Then come back. We'll talk."

"You're not going to do anything rash while I'm gone?" It's the question of a child seasoned in suicide, and I wish she didn't have to ask it.

"I promise. Scoot."

I hadn't planned to tell Anne, at least not yet; but George is getting sicker by the day, his mother is about to arrive for several weeks,

Christmas is coming, and I don't think I can deal with this new complication alone. I have George's permission to tell whomever I wish. "I want you to write about this," he says. "I want you to write about us." For himself, he has never revealed it to anyone except once, early on, the psychotherapist with whom we've worked, together and apart, over the years. But he believes in the value of what I try to do in my work: in reclaiming human experience, insofar as I can find it embodied in my own experience, from the morass of secrecy and shame into which Christian and pre-Christian social taboos have plunged it, to rescue and restore God's good creation. (And if at times the work proves as smelly as pumping a septic tank, well, shit is God's creation, too.) George supports it, but the work itself is mine. If any bad tidings are to be borne, I am the one to bear them.

"But Mom," Anne says when I've finished my tale of woe, "men *do* these things." Transcribed, these words might look like a twenty-five-year-old's cynicism, but in fact her tone rings purely, and characteristically, pragmatic. It's just the tone I need to jerk my attention back from private misery to the human condition. She's right, of course. In the Judaic roots of our culture, as Uta Ranke-Heinemann points out in *Eunuchs for the Kingdom of Heaven,* "A man could never violate his own marriage. The wife belonged to her husband, but the husband did not belong to his wife," and a couple of thousand years of Church teaching on the subject of marital fidelity—not all of it a model of clarity and consistency—has never entirely balanced the expectations placed on the two partners. *People* do these things, Anne means (I know: I have done them myself); but ordinary men, men possessed of healthy sexual appetites, have been tacitly *entitled* to do them. They're just *like* that.

Except for my man. One reviewer of my first book of essays, *Plaintext,* wrote: "The reader will also wish to see more closely some of the people who simply drift through these essays, especially Mairs' husband, who comes across as a saint, staying through extreme mood swings, suicide attempts, severe illness, and a number of love affairs." That's *my* man: a saint. Through my essays I've publicly canonized him. Any man who could stay with a crazy, crippled, unfaithful bitch like me had to be more than humanly patient and loving and long-suffering and self-abnegating and . . . oh, just more than human.

Admittedly, I had help in forming this view, especially from other women; a man whose bearing is as gentle and courtly as George's can seem a true miracle, one my inconstancy plainly didn't merit. "But hasn't he ever slept with another woman?" more than one person has asked, and I've said proudly, gratefully, "No. I've asked him, and he tells me he never has." I often told myself that he "ought to go, get out now, while he's still fairly young, find a healthy woman free from black spells, have some fun. No one could blame him." And occasionally, trying to account for his physical and emotional unavailability, I'd conjecture: "Perhaps another woman—he's so attractive and romantic that that thought always crosses my mind." My guess was dead on, it turns out, formed at the height of his affair with just the sort of healthy woman I'd had in mind, but I took him at his word and felt humbled—humiliated—that he had responded to my infidelities with such stead-fastness.

A saint's wife readily falls prey to self-loathing, I discovered, since comparisons are both common and invidious, and recuperation, if it occurs at all, is a protracted and lonely process. One evening a couple of years ago, when I'd been invited to discuss *Plaintext* with a local women's reading group and the conversation turned, as such conversations always seem to, to my infidelity and George's forbearance, I blurted: "Wait a minute! Did it ever occur to you that there might be some advantage to being married to the woman who wrote *Plaintext?*" At last I'd reached the point where I could ask that question. But as I sipped coffee and nibbled a chocolate cookie in the company of these polite and pleasant but plainly distressed strangers, my chances of getting an affirmative answer seemed as remote as ever. In this tale, I was decidedly not the Princess but the Dragon.

George has conspired in his own sanctification. Why wouldn't he? The veneration of others must be seductive. And if, in order to perpetuate it, he had to affirm—to me, and through me to others familiar with my writings—his faithfulness even as he shuttled between Sandra and me, well, what harm was he doing? For her own reasons, Sandra was just as eager as he to keep the affair clandestine. They seldom went out and never got together with friends; he never even encountered her child, who was always, magically, "not there"; she'd even meet him in a parking lot and drive him to her house so that the neighbors wouldn't see his car. He could maintain this oddly hermetic relationship without risk to the sympathy and admiration of friends, family, and book reviewers alike. No one need ever know.

Until, ultimately, me. That is, I don't need to know, not at all, I've done very well indeed without knowing, but he has come to need to tell me. At first, he thought merely breaking with Sandra would calm the dread his father's death and the discovery of melanoma in a lymph node stirred in him, but now he needs a stronger remedy. "I feel this awful blackness inside. I just want to die," he says after confessing, and I shudder, because an awful blackness is precisely what he has inside—a six-centimeter melanoma attached to his small bowel—and I don't want him to die, he can tell me anything, I'll accept whatever he confesses, any number of awful blacknesses, if only please he won't die. He hasn't any control over that, alas, but at least now he has cleared his conscience thoroughly. I think he's after another clarity as well, one that involves putting off sainthood and standing naked—bones jutting under wasted flesh, scars puckering arm and belly, penis too limp now for love—as a man. He wants to be loved as he is, not as we—his mother, my mother, my sisters, our daughter, his students, our friends, maybe even Sandra herself—have dreamed him. I most of all. I look anew at the reviewer's words: "The reader will wish to *see more closely* some of the people who *simply drift* through these essays. . . ."

George is accustomed to holding himself slightly aloof. The only child of adoring parents, he grew up believing himself entitled to act on his own desires without regard for the needs of others: There weren't any others. If he wanted the last cookie, it was his. (In fact, even if he didn't want it, his mother probably made him take it.) No noisy wrangles, no division of the coveted cookie followed by wails that "he got the bigger half," no snitching a bite while the other's head was turned or spitting on the other's half to spoil it for both, just complacent munching down to the last sweet crumb. But, by the same token, no whispers and giggles under the covers after Mother has put out the light *for absolutely the last time*. No shared cookies. No shared secrets, either. No entanglements, true. But no intimacy.

Having grown up in an extensive family linked by complicated affections, with a slightly younger sister who still sometimes seems hooked into my flesh, I don't think I ever quite comprehended George's implacable self-sufficiency. Maybe for that reason I allowed, even encouraged, his remoteness. And I did. The reviewer is talking, after all, not about George's nature but about my essays. If the reader wants to "see" George "more closely," then I have not seen him closely enough. George "drifts" through my essays because I permitted him to drift through my life. "I couldn't imagine," he tells me now, "that what I was doing, as long as I kept it in a separate little box, had any effect on the rest of you." Like his indulgent mother, I let him persist in such manly detachment. I'd have served him better as a scrappy sister.

What I might have thought of, in good aging-hippie fashion, as "giving him space," letting him "do his own thing," strikes me now as a failure of love. Respecting another's freedom does not require cutting him loose and letting him drift; the lines of love connecting us one to another are stays, not shackles. I do not want to fail again. After the children and I have each spoken with him separately about the affair, I say to him: "You may have hoped, in confessing to us, that we'd punish you by sending you away, but now you see that we won't do that. If you want to leave, you'll have to go on your own initiative. As far as we're concerned, you're not an only child, you're one of us. We love you. We intend, if you will let us, to keep you."

"You will love me?" George asked at the beginning of this terrible test, and I find, to my relief, that I can keep my promise. "But can you forgive him?" asks our friend Father Ricardo when we seek his counsel, and I reply without hesitation, "I already have."

I *have?* How can this be? I have never felt more hurt than I do
now. I am angry. I am bitter. I try to weep but my eyes feel blasted,
although occasionally I shudder and gasp in some stone's version of
crying its heart out. I dread going out into the city for fear I'll encounter Sandra. I torment myself with images of George pressing his lips to
hers, stroking her hair, slowly unbuttoning her blouse, calling her
"sweetheart" too. *She got the sex*, I reflect sardonically as I keep my
vigil through surgery and its horrific aftermath, then through chemotherapy, *and I get the death*. I despise her for her willingness to risk my
marriage without a thought; and yet in a queer way I pity her because,
as it has turned out, she has to live without George and, for the
moment, I do not.

Worst of all, ghastly congratulatory cheers ring in my head:
*Good-o, George! You've finally given the bitch her comeuppance: tit for
tat, an eye for an eye, and not a whit more than she deserves*. "What do
you care what people think?" He shrugs when I tell him of this fantastic taunting, but the truth is that, with new comprehension of the
suffering my adultery must have caused him, I'm tempted to join the
chorus. Still, although our affairs may be connected chronologically
(mine all took place before his) and causally (bitterness about mine
offered him permission for his), morally they stand separate. I don't
merit the pain I'm now in, any more than George ever deserved to be
hurt, but we have unquestionably wounded each other horribly and we
each bear full moral responsibility for the other's pain. George is right
to dismiss my demonic chorus: What matters is not mockery and
blame, whether our own or others', but mutual contrition. Over and
over when he clings to me and weeps as I cannot and says, "I'm sorry,
I'm sorry," I hold him, stroking his back and murmuring reassurances:
that I love him, that I'll be all right, that he hasn't "spoiled" us, that
through this pain we can grow. Forgiveness is not even in question. It
is simply, mysteriously, already accomplished.

Week after week he has stood beside me telling me what I have not
wanted to know: *I confess to Almighty God, and to you, my brothers and
sisters, that I have sinned, through my own fault, in my thoughts and in
my words, in what I have done and in what I have failed to do*. Now that
he's divulged the specific contents of his conscience to me, I'm curious

what this little ritual of general confession meant during the time he so plainly wasn't sorry for what he was doing. "Did you ever think about Sandra as you said those words?" I ask. "Did you think what you were doing might be wrong?"

"Well, yes, I knew it was. But I also knew I didn't intend to stop. So I just had to hope that God had a sense of humor." Fortunately for George, God has a much better sense of humor than I do. But I've been working on it. Meanwhile, week after week his voice has spoken aloud at my side: *And I ask Blessed Mary ever virgin, all the angels and saints, and you, my brothers and sisters, to pray for me to the Lord our God.* As bidden, I have prayed for him, as for myself and for all the disembodied voices floating up behind me, that God might have mercy on us, forgive us our sins, and lead each one of us to everlasting life. Believing myself forgiven by God, I must believe George equally forgiven. And if forgiven by God, surely no less by me.

One of the elements that drew me into the Catholic Church was the concept of grace, although I've never been able to make more than clumsy sense of it. I am moved by the idea that God always already loves us first, before we love God, wholly and without condition, that God forgives us even before we have done anything to require forgiveness, as we will inevitably do, and that this outpouring of love and forgiveness fortifies us for repentance and reform. I am moved—but not persuaded. I am simply incapable of grasping an abstraction unless I can root it experientially, and nothing in my experience has revealed quite how grace works. Until now. The uncontingent love and forgiveness I feel for George, themselves a gift of grace, unwilled and irresistible, intimate that grace whose nature has eluded me.

For the most theologically unsophisticated of reasons, involving a dead father who went, I was told, to heaven up in the sky, together with continual reiterations, from about the same age on, of "Our Father, who art in heaven . . . ," I always expect spiritual insights to shower like coins of light from on high. When instead they bubble up from the mire like will-o'-the-wisps, I am invariably startled. Grace *here*, among these lies and shattered vows, sleepless nights, remorse, recriminations? Yes, precisely, here: Grace.

But forgiveness does not, whatever the aphorism says, entail forgetfulness. Never mind the sheer impossibility of forgetting that your husband has just told you he's had an affair, a strenuous version of that childhood game in which you try, on a dare, *not* to think about a three-legged green cat licking persimmon marmalade from the tip of its tail. Never mind memory's malarial tenacity, the way that, weeks and months and even years after you think the shock has worn off, as you recall a trip you made to Washington to receive a writing award, it occurs to you that in your absence they may have made love for the first time and all your words, the ones you'd written before and the ones you've written since, shrivel and scatter like ashes. Never mind.

Mind what matters: his presence here, for now. Love is not love, forgiveness is not forgiveness, that effaces the beloved's lineaments by letting him drift, indistinct, through the lives of those who claim him. That way lies lethargy, which is the death of love. I am not married to Saint George, after all. I am married to a man who is, among many other things neither more nor less remarkable, an adulterer. I must remember him: whole.

The Disassociation Game

Patton Hollow

My father loved planes and trains, hated cars. I suspect he hated traveling by car because distance covered is so much more obvious—the precisely demarked speedometer, the monotonous thrum of expansion joints, the constant reminders along the way of how far you've come and how far there is yet to go. If the relationship between time and velocity is relative, then the relationship between time and distance, at least when my father was driving, appeared absolute. Even in the late sixties and early seventies, before the speed limit shriveled from seventy to fifty-five, it took my father over thirteen hours to drive our family the six hundred miles from our home in Athens, Ohio, to the maternal grandparents' house in Brownsville, Tennessee, near Memphis. My mother's explanation for this warp in the laws of physics would have been that my father—a second-generation American, a young man who grew up in Dallas and went off to college in New York City, a Catholic who began courting my mother around the time that John F. Kennedy, Catholic, campaigned for the presidency against Richard M. Nixon, Quaker—never felt welcome in the Reformed, small-town southern society of Brownsville. It was a society founded, and at that time still dominated by, my mother's relatives, who had been in this country, as she often pointed out, "long enough for their blood to become very, very blue."

My younger sister and I made fun of my father under our breath from the backseat on those long trips from eastern Ohio to western Tennessee. We mocked him in his own language: "Come on, you're lollygagging," we'd say; or, "Let's go! We're moving slower than Christmas around here"; or "Chop-chop!" with an accompanying double clap of the hands.

My father said traveling with a family was slow going, no matter what the speed limit.

Is this a memoir featuring (heaven forbid!) a family trip to Grandma's house? A tired-out, adolescent experiment in point of view: two children read the world and their own piddling family cosmos from the backseat of a Buick Skylark? Flannery O'Connor pulled it off in "A Good Man Is Hard to Find," but of course she turned the tableau on its side: the grandmother takes charge of the trip from her place in the backseat between the two children, and the house she leads them to doesn't exist. That's really what this is about. You think you're traveling one direction, on a well-planned trip, with miles of clear road ahead, then abruptly discover that there really were no maps in the first place, that it's all something you made up along the way to keep yourself going. This is a cancer story, and because it's a cancer story, it's a story about preparation—about the shock of being "given" only months to live—and a story about grief, about every single word and touch and moment in time now suddenly missing, and, inevitably, a story about telling the story. I must choose what of my father and myself I wish to share, and I must carefully cast each image, each description, each link. I am my father's advocate here, his second, his envoy; he cannot speak for himself.

Do I talk about how far apart we were, how close we had become? Will the essay be about regret or redemption? Will it be about Love, that earnest, protective touch, that unending moment of revelation, that crusty accretion of sentiment, that burdensome weight, that ball and chain, that moonlight caught within a chamber, that homage to our own ability to hold and hoard, to name and describe, to clean up, fluff up, brush, pet, and polish?

It's about the assignation of meaning, transfiguring the incomprehensible concrete into fathomable abstraction.

For three months our family doctor had my father on different courses of antibiotics to treat what they thought was a prostate infection. In August our whole family met in Wilmington, North Carolina, for a week at the beach, and I saw my father for the first time since Christmas. He looked tired, hollowed out, like a powdered version of his usual self. His skin was the skin of a much older person, without the wrinkles: a scentless, inelastic lacquer over the veins in his temples and the underside of his forearms. My mother said she couldn't tell if he'd lost weight since she saw him every day, but my sister and I insisted that he'd dropped at least ten pounds. We made him promise to go back to the doctor when they got back home. Though he tried not to seem so, he must have been concerned. He said the next step would probably be to see a specialist, and cursed. His theory about specialists was that they didn't view their patients as people, but body parts. Hence, the specialist he would have to visit for this particular problem would see him as an "asshole." He'd rather have had a brain tumor than colon cancer, I think. The Friday after we all left the beach, my mother called with the news.

When I try to imagine, after the fact, how I would have imagined a trip back to the bedside of my dying father, the trip becomes an epic physical and psychological ordeal, very different from what it actually was: a three-hour plane ride, passed, without the hope that time engenders, eulogizing the not yet dead. What if the phone call from my mother had come 135 years ago, on August 12, 1859, rather than on that date in 1994? The year 1859 is usually associated with the publication of Darwin's *Origin of Species*. Other events of that year would have interested my father more. Arthur Conan Doyle was born; George Eliot published *Adam Bede;* Tennyson's *Idylls of the King* appeared, as did Mill's essay *On Liberty;* the first oil well was drilled in Titusville, Pennsylvania. The huge eight- and ten-wheel Baldwin steam locomotives my father enjoyed so much were just beginning to freight significant numbers of passengers from the cities in the East to the developing frontier.

It wouldn't have been a phone call, of course. I would have received a telegram, probably hand-delivered from the local Western Union office. "Your father is much sicker than we thought. Hurry home." I would catch the first train headed west on the New York and Erie line through Binghamton, joining my sister who, coming from Manhattan, would already be aboard. We ride in a sleeper car, a chicken coop for people, yet not so bad as the immigrant cars at the end of the train, with their rows of pewlike benches packed with Irish and Italian families heading to Chicago and beyond. The late summer heat seems to radiate up from the dusty floorboards. During the day, Elizabeth and I ride in unpadded seats, the wood polished dark with a patina of sweat and soot. At night, if we wish, we can drag ratty tick mattresses from a stack at the other end of the car and lie down in one of three tiers of sleeper berths. But we won't sleep. If our thoughts don't keep us awake, then the noise and the heat, the jolting ride and the insects, will. The bedding holds the smells, the permanent impress, of previous passengers' bodies, and, in the darkness, in that confined space, with ears ringing in the first hissing silence of a stop for fuel and water, I feel something that is both memory and premonition, a vision, gone in an instant, of that last, irretrievable moment before death. It comes like a revelation: Death is a terrible mistake! Tell him it's a terrible mistake. Get home now and tell him before it's too late.

When my father was admitted to the hospital, his colleagues in the English department at Ohio University rushed over with flowers and cards. Tom Andrews, a poet who, as a hemophil-iac, knows about living with illness, wrote him this note:

8-16-94

John-

In *Intoxicated by My Illness*, Anatole Broyard wrote: "It seems to me that every ill person needs to develop a style for his illness."

You don't need to, of course—you have style and grace to spare.

Be well soon.

Tom

No one but us, his immediate family, knew how sick my father was. Because of the three months of misdiagnoses, by the time my father was admitted to the hospital the radiologist's report showed that he had a grapefruit-sized tumor in his large intestine and that the cancer had metastasized to his liver and his lungs. He went into the hospital on Monday morning for tests to precisely locate the tumor in his colon, and he died Wednesday night. He was fifty-five years old. He didn't have time to reconcile himself to how sick he really was; he didn't have time to develop a style for his illness. So it was we, my mother, my sister, and my brother, in the way families must, who imposed a style upon my father in his death, a style, a closing narra-tive, that we can only hope would have pleased him and represented him finally to the world in a manner he would have chosen.

The Jagers Funeral Home, a sturdy two-story barrackslike building at the top of the hill on Morris Avenue, stands four blocks from my parents' house on Maplewood, and even closer if you cut diagonally across the East Elementary playground. After you pass the playground equipment—severe, knobby-jointed, lead pipe handwalkers and jungle gyms, tokens of an early Cold War notion of recess: an hour each day devoted to the training of a fearless and physically fit children's militia—and, up at the top of a rise, the basketball court, you come to a seven-foot stone retaining wall, a mossy ruin now bound together by an arterial web of roots and wild vines. This wall leads up to the funeral home parking lot. During the summers, we neighborhood kids, including the Jagers boys, gathered in the early afternoon to play baseball or basketball. When we got too hot, and if Chris and Jamie Jagers were sure there was no service in progress, we'd climb the wall to the funeral home and file in for drinks of water from the fountain. I remember expecting the place to smell of formaldehyde, but I don't remember that it smelled like anything at all. I remember wall-to-wall teal carpeting and matching drapes pulled closed over the long windows, sunlight leaking in around the edges. Dust motes, or maybe a lucent mist of pollen—trace evidence of a morning service—jumped and looped in the light, and sometimes, in a room off the entrance hall, would be a body lying in state. In that dim quiet, my lean, sweat-slicked adolescent body, with all its new sproutings of hair and smells and muscle, felt, suddenly, obscenely vigorous and alive.

We made up stories, Elizabeth and I, on those trips to Tennessee, about the people who passed us by—and trucks, motorcycles, cars full of all kinds of people, always seemed to be passing us, leaving our poky family behind. A car or truck would come up alongside us, and my sister and I would stare like mesmerists at the driver or the front bumper, trying to hold off the assault with our minds. Often the car passing us would then sag back a little as if building momentum, proving our theory that passing people on the highway had psychological as well as physical costs, tolls our father was unwilling to pay. As we gritted our teeth and beamed our thoughts against the driver of a red pickup, sitting upright and stiff in his seat, we would remake his life. He became a pig farmer with six daughters, who had just used the shovel and wheelbarrow in the back of his truck to bury the family dog, killed in a hunting mishap. He hadn't told his children of the tragedy yet, and he was thinking of the best way to break the news. Then the man and his truck would break free of our thoughts and pull away, along with his story, diminishing and finally flattening into the horizon.

The best game, the fastest moving and most challenging travel diversion, was the Disassociation Game. The object was to take turns naming things. The first person would start by pointing out something everyone could see through the windshield: a cow, or a Stuckey's, or a serpentlike strip of retread tire. The second player then had to name something, an image, as it popped into his or her head. In fact, after starting the game off with an object visible outside the car, all subsequent "plays" or "moves" in the game had to come from inside, from the imagination, had to be complete fabrication. The second person had to produce an answer quickly, and the thing named had to be absolutely discrete from the first person's thing named. If Elizabeth looked out the window and said "corn," I would then have two to three seconds to say something like "oil derrick," and then I had to hope that she couldn't trace a connection, no matter how thin, abstract, or complicated, within the few seconds following my utterance. If my oil derrick stood in the middle of her cornfield—I often had to cheat to stay in the game—she only had to point that out to win. If she couldn't prove within seconds that I had somehow derived "oil derrick" from the concept of "corn," or from any external cue, she then had to continue, coming up with her own untraceable something. Each round lasted until one of us demonstrated a link between answers or stumbled and stuttered too long in the search for a new "disassociated" thing.

Sometime the night before he died, standing outside his hospital room with my mother, I asked her, not how my father took the news, but what they'd done after they heard. She said they set up the lawn chairs in the backyard, under the walnut tree. Green-husked walnuts pocked the grass around them like perfect malignancies. The doctor had said it's hard to tell, two or three months, maybe a year or possibly even two with aggressive treatment, who knew. That was all the information they had at that point. They sat quietly for a long time. My mother couldn't remember if they told my brother, who still lived at home, before they went outside, or if he came home at some point while they were out there. She remembered my father saying, "This isn't what we planned at all, is it?"

These days people put off those things that we tend to most carefully make note of when they die—marriage and children. Is it the longer life expectancies or that we hope to make some mark on the world before we're thirty? *"Carpe diem,"* the Robin Williams character tells his students in *Dead Poets Society*. Bullshit. Some things take time. In Jorge Luis Borges's story "The Secret Miracle," the Nazis sentence Jaromir Hladik, a Czech Jew, to death by firing squad. In his cell, Hladik reviews his life, finding it "uninspired" except for his unfinished verse drama, *The Enemies*. He decides he exists only as author of *The Enemies*, and asks God for the year he requires to complete the play. He doesn't need paper or pen or manuscript; the metrical lines live in his memory. On the scheduled execution day, guards place Hladik against a wall and raise their rifles. At the last instant God suspends time, but only for Hladik. A raindrop pauses on Hladik's cheek; the shadow of a bee freezes on a stone. Hladik lives a year in his mind with guns leveled at his heart, writing and rewriting his play, "his lofty, invisible labyrinth." He perfects a final, flawed phrase, time commences, bullets fly.

My uncle painted a portrait of my father when Dad was about the age I am now. I now ask myself if that moment of time, caught in oils, provided my father with the sort of interior labyrinth of possibility and doubt that Hladik had. My uncle made a living painting portraits, and if you asked him why he painted portraits rather than landscapes or battle scenes or objects, he said it was because he had nothing to say. Of course, it's impossible to have nothing to say, impossible not to mean something, no matter how muddled or undeveloped; no presentation is completely transparent. Picasso's cubist portrait of Ambroise Vollard—in which the image falls away in smoky shards from the center of the canvas, fragmenting under the weight of the artist's attempt to foreground every element—has much greater formal density than my uncle's painting of my father. Perhaps my uncle only more quietly admitted his inability to show everything.

Yet there is something missing in my uncle's portrait of my father, and I wonder if that thing left out spoke to my father, if it told him anything about himself. In his portrait he wears a goatee rather than a full beard; he's in his early thirties. It is at once a scary and kindly mien: the goatee, the dark hair and sideburns, the thick-framed Buddy Holly–style glasses, and the high forehead cleft by a sharp widow's peak. He wears a forest-green knit shirt, making him look at once professorial, which he was, and cavalier, which he wasn't but always wished he could be. A dark background of thick rusts and browns accents what I always saw as the draconic in my father, but there is still that knit tennis shirt, the large eyes behind the glasses, that little bit of softness and rebellion against a carefully studied and constructed severe self. I've never thought of my father as a person to have his portrait painted. In my reading of my father's face in that picture, he is a man who wants to see what the painting can teach him about himself; he wants to know, not how others see him, but how his view of himself might be somehow incomplete, inaccurate, how he might not be recognizing his own potential; he hopes that each glance at this caught former self will be an added line of dialogue, an externalized and therefore more dynamic and malleable version of a previously internal conversation.

He hopes it will give him the key to remaking his life.

The face, the man in the portrait, intimidates, but in a self-protective rather than an aggressive way. Mostly my father was, despite how he looks in that picture, an optimist, a man who wished, over and over again, with all his might, and with the kind of fear and doubt only a true optimist can realize, for the world to be at least a tolerably fair, just, and accommodating place.

Does my uncle's painting have the kind of meaning Picasso's has? No. My uncle's painting allows me to reconstruct my father too literally. That tennis shirt has accumulated meaning for me, referentiality, is an endless branching of associations constructed of memory and imagination. The painting doesn't force me to do enough work. I don't create anything new as I study it; it is the difference between simile and metaphor. My uncle was right. He had nothing to say. The portrait relies on prefabricated, reconstituted content; by being full, it is empty.

All resemblance, all that I recognize in the rendering overruns and obscures any effect the painting could have on me, or my father for that matter, as an object, as a thing very different from other things I associate with him—the collection of Tarzan first editions, Oreo cookies and milk, my dead grandfather's old three-fingered baseball mitt.

I have the comfort of knowing that when I visit my mother in Ohio, the portrait of my father will be there, and I will appreciate it for allowing me my sentiment, for the shape and weight all its easy associations grant my emotions. It accommodates the formation of a narrative, of a story; it asks to be part of something larger than itself, one facet of an impossibly complex identity.

The Jagers Funeral Home, now fifteen years later, is the same as I remembered it, only more so. My mother made this appointment last night at the hospital, and Joe comes down the hall to meet us as we enter. The Jagerses of the Jagers Funeral Home are Joe and Jerry, brothers who must be in their early sixties. They both wear short-sleeved white oxford cloth shirts with conservative ties. Jerry nods his respects, but hangs back quietly while Joe does the talking. I wonder, as I watch them, if they take turns greeting the grieving, or if, after so many years in this business, they each attend to specific duties. It is Joe who has the rounded features, while Jerry is smaller, more angular, darting. Joe is solid and upright, a stone polished soft by sorrow. Though Mr. Jagers probably knows who "the Hollow children" are, my mother formally introduces us. Mr. Jagers remembers Elizabeth immediately; his son was in her high school class. My mother keeps a comforting hand on my brother, Joseph, who, at twenty-two, is the baby of the family.

Joe Jagers is a tall, friendly-looking man. He ties his tie just about an inch or two too short, so the tip doesn't quite reach his belt buckle. For some reason I find this endearing. He also seems to stand on his heels, his shoulders pulled back as if he's harnessed to an invisible stake and can rove only so far. He leads us into a sitting room, still tilting away as he walks, expertly gauging the space we need, careful not to crowd in or impose himself upon us.

We, the family, sit in a semicircle, my mother and I on a small sofa, Elizabeth and Joseph flanking us in straight-backed chairs. Joe Jagers faces us from across the room, his elbow crooked on a spindly writing table. Jerry Jagers has disappeared into a back office, and I can hear him talking on the phone, his voice muted and unmodulated, a sort of drone.

"First, Mrs. Hollow," Joe Jagers says, "we should decide when you want to have the service, and what sort of service you would like it to be."

"Well, I think it should be tomorrow, don't you?" My mother looks at us all for confirmation. This is something we agreed upon this morning.

"The notice will be in the paper this afternoon," Mr. Jagers says. "Is that enough time?"

"Yes. A lot of the people John worked with at the university are out of town right now. Athens just empties out in August." She studies us again for confirmation, or strength. "Yes. We'd like to have it tomorrow afternoon sometime, if that will work for you all."

"Yes. Anytime tomorrow afternoon." Mr. Jagers seems surprised that we want a service on Friday rather than Saturday, but also a little relieved. "Of course you can have a memorial service anytime after everyone gets back into town."

"That's right." My mother sits on the edge of the sofa. In her hands she holds her folded list of things to do this morning. Joseph hasn't shaved, and, to me, this unscrubbed look connects him still to last night in the hospital, to the room lit only by the insistent white fluoresce of the hallway fixtures, by the red glow of the call button over the bed, by the blinking green of the morphine drip.

I wonder where my father's body is. "Somewhere upstairs" is all I can bring myself to think. Then I wonder, absurdly, if the person who prepares the body for burial will be as shocked and overwhelmed by the extent of my father's disease as we were, as my father was when he finally got the news.

Following Mr. Jagers's practiced lead, we settle some of the details. The service will be at four o'clock, with a visiting hour here at the funeral home from three to four. Reverend Morgan from the Episcopal

Church stops by, looking shattered at first, but calming down quickly as he sees that we are determined to be in control. He agrees to perform a brief service from the Book of Common Prayer.

"So there won't be anything at the grave site, correct?" Joe Jagers asks, looking first at my mother, then at Reverend Morgan.

"We want to bury him in Tennessee," my mother says.

There is nothing apocryphal about hospital lighting. During the day the bright hallways and rooms, with their uniform, unshaded lighting, offer a kind of liminal free passage, an anesthesia against the real essence of hospitals; everything speaks of cleanliness, institutional efficiency, wakeful hope. At night the message is different, but feels just as authentic, just as intentional. The contrast with the outside darkness is not inviting. These are not the ethereal hallways of so-called near death experiences. Nothing about a hospital at night says "Follow the light. Follow the light to rapture and tranquillity, to a dignified, eternal peace." The light isolates the patients in their darkened rooms. The hums, the rhythmic clicks and articulations of the machinery well up to the surface and take over, filching any comfort or rest the dark might provide. And the after-hours visitors feel exposed at night, alien, desperate, and humiliated. Having neither the tangible need of the patients, nor the healing or comforting power of the doctors and nurses and their tools, the visitors must steel themselves for every trip out of the room and into the light, and then must brace and fortify themselves once more when they return and practice again their private art of the word, their personal loving witchery and laying on of hands.

Contexts, associations, connections. Is it a game if there are none, and is it real if there are? My mother spent weeks following my father's death searching through his papers, his books, his computer files for some kind of message. Wasn't there something they could have said to each other that would have brought some sort of closure to thirty-two years together? Why hadn't they realized in time that it was cancer? Why, she asked herself, hadn't she been able to tell him, in the last hours of his life, that he was going to die?

For almost a year after Dad died, I saw only his final twenty minutes, over and over, like a spliced-together loop of videotape in my head. No other memories seemed to exist. Those twenty minutes, compressed, came back morbidly in everything I read, came back in every quiet, voiceless moment of my life.

From Gertrude Stein's 1914 prose poem, *Tender Buttons:*

A CHAIR

> *A widow in a wise veil and more garments shows that shadows are even. It addresses no more, it shadows the stage and learning. A regular arrangement, the severest and the most preserved is that which has the arrangement not more than always authorized.*
>
> *A suitable establishment, well housed, practical, patient and staring, a suitable bedding, very suitable and not more particularly than complaining, anything suitable is so necessary.*
>
> *A fact is that when the direction is just like that, no more, longer, sudden and at the same time not any sofa, the main action is that without a blaming there is no custody. . . .*
>
> *Hope, what is a spectacle, a spectacle is the resemblance between the circular side place and nothing else, nothing else. . . .*
>
> *Pick a barn, a whole barn, and bend more slender accents than have ever been necessary, shine in the darkness necessarily.*
>
> *Actually not aching, actually not aching, a stubborn bloom is so artificial and even more than that, it is a spectacle, it is a binding accident, it is animosity and accentuation.*
>
> *If the chance to dirty diminishing is necessary, if it is why is there no complexion, why is there no rubbing, why is there no special protection.*

A FRIGHTFUL RELEASE

The poem is famous for meaning nothing. Perhaps it's an elaborate cryptogram, this dissociative study of comforting objects, food, and rooms, and for me, in those moments when I must have a context for my father's death, when I must hold off the vivid frames of the videotape, such passages, individual words themselves even, help me shape what I saw and felt into a more occult and diffuse narrative; words presented as shared experience rather than hard image.

        Mr. Jagers keeps recouping things, repeating the details aloud to himself. I can see this worries Elizabeth. She has been a book editor in New York for the six years since she graduated, and she carefully gathered the facts of our father's life early this morning, piecing them together in a short, elegant narrative. She tries to give Mr. Jagers the obituary she has written, but he says he needs to fill out the forms anyway, and that he will be sure to send her text directly to *The Athens Messenger* as soon as we're done here. We go through the expected questions: when and where Dad was born; his full name; his parents' names; brothers and sisters; where he went to college; when he and my mother were married; where he did his graduate work in literature.

Then we get to the matter of my father's two years in the army. Mr. Jagers stops his deliberate writing and repeating.

"Where did he serve?"

"Fort Hood. In Killeen, Texas," my mother says.

"You said 1963 and '64?"

"Yes. That's when we had Pat."

"You know, as a veteran, John is entitled to have a flag displayed at the service."

Elizabeth groans and leans back in her chair, then raises her eyebrows apologetically.

"Oh, I don't think we'll need that," my mother says. "He was director of the motor pool. He had to keep the jeeps and armored cars running, and he wasn't at all mechanically inclined. He hated the army."

"We can display it folded, in a small glass case."

"I don't think so," Elizabeth says.

Mr. Jagers looks, for a moment, startled and slightly bruised by the fight in Elizabeth. "We can place it anywhere, the back of the room," he says. He seems to feel we must not be thinking clearly.

"The back of the room is fine," Elizabeth says.

Mr. Jagers turns back to the forms he's filling out. "And where did you say John's family was from?"

"John's father was from Missouri," my mother says, patiently. Elizabeth looks as though she might scream. Joseph looks like he wants to help answer questions and make decisions, but that everything is just going too fast for him to even try to keep up.

"You know," Mr. Jagers says slowly. "Well, I'll be darned. You know, during the Korean War I was stationed at Fort Leonard, Fort Leonard Wood. That would have been in fifty-two and fifty-three—I'm older than John was—and during weekends I used to get a ride into Rolla, Missouri. Was your husband related to any of the Hollows in that part of Missouri?"

"Well, yes. John's grandfather and grandmother came here in, oh, early nineteen something, and they ended up in Rolla of all places."

"I'll be darned. Would that have been a Jim Hollow?"

My mother laughs. "Sure," she says. "Jim Hollow was John's grandfather."

"They owned a funeral home there in Rolla, you know."

This is a story I've never heard. I know about my father's mother's side of things, how they started the Enns milling company in Inman, Kansas. I know about my grandfather, Walt Hollow—the St. Louis Cardinals signed him out of high school to play baseball for ninety dollars a month, but he turned the offer down to get a degree in petroleum engineering and go out prospecting for oil. I've heard nothing of a funeral parlor. No wonder Dad was such a strange mix of dirgelike earnestness and dreamy discontent. I glance over at Elizabeth and she arches an eyebrow, as if to say, "This is just too weird."

Jerry Jagers checks on us, peering in quietly like a stoic, flightless bird, then vanishing again into the back.

Joe Jagers says, loudly, "Well, I'll be darned."

"There were three brothers," my mother says. "Only one of them stayed in Rolla with Jim."

"You know what I would do? I was only eighteen or nineteen, you know, and I got kind of lonely and homesick out there at Fort Leonard, so I looked in the phone book for funeral parlors, and I could never tell you why I picked that one, but I picked the Hollow Funeral Home and I went to visit them."

"You're kidding."

"I'd get a ride in on weekends and they let me stay there overnight. I'd answer the phones, do other little things. They were real kind to me. I can't believe that's the same Hollows."

I try to picture Joe Jagers as a young man about my brother's age, sitting down to Sunday dinner with my great-grandfather. I realize Mr. Jagers knows parts of my family better than I do.

"I'll be darned," Joe Jagers says. "It really is a small world."

After Fort Hood and the army, my parents moved to Rochester, New York, and then Charlottesville, Virginia. They lived in graduate student housing in both places, and I remember some of the furniture, though I was only three or four years old. There was a big red couch. I remember that because I wore out the springs by jumping up and down on it. There was an old-fashioned wood and cast-iron school desk, with an inkwell and a seat that folded down for the person in front of you. I suppose I remember the desk because, on two separate occasions when we returned from those long visits to family in Tennessee, I ran down the hall to my room, slipped on my cord rug, and bashed out some front teeth on the hand-beveled edge of the writing surface.

I seem to remember furniture, but not rooms. I remember movement and doorways, chosen objects.

We tried to make my father's hospital room more comfortable for the short time he was in it. If we'd had more time, we would have taken him home. There were flowers, of course, and my sister taped to the beige walls some pictures she'd taken at the beach. Last year I gave my father ceramic Calvin and Hobbes figures for Christmas. My mother set them out on the rolling tray table at the foot of the bed. Sam Watterson's comic strip was Dad's favorite, perhaps because Calvin is constantly at the mercy of his own vivid imagination, and is harassed more often than comforted by his lanky and understuffed toy tiger, Hobbes.

When I returned to the hospital the morning of the day my father died, the sun cast a bright square of light across the foot of his bed. Hobbes stood in the sun, but a basket of flowers shaded Calvin. Though my father had a difficult time talking, my mother reported that he had asked her to move Calvin because he was afraid the sun would be in his eyes.

For me, there is a lot in this. My father, as my mother remarked when it was over, remained remarkably calm during the last week of his life. He roused himself when visitors came into the room and made jokes with them, letting them know that he had some fight left in him, even if we were all hovering around "gathering firm for that last Onset." So the request for my mother to move Calvin under the shelter of a bouquet could have been a small gesture of control, a bit of achieved grace in a morning that would later bring news that the tumor had perforated his abdominal wall. It was also an example of how seriously he took what he always viewed as the proprieties of being the father and husband. He never wanted to bring attention to himself, and it was just like him to want us to pay a little attention to Calvin instead.

And I wonder, as strange as it may seem, if my father wanted to be certain that Calvin could see him clearly. With the rest of us so shocked and upset, so rapaciously grim, it must have been cheering to have Calvin survey the situation and remain unfazed. There he was, stalwart as ever in the face of terrifying adversity, beaming and unconcerned.

Joe Jagers leads us upstairs to the coffin room. It is a bare, rectangular room with bright white walls and polyurethaned hardwood flooring. There are fifteen or more coffins on display, all open, and all with "Total Cost" price tags written out on index cards. There are stainless steel coffins, high-carbon-steel coffins, and wooden coffins. The steel coffins look ready for space flight; they have a glistening, airbrushed shine. We pick an oak casket with a subdued finish.

Mr. Jagers says they will take care of everything. They will drive the body to Columbus and put it on a plane that will take it to Memphis, where it will be picked up by the Brownsville Funeral Home. "We just have to make sure there is enough time between connecting flights," Mr. Jagers keeps reminding us. He is pretty sure the body will be in Brownsville by Saturday, but recommends we arrange for a Sunday burial, just in case.

My mother looks at Joe and says, "Now, we want the casket closed during the service tomorrow."

"Are you sure? He'll look just fine."

My mother shakes her head. We agree to bring over clothes later in the afternoon for my father to be buried in. "He asked to be buried in his blue jeans," my mother says. "So that's what he's getting."

From *The States Graphic*—Friday, June 29, 1962:

SOCIETY

Wedding at Home of Parents unites Miss Patton, Mr. Hollow
Elizabeth King Patton, John Walter Hollow, Pledge Vows in Wedding Here Wednesday Morning

In the presence of their immediate families and a few close friends, Miss Elizabeth King Patton and John Walter Hollow were married at ten o'clock Wednesday morning, June 20, in the home of Mr. and Mrs. William Leon Patton, 605 North Washington.

Mr. Hollow is the son of Mrs. Walter Byron Hollow of Dallas, and the late Mr. Hollow.

The Rev. Edward Walenga of Humbolt performed the double ring ceremony before the fireplace which was decorated with bouquets of gladiolus, snapdragons, baby's breath, and greenery in white heirloom vases. Mrs. William H. McDow presented the wedding music, four Schubert Impromptus.

Lovely Bride

Given in marriage by her father, the blond bride wore a dress of candlelight peau de soie, fashioned with a scoop neckline and elbow-length sleeves.

The floor-length skirt fell in soft folds with an obi sash trimmed with lace medallions traced with seed pearls. Her fingertip veil was attached to a small pillbox of matching peau de soie. Her bouquet was of white lilies of the valley, centered with an orchid. Her only jewelry was a simple strand of pearls, the groom's gift to her.

Miss Mary Ann Thompson, daughter of Mr. and Mrs. E. D. Thompson, was maid of honor and the bride's only attendant. She wore a green silk linen dress and carried pale yellow majestic daisies.

John Buford Foley of Wichita, Kansas, was Mr. Hollow's best man.

Mrs. Patton's dress was a sheath of antique white silk, and her corsage was of green orchids.

Mrs. Hollow chose a sky-blue linen jacket dress to which she pinned a white orchid.

Mrs. J. C. Dickinson, maternal grandmother of the bride, wore blue silk with a white orchid.

Mrs. W. B. McConnico, the bride's great-grandmother, was a special guest at the wedding.

After a brief wedding trip, the couple will be at home in Houston, Texas, where the bridegroom is a graduate student at Rice University.

We leave the Jagers Funeral Home and drive down East State Street to the Athens Flower Shop. There we look through a stack of books filled with wreaths and sprays. We don't find anything appropriate, so my mother challenges the woman there to fashion something "loose and thick and a little bit wild" with all different kinds of greenery.

Later that afternoon I drive to Columbus to pick up my wife, who has flown in from upstate New York. By the time we get back to Athens, there is a stack of newspapers on the dining room table, and

Elizabeth has already phoned the *Messenger* to let them know how infuriated she is at the way they botched the obituary.

"It couldn't say what he was really like, and they had to go and ruin what little about him there was," she says.

And she's right. There was no space to say how he liked airplanes, how he liked to build balsa wood and tissue models of World War II fighters. There was no room to speculate about why. Was it because piecing together the models reminded him of a long six months he spent, just after the war, when he was six or seven or eight, sick with rheumatic fever and cooped up inside? Was it that the delicate materials of the airplanes forgave no mistakes? There was no room to write about how he liked trains, the naked, working mechanicals of old steam engines, the impossible, curve-of-the-earth length of modern, five engine series. How he liked to collect antique toy boxcars and piggyback flatcars with advertisements for products such as Gold Medal Flour, and Union 76 gas. There is no mention of how much he liked science fiction or red wine, or the sadness in Bessie Smith, or the sheer mastery in the sound of Sidney Bechet on the clarinet. Somehow the people at *The Messenger* have managed to invent a whole paragraph of activities for my father at the Church of the Good Shepherd; they've misspelled the titles of his books, and rearranged the chronology of his life. They have cut down Elizabeth's long, lamenting sentences into pithy, journalistic fragments.

         Kentucky, on the twelve-hour drives to and from Brownsville, was the easy part of the drive. We often stopped in Bardstown, eating a lunch of pimento cheese sandwiches, potato chips, apples, and warm Cokes, in My Old Kentucky Home State Park. The house, an unspectacular but stately two-story Georgian, stood up on a rise, and I remember the grass being an impossible emerald green, and the huge old trees unfurling dark, rough-edged carpets of shade. On the way into town my father would sing lines of Stephen Foster songs: "Camptown Races," "Swanee River," "My Old Kentucky Home." "Oh, the sun shines bright on my old Kentucky home. 'Tis summer,

the . . ." he'd sing, letting his voice trail off at that point in a face-
tious reminder—though it was a long time before I understood it—to
my mother that there were things about the South we children needed
to be protected from.

After lunch, during the interminable drive across Tennessee, from
Nashville to Memphis, it was time for the Disassociation Game. Elizabeth seemed to have an endless supply of dissociated things stored
away. At least that's how my male brain tried to explain the ease with
which she blurted out her answers. I was the one who had to plan for
the game, had to have prepared responses. She cleared her mind while
I filled mine up, and her responses, the strange metaphors she constructed, were much more interesting than mine. I was clever at decod-
ing the associations, or, rather, at inventing the connections. I could
build bridges, set up ladders to get from one point to another, but had
a difficult time creating something whole and new.

The physics equivalent of Elizabeth's metaphors would be singu-
larity. No before, no context, no cause necessary. She discarded the
usual model of fusing two known elements to create something new or
reveal new properties of the old, and instead continuously smashed
together the pristine and the unalloyed. The resultant particles formed
little, short half-life artifacts, white-hot tracers of surprise as bits of her
unconscious vented out into the air. Words and objects presented to the
world free of all sentiment and meaning. New ways to see, new ways
to feel.

We get to the funeral home early, well before
the three o'clock visiting hour. The Jagers brothers greet us at the
door again, and Joseph gives Jerry Jagers a tape of Pete Fountain
clarinet tunes. He spent the previous evening trying to pick out and
record my father's favorite jazz pieces. But after Cole Porter's "Let's
Misbehave" made my mother cry, we settled for an all Pete Fountain
background during the visiting hour, and then Louis Armstrong's
"The Faithful Hussar" to be played as we all file out at the end of the
service. My mother has worried, in a flitting, unconvincing way, that

Louis Armstrong isn't appropriate for a funeral, though my father always said to her, happily, as he washed the dishes after dinner, and blared the song over the kitchen speakers, "I want you to play this song at my funeral."

And so there he is, in the closed oak casket on a dais at the near end of the room. He's wearing his jeans and a comfortable knit shirt and a favorite sweater, and we plan to play his favorite song. The spray is wild and wonderful. It droops and sprawls over the wood, an intricate weaving of vegetable textures and foliate hues. On plant stands beside the coffin are more flower arrangements and wreaths. They come from California, from Tennessee, Texas, Kansas, some from friends of Elizabeth's in New York, some from friends of mine here in Athens and in Columbus.

Elizabeth takes the glass-encased flag and hides it in a back corner of the room. I guess that there are a hundred folding chairs set up.

The room starts to fill with people. People hug and kiss. The sound of voices in my ears is subdued and ringing. People I haven't seen in years show up. They have sad, cautious, kindly expressions. I find myself feeling genuinely happy to see them. They approach me, shake hands, and say how sorry they are, and I hear myself say, "David, Andy, Steve, it's great to see you."

"I just wish it could be under different circumstances," they say, standing a little away from me.

"No," I want to tell them. "No. Don't be sorry. Tell me what's happening with you, what's changed, what's new in your life? It's a beautiful afternoon," I want to say. "Let's get out of here and shoot some baskets. Let's have a beer."

A memory recently returned to me by time petrified, stone for tissue, like a fossil:

I'd always loved to run at night. I remember being ten and eleven years old, and even after a summer morning spent weeding the cracks in the driveway, a long afternoon swimming at the city pool, I would go out in the evening when the sky turned purple and the streetlamps came on. I'd run around the block, run over to the playground, run around and around the school building, veer off down our street or some other, right down the center. It might have been the stillness of the air at night, I don't know. I felt faster at night, running through pools of phosphorescent light, my striding shadow circling me like the gnomon of a sundial—traveling through time, days clicking off in seconds, light to dark, light to dark, light to dark.

I ran track in high school. The quarter-mile relay, the high jump, the 220-yard dash, the quarter mile. I don't remember my parents coming to many meets, but that may be my angry adolescence distorting things. My senior year, though, they did come to the Athens Relays, the first big meet of the season. Many teams participated, so the events started in the afternoon and went on into the night. I won the high jump, ran the first leg of the quarter-mile relay. It started to get cold. I have a picture in my head of my father, up in the rickety stands, English driving cap on, hands in his pockets, hunching up his shoulders to keep warm. My legs were cold and tight for the 220, and I dove at the finish line, coming in second, skidding on the cinder track. Fourteen years later, I still have cinders in my back and under the skin over my kneecaps. The team trainer took me into the field house to clean me up; I stayed in there to keep warm, asking him to come fetch me for the mile relay, the last event of the meet. I don't know if my parents thought I was done for the night or if they just got too cold and left. When I came out to anchor the mile relay, they were gone. Almost all the spectators had left. Most of the athletes had packed up their stuff and boarded the buses off in the parking lot. I don't remember any cheering, just the bite of the runners' steel spikes as they strode past. I took the baton in second place, behind by seventy or eighty yards. An impossible distance. When I hit the back stretch, I went from thinking I'd never catch the guy to knowing—to seeing—the exact spot under the stadium lights where I would come up on his shoulder and pass him.

I remember being angry and scared. I had four medals around my neck, and had the Outstanding Athlete trophy crooked up between the passenger seat and the door, where I could glance at it as I drove. The road was dark and the headlights didn't seem to reach past the front end of the car. I was so angry at my parents, at my father, for missing that last race. I was so terrified I might get in an accident and die before I could show my father the trophy, I'd guess I drove the ten miles from the high school back home slower than I could have run it.

My father loved that story.

We linger after the service. The prayers felt right, and the readings were fine—chosen and presented by three of his colleagues. Louis Armstrong closed things on a more personal note. We gather the guest book, which turns out to have over two hundred names in it, and my mother asks Mr. Jagers to deliver the flowers we don't have room for to the nursing home.

We are about to leave, when Joe Jagers comes down the hall from his office. He stops in front of my mother, still leaning away from her as always.

"I wanted to show you this," he says, and he hands her a stationery-sized, white plastic clipboard. Green lettering across the top of the clipboard says THE HOLLOW FUNERAL HOME.

"You kept this all these years," my mother says.

"I knew I had it somewhere. I went back to my office and dug around and there it was."

"Well, they must have been really nice to you." My mother hands the clipboard back. "I'm glad you showed that to me."

We get outside, and the afternoon sun stretches our shadows out long and prayer-thin. My mother takes my arm and I walk her to the car. "Don't you think it's nice," she says, "that Mr. Jagers had that connection to your father?"

We bury my father late Sunday morning, at Brownsville's Oakwood Cemetery. He is laid to rest in the family plot, head to head with his father-in-law. Earlier in the morning it rained, but now the sun is out, and tall, gleaming white clouds hover low in the sky. It is as if we are all part of a cartoon, and the clouds are our enormous thought-bubbles. We huddle under a tarp, and as Reverend Joe Thornton speaks, the following things happen: a rush of wind whips at the canvas, sending down a mist of sun-warmed rainwater; a train sounds its whistle as it charges toward a crossing outside town; and, as the reverend finishes and we stand to leave, a jet roars over-head, its vapor trail scarring the sky.

The Second Divorce

LAURA PHILPOT BENEDICT

*My second husband left me. One spring evening
I came* home from work to find a brief note on the kitchen table, and
his robe and toothbrush gone from the bathroom. Every day for a
week I'd come home to find something else of his missing: suits and
ties, socks, shirts, videos, suitcases, shaving gear, baseball gear, and
finally, his tattered Indians cap. He wouldn't take my calls at work.
The note he left on the first day was our only means of communica-
tion. I wrote on it, below his words, asked him to call me to talk. But
instead there was only another reply on the paper. Over the week, the
paper filled on both sides until the margins were gone, sentences
curved around its corners; it looked like something passed back and
forth between two junior-high kids. That paper must have been the
documented measure of our cooling-off period, because when it was
filled up we were finally able to talk to each other in hushed voices
over the phone. I still have the sheet, folded into quarters and stuffed in

the manila envelope that contains the paper trail of my life, including the decree of my first divorce. I haven't looked at it since I stuck it in there because the things we wrote to each other are too naked in their pain. It's shameful stuff.

Every marriage has its beginning, middle, and end. Here is the end of this one: I deserved to be left. Two months before I had gone away for an *all-girls* vacation on Hilton Head Island and had a brief affair with a man I met there. My husband Eric found out about it. He left.

There was bound to be a second divorce. I had known, standing at the altar, even as I promised before God and the assembled company that I would be joined to Eric forever, that I was making a mistake. I'd had feelings of doubt at my first wedding too. Only I was eighteen then, and no one, not a single friend of mine or family member thought that particular marriage was a good idea. But the second wedding was much-anticipated, and far more elaborate, with brides-maids and families and caterers and a bitchy, expensive photographer. Calling it off in the middle of the ceremony would have been extremely embarrassing. I confess I was hopeful too, that I was wrong, that everything would turn out fine and we would buy a house, have children, and grow old *together*.

People in my family stay married. My parents, my grandparents, aunts and uncles, cousins. Rumor has it that my paternal grandfather was married and divorced quite young, many, many years ago, but there are hints of mystery surrounding it, and no one will tell me the details. And I wonder sometimes at the content of my maternal grand-parents' marriage. I have the sense that it was an uneasy arrangement, and I recall a lot of tension in their house, but I never, ever heard even a suggestion that the two of them would part before death. And even though my parents argued vigorously within the hearing of my sisters and me, the word *divorce* was never used. I come from working-class, predominantly Catholic stock, but there is nothing magical about that mix when it comes to marriage. I prefer to think that my family is just *good people*. My first divorce meant that I had already failed to measure up to my family history, so, maybe a tiny part of me expected to fail again.

. . .

His third-floor one-bedroom apartment in a hip but deliciously dangerous St. Louis neighborhood.

Our second date. We dance to Nat King Cole with the slowness of ritual. My fingers slide over his sharkskin suit. We are a little drunk on sake. He has taken me out for my first sushi dinner. A seven-foot-high pastel face of Quetzalcoatl (a fiberglass set piece he salvaged from an industrial show) looms behind us. We make love all night on his futon. In the morning he cooks omelets and tells me that no woman has ever dumped him, and that what he really wants to do is leave his corporate job and be an artist.

Light-haired and slender, Eric looked like he could have been my brother rather than my husband. There are other adjectives that come to mind when I think of him: immature, cunning, innocent but sometimes cruel, inflexible. But those are adjectives jaundiced by my own insecurities. When I met him, I was overwhelmed by his *cool*. He worked among the corporate suits, but was brilliant at not appearing to be one of them. In him I saw a beat poet, although he never wrote. In him I saw a tortured artist crying for release. A tiny sun room perched at the end of his apartment served him as a studio, where he worked in pastels and charcoal. After college he had tramped around Europe for a summer; he showed me the notebooks he had filled with sketches of buildings and people, their forms suggested by lines that looked frayed and broken, as though by a sudden wind. Within the company we worked for, a company that was, in fact, packed with designers, graphic artists, photographers, and multimedia production types, he was the one true romantic. I was warned, I confess, by even his close friends, that he wasn't what he seemed to be. I wanted to tell them that *I* wasn't what I seemed to be, and, in fact, who was? In him I saw the suave sophistication of a post–World War I man-about-town—I saw myself as Nora to his Nick Charles. If I saw it, it was real enough for me.

Our courtship was erratic. I worked long hours. My primary entertainment was working out five days a week at a fitness studio. This was something new to me. I reveled in the exertion and the sweat. Most of all, I loved the effect on my body, the careful sculpting of my muscles: I developed gently rounded calves, firm triceps, and a taut stomach. It was exhilarating. I felt primed, particularly for an intensely physical sexual relationship with a man. My best friend Maggie and I spent long hours in Central West End bars dancing, nursing beers, and talking about nothing and everything. At home I read books from the University City public library and slept off hangovers. From the beginning Eric made it clear that he was *busy.* He played baseball, went to the batting cages, spent time with his musician friends, did his artwork. I let him call me when he was available. I never asked him for dates. This was a man I wanted, and long experience had taught me that pursuing a man will only drive him away.

For a month we played what my grandmother would have called a game of *come away closer,* until, finally, he was convinced, and we got down to the serious business of courting. We took long walks in wooded places. We went to parties where we would talk to no one but each other, our bodies magnetically close, then leave early. We cooked for each other, tried Thai food together, adopted a favorite Italian restaurant, complete with accordion player, plastic grapes, and peeling murals. We gave up smoking together. We talked *possibilities:* trips to Europe, graduate school (for him), living in Boston or London or Barcelona, how my furniture would look in his apartment. We stood on the riverbank in evening clothes and watched the sun rise over East St. Louis. We held hands at the movies. We went to the zoo.

A private New Year's Eve party at a downtown bar.

I wear a dress that I consider devastating. He has been cool and standoffish all night. The band is dreadful and I want to leave. A few minutes before midnight the band stops and someone turns on the giant television. Times Square, almost 1986. The ball drops and Eric pulls me into a dark corner and whispers in my ear that he loves me. The moment has the feel of a well-rehearsed play, but his kiss is tender and I am smitten anyway.

After deciding that it was foolish to keep paying rent on two apartments when mine had become nothing more than a place for me to launder and change my clothes, we found and rented an apartment together. (Coincidentally built in 1933, it had hardwood floors, vaulted ceilings, bizarre molded plaster ornaments, and mullioned windows. It had surely been chic beyond belief in its day. I was in heaven.) From the moment our furniture was commingled, the question *will we marry?* hung in the air. We were firmly and resolutely in love.

Elephant Rocks, a park an hour out of town.
I know why we are going to Elephant Rocks. As we drive, we both pretend that I don't. The sky is clear and the wind is sharp and it is not quite winter. The rocks in the park are like giant bird eggs half-buried in the earth, smooth, gray, and shell-white with horizontal striations. A frothy, quick-moving stream cuts through the rocks, dividing the park into jagged halves. There are lots of other tourists climbing over the rocks, parents and children, a gang of college students, hip in their grunge clothes, backward baseball caps, limp ponytails. He leads me from rock to rock until he finally selects one, and turns me so my back is to the wind. When it's over and he has asked me to marry him, and put the ring that we had chosen together weeks before on my finger, it is time to leave. He suggests that we jump the four feet across the stream instead of going all the way back to the bridge. Without warning, he jumps nimbly over to the other side, but I am afraid, and hang back. The college kids are standing near him and they urge me on. One of the young men holds his hand out and I take it. I jump, the lower half of my body slapping against the far rock as I fall. The young man pulls me out. Everyone laughs except Eric and me. As we drive back to town I shiver in my wet jeans and think about omens.

. . .

It was a beautiful wedding. My parents poured all the energy and enthusiasm into it that they hadn't been able to muster for my first wedding. Eric's parents very generously paid for the reception at their country club, so I was able to be extravagant with dresses, flowers, decorations, and music. We had a string quartet play during dinner. The color scheme was ivory and black (in that my dress was ivory-colored raw silk, and the bridesmaids wore black velvet), the flowers were rare and tropical and jewel-toned. Eric and the grooms-men were dashing and elegant in their deep gray dinner jackets. The cake had the thinnest, most delightful spreading of sweet raspberry jam between each layer. The whole evening was spectacular. Everyone said so.

Cancún in February. The honeymoon.

We sit on the beach in our wool clothes, waiting for our hotel room to be ready. Eric is dressed all in black, like a refugee from a funeral. His skin is pale and even more fair than my own. We are ice people out of place among the thatched cabanas and the thong bikinis and the endlessly blue water. The first four days of our stay we are too hot and too sick to make love, and when we finally do it is only because we are leaving and it would feel too much like failure if we didn't.

Everything after the honeymoon happened in perfect order. I got a raise at work. Eric left his dead-end multimedia job and got a new job selling and designing media systems for a small, aggressive company. We talked about buying a house. We both agreed that we didn't want children right away, but we wanted a place big enough for a growing family. One Sunday we mentioned our plans to his parents. They were thrilled, and seemed determined to get us into a place of our own as soon as possible.

Eric's mother didn't like me from the start. Given my generally low self-esteem, I could hardly blame her, but I couldn't dislike her for it; I could only wish that it weren't so. She was an amazingly industrious homemaker who had stood by her husband through some hard financial times, designed and built their dream house, raised three children, took good care of elderly relatives, and put her laundry in the car each week and drove it to the Laundromat to wash and dry it even though she could have afforded a thousand washers and dryers. She was a tough woman. I don't know what she saw when she looked at me. She knew I'd been divorced. I was marrying her youngest, dearest son. I changed hairstyles almost weekly. I suspect she thought I was prissy, and not at all her sort of person. Eric's father was different. He was charming and courtly, and at the same time flirtatious. The pictures from his youth show him to be a handsomer version of Eric, Jr. The fact that I was young and blue-eyed and slightly flirtatious myself seemed to win his approval.

In short, they made it possible for us to buy a house. I think now that it didn't have a happy effect on their son. He lost all enthusiasm for the project when they got involved. We never talked about it, but I think he would've liked to have done it on his own: saved the down payment, negotiated the mortgage, attend the official inspection. When his parents got involved, he bowed out, and left it in their capable hands.

Tulsa, Oklahoma. His sister's house.
I watch Eric push his nephew on a swing. He is the relaxed visiting uncle, joking with his older sister, who looks a lot like me: blond and thin and vaguely Germanic. I think that he and I will someday have slight, towheaded children who will be tiny versions of ourselves. I think that he will not like to have children interrupt his life.

I wish I could pinpoint some moment in our brief marriage when things began to go wrong. I fear that something was wrong from the beginning. We were just half a beat off the whole time. It was as though we each had similar programs in our heads, programs that prescribed how our lives were supposed to go: careers, dating, marriage, house, children, children to college, retirement, death. He was always fighting that program, and at the same time living it. I believe he honestly and sincerely wanted to be an artist instead, but he was too afraid of disappointing his family, and himself. I can't really say for sure though, because I never got the chance to ask him. Me, I had already screwed up the program once, and so was too intently focused on getting it right the second time to realize that the things that had drawn me to him—his art, his imagination, his ambition to create and be recognized for it—were the same things that needed to be nurtured in me. Neither of us belonged on the program.

We had no activities in common. Physical fitness and books weren't for him, baseball wasn't for me. Our conversation at home was mostly limited to gossip about our workplaces. I needed something new, some sort of intellectual stimulation. I had been writing most of my life, in journals, mostly. It was erratic, foolish stuff, but I decided to take it more seriously and I went back to college for some writing classes. I wrote story after story, most of them implausible tales about twisted old women or mountain people or troubled children. My first story came back to me with an A plus, and I was elated. I gave it to Eric to read; he was unimpressed. No. Unimpressed is not the word. More like unaffected. In fact, he looked vaguely puzzled. *What do you want?* he asked. *Are you thinking of getting another degree?* I didn't bother to show him any more stories.

The company Christmas party in the gymnasium of a downtown Catholic school.

We argue about nothing on the way there. He is effortlessly handsome in his dark suit. After dinner I see him sitting at a back table with a woman. She is dark: dark eyes, dark hair, dark red lipstick, dark breasts that well up from a deep red dress. Their chairs are side by side, but his body is angled toward hers, and hers to his, like two conspirators. Her darkness swallows the brightness of his smile: a shy, self-deprecating smile that begins in his eyes and gently pulls up the corners of his mouth, a smile I recognize from the days when he would lean over my desk, asking me for a date, just one date. They dance once, pressed close, and I watch, hypnotized, as though I'm seeing some fantastic illusion. Others stare at them. I cry in the bathroom. I dance and flirt with a married friend who is very drunk, hoping Eric will notice. The band is packing up its instruments when I finally approach their table. They shake hands good-bye. Her smile for me is innocence itself. On the way home he is silent, and I take it as a dare for me to cry, scream, accuse, but I decide to be terribly clever and attempt to unnerve him by talking about how bad the food was instead.

The idea that Eric might be actually unfaithful to me, or I to him, honestly never occurred to me in all the time we were together. Call it egomania on my part, or, perhaps, faith. After we split up, friends came forward and offered evidence against him, but I was too consumed with my own guilt to give a damn.

The guilt started in Hilton Head. Eric saw me into the van of the woman who was driving us there in the cool of an early March morning. He stood sleepy and barefoot in the dewy grass, wearing jeans and a ripped T-shirt. He kissed me good-bye on the forehead like an indulgent father. I fretted over what he would eat while I was gone, and whether or not he could keep the cat from escaping the house, but he shut the van door and waved us off.

There's something about the company of a group of women that brings out the worst in me. I don't trust most women. I know too many of them to be insincere and calculating. They keep secret agendas that I find too hard to guess at. I know the secret language, how a deferential *I just love your dress* can actually mean *I bow to your greater charm and beauty and will stay out of your way, so please don't pick on me this evening* or *Personally, I wouldn't be caught dead in such a rag* or twenty or thirty other awful things. Women are born with internal knowledge of this language. But imagine five women together, engaged in constant conversation for a week, with mountains of subtext beneath every word, every sentence, every gesture. It was unbearable, and I was overwhelmed. Within hours I was reduced to the quavering teenager that I had once been, the girl who forever hovered around cliques of girls who had no interest in her. I had no fashion sense, no handsome older brother, no money, no talent for volleyball or cheer-leading, no clue how to apply eye shadow. The one thing I had that they didn't was a steady stream of boyfriends, and that was because I was willing to offer sex for companionship and affection, and they weren't. And so, finding myself all grown-up and far from home, a home where affectionate attention had, for the most part, disappeared, and in the company of too many women, I fell back on old, old habits. I took up with a man.

I won't go into the ugly details. He was low dog in the pack of other young males he ran with. He was four years younger than I, wiry, and just this side of ugly, and he had a peculiar habit of wearing a red bandana tied tightly around his head, day or night. He was everything my pitifully low self-esteem demanded.

Although none of the other women had behaved as I had (most of the fun had been of the flirtatious, innocent sort) before we went home we swore one another to secrecy like the teenagers we had become. Later I sat wedged into the back of the van, my knees to my chin, looking out the window and wondering when and how Eric would find out what I'd done.

Before I was home a day, the guilt made me physically ill. I couldn't keep down any food, and my bowels were cramped and liquid. I thought about dying: suicide, accident, lightning bolts. I unpacked immediately; usually I'd have suitcases sitting around for at least a week. The house got a thorough cleaning: furniture vacuumed or waxed, cupboards cleaned out, windows washed. The place had never looked so good.

Life with Eric was outwardly no different from before. We went to work, came home, ate together, watched television or worked in the yard. I'd always had secrets from him, things I wasn't quite ready to tell him, bits of myself I was too ashamed to reveal, and I knew he was the same way. He didn't like to answer questions about himself. I had learned that early on. I think it was part of his mystique.

Finally, though, I had to tell someone. Yes, there had certainly been witnesses to my infidelity on the island (one of whom was the wife of Eric's only brother). I had made sure of that. What I was desperate to do was to confess. Confessing the thing would have named it. Naming a thing bestows it with reality and substance and truth. These many years later, I am reminded of the story of Cain and Abel. Cain lies when God asks him where his brother is. But instead of striking Cain down without a word, he names Cain's crime of murder before assigning punishment, or, further, showing mercy. I had to name my crime before I could move on to the consequences.

I had been back almost two weeks, and I was a wreck. The lack of food and my stepped-up exercise program meant that I was light-headed all the time, and I couldn't concentrate on work. One afternoon I left the office early and went to the bar where Maggie was working. It was after the lunch crowd had gone, three college kids sat drinking soda in a corner booth, and a woman in her fifties with hundreds of silver bracelets up and down her arms sat at the bar sipping white wine and watching satellite TV. I sat on a barstool, my hands shaking. I had bought a pack of cigarettes from the machine and I smoked one after another. Maggie sat with me at her break and I told her everything. I'll never forget the shock in her voice when she asked me if I was joking. I realized then that I'd crossed some sort of line. I was an adulteress. It was yet another milestone for me that distanced me from the rest of my family and the civilized world. I could never go back.

Our house, a Wednesday evening.

He has gone straight from work to the studio space he rents from a photographer friend. I call and the line is busy. I call every fifteen minutes. At midnight I imagine someone has broken into the building. I imagine he is hurt. At one o'clock I want to call the police, but I know Eric would be embarrassed for me to do that. At two o'clock I consider driving to the studio, but I am too afraid. The busy signal is so familiar that I listen to it carefully for minutes on end to see if it varies or is trying to impart some sort of important information to me. At two-thirty I fall asleep on the couch. At four-thirty the sound of his key in the lock awakens me. He looks

*tired and surprised, tells me he and a buddy went for drinks across the river.
"Across the river" means strip bars, but I am too relieved to see him alive
to be angry. We go to bed.*

The two months in between my infidelity and
Eric's leaving are almost impossible for me to describe. I was a poor
actress. Our relationship deteriorated to the point that we never dis-
agreed about anything. He spent almost every evening at the studio he
had rented downtown. I was desperately afraid that I had contracted
herpes or AIDS or venereal disease or syphilis or genital warts or some
other hideous disease from the man I'd been with, and I couldn't bear
the thought of passing it on to Eric, and so I made excuses when he
wanted to make love.

The idea that I could not share my body and my deepest self with
the person I had married—the person to whom I had been joined so
that we were to be of one mind and one heart—led me to despair. I felt
despicable and sinful and unworthy. I remember lying alone on our
marriage bed thinking, *This is what it feels like to be trash.*

A Monday in early June, almost the end.
*He takes me for a ride around the neighborhood in his new car when I
get home from work. I hadn't known he was buying a new car. That night,
instead of fixing dinner, I tell him I have been unfaithful with a stranger.
He sleeps on the couch in the family room. I lie awake in our bed until
morning.*

In my first marriage, I had been the one to
leave. I moved out on April Fool's Day, thinking myself terribly
clever.

The way I see it, everyone is entitled to one mistake in marriage. A
marriage is too complex a thing, too demanding for the very young. I
was first married a month after my eighteenth birthday, and divorced

just before my twenty-first. My twenty-year-old husband and I had three things in common: sex and drugs and youth. Not much to base a marriage on, though I will say that we loved each other in the solid, innocent, true way that only adolescents can love: with blind confidence in each other and, more important, the concept of love. But that kind of love is easily tarnished and disillusioned because it is rarely flexible. It is incapable of the transformation that marriage demands.

Michael and I moved in together the summer after I got out of high school. My parents were moving away, and I wanted badly to stay in Louisville. *Whatever you do,* my mother said, *don't get married. You're too young.* It was, of course, for a rebellious eighteen-year-old, tantamount to an order to marry him.

Our wedding, on reflection, was both sweet and pathetic. I bought my dress on sale at J. C. Penney for seventy-five dollars. My attendant wore a borrowed prom dress. Michael wore rented white tails. We had only fourteen guests; they sat scattered among the pews, looking tiny and insignificant in the cavernous Baptist church. Michael's father took the wedding pictures because we couldn't afford a professional photographer. I still have them, stored in the same envelopes the Walgreens people put them in.

One picture is an eloquent illustration of the way things were that day. It is a shot looking back into the church from the front, and all the guests are in it, and none of them are smiling. Michael's mother sits at one end of the front pew, and my mother is at the other, with about fifteen feet between them. Michael's mother is wearing her corsage, looking a little vague (she was vain about wearing her eyeglasses), and my mother stares straight ahead, looking past the camera. My father-in-law must have noted the sad nature of the picture he had just taken, because in the next picture in the stack, my mother and mother-in-law are sitting cozily together in the center of the pew, looking at the camera with laughing, nervous smiles.

The ceremony was brief. As Michael put the gold band on my hand, I remember thinking, *What am I doing here? What if we are too young?* I could hear my closest friend Julia sobbing audibly from the back pew.

Michael was a carpenter. I loved that he worked with his hands. He would come home from work dirty and exhausted. I loved to do his laundry. I loved to go to the grocery store, and come home to make thrifty, nutritious dinners. I loved to lie next to him in our water bed and run my hand over the muscles in his arms and back. We were young and poor and married, and I thought it was all very romantic.

Rather than start college right away, I spent four months working at a dry cleaner, ironing men's shirts. It was miserable, hot work, and I earned only three fifty an hour. I did it as some kind of penance, I think, for rejecting what I thought my parents wanted for me: college first, then marriage to someone much higher up on the food chain than a blue-collar worker.

The job didn't last long. Even though I found some small satisfaction in completing my work each day, I was desperate to go to school. But I think the job wasn't a complete waste of time. I was ready for college, and I was ready to appreciate it.

I have never asked Michael for his explanation of why our marriage broke up. Education, I think, was one of the things that drove us apart. My ambition was another. I never lost respect for Michael and his work. He was good at his job, he was in demand. There was never a doubt in my mind that someday he would build his own business and become what I, and my parents, considered to be a success. (He did, of course, in the years after I left.) I was ambitious for him. And even though I respected him, I began to push, to try to make him the sort of person I thought he should be. I wanted him to dress better when we went out. I wanted him to go to museums and college events with me. I wanted him to go to college, like me. I was at my most arrogant, wanting to mold him into the man that would be worthy of the woman I wanted to become.

He responded to the pressure by drawing into himself and ignoring me. I found myself having loud, one-sided arguments. I screamed at him, threw things; once it was an open green-bean can that missed his head by an inch and left a nasty gash in the wall. He developed stomach ulcers, and aggravated them by drinking too much. I gave up smoking marijuana because it made me feel out of control, and I was afraid of being arrested; he smoked more because he wanted the escape.

We were never unfaithful to each other. We didn't want to be. For all our immaturity, we loved and respected each other a great deal.

In the end, we just both gave up. I remember the afternoon I decided to leave. I was talking to Julia on the phone, and she asked me if I was unhappy. I burst into tears, and told her that *yes, I was miserable*. Three days later, her boyfriend helped me move out. I had told Michael that morning that I was leaving, but I don't think he believed me.

My recovery from that divorce was emotionally expensive. Ask any divorced person and he or she is likely to tell you that few friendships survive a divorce, regardless of whether or not the friendships involve mutual friends of the divorcing parties. Unless they're sadists, friends don't like to see their friends suffer. And so, finding myself alone, I turned to my family. I moved from Louisville to St. Louis to live with my parents, dropping out of my junior year of college. It was a tough year. But they gave me what I needed, and I was able to finish school and restart my life without hardship. I hope, too, that I gave them back something of myself in that time: a less angry and more loving self than had left home three years before.

Perhaps the most important part of my recovery came through a year of professional therapy. It began a process of self-discovery for me that I have cultivated and developed continuously since then.

I'll never be *over* the ending of that marriage. I don't want to be. It lives enshrined within me; it is the constant companion of the troubled young woman that I was. It is her comfort. The memory of it belongs to the woman I am now only as a piece of treasured jewelry would; it is an enhancement, a reward, sometimes a decoration.

It is the second divorce that is the unforgivable one.

Tuesday morning, before work.
I sit on the stairs in my bra and panties. Eric stands looking up at me from the living room. He is dressed for work, holding his car keys. I want

us to stay home and talk. He says we will talk after work, and I believe him. He leaves.

Eric wasn't coming back to me. I knew instinctively that I had wounded him in the worst way a woman can wound a man. I had played him for a fool—unintentionally of course. I imagined, in my own misguided way, that I had given him a gift: his freedom. He didn't have to do a thing. I didn't want to know if he'd been unfaithful to me. I wanted all the guilt for myself.

I don't believe that I cuckolded him only because I was bored and lonely and I'm a rotten person. But that's what I wanted him to think. I know it's what his family thinks. Fine. I know it is far more complicated than that. My act, and my confession, came at him from out of left field because there was no precedent for it. I was faithful to him, until I wasn't. I didn't even think about other men. I didn't think about the man I was unfaithful with. I just did it. I remember my sister-in-law saying to me in Hilton Head that she thought I was mentally ill, that something was seriously wrong with me, that she'd seen me change overnight into a stranger. Those days and nights on the island (which is not a tropical, dreamy sort of place at all, but more like an upscale Atlanta suburb dropped on a beach), I did have a sense of not being myself, of watching myself be defiled from a distance. At the same time, I knew the concupiscent nature of my actions. My lover was skilled and generous. My body was definitely alive to his attentions.

Committing adultery was akin to dying and being reborn for me. The moment my lips met those of my lover, Laura, Eric's wife, died, and Laura, the adulteress, was born. I get to live with that bit of self-knowledge for the rest of my life.

I went to work like a zombie, going through the motions of my job. I kept the door to my office closed all the time because I never knew when I was going to burst into tears. My grieving for our marriage started right away because I knew there would be no reconciliation. And on top of the grief, I experienced a vast sense of failure. I would have rather pulled my fingernails out one by one than acknowledge that I had failed at something.

As he quietly removed traces of himself from our house, Eric never took any of our common belongings. I think he was sending me a message: I'm not taking anything else because it needs to be here, where I can claim it when you're gone. And so things stayed where they were, gathering dust. The house was like a corpse I couldn't quite approach: if I changed anything about it, it might be profaned.

After two weeks had passed and we had finally begun to communicate by telephone about checking accounts and canceled plans, I began to feel like a squatter, living in someone else's house.

Eric was staying with his parents. I wondered what he told them about me. I imagined their conversation and their silences. I imagined that I could feel their anger and their hurt.

What I wanted was to be with my own family again. I wanted an understanding sister with a shoulder I could cry on, a childhood bedroom with faded floral wallpaper, and a closet where I'd written on the walls when I was four. But even if any of my family had been living in St. Louis at the time, I wouldn't have gone to them. I told them over the phone that Eric and I had split up. I didn't tell them why. I couldn't stand the thought of their being ashamed of me. My family has always been intensely worried about what other people think of them, or at least what they imagine other people think of them. Keeping them ignorant of what Eric's family and friends were saying about me could only be a good thing as far as I was concerned. We're not a close-knit bunch, but we're big on sparing each other pain.

A good friend at work said I could move in with her for a while, but she lived in a house with furniture and carpeting that was, for the most part, pure white and antiseptic; I couldn't bring the sopping, ugly mess of my life with its dirty secrets and loose ends onto that sparkling, brilliant stage. What I really wanted was a cave, or some hideous vermin-filled tenement. But I'm no romantic heroine. I wasn't up to punishing myself so completely.

My first desire was to escape our comfy suburb. There were apartments nearby that I might have afforded: fresh, anonymous, planned communities for single people, places with names like Seven Oaks and Indian Trace. But I needed something different. I needed a neighborhood where people had roots because I had none of my own. I looked in University City, where I had lived when I met Eric, but everything I looked at there had an air of menace about it. My perception was due, surely, to my own fragile state, or perhaps it was that in one of the nearby houses the mother of a friend of ours had recently been murdered, stabbed by her husband of some years. I don't know.

I finally found what I was looking for on the Hill, an old Italian working-class neighborhood. The apartment was the downstairs unit of a 1940s duplex. The day I moved in, several neighbors helped me unload my car and brought me food. I felt like I had come home.

After I left my first husband, I went on a sexual binge that lasted two years. This time I didn't even bother looking for answers or comfort in temporal diversions. Two things brought me to a place where I could even begin to see the end of my pain and the beginning of my life: therapy and prayer.

I went back to the same therapist I had seen after my first divorce. Instead of the one-on-one sessions I expected, he put me into a group. I was reluctant. I don't like talking about my private life in front of strangers. But after a few weeks, I found that I was learning to listen as well as learning to talk. No one condemned me, and they wouldn't let me condemn myself. As I talked and listened, I discovered that I didn't necessarily need to try to make sense of the previous few months, but instead I needed to acknowledge and treat my own suffering, regardless of whether or not I considered it self-inflicted.

Soon after I moved into my new neighborhood, I started taking long evening walks. It was summer and people sat on their porches talking, or just watching the cars pass by. When it got dark, they went inside, and I could see their lives through their lighted windows. I liked that. As I walked, I began to notice the churches on my routes. Then I found myself looking for churches. I found four Catholic churches, one Episcopalian, and one Presbyterian. The Presbyterian church was the brightest, grandest, and most intimidating; the others were all small, on tiny plots of land, but built of large, carefully hewn stones. I would mount their stairs, try the doors. They were always locked on those evenings. I wanted just one of those doors to be open so I could go inside and pray. I didn't want a Sunday congregation. I wanted my own private audience with God. It was a romantic notion, but it kept me walking and walking, trying one church after another. For weeks I walked almost every evening, but not so much as building maintenance was going on in any one of them.

One evening in early August I sat on the steps of St. Mark's Episcopal Church, letting the dusk fall around me. A light, cleansing breeze brushed my face, and I was chilled. Suddenly, I knew my walks were over, and that I would never see the inside of any of those churches. I realized that I had been looking for divine help in human constructs: a confessional, a rose window, a dimly lit sanctuary. I began to pray on my own. But I believe that the sound of my feet on the concrete as I walked had been the real beginning of my prayer.

The divorce took four months. Eric and I never actually talked about getting divorced; it was just assumed. I wonder sometimes how long it would have taken him to make the first move.

Once I got into the process of the divorce—the filling out of forms, calls to and from lawyers, the formal division of property— things changed for me. Or, rather, I changed. My life, which had felt like it was veering out of control for so long, began to be important to me again, and I wondered if the divorce hadn't been what I was after all along, and I'd just created the excuse. The idea that I might have subconsciously manipulated events to put myself and a person I loved through months of torture appalls and frightens me.

Eric didn't show up at court the day our case was scheduled. I had half hoped that he would be there, mostly out of curiosity because I hadn't seen him since the morning he left. Had he changed? Was his hair different? Was he wearing a new suit? Would he shake my hand or even acknowledge me? Instead, it was just the judge, our lawyers, and a dozen other people waiting for their own decrees of dissolution in the stark courtroom, unornamented but for the state seal on the wall. My lawyer was a nice woman who appeared to be doing paperwork for another client while my case was being reviewed. I couldn't blame her though. I think I was paying her all of five hundred dollars for her services. But if she was disinterested, Eric's lawyer was determined to earn both their fees. He was a bristly old man with a voluminous voice, and delicate white hairs sticking out of his ears. I might have been intimidated by him save for the fact that he became so exercised and excited while he questioned me on the stand that I thought he would have a good old-fashioned apoplexy. *You understand, young lady, that the papers you have signed mean that you will never have any claims to any financial resources, present or future, belonging to Mr. Hoffman?* His voice rang out as though he had discovered my secret ambition—to haunt Eric for the rest of his life, lying in wait for the moment when he hit it big in Vegas, or invented some remarkable new slide projector. I wanted, really wanted to say, *Oh, please. You can't possibly be serious.* But I have a childlike respect for institutional forms of authority, and I had never been on the witness stand before, and so I could only offer a quiet *Yes, sir.* The judge asked if either of the lawyers had anything else to say. They didn't. He told me I could get down from the stand. Before I reached the table where my lawyer sat, he declared the marriage dissolved. Just like that.

Dressel's, a Welsh pub in the Central West End, a few days before our divorce becomes final.

The bar is crowded. It is the first time I have seen Eric in almost four months. We both smoke cigarettes, something we had both quit doing before we married. Our words are tentative; we are careful not to argue or accuse. I know that he is dating the secretary at his new office. I tell him that his lawyer was cruel to me at the divorce hearing. He tells me he is sorry. I tell him I am sorry. He says that he never should have married me, that he wanted only the ceremony, the party, the recognition from his family. As he talks, all I want him to do is to say he forgives me, that he forgives us, that he wants me back. Instead of telling him that, I tell him to let his new girlfriend love him and take care of him. Then I begin to cry. I see tears

start in his eyes. It is something I have never seen before. He tells me he
has to leave, and I don't try to stop him.

I wish I could be more like my father. He is compassionate without being weak. He is strong, but not overbearing. He knows the value of self-restraint, but is never cold. He is a hard-working and driven man who constantly looks for ways to improve his work, his station in life, the quality of others' lives. I've come to admire him enormously.

My father worked for the same company for twenty-seven years, rising steadily through its ranks until he became an executive officer. Then, in 1991, he was ceremoniously ousted. It was a shock to everyone who knew him. My mother and I spent long hours on the phone worrying about him, and what would happen to them both. She was very angry for him. But she told me he never complained. In the years that followed, he went through two more traumatic job changes, until, finally, the company he'd worked so long for asked him back.

I recently asked him how he had kept himself going throughout those years when his life was turned upside down, and he told me that early on he had schooled himself to look at negative experiences as part of the learning process. That it was his way of insulating against fear and uncertainty. He never once looked at any of his setbacks as failures.

I can't believe that I lived with him for so many years without absorbing his positive attitude toward life's challenges. So many times in my life I've failed or almost failed at things simply because I was so afraid of failing that I made a poor job of them or just gave up. I took piano lessons for seven years, then quit, telling everyone that they were useless because I had no talent. The truth was that I couldn't bear for anyone, not even my family, to hear the mistakes I made as I practiced, and so I didn't practice. My grades in high school worsened as the work got harder because there were always students with better grades, and I didn't want to have to compete. So I did only what I had to do to get by. I dallied for years with my writing; I would read books written by people who were my age or younger, and tell myself that I'd never catch up, that I'd already blown my chance at a career because I hadn't started in college.

The sad irony of perfectionism is that human beings are imperfectable. I'm sure my parents tried to teach that to me, but I am hardheaded and stubborn, and I had to learn it for myself.

It is only in the past two years or so that I have come to realize that I wouldn't be the person I am today, that I wouldn't have the wonderful life that I have now if I hadn't failed at my first two marriages. And I do feel that I actively failed them. I'm not so egotistical as to think that I was the only one responsible for their success or failure, but perhaps with more effort, or more maturity on my part, I might have helped one of them succeed.

If my first marriage had been successful, of course, there would not have been a second one, or a third. I think about that a lot. I imagine sometimes what it might have been like if I'd stayed with Michael, and toughed it out until we both grew up a little more. I imagine the children we might have had. No doubt they'd be in their early teens by now. I wonder what sort of house we would have lived in and what sort of relationship he and I might now have had; it would be a strong one borne of those hard early days. And I wonder if he would have become the successful person he is today if I had stayed with him.

I don't have similar thoughts about my marriage to Eric, because I think we never should have married in the first place. I know he feels that way, because he told me so. I wanted, really wanted, our marriage to succeed, but only because I feared so desperately that it would fail, and so helped create a self-fulfilling prophecy.

I complained to my friend Maggie once that I felt jaded and slightly ludicrous about having been twice-divorced before the age of thirty. She said that I just had the bad habit of making husbands of men who should have remained boyfriends. I think she may be right. In many ways, my third marriage feels like it is my first *real* marriage, in the sense that for the first time I am ready to give it everything within me—plus all those hours I should have been pounding away at the piano and studying my schoolbooks. What I've found is that I know better now: I know myself better, I know when things are beyond my control, and I know when I'm being dishonest with myself or with my husband. There are those times when the fabric of our marriage tears just a little and the specter of failure peeks through and says *it could happen again, you know*. But the terror lasts only a moment, and I embrace it.

We have a daughter who is five years old. I see myself in her, the same willful determination not to fail, even if it means giving up. When she loses at a board game, she throws a temper tantrum, and then won't play it again for weeks. She rarely looks at books by herself because she says she doesn't know how to read, and that it's too hard to learn. When she is sick, she says she doesn't want anyone but me to see her because she looks ugly. The panic I feel when I see these things in her is almost unspeakable. As a parent, I want to lay out my life before her as some cautionary tale. But even if that would be useful, five years old is a little young to be chatting about ex-husbands and adultery. Instead, I beg her to keep playing the game she has lost until she wins; when I lose, I say *It's okay, I might win next time*. I read books to her as often as she likes, practice writing the alphabet with her, and talk about what fun it will be for her to read when she is ready. Even as I do these things with her, and try to ease her way, I know she will have to learn for herself that she will not be satisfied with herself or her life unless she learns to accept her own shortcomings and failures as part of life's learning process. And that perfection is only an illusion.

Someday I will be able to tell her that I do not regret my second divorce, or my first one. I find some of the circumstances regretful, but not the fact of them. When I look into her face, and see the intensity and determination in her blue eyes that so resemble my own, I know that to have any regrets would be to regret her very existence, and that, I truly cannot imagine.

The Vision

A L A N   S H A P I R O

The day before she died I had a vision of my sister. I was lying on the floor beside her bed, my feet up on a chair, the only position that relieved the back pain I'd been having ever since I moved into the hospice with her four weeks earlier. Her half-filled urine bag was level with my head. On my other side my father, nearly blind, had pulled a chair just inches from the television screen so he could watch the O. J. Simpson trial. Or appear at least to watch it, for, as he always would, he fell asleep as soon as he sat down, his head nodding lower and lower till now and again he'd start awake and say, as if to prove he wasn't sleeping and hadn't missed a moment of the court proceedings, "He's gonna walk, I'm tellin' ya, guilty as sin, he's gonna walk. . . ." On the couch beyond him, my mother and brother were leaning forward over the book of crossword puzzles open before them on the ottoman. They'd started the book three weeks ago and now were working on the final puzzle. From time to time, one of them would ask my father or me for help—my father for the sports questions, me for the literary ones.

"Defensive end of the Steel Curtain, begins with M, ends with E, thirteen letters."

"Mean Joe Greene," my dad would call out dreamily, not even opening his eyes.

"Okay, professor, de Beauvoir's beau, six letters."

"Seven letters" was how I usually responded, whether or not I knew the answer. "Means 'no I don't, couldn't be bothered, get lost,' begins with F, ends with F, two words, first word rhymes with puck."

The room had a familial intimacy, spacious yet cozy, the furnishings, the walls, even the painting, propped on a cabinet shelf, of a horse and English rider, were tastefully done in soft tones, varieties of beige and brown, designed to make us feel if not at home exactly, then as far from a medical institution as a medical institution could be. If my sister hadn't been there dying, you'd have thought we were a normal family on a normal day, absorbed in ordinary and habitual pleasures, pursuits, preoccupations. What we, in fact, were doing, had been doing now for several weeks, was performing ordinary life, and the better and more convincing the performance, the more estranged we felt from the lives we left behind us when my sister began to die in earnest.

Beth's dying had become a new reality, too all-encompassing to be constantly perceived or felt, yet too heightened in its strangeness to be ever out of mind. It shadowed the most mundane activities we used to do unthinkingly and now could not do without thinking how peculiar it is that we were doing them at all. Day in, day out, sitting beside my sister, I would ask my father how the BoSox did last night, did the Yankees win, could Roger Clemens ever come back from his elbow problems, and do the bums really have a chance without him, and while I spoke I'd hear myself speaking, see myself turned to my father, listening as he answered, wondering at our intonations, at our gestures, how our hands waved to emphasize a point, each of us arguing our positions as if nothing in the world were more important. Or afternoons when I'd go out to get our lunch at the local supermarket, as I picked this or that thing off the shelf, or stood waiting while the woman at the deli took her sweet time making the sandwiches I ordered, or as I placed my basket on the checkout counter, answering the bagger that I wanted plastic, please, not paper, and then paid, and lugged my few bags to the car, I'd think how much I must have looked like any other customer on just another day of errands, and not someone whose sister was dying just a mile down the road. I seemed to hover outside my body in the charged atmosphere of Beth's impending death, while my body went on pretending I was who I always was. I lived, we all lived, with a doubled, dreamlike consciousness of what we all were going through, bewildered most by what remained familiar, like anthropologists discovering that the never before encountered culture they're observing is their own.

We had fallen abruptly out of life into a virtual existence in which time was measured mostly by my sister's failing body, her moment-to-moment changes in respiration, temperature, intake of food or fluids, by how long it took her urine bag to fill, how often she needed morphine, and in what amounts. The hospice room became a universe in which the terms of life were simultaneously narrowed and intensified. And in keeping with the inherent doubleness of every state of feeling, however much we suffered as we watched my sister die, we didn't merely suffer. There was joy, too, or something like joy, in the suffering itself. Joy in the self-forgetfulness that came with tending Beth, with grieving her, and in caring so tenderly for each other as we grieved; joy in the dissolution of the opaque privacies of daily life, in the heightened clarity of purpose and desire, in the transparency of understanding we all felt for the first time as a family: joy, in other words, in an intimacy whose very rarity added sadness to the joy.

By "we," I should add, I mean my mother, my father, my brother, and me. That familial intimacy, however, intense as it was, still had to compete for each of us in varying degrees with other claims on our attention. My father, for instance, was intermittently distracted by his various ailments, his Parkinson's syndrome, the fatigue from his insomnia, his general disorientation at being far from home. My brother, an actor, arrived from Pittsburgh at the end of the first week when the show he was doing there had ended. A week later he went to New

York for another job and then returned to Houston during the final week. During this time as well, his daughter in California had gotten sick. Hepatitis was the initial diagnosis. It turned out not to be, but for several days he was very worried about her, always calling home. Shortly after I arrived in Houston, my wife badly sprained her ankle, generating a flurry of calls to her, to my children. Like my brother, I too felt the need to be in two places at once. Only my mother remained completely focused on Beth throughout the whole ordeal, her attentions unclaimed by any other need or obligation.

My sister's husband, Russ, was a peripheral figure at the hospice. Usually Russ visited only in the early evenings after picking their daughter, Gabbi, up from horseback riding camp. Tired, hungry, and every bit her seven years of age, Gabbi would get antsy almost right away, especially once Beth had lost her ability to speak or respond, and Russ would have to take her home. Gabbi, it was clear to all of us, to Beth especially, provided Russ with a reason not to stay too long. That's why he never came without her. Once Beth was moved into the hospice, and her condition worsened, he withdrew—from her, from us, perhaps from the overwhelming sorrow of it all. Beth at times seemed wounded by his absence, and for her sake I was angry with him. At the same time, I knew he had his reasons. He was diagnosed with heart disease around the same time Beth was diagnosed with cancer. I can only imagine what his anxiety and fear on Beth's behalf was doing to his already weakened heart. And then there was his history: his mother's death from cancer (the same cancer that was killing Beth) when he was five, his father's of a heart attack a year later. I knew that Beth's illness had awakened all the devastating traumas of his childhood. I also knew that as a black man married to a white woman he never felt entirely at ease around her family. And his history with us, my father especially, was not a happy one.

For years my father would not accept Russ as his son-in-law. Early in Beth and Russ's relationship, my father refused to let Russ visit on the holidays. He refused to introduce him to his family back in Boston. And when Della and I got married, he threatened to dis-invite his relatives from the wedding if Della and I invited Russ. We did, of course. But Russ decided not to come, not wanting to go anywhere he wasn't welcome. Through it all, while Beth raged at my father's ignorance and selfishness, Russ himself remained imperturbable. From hard experience, he'd long since come to expect nothing else from most white people. He even calmly tried to talk my sister into going to the wedding out of loyalty to me. After Gabbi was born, my father came around enough at least to recognize Russ as his daughter's husband, if not to love him as he loved my brother's wife and mine.

For years I thought it was only for Beth's sake that Russ would always somehow put aside his anger and become around my father more cordial, more attentive, warmer, than he usually was. In May, though, on my previous trip to Houston, I learned it was, if not his only, then his most reliable strategy for living in a white world.

After weeks of searing headaches and erratic behavior (the former her doctors diagnosed as sinus problems, the latter as depression), Beth went into a catatonic state. A CAT scan showed us what we all suspected: that the breast cancer had now metastasized to her brain. With steroids, she regained consciousness only to be told that she had months, at best, to live. The day I arrived, we had our meeting with the neurosurgeon to discuss the feasibility of surgery, given the location of the tumor and my sister's history. Russ and I were sitting on one side of the bed, the doctor was standing on the other. The doctor talked for a while about the probable complications surgery would entail, and that anyway, even if it went without a hitch, the operation would give her only a few more months of life, and in what condition he couldn't say. What he *could* say with certainty was that the tumor couldn't be removed without damaging her brain. The Beth who went into surgery would not be the Beth who came out of it, no matter how well the operation went. I asked for more details about which mental faculties would be destroyed or compromised, and he answered courteously and at length. Then Russ asked how the cancer would progress if we did nothing, no surgery, no radiation. Instead of answering, the doctor asked, "And who are you, again?" My sister quickly interjected, "He's my husband." The doctor must have assumed that I was Beth's husband and that Russ was a family friend. An understandable mistake given that Beth and I have the same last name. Yet even after knowing who Russ was, the doctor refused to acknowledge him, the whole time looking either at me or my sister. Russ continued to participate in the discussion, his voice never once betraying any annoyance whatsoever. Throughout the conversation, he remained implacably calm and measured—determined, it seemed, in his dignified and intelligent demeanor to contradict all the assumptions that the doctor made about him. Later, I told Russ how appalled I was. In a voice I'd never heard so full of weariness, he said, "Dumb nigger till proven otherwise. That's how it always is."

For the first time, I could sense the bitterness behind the dignified facade, the rage behind the even temper. How hard Russ had to work to eat his anger and humiliation, to convert his indignation over every racial slight and innuendo into workable cordiality. And if it exhausted him to deal with clerks, doctors, mechanics, people he didn't know and whose prejudice was therefore more impersonal, easier maybe to dismiss, how much more painful and exhausting to have to overlook, put aside, ignore, and continually forgive the prejudice, the history of prejudice, within his very family? And how much more exhausting at a time like this, now that his wife was dying, and he no longer had the reserves of energy required to forbear, if not forgive? And the more we—my parents, my brother, and I—grew closer as a family and closed ranks around my sister's bed, the easier, I think, it must have been for Russ to think he wasn't wanted there, or needed.

One afternoon after he visited with Beth (we usually cleared the room when he arrived so he and Beth could be alone together), Russ told me he felt trapped in a nightmare whenever he came to the hospice, a nightmare I can understand only in terms of racial anger, childhood trauma, grief, and terror over what his wife was going through, over how difficult his life would be without her. In the first ten days or so, when Beth was still entirely lucid and felt wounded by his absence, I resented Russ for withdrawing from my sister at the very time that she needed him the most. By the last days, though, I felt mostly sorry for him, because it seemed to me he'd lost or given up the privilege of caring for his dying wife. At the same time, I felt ashamed, too, for anything we did or didn't do that might have made it easier for him to lose that privilege.

That privilege notwithstanding, by that last day we ourselves were tired of the vigil, tired for Beth, of course, but tired for ourselves as well. It had been two days since Beth had spoken. She lay in a coma, her open eyes flitting from side to side, her body at once bloated from steroids and emaciated from lack of nourishment, her swollen cheeks as hard as muscle, her shoulders, her arms, her wrists, her finger bones, especially, now nothing but twiglike points and angles. We were tired of seeing her languish, tired of the degradation we were helpless to do anything about. We were tired of our helplessness, and guilty for being tired. That we were all impatient to go home was our unspoken wish, our dirty secret.

But I had another wish as well, another dirty secret. However much I wanted to be with my sister when she died so I could comfort her as best I could, lessen what I imagined would be a terrifying loneliness once death was imminent, I also wanted, for purely selfish reasons, to see her die. Even as I feared and mourned it, I looked forward to the moment of her dying with an almost prurient curiosity. How would she look then? Where would she go? All of our notions of an afterlife seem just as implausible to me as that my sister with her unique vitality, her rich and complex and never-to-be-repeated history, would simply vanish into nothing. Wouldn't the conservation of energy principle contradict the fact of death as pure extinction? Wouldn't her existence have to continue in some way, if only as a fading but never completely faded energy impression on the universe? Some primitive part of me believed if I were with her when she died, if I were vigilant enough, I'd get to peek into the mystery as the soul passed from her body, out of this world into who knows where.

In the preceding days, as she slipped in and out of consciousness, her wakefulness each time a little briefer, a little fainter, I grew increasingly reluctant to leave her side. I stopped going over to her house in the mornings to help Russ get Gabbi ready for camp. I stopped returning to the house in the evening hours to relax, to have a drink with Russ, to talk about the day, how Beth was doing, how my folks were holding up. And at night I'd drive my parents back to their hotel and instead of sitting up with them an hour or so before returning to the hospice, I'd simply drop them off and hurry back to Beth, afraid that if I weren't there, she'd die without me. Was this fascination with her dying a way to keep from thinking of the grief I'd feel once Beth was dead, the depressing blunt truth of her absence? Or was it my own death I was really thinking of, obsessing over, grieving for, as if Beth's dying enabled me to watch, experience, and understand what it would mean for me to die? What at that point was going on inside her, what portion of self, of memory, of awareness, still remained to her? Was she ready to die? Did she even know by then that she was dying? And would my presence at the moment of death itself make any difference to her?

What was she now but a blank page written over by what each of us—out of our own particular relationship to her—was predisposed to write. Beth and I were friends as well as siblings, the "intellectuals" in the family, who had made a life of teaching, writing, learning. We were confidants, consolers, caretakers of each other's problems. And since we talked incessantly in the last two years about her illness, what it meant to die, it was consistent with our friendship that I should wonder now about her death and want to be there with her when it happened.

I was so far inside this fascination with her dying, so curious about what dying would be like, I wondered why my parents and my brother didn't seem to feel it too. I marveled at my mother, especially since she was more involved with Beth than anyone. I'd watch her say good-bye to Beth each evening, knowing that it was more than likely Beth would not be with us by the time the morning came. She'd cry as she kissed her, but she never lingered, didn't want to linger. Unlike me, my mother had no desire whatsoever to spend the night.

As I watched her feed Beth, help turn her body from one side to the other to make her comfortable, anticipate her needs and meet them tactfully before Beth had to ask, or just sit there holding her hand, talking quietly as she massaged Beth's forehead sometimes for hours at a time, it seemed to me at first as if Beth's illness had returned them both to a less complicated time in their relationship, to a time before Beth's tumultuous and divisive teens and early twenties, when her political rebellion as a founding member of Students for a Democratic Society in the mid-sixties, and her sexual rebellion (her boyfriend at the time was black) had badly damaged her relations with my parents. For years my parents would have nothing to do with her, and even after they were reconciled, their relationship was always strained, muddied with ambivalence, my parents never approving of my sister's boyfriends, who were never Jewish and seldom white, my sister never entirely forgiving them for throwing her out at such a young age, for continuing not to accept her in all her differences, for continuing to cling to their idea of who she is or should be, preferring that sanitized abstraction to the person she'd become. With Beth reduced to infant-like dependency and need, it seemed as if that painful history had vanished, dissolved along with Beth's feisty independence.

And yet the more I watched the two of them, the more I realized that this intimacy wasn't a return to some less complicated time in their relationship, but the creation of something new and different, something that never existed between them and never could have existed, something the very structures of mothering and being mothered don't ordinarily permit. Beth's illness had put an end to the contest for autonomy and self-definition that the two of them had always waged, as daughter, as mother, as wife, and more generally as women independent of these familial roles. It was as if her illness had given them both the permission to be more generous, more imaginative than they had ever been before. Because my mother knew Beth had no choice but to accept the care she had to give, she gave it tactfully, respectfully, so that it came as much as possible without the stigma of submission; and because my sister, knowing how painful it would be for her if it were Gabbi who was dying, and she were caring for her daughter the way her mother now cared for her, accepted graciously, compassionately, everything my mother tried to do. What seemed most remarkable was the mutual forbearance, restraint, and profound courtesy in their attentions to each other. My mother could have overwhelmed my sister with maternal care; Beth's abject neediness would have justified it. My sister could have accepted grudgingly or bitterly the care she couldn't do without, compensating for the humiliation of her helplessness with understandable impatience, irritability, anger. Neither of them did.

The unique maturity of their relationship was nowhere more apparent than in the last few days when Beth, still conscious, stopped asking for food or liquid, and my mother stopped offering, even though she knew not getting her to eat or drink would hasten her death. That she could let go of her daughter and, once Beth lost consciousness, tell her it was all right to die, to take God's hand, was the ultimate expression of the intimacy the two of them had finally achieved. That they had achieved it is why, I think, my mother had no desire to be there with her daughter when she died. The very way she'd been with Beth throughout each day of those last four weeks was how she'd said good-bye, and having said it, she'd done everything that it was possible for her to do.

I was thinking about all of this that last day as I lay on the floor beside my sister's bed. I was thinking about Russ and Beth, Beth and my mother, Beth and me, always Beth in relation to one of us. It had been two days now since she had spoken, only a faint wheeze or whimper coming from her chest. In the days before she slipped into the coma, every now and then I'd ask her how she was feeling, what she was thinking of. "Nothing," she'd murmur, "absolutely nothing." The massive amounts of morphine needed to eat up the pain had left her either deeply asleep or drifting in a sort of waking dream. Yet on the morning of the last day she had spoken, she woke and told my mother, "I think I'm getting better." An hour later the doctor asked her if she was okay, and she said, "I think I'm okay somewhere inside." And when the nurse arrived to change her urine bag, Beth answered her cheery "Hi, Beth!" with "I want to get out of here."

The nurse thought "here" meant the hospice, that Beth was asking to go home. But I was certain that it meant the body that betrayed her, that she felt better, "okay somewhere inside," because she knew that death was near and she was ready for it. Those were the last words she had spoken. And two days later she was still alive. The whimpering in her chest had persisted for twelve hours now. All through the night and morning, it was horrible to listen to because I couldn't tell, and the nurses couldn't tell me, if it was just some physiological event, the onset of the death rattle, or if it meant that Beth was trying unsuccessfully to tell us something, to communicate one last time. I was thinking as I lay there, before the vision came, of how completely inaccessible my sister was to all of us as the life within her petered out. The nurses told us that the hearing is the last to go, that we should still be careful of what we say around her. But did she hear us? And though unable to communicate, did she still feel in our presence some remnant of who she'd been for each of us? And was there, then, some pressure to continue being, to conform to who we each of us unconsciously still needed her to be? And was that whimper then some feeble protest that she was tired of us all, that she wanted to be left alone? Or did it simply mean that her life had thoroughly dissolved past her identity into the mere machinery of slowing heart and lung?

Flat on my back, my feet up on a chair, my eyes closed, suddenly I saw my sister. She was lying on a made bed, the covers under her. She looked like her old self, only thinner than she'd ever been, sleeker, and she was dressed like a dancer, a Rockette, in black tights, black shirt, and vest, the costume all awash in sequins, her top hat tilted stylishly down to just above her eyes. She was smiling not at me but in my direction, as if I'd only accidentally crossed the path of her attention—like someone you think is greeting you and whom you've therefore waved and smiled at and then discover as she nears that she has all along been looking past you, at someone else, she doesn't know that you exist. The smile widened. It went on widening into a grotesque Cheshire cat smile, and suddenly I realized that what I thought had been a smile was only flesh disintegrating, disappearing like an ebbing tide beyond her lips and cheeks, up over the forehead, down her neck, into the collar of her black shirt, till just the skull lay on the pillow, the top hat now slumped forward over the eye sockets, the tight-fitting clothes now loose and billowy as they settled to the bones that could have been anybody's.

from *Darkness Visible*

WILLIAM STYRON

For years I had kept a notebook—not strictly a diary, its entries were erratic and haphazardly written—whose contents I would not have particularly liked to be scrutinized by eyes other than my own. I had hidden it well out of sight in my house. I imply no scandalousness; the observations were far less raunchy, or wicked, or self-revealing, than my desire to keep the notebook private might indicate. Nonetheless, the small volume was one that I fully intended to make use of professionally and then destroy before the distant day when the specter of the nursing home came too near. So as my illness worsened I rather queasily realized that if I once decided to get rid of the notebook that moment would necessarily coincide with my decision to put an end to myself. And one evening during early December this moment came.

That afternoon I had been driven (I could no longer drive) to Dr. Gold's office, where he announced that he had decided to place me on the antidepressant Nardil, an older medication which had the advantage of not causing the urinary retention of the other two pills he had prescribed. However, there were drawbacks. Nardil would probably not take effect in less than four to six weeks—I could scarcely believe this—and I would have to carefully obey certain dietary restrictions, fortunately rather epicurean (no sausage, no cheese, no pâté de foie gras), in order to avoid a clash of incompatible enzymes that might cause a stroke. Further, Dr. Gold said with a straight face, the pill at optimum dosage could have the side effect of impotence. Until that moment, although I'd had some trouble with his personality, I had not thought him totally lacking in perspicacity; now I was not at all sure. Putting myself in Dr. Gold's shoes, I wondered if he seriously thought that this juiceless and ravaged semi-invalid with the shuffle and the ancient wheeze woke up each morning from his Halcion sleep eager for carnal fun.

There was a quality so comfortless about that day's session that I went home in a particularly wretched state and prepared for the evening. A few guests were coming over for dinner—something which I neither dreaded nor welcomed and which in itself (that is, in my torpid indifference) reveals a fascinating aspect of depression's pathology. This concerns not the familiar threshold of pain but a parallel phenomenon, and that is the probable inability of the psyche to absorb pain beyond predictable limits of time. There is a region in the experience of pain where the certainty of alleviation often permits superhuman endurance. We learn to live with pain in varying degrees daily, or over longer periods of time, and we are more often than not mercifully free of it. When we endure severe discomfort of a physical nature our conditioning has taught us since childhood to make accommodations to the pain's demands—to accept it, whether pluckily or whimpering and complaining, according to our personal degree of stoicism, but in any case to accept it. Except in intractable terminal pain, there is almost always some form of relief; we look forward to that alleviation, whether it be through sleep or Tylenol or self-hypnosis or a change of posture or, most often, through the body's capacity for healing itself, and we embrace this eventual respite as the natural reward we receive for having been, temporarily, such good sports and doughty sufferers, such optimistic cheerleaders for life at heart.

In depression this faith in deliverance, in ultimate restoration, is absent. The pain is unrelenting, and what makes the condition intolerable is the foreknowledge that no remedy will come—not in a day, an hour, a month, or a minute. If there is mild relief, one knows that it is only temporary; more pain will follow. It is hopelessness even more than pain that crushes the soul. So the decision-making of daily life involves not, as in normal affairs, shifting from one annoying situation to another less annoying—or from discomfort to relative comfort, or from boredom to activity—but moving from pain to pain. One does not abandon, even briefly, one's bed of nails, but is attached to it wherever one goes. And this results in a striking experience—one which I have called, borrowing military terminology, the situation of the walking wounded. For in virtually any other serious sickness, a patient who felt similar devastation would be lying flat in bed, possibly sedated and hooked up to the tubes and wires of life-support systems, but at the very least in a posture of repose and in an isolated setting. His invalidism would be necessary, unquestioned and honorably attained. However, the sufferer from depression has no such option and therefore finds himself, like a walking casualty of war, thrust into the most intolerable social and family situations. There he must, despite the anguish devouring his brain, present a face approximating the one that is associated with ordinary events and companionship. He must try to utter small talk, and be responsive to questions, and knowingly nod and frown and, God help him, even smile. But it is a fierce trial attempting to speak a few simple words.

That December evening, for example, I could have remained in bed as usual during those worst hours, or agreed to the dinner party my wife had arranged downstairs. But the very idea of a decision was academic. Either course was torture, and I chose the dinner not out of any particular merit but through indifference to what I knew would be indistinguishable ordeals of fogbound horror. At dinner I was barely able to speak, but the quartet of guests, who were all good friends, were aware of my condition and politely ignored my catatonic muteness. Then, after dinner, sitting in the living room, I experienced a curious inner convulsion that I can describe only as despair beyond despair. It came out of the cold night; I did not think such anguish possible.

While my friends quietly chatted in front of the fire I excused myself and went upstairs, where I retrieved my notebook from its special place. Then I went to the kitchen and with gleaming clarity— the clarity of one who knows he is engaged in a solemn rite—I noted all the trademarked legends on the well-advertised articles which I began assembling for the volume's disposal: the new roll of Viva paper towels I opened to wrap up the book, the Scotch-brand tape I encircled it with, the empty Post Raisin Bran box I put the parcel into before taking it outside and stuffing it deep down within the garbage can, which would be emptied the next morning. Fire would have destroyed it faster, but in garbage there was an annihilation of self appropriate, as always, to melancholia's fecund self-humiliation. I felt my heart pounding wildly, like that of a man facing a firing squad, and knew I had made an irreversible decision.

A phenomenon that a number of people have noted while in deep depression is the sense of being accompanied by a second self—a wraithlike observer who, not sharing the dementia of his double, is able to watch with dispassionate curiosity as his companion struggles against the oncoming disaster, or decides to embrace it. There is a theatrical quality about all this, and during the next several days, as I went about stolidly preparing for extinction, I couldn't shake off a sense of melodrama—a melodrama in which I, the victim-to-be of self-murder, was both the solitary actor and lone member of the audience. I had not as yet chosen the mode of my departure, but I knew that that step would come next, and soon, as inescapable as nightfall.

I watched myself in mingled terror and fascination as I began to make the necessary preparation: going to see my lawyer in the nearby town—there rewriting my will—and spending part of a couple of afternoons in a muddled attempt to bestow upon posterity a letter of farewell. It turned out that putting together a suicide note, which I felt obsessed with a necessity to compose, was the most difficult task of

writing that I had ever tackled. There were too many people to acknowledge, to thank, to bequeath final bouquets. And finally I couldn't
manage the sheer dirgelike solemnity of it; there was something I
found almost comically offensive in the pomposity of such a comment
as "For some time now I have sensed in my work a growing psychosis
that is doubtless a reflection of the psychotic strain tainting my life"
(this is one of the few lines I recall verbatim), as well as something
degrading in the prospect of a testament, which I wished to infuse with
at least some dignity and eloquence, reduced to an exhausted stutter of
inadequate apologies and self-serving explanations. I should have used
as an example the mordant statement of the Italian writer Cesare
Pavese, who in parting wrote simply: *No more words. An act. I'll never
write again.*

But even a few words came to seem to me too long-winded, and I
tore up all my efforts, resolving to go out in silence. Late one bitterly
cold night, when I knew that I could not possibly get myself through
the following day, I sat in the living room of the house bundled up
against the chill; something had happened to the furnace. My wife had
gone to bed, and I had forced myself to watch the tape of a movie in
which a young actress, who had been in a play of mine, was cast in a
small part. At one point in the film, which was set in late-nineteenth-
century Boston, the characters moved down the hallway of a music
conservatory, beyond the walls of which, from unseen musicians, came
a contralto voice, a sudden soaring passage from the Brahms Alto
Rhapsody.

This sound, which like all music—indeed, like all pleasure—I had
been numbly unresponsive to for months, pierced my heart like a
dagger, and in a flood of swift recollection I thought of all the joys the
house had known: the children who had rushed through its rooms, the
festivals, the love and work, the honestly earned slumber, the voices
and the nimble commotion, the perennial tribe of cats and dogs and
birds, "laughter and ability and Sighing, / And Frocks and Curls." All
this I realized was more than I could ever abandon, even as what I had
set out so deliberately to do was more than I could inflict on those
memories, and upon those, so close to me, with whom the memories

were bound. And just as powerfully I realized I could not commit this desecration on myself. I drew upon some last gleam of sanity to perceive the terrifying dimensions of the mortal predicament I had fallen into. I woke up my wife and soon telephone calls were made. The next day I was admitted to the hospital.

To the Lifeguard

CHRISTOPHER DAVIS

        Ben, my younger brother, was murdered in 1979 in Whittier, California. The murderers were two local guys. David Kuns actually did the stabbing: despite his German name, he was a light-skinned Hispanic who, in his fifteen years, had been shoved from foster home to foster home. Fred Munoz, who drove the white station wagon in which Ben was stabbed, was my age, eighteen, and would have been my classmate at Whittier High School had he not dropped out.

On the night of April 29, Kuns and Munoz were high on PCP, "angel dust." Ben was stumbling home from a party. He was drunk, stoned, and woozy from Valium he'd stolen from our mother's purse—a trick he'd learned from me. Kuns and Munoz picked him up. In the backseat, Kuns stabbed him twenty-seven times, then, at the edge of a cliff, beat him and threw him down into Turnbull Canyon. Perhaps Ben's inebriation in those moments was a blessing.

Kuns and Munoz may have recognized Ben's brilliant orange-red hair: before Ben had had it "permed," it had been long, and in the spring of 1979 the pile of fiery curls surrounding his head was famous in Whittier. Earlier that afternoon, our mother had warned him that he should wear a cap to avoid attracting attention: after Ben died, they would seem to have been premonitions to her, these thoughts that as an upper-middle-class Anglo kid with schoolteacher parents, he was in danger of drawing the hate of the less privileged.

The cause given for Ben's death was "blunt force trauma": an injury to his head he had sustained as he fell into the canyon (unless Kuns had picked up a large stone) caused his brain, finally, to explode.

A few years after Ben's death, I was tormented by a constant sexual impotence which I frantically, obsessively challenged, grieving in my body for the brother with whom, throughout my childhood, I'd had sex, and who had whispered to me, as we huddled in our room downstairs and listened to our parents rage against each other, "Why don't they just get a divorce?" By 1984 my mother and father *were* finally divorced: my father was living in North Hollywood with a man, his lover, and my mother, whose alcohol-red eyes had been blackened and who had had lard rubbed into the curls of her hair, was appearing on television talk shows as a "victim of murder," weeping beside neo-Nazi bikers.

Ironically, given the destruction of her dreams of a family, my mother's career had been the teaching of home economics, that postwar pseudo-subject invented to keep newly ambitious women in the kitchen. Perhaps my mother's dreams, being dreams, were meant to be destroyed by realities even larger than her bad marriage and her murdered son. Since 1952, when, with her bachelor's degree from Oklahoma University and her master's degree from UCLA, both in home economics, my mother began teaching at Whittier High School, most of her students had been Hispanic girls with frosted hair who either ignored or hated the posters around them advertising Thanksgiving, "vitamins," grinning white faces, and food groups containing brussels sprouts and Swiss cheese.

.   .   .

Throughout my childhood, I visited my mother's classroom, which was below ground level in a building that had been built in the 1930s, and looked like the Emerald City in *The Wizard of Oz*. I felt "special" there. The room had a sweet stench to it, a corrupted earthiness, the smells of baking inseparable from those of cleansers. The wood closets were brightly lacquered: I sniffed the glittering, confectionary surfaces of the doors, and seemed to smell the stained boxes of evaporated milk, Bisquick, and brown sugar on the shelves behind the doors.

My mother was an outgoing, imaginative teacher. Did her students intuit her suffering? Perhaps because of her marital insecurities, she worked especially hard for their affection, lecturing from atop a stepladder painted cardinal red, the school color, blowing whistles like a coach, teaching students about international cuisine by bringing in cans of kangaroo soup from Australia. One day during her first year on the job, an enormous girl stood up and interrupted my mother's lecture to ask to be allowed to use the rest room. My mother asked her to wait. The girl pulled up her skirt, squatted, and urinated on the floor. On another occasion, a sink was clogged. My mother stuck her hand into the drain, where her fingertips felt the whiskers, nose, and teeth of a dead rat, which one of her students had presumably stuck down there.

Most of my mother's colleagues lived far away from Whittier, not wanting their students or the parents of their students to see into their privacy. But Ben and I were destined by our street address to attend the same public high school at which our mother taught. Before I received my driver's license, my mother drove me to Whittier High School with her in the morning. She seemed unembarrassed by my obesity. Throughout my adolescence, my weight increased. Near the end of my senior year, I weighed 285 pounds. Apparently she hadn't understood me when I'd shrieked, "You made me into a freak!" Couldn't she see that in public I was a target for ridicule? The Chicano boys, with their hard, handsome bodies which I stared at in the locker room and sucked off in my dreams, hung out smoking cigarettes in the mornings around an oak tree covered with initials, dates, and other scars. That was exactly where my mother parked.

"Mother," I begged, *"please* drop me off on the other side of school, not here." Like her, I was, to use her own mother's word, "headstrong."

Five or six grinning Chicano studs stared at us. Each wore a plain white tank top over a perfect torso, and a red headband around slick black hair.

Tears erupted in my mother's eyes. Her voice simultaneously whined and growled. "Everything I *do* is wrong. It's just one *pick* after another." There was a light purple bruise on her arm, below the wrist. She sobbed, "Don't you want to be seen with me?"

I blazed inside, but couldn't organize my thoughts quickly enough to respond. I pouted as we both unlocked our doors and waddled out, her necklace of whistles and keys jangling against her breasts. As she bent into the backseat for her cardboard box filled with grade books and recipes, I felt humiliated by the comparison the Chicanos were undoubtedly making between my swollen body and my mother's chubby, polyester-clad awkwardness.

Once, I calmly watched a crowd of girls drop an overripe tomato onto her head as she passed under their second-floor window.

Every night, it seemed, Ben and I eavesdropped on a verbal battle we at first could hardly understand. "Tell your queer friends to stop calling here," she would shriek. We would laugh about the night in a campground when, her voice seething, she whispered, "Do you remember the last time we made love? It was when we saw *The Godfather* in Oklahoma City." We wondered what had aroused them. Had it been the scene in which the man wakes up in his sunny bed to find himself covered with blood, a severed horse head near his feet?

Sometimes, when the shouts segued into slaps, our mother would totter downstairs and beg us to come up into their bedroom to protect her from our father: while Ben watched, I, being the oldest and the largest, would be placed like a shield before my mother's body. I would see my father literally backed against a wall. He was tall, intelligent, a thin Elvis Presley in glasses, unable to articulate his shame, his feelings of having been betrayed. Long ago he had started his fiercely defensive turn inward, away from the loud disappointment of his wife, and, as I would soon understand, toward relationships with other men. The violence never seemed to be his fault. In his distance and his delicacy, he was attractive.

"Mister Rogers," my friends mockingly called him, comparing him with the effeminate, gentle host of the children's program, *Mister Rogers' Neighborhood*. My father had been sensitized by childhood trauma and instability: after his adoptive parents divorced, his mother could not, in the Depression, support him, and left him first with her ancient parents, then with her former husband, now remarried to a much younger woman. My father's stepmother, blond, svelte, and close to my father in age, exuded enough erotic attentiveness to complicate his ability to trust her as a source for maternal comfort. My father's father was an attorney in Oklahoma City. He investigated, and learned that my father's natural mother had died soon after giving birth. He thought it right to acquaint my father with the sister of his natural mother, who became another pseudo-parent. My mother's family, large, rural, and simple, must have seemed security itself.

"Even at the beginning," my mother's mother once said to me, "it seemed like something was missing between them. They never touched each other, and they always talked so much about buying things." Embodying the ideology of young heterosexual couples of their time, they wanted to work hard, save money, own property, and have children. Even the exciting move to the West Coast was standard. At age twenty-six, my mother created the blueprint for the large home on a hilltop, a dream home they could afford through their obsessive work, teaching extra classes, making their own clothes, sharing one car.

My father had a bachelor's degree in English from Oklahoma University (where they met) and, eventually, a master's degree in communications from UCLA. His career as a radio script writer and actor died at the hands of the television industry; he taught English and history in several suburban public high schools until, in the late sixties, he was caught (possibly entrapped) having sex with a male student. That crisis, in which suicide had seemed an option for him, passed in nights of threats and screams which were inseparable to me from the others. Through contacts, he was hired into the telecommunications department at the University of Southern California, and was soon a pioneer in a combination of the fields of gerontology and communications, receiving large government grants to study the roles of the media in the lives of the elderly. My father's ability to escape Whittier and his marriage for conferences and weekends of anonymity in other cities haunted my mother.

During Episcopal sermons, I would close my eyes and project onto their black screen my own David Lean–style epics, imagining enormous mountain battles between British redcoats and armies of Hindus. After Ben's murder and during my defensive self-exile from California, my ability to write poetry became my primary stabilizing obsession, my only way to transform pain back into love.

Every summer, the family journeyed to Idyllwild, a mountain town above Palm Springs, where Ben and I took courses at an "art camp," an extension of USC. My creative writing was encouraged by Norman Corwin, the resonant gentleman who thought *Jonathan Livingston Seagull* was "twaddle," and who had written the great radio plays of the war era. He played for his students the recording of *My Client Curly*, about a pet caterpillar turning into a butterfly: the cinema in my head easily transformed his words into a black and white film. It was less easy to picture *On a Note of Triumph*, his V-E–Day propaganda piece consisting of speeches to an audience tired of adding private imagery to radio reports from a real war.

My poetry depicted my war. Norman praised a piece in which a child listens, uncomprehendingly, to his parents' furious bickering, then proclaims, "I am Aries, sign of fire! Upon this page, I burn!" Norman seemed to love my long, Sandbergesque poem, "Build Me Up a Castle Here," expressing a desire to turn the mortal, vulnerable body into marble: with my long, straight hair, my Mama Cass face, and my endomorphic "form," I had been mistaken for a girl by one workshop participant, an older man who apparently could not hear Norman's attempts to correct the man's use of the pronoun "she" in reference to me.

In the mid-seventies, my parents bought a small house, "the cabin," in Idyllwild. At the center of "the cabin" was an enormous fireplace. The original owner of the lot had built this fireplace, using field stones and grave markers, but his wife had died before he could build their dream house around it. The lot's second owners constructed an awkward building around the monument. Apart from writing, my summer world consisted of trying to discern, then avoid, the intensity of my parents' anger toward each other, and of trying to blow whatever friend Ben had brought to Idyllwild with him. Once, I offered, unsuccessfully, his friend Jim my copy of the *Yellow Submarine* album. Or my brother: sometimes when we showered together I knelt to take his substitute nipple into my mouth. I looked up at his red hair, his marble-white belly.

David Bowie, beautiful, exhilarating, permissive, became the pop star on whom I modeled my adolescent fantasies. My interest in the Beatles died into a loyalty to John Lennon: as I shrieked the final moments of "Mother" along with him, he and I expressed the ugly reality of adolescence. When, in 1977, the Sex Pistols emerged, punk rock devoured me wholly. Finally, I obtained my driver's license. By draping my obese body in a green army trench coat and driving into Hollywood, to the Whiskey A-Go-Go, to pogo to Devo, I could worship the loser, the outcast, the monster: myself.

My senior year in high school was a blur of automobile wrecks and other disasters. I worked for a catering outfit, and each night I drank cheap brandy with the other employees until, early in the morning, I had a chance to relieve Hank or Russell in the walk-in refrigerator or on the front seat of my Pinto. In the mornings, after my mother had left, I would open her liquor cabinet and gulp mouthfuls of vodka. Stumbling into my second-period class, I'd sit, and lean my bleary-eyed, burping head against the wall. I presumed that the instructor would be too embarrassed or puzzled to talk about me with my mother, a colleague.

Once I'd graduated from high school in 1978, I began to lose weight. The comments of others had worked their spell: Gary, the queeny Hispanic waiter, had cornered me in the walk-in, shoved cole-slaw into my mouth, and sneered, "Eat, beefy, eat!" By New Year's

Day of 1979 I weighed 185 pounds. Despising the idea of college, I moved into a ranch house on the other side of Whittier with my friend Paul, with whom I'd formed a kind of imitation glam rock band. I left the catering company (perhaps I was fired) and took a job at Whittier's local newspaper, where I distributed the United Press International wire copy to the appropriate desks, and where I wrote the obituaries.

Even at Christmas, I avoided the family home. The angry expression on my face felt like a reflection of my mother's face; the aggression bubbling in my body seemed stirred by the invisible fists, thrashing in every direction, of my father. I craved independence. Toward that end, like most of my friends, I enrolled in est, "Erhardt Seminars Training," a two-weekend pop-psych process during which the "trainers" theatrically bullied participants into egolessness, pushing people beyond the comfort of their familiar identities, then building in participants' imaginations a sense of self that was stronger, larger, more transcendental, capable of containing multitudes. As an est graduate, I thought, I could "accept responsibility for my creation, my universe," whatever that meant.

I saw Ben only once in 1979, before he died: his room was a picture of a "den of iniquity," with fake Turkish blankets billowing from the ceiling, and with Pink Floyd posters, incense, and water bongs everywhere. If I tried to talk with Ben about the difficulties of living with Mom and Dad, it's likely that my voice had an edge to it, but maybe it was my large physical appearance (my insecurities distorted by my dyed-black hair) and his shame at our earlier habit of sex play that made him draw back into silence, and keep his body away from mine.

That was the last time I saw Ben fully alive. When his blood-stained short pants were delivered to my mother by a nurse, we found, in one of the pockets, a slip of paper with my phone number on it.

On the Saturday afternoon of May 29, my mother watched Ben put on those white shorts and a lavender shirt, then, following her advice, a cap. "Thanks for letting me go to this party," he said, and proceeded to make a small speech to her, saying that he realized how difficult it must be to have a teenager, and then when he had children he would try to have the same kind of relationship with them that he had with her.

Through the large, panoramic kitchen window, she stared at him as he rode his skateboard down the driveway, out into the street, away. Acting on an impulse which would later seem to her to have been another premonition, she telephoned her mother, her sister, and even my father's adoptive mother, with whom she never spoke, to talk about how her younger son was coming out of his shyness. She was lonely. She tried to call my father, who was in San Francisco for a Gerontological Association conference: he'd left word at the front desk of his hotel that he was not to be disturbed.

That evening, I was either in Hollywood, or in a coffee shop with Paul, trying to write song lyrics. Ben, meanwhile, was popping Valium, drinking, and smoking pot in a house rented by a girl who, earlier that day, had gone to the home of David Kuns to ask him to return a record she'd lent him. He'd pulled out a knife, held it near her face, and forced her to leave. When Kuns and Munoz, high and mighty on PCP, stopped by the party to insult the hostess, she had her chance to tell them to get out.

Eventually, Ben, forgetting his skateboard, began to stumble through the dark residential streets toward his home, which was miles away, and on a hill high above the homes of his low-income friends. He passed the little park where he and I had released a golden carp into the fishpond. The walk home would have taken him hours. Had he not been picked up by two boys in a white station wagon, he probably would have passed out underneath a bush.

It all came out in the trial. David Kuns was in the front passenger seat at first, but after Ben nodded that he did want a ride, Kuns slid into the backseat next to him. Months later, detectives found Ben's dried blood in the cracks in the upholstery. When I saw David Kuns in court, I was surprised by his slightness, and by the feral silence in which he held himself, not looking at anyone. Although David Kuns knew who Ben was, where he lived, who his mother was, he might not have been thinking about the person inside the body he began to stab, in the back and in the sides, as Fred Munoz drove the car to the outskirts of Whittier and up into Turnbull Canyon. After tossing Ben over the canyon's edge, the two boys returned to the party. Kuns told the hostess what he had just done, then went into the bathroom and vomited.

After Ben died, my mother dreamed incessantly about his torn body curled down in the canyon, in the ivy and weeds. She dreamed about animals smelling the blood, and coming to nibble him. In the hospital, maggots were cleaned from his wounds. That first night, shocked and stoned, Ben went into a coma; on Sunday morning, he was still alive. As the warm day progressed, my mother began to worry, and to drive around Whittier looking for her son. She called the police, who suggested that he had run away from home, a possibility she angrily denied.

On Monday morning, Ben, who had been lifting weights for a year, regained consciousness enough to tug himself up out of the canyon, grabbing the ivy tendrils and the brittle Indian gum stalks. "That was his gift to us," my mother said later. "It would have been so much worse if he had died in the canyon." He lurched out onto the road, and sat on the retaining wall. Eventually, a second pair of young men, this pair in a pickup truck, stopped, astounded to see a boy covered in blood. Ben could only mumble, and would not let them touch him. They rushed him to the nearest hospital, from which he was transferred to the Queen of the Valley Hospital, far from Whittier, where his condition could be better monitored.

Although desperate with anxiety, my mother had gone to teach. At four in the afternoon, a secretary from the principal's office came to my mother's classroom and told her that there was a phone call for her about her son. The nurse on the other end said, "Mrs. Davis, you can come pick up your son and take him home." Had the nurse told the truth, of course, which was that my mother's youngest son would never leave the hospital alive, my mother might have wrecked her car.

In the hospital lobby, my mother was intercepted by a policeman, who tugged her into a small room and asked her to sign some documents. "I just want to see my son," my mother sobbed. The policeman told her that her signature was necessary "in case this comes to trial." My mother did not know what he meant. At last she was taken to the intensive care unit in which her son lay, his beautiful hair shaved off, his eyes blackened, reduced to two small slits, a long gash crossing his chin. "I love you, Ben," she said.

He answered, "I love you."

My mother stayed in the hospital as Ben slipped in and out of consciousness. She could not telephone me: I had chosen not to give my parents my phone number at the ranch house, although she could have guessed that I was at work at the *Daily News*. She was finally able to leave a message for my father with a colleague of his. Late at night on Monday, May 1, I received a call from Brad, a friend of both Ben's and mine who had spoken with my mother: he told me that I should go meet my mother at her house in the morning. In San Francisco, my father was able to get a flight for L.A. that left at dawn.

I met my mother, and we rushed to the hospital. In the car, as she told me the news, I felt disbelief, then numbness.

Ben seemed flat under the thin blanket. The outline of his body was insubstantial, as if he had been drained. His white arms, stretched along his sides, were covered with tubes and tiny wounds. The black discoloration around his swollen eyelids, through which tiny glimmers of retina shone, looked almost like mascara and eye shadow. The sides of the clear plastic tube in his nose were painted with cloud when he exhaled: when he inhaled, the cloud disappeared. Ben's brain was swelling, and an operation needed to be performed to take pressure off the brain.

I left Ben's intensive care room. I told my friend Mary, who was sitting in the hall, that I needed to walk around alone. I wandered down a fluorescent, heaven-sterile hall. In the men's room, I pressed my skull against the white, cold tiles of the wall, and then against the mirror. I felt numb, detached. I could not cry or tremble. Guarding myself against chaos as I'd learned to do in the face of my parents' violent marriage, I refused to shriek, to break my fists against the mirror. When Mary saw me again, she said, "You seem a thousand miles away."

My mother pleaded with the doctors to transfer Ben to a familiar hospital, where he could be treated by the family physician, Gerald Evers: the doctors must have known that Ben would not live, and could not be relocated now. We believed he would live as he was wheeled into the operating room, that once the skull had been opened and pressure had been taken off the brain, he would snap back into consciousness. Mary, my mother, and I sat in the cafeteria and waited.

I stood in the lobby, smoking a cigarette in the "smoking area," when my father came through the revolving door. Panic filled his face. "Where is he? Where is he?" tumbled from his lips. When he came into the cafeteria, my mother saw him, and looked away without saying anything. Later, screaming at him in the night, she would say, "Ben died because you weren't here to pick him up from that party."

A doctor shepherded us into a conference room. Ben, he told us, would not regain consciousness. He was brain dead. Eventually his body functions would stop. He would die. We had the option of keeping him attached to the life support system, or of having it removed. After mumbling to one another through our tears for a few moments, we chose the latter option. A nurse asked my mother if she would like to keep Ben's hair: matted with blood, it was in a plastic bag which she handed to my mother, who put it in her purse.

Family friends, Pat Mogen and her daughter, Becky, met us in the lobby. Pat insisted that Becky stand in Ben's room with the rest of us as, early in the morning on May 2, the snakelike pulsations of the thin green line inside the electroencephalograph screen were smoothed down until the line was motionless and flat, and Ben was dead. Later, my father said, "I felt nothing but empty, helpless despair."

My mother told me, later, that although she and my father had not had sexual contact for many years, two nights after Ben's death her husband suddenly turned to her in bed and made intensely passionate love to her, sobbing and trembling as he moved his hips on top of her. The next morning, for a moment, there was an impossible tenderness between them.

The weekend after Ben's death, I attended an est "post-training session": in the large convention auditorium of a hotel on Wilshire Boulevard, I stood up to share with the hundreds of citizens of "my creation" that I had accepted responsibility for my brother's murder. There were gasps. To est disciples, the idea of "responsibility" as a metaphysical and psychological posture was most often actualized in relation to simple, common situations such as angry bosses. To ears untrained to est ideology, my statement could have constituted grounds for arrest. After the session, a woman thanked me for sharing.

On Sunday, a memorial service was held at the Episcopal church. Many, many people attended. Ben's murder had been front-page news in Los Angeles: the newspapers had mistakenly called it a "gang-related" incident, and it seemed the first time in Whittier at least that a privileged Anglo kid had been killed by Chicano "gangsters." And Ben had been the son of a teacher whose ex-students populated the town. My mother insisted that some of Ben's Hispanic friends sit in the pew beside her: I was made to sit in the pew behind her, but I reached over my father's shoulder and held his hand. Paul played the flute, then the minister read a speech I had written in which I proclaimed that we all had to take responsibility for our universes, our creations. When he finished, I stood up, and walked alone down the aisle, the anger on my face having become a mask of acceptance.

My mother insisted that no one from my father's university be allowed to attend the reception at the family home, especially not his close friend, whose name was also Paul. Food covered the dining room table, which, for years, had been ignored: because mealtimes had been opportunities for hostilities to be renewed, Ben and I and our father had learned to eat away from home. As I filled my plate with ham, a woman named Friedel said, "You're strong now, Chris, but you'll have to feel the pain later." My mother ordered Charlotte, a born-again Christian, to leave after the latter said, "God must be punishing you, Coleen."

Was God punishing us? The summer throbbed on. The need for my mother and father to torture each other increased. I could "accept responsibility for the universe, my creation," but a part of it had collapsed as the life had left Ben's body, which had seemed tiny under the white sheet, those last minutes of his life. I decided to go away, with my friend Paul, to Humboldt State University in northern California. This began a decade-long period of wandering around the universe, during which I felt as if I lived in a kind of shocked solitude, the delayed and expanded emotional "fetal position" of grief. I was impotent: I refused to let Ben's grieving brother inside my body be touched.

In the weeks after Ben's murder, the *Daily News* ran stories about the search for the murderers. Although I'd been spared the task of writing Ben's obituary, I was pained by my father's horror at the publicity attending what, for him, was an exclusively personal tragedy. My mother took the tragedy into the public realm, talking about it everywhere, including in the classroom, but she was furious at the anti-Hispanic slant of the coverage. I asked the editor in chief to stop running stories about Ben's murder. "News is news," he said. A sense of the world as unreal, an alien place, was deepening. God was punishing us.

Throughout July and August, I prepared for college by painting. On a huge canvas, I created a panorama of greenery: a few of the brush strokes, in the shape of an inverted pyramid, or a V, suggested a canyon and there was a small red dot in the lower corner of the painting, where a signature should have been.

My mother immersed herself in Parents of Murdered Children, a support group (which would later involve her in talk show appearances and in high-level political advocacy) for people whom she and her associates called "victims of murder," the absurd life-denying irony of the phrase never obvious to them. The administration of Whittier High School asked her to take a sabbatical: they were disturbed by her openness with students about what had happened to her. Her face was red from crying and anger and alcohol and, probably, menopause.

My father's pain was silent. When I visited the family house, I found him hunched in front of the television, watching, in effect, nothing. One afternoon, I found, in his desk, a short, furious poem, a raw expression of outrage and grief at the loss of his son, with hair "so beautiful."

Munoz had fled to Colorado, where his parents owned a house. He was quickly caught. Kuns attempted to disappear into the navy, but was expelled for some illegal activity, then, on my mother's fiftieth birthday, was arrested by the FBI. Finally he was sentenced to a minimum of fifteen years in the regular prisons; Munoz would be held by the California Youth Authority until he reached the age of twenty-five.

That fall, my father would come home from USC each night to find his wife, already drunk, brooding in the living room. What words passed between them were words of frustration, anger, disappointment, loneliness.

At Humboldt State, I wore white shirts, acquired an almost-delicate thinness, read T. S. Eliot, and, anxious to distinguish my frantic, "damaged" life from the mellowness of the hippie culture around me, made a point of listening to Talking Heads, rather than Grateful Dead, records. I laughed too loudly, hysterically. I wept in the office of Jorie Graham, my poetry workshop instructor: "You don't have to write poems about all this pain if you don't want to face it," she said, but, in teaching me how poetic imagery could be a liberating deflection away from the known self, revealing subtle, mysterious elements of character, she showed me a way not simply to release emotion, but to transmute it, and, possibly, to heal from grief. The northern Californian landscape was beautiful. I stared down into the forest undergrowth, scraping away fallen pine needles, exposing ivy tendrils crisscrossing the roots of evergreens.

Separated from my parents but not from the anxiety of my relationship with them, and surrounded by friends from poetry workshops with whom I could articulate my agonies indirectly, through my poetry, the repressed violence in me began to seep out. The fact that a female classmate and I seemed to be dating made me twitch with uncomfort. Although Jorie was only thirty, her "nurturing" made her seem a kind of substitute mother, one to whom I could show the fury I felt toward my literal mother. The winter rains stopped, spring erupted, and I wrote a poem called "The Murderer," in which a murderer with a voice sounding more like mine than that of David

Kuns narrates a dream. The poem ends with the line "I hardly know what I've done."

As I wrote, and tried to adjust to unfamiliar people and situations, and buried my sensuality in my thin, untouched body, I developed, within myself, a wordless private vocabulary of nonfigurative imagery that spontaneously illustrated my emotional responses to events. Driving up and down California, I felt the length of the state inside me. I felt my dependence on my mother and father as a kind of elastic weight in my nervous system.

I had the opportunity to transfer to Syracuse University: because it, like USC, was a private university, the two schools had established a student exchange program, and as the child of a faculty member at USC, I could attend either school tuition free. Close to New York City, I thought, my punk identity could flower; I had not imagined the ways in which my gay identity would grow. In their dark-haired urbanity, New Yorkers seemed unable to perceive my fragility. Anxieties rippled through my body, and tugged words down my throat, away from my mouth. In therapy, I tried to express a sensation of being pulled backward across the continent to Los Angeles, as if a caul surrounded me and my mother held the other end.

A graduate creative writing student and I entered into a relationship which seems paradigmatic of my social life throughout the eighties and early nineties. George may have been schizophrenic: he was smart, aggressive, and despised whatever in me struck him as self-indulgent, puerile. He introduced me to writers who were involved in aesthetic, cultural, and linguistic, not psychological, issues. I wanted the uncomfort and the sexless intellectualism of our friendship. Sitting in his Volkswagen Bug, unable to see my face in his rearview mirror as the sunset made it glint, I imagined that rectangle of fire inside my mind, a symbol for the self as abstraction, its density and weight, like words, pulling me down.

On weekend nights, I would walk around the Lower East Side. I was unafraid of homeless people warming their fingers over trash cans of burning garbage. I felt almost invisible, invincible: touching death had inoculated me, and now I was immune to death.

In 1983, my father finally left my mother. He moved to Hollywood, where he remained afraid that she would find him. That summer, I moved to Iowa City, where I would attend the Iowa Writers' Workshop: when he visited me there, I received a phone call from a new boyfriend, Steve, which provided my father and me with an opportunity to awkwardly "come out" to each other. I, too, "divorced" my mother. My father told me that during the divorce proceedings, she raved in the courtroom over the division of property; I was glad I was not being divided, I thought, although friends questioned me as to why I was involved with Steve, who treated me unkindly.

Every poem seemed an attempt to articulate my response, my responsibility, to violence, if not death itself. I remembered that at the art camp in Idyllwild I had shoved a female lifeguard into the swimming pool: I'd snuck up to her back as she'd been showing us how to dive from the side of the pool. I could remember (well enough to describe the feeling in a poem) putting my lifelines on the small of her back, and I could imagine my father shoving my mother.

Was I immune to death? Had I, so to speak, shoved my lifeguard into the water? Years later, in the summer of 1993, in Taos, New Mexico, I had an affair with a man who was HIV positive. He did not reveal his health status to me until the end of the summer. Although I was not infected, he was my David Kuns: given the tensions in my life between sensuality and solitude, he stabbed something essential in me. But I, unlike Ben, escaped. I want to believe that this crisis was "survival guilt" 's last stand in what will be a long life.

I was a resident at an artist's colony, the Wurlitzer Foundation. David was a local Hispanic elementary-school teacher. At first he seemed intensely warm; after I knew his health status and returned to Charlotte, where I was then living and teaching, he seemed narcissistic, selfish, consuming. Desperate for sexual fulfillment, at his insistence I abandoned my cabin at the Wurlitzer Foundation and moved in with David, trading my identity as a poet, the reason I was in Taos that summer, for the exotic, happy atmosphere of his "Spanglish"-speaking family. On the Fourth of July, he and I smoked strong dope and watched scarlet fireworks explode in the black sky. He stood behind me and wrapped his warm arms around my waist. I wondered why he had a "special doctor" in Albuquerque, and what, exactly, his health status was, but, for so many reasons, I avoided interrupting that romantic moment to ask him hard, life-protecting questions.

Once, he asked me, "Aren't you afraid of being with someone like me, all dried up?"

Another afternoon, he said, "Whenever I'm with you, *lindo*, spiritual, religious things go through my mind."

When we made love, he would touch my anus, showing me that he wanted to be inside me. I resisted, unwilling to do something typically out of my range. I was scheduled to leave Taos on August 6, Ben's birthday; during my last week, I decided to give him the pleasure he seemed to crave. He ejaculated outside my body. The condom had been broken. "Oooh," he hissed, "that's not good."

Stretched out against him on his bed, the insight I had repressed a month ago began to form into a question. I felt terrified, but coldly in control. "Have you been tested?" I asked.

"Yes," he said.

"And did you test . . . positive?"

"Yes."

I turned onto my side, away from him, and was quiet. So that's that, I thought. I'm doomed. That would be my fate, wouldn't it.

My long silence was passively aggressive.

Finally, David said, *"Mijito*, you gave a lot to me, but I'll tell you, you will always have a lover in me."

Eight years previously, his lover (who, I now learned, lived in San Diego) had infected him: as he told me this, his tears revealed the reason he had craved endangering me: he wanted to expiate his rage by reversing the roles. And I did want a lover. And wasn't I used to feeling close to death? That part of me which remembered being the shield before my mother's body, which, in a lethal situation, felt totally involved and totally helpless, was in danger now of drowning in the warmth, and needed a lifeguard.

My last day in Taos, I took the last bit of marijuana from David's kitchen drawer and drove down to the edge of the Rio Grande, to the hot springs. It was a blazing afternoon. A beautiful nude boy sunned on a boulder. He had long red hair. Stripping off my clothes, I loved the feeling of the sun on my shoulders and my belly. My body seemed to swell and glow with stoned excitement. I sunk down into the muddy, amniotic hot spring.

The boy's eyes were closed. The sun pressed its heat down against his chest, his torso. His cock lay on his thigh, and twitched into hardness, but still he did not open his eyes. Even when he rose, tiptoed to the hot spring, and lowered his turned-on body down into the fluid, he still refused to look at me. He reached around behind his head to a crack between two boulders. He pulled out a pot pipe, lit it, and puffed. For quite a while we sat together, his white cock bobbing in the murky water. I touched his knee. He shoved my hand away, then opened his eyes and glared at me.

Why was he saying no? My stoned thoughts wandered. What about my current nightmare? What if I'm sick? Will I be able to write poetry about it? Furious, primal poetry, my dreamlife finally free from the citizenly need for repression? If I'm sick, I thought, my longevity will be a sacrifice to my poetry, through which I'll finally be able to understand what this mysterious presence of death, so essential in my life, is all about.

From the landing where my truck was parked, the shouts of two other young men tumbled down to the hot spring. The boy opened his eyes. He waved to his two friends as they approached. They stripped. They giggled. They said hello to me as they descended into the spring. Another pipe was passed around. The sun started to set. From some hints and innuendos, I guessed that the boy had been waiting for his pals, and that, once the darkness hid their faces, their love-in would begin.

The guy with the strongest personality worked to engage me in conversation. Now the air was dark. I was very stoned: the cool breeze over the warm water touched my face, and made me shiver. I also shivered from my thoughts of my possible death, and the articulation I could wring from dying; my inner articulation was so different from the chatter shared by these three boys, and I felt like an intruder, a voyeur, and then like an embarrassing old man, desperate, solipsistic, pathetic. Actually, I thought, my whole life has seemed like this: impossible to be happy in, impossible to survive. The leader snickered. "Hey guy," he said to me, "I don't know if your truck'll be safe up there once it gets dark. Sometimes the Mexicans come and mess with people's cars up there . . ."

His words had their intended effect. If I hadn't been jittering, I would have shrugged.

Fate is fate, I thought.

The tiny amount of tear-moisture in my eyes seemed to make the stars jitter, far away in their lonely silence.

The lifeguard inside me began to whisper to the fat, passive, loyal little boy inside me. "Get up out of this mudhole, Chris," the lifeguard said. "Can't you see it's eroding your life? Listen to what these goofballs are talking about. Nothing."

When I stood up, the night blew on my wet nakedness.

Fate *is* fate: that is the element I could have drowned in. Self-awareness, self-love, that is my lifeguard.

Back in Charlotte, I waited for the test results from the health center. Curled on my bed, I imagined being outside, riding my bicycle down the sidewalk, passing under the leaves of the huge old East Coast trees I couldn't name. The leaves at the edges of the treetops glowed like emeralds, and seemed almost swollen with daylight; the shadows of the treetops almost covered the sidewalk, but not quite. I imagined feeling, on my bare shoulders, sudden, quick fingers of warmth, then the coolness of the shadows as I darted from tree to tree, life and death touching me again and again as I continued my journey toward some distant conclusion.

Near David's house, in a town called Arroyo Seco, "dry ditch," there was a Penitente *morada*, or chapel. A sign on the gate asked tourists to refrain from taking pictures. The windows of the old house were boarded up. The Penitentes, of course, were famous for their ritual self-floggings. Tourists were excited to read, in their guidebooks, that the inner walls of the *moradas* were stained with blood. In the grass behind the chapel stood a large, simple crucifix of wood: in earlier days, before publicity, men had chosen or had volunteered to hang on the cross at Easter, reenacting Christ's worldly death.

David's mother, who had lived all her life in Arroyo Seco, told me that back in her childhood, on religious holidays the Penitentes would organize circuitous processions through the town. The church elders, dressed in black, would shuffle along the dirt roads, singing their slow, sad hymns, their *alabados*, describing frightened sheep lost in the canyons, crying to be found.

Young initiates would walk behind the elders and beat tambourines or blow on whistles. The old Penitentes, she said, were frightening in their sternness and sorrow. Behind their backs, she and her friends snickered at them; if the laughter were heard, the girls would be punished by fierce glares from the eyes of these inhabitants of an emotion in which love and death were unified, these men who lived their lives symbolically, in imitation of the life of one man for whom material existence had been entirely symbolic, the shadow of the deathless realm which the Penitentes, like all transitory mortals, could only guess at, and never, in this life, see or know.

To the Penitentes, the injuring of the flesh was that guess, the body bent into a question mark.

Was it strange, the life and death of my brother, or was it only an exaggeration of something quite common? No one else had hair like Ben's, such a brilliant red. No one else was discarded in a canyon, left to die in a green crevice of the world. No one else crawled back up into the sun to refuse to let himself be touched, and to say "I love you" to his mother before dying.

Why had Ben and I made a childlike kind of love, both of us seemingly encouraged to do so by the forces of male power that surrounded us, as if, in our incest, there were the seeds of an orderly masculinity?

David's mother said that the Penitentes were the governmental leaders of the village, voting on, and enforcing, town ordinances, see-ing to the early educational needs of the children, and providing meet-ing places for the citizens. This seemed profound to me. These men, for whom worship meant flirting with suicide, were community-minded, and were not interested in turning away from other people into private worlds of extreme gratification. They were responsible fathers.

As I slowly recovered from my brother's murder, it was impossible for me to separate the violence of my parents' marriage, and the violence of sexual complexities within the family, from the act of violence that took my brother's life. But perhaps three wrongs make a right. Had Ben never died, and had his death not sent a nearly electro-cuting shock through the crisscrossed wires of my emotional system, I might never have left home, might never have begun the process of "individuation," to use the Jungian word: my characteristic helpless involvement might have consumed me, my life dissolving into drug addiction or some other hell.

I cannot say that the universe is "my" creation, but I am willing to take responsibility for what, in the universe, touches me. Within my body, I contain, not Whitmanic multitudes, but a violent ability to respond. This is a source for energy, for destruction and love.

Now I have a lifeguard in me called self-knowledge who protects me from drowning, not in water, but in fire. If the sacrifice of the erotic body, totally helpless, totally involved, is the point of entry into the core of life, I am lucky to have survived thus far my journey through that core, burning like the hair around Ben's mind, toward self-knowl-edge.

Someday, with more luck, stretched out naked on the shore, I'll feel the sun.

Mirrorings

LUCY GREALY

There was a long period of time, almost a year, *during which* I never looked in a mirror. It wasn't easy, for I'd never suspected just how omnipresent are our own images. I began by merely avoiding mirrors, but by the end of the year I found myself with an acute knowledge of the reflected image, its numerous tricks and wiles, how it can spring up at any moment: a glass tabletop, a well-polished door handle, a darkened window, a pair of sunglasses, a restaurant's otherwise magnificent brass-plated coffee machine sitting innocently by the cash register.

At the time, I had just moved, alone, to Scotland and was surviving on the dole, as Britain's social security benefits are called. I didn't know anyone and had no idea how I was going to live, yet I went anyway because by happenstance I'd met a plastic surgeon there who said he could help me. I had been living in London, working temp jobs. While in London, I'd received more nasty comments about my face than I had in the previous three years, living in Iowa, New York, and Germany. These comments, all from men and all odiously sexual, hurt and disoriented me. I also had journeyed to Scotland because after more than a dozen operations in the States, my insurance had run out, along with my hope that further operations could make any *real* difference. Here, however, was a surgeon who had some new techniques, and here, amazingly enough, was a government willing to foot the bill: I didn't feel I could pass up yet another chance to "fix" my face, which I confusedly thought concurrent with "fixing" my self, my soul, my life.

Twenty years ago, when I was nine and living in America, I came home from school one day with a toothache. Several weeks and misdiagnoses later, surgeons removed most of the right side of my jaw in an attempt to prevent the cancer they found there from spreading. No one properly explained the operation to me, and I awoke in a cocoon of pain that prevented me from moving or speaking. Tubes ran in and out of my body, and because I was temporarily unable to speak after the surgery and could not ask questions, I made up my own explanations for the tubes' existence. I remember the mysterious manner the adults displayed toward me. They asked me to do things: lie still for X rays, not cry for needles, and so on, tasks that, although not easy, never seemed equal to the praise I received in return. Reinforced to me again and again was how I was "a brave girl" for not crying, "a good girl" for not complaining, and soon I began defining myself this way, equating strength with silence.

Then the chemotherapy began. In the seventies chemo was even cruder than it is now, the basic premise being to poison patients right up to the very brink of their own death. Until this point I almost never cried and almost always received praise in return. Thus I got what I considered the better part of the deal. But now it was like a practical joke that had gotten out of hand. Chemotherapy was a nightmare and I wanted it to stop; I didn't want to be brave anymore. Yet I had grown so used to defining myself as "brave"—i.e., *silent*—that the thought of losing this sense of myself was even more terrifying. I was certain that if I broke down I would be despicable in the eyes of both my parents and the doctors.

The task of taking me into the city for the chemo injections fell mostly on my mother, though sometimes my father made the trip. Overwhelmed by the sight of the vomiting and weeping, my father developed the routine of "going to get the car," meaning that he left the doctor's office before the injection was administered, on the premise that then he could have the car ready and waiting when it was all over. Ashamed of my suffering, I felt relief when he was finally out of the room. When my mother took me, she stayed in the room, yet this only made the distance between us even more tangible. She explained that it was wrong to cry *before* the needle went in; afterward was one thing, but before, that was mere fear, and hadn't I demonstrated my bravery earlier? Every Friday for two and a half years I climbed up onto that big doctor's table and told myself not to cry, and every week I failed. The two large syringes were filled with chemicals so caustic to the vein that each had to be administered very slowly. The whole process took about four minutes; I had to remain utterly still. Dry retching began in the first fifteen seconds, then the throb behind my eyes gave everything a yellow-green aura, and the bone-deep pain of alternating extreme hot and cold flashes made me tremble, yet still I had to sit motionless and not move my arm. No one spoke to me—not the doctor, who was a paradigm of the cold-fish physician; not the nurse, who told my mother I reacted much more violently than many of "the other children"; and not my mother, who, surely overwhelmed by the sight of her child's suffering, thought the best thing to do was remind me to be brave, to try not to cry. All the while I hated myself for having wept before the needle went in, convinced that the nurse and my mother were right, that I was "overdoing it," that the throwing up was psychosomatic, that my mother was angry with me for not being good or brave enough.

Yet each week, two or three days after the injection, there came the first flicker of feeling better, the always forgotten and gratefully redis-covered understanding that to simply be well in my body was the greatest thing I could ask for. I thought other people felt this appreciation and physical joy all the time, and I felt cheated because I was able to feel it only once a week.

Because I'd lost my hair, I wore a hat constantly, but this fooled no one, least of all myself. During this time, my mother worked in a nursing home in a Hasidic community. Hasidic law dictates that married women cover their hair, and most commonly this is done with a wig. My mother's friends were now all too willing to donate their discarded wigs, and soon the house seemed filled with them. I never wore one, for they frightened me even when my mother insisted I looked better in one of the few that actually fit. Yet we didn't know how to say no to the women who kept graciously offering their wigs. The cats enjoyed sleeping on them and the dogs playing with them, and we grew used to having to pick a wig up off a chair we wanted to sit in. It never struck us as odd until one day a visitor commented wryly as he cleared a chair for himself, and suddenly a great wave of shame overcame me. I had nightmares about wigs and flushed if I even heard the word, and one night I put myself out of my misery by getting up after everyone was asleep and gathering all the wigs except for one the dogs were fond of and that they had chewed up anyway. I hid all the rest in an old chest.

When you are only ten, which is when the chemotherapy began, two and a half years seem like your whole life, yet it did finally end, for the cancer was gone. I remember the last day of treatment clearly because it was the only day on which I succeeded in not crying, and because later, in private, I cried harder than I had in years; I thought now I would no longer be "special," that without the arena of chemotherapy in which to prove myself, no one would ever love me, that I would fade unnoticed into the background. But this idea about *not being different* didn't last very long. Before, I foolishly believed that people stared at me because I was bald. After my hair eventually grew in, it didn't take long before I understood that I looked different for another reason. My face. People stared at me in stores, and other children made fun of me to the point that I came to expect such reactions constantly, wherever I went. School became a battle-ground.

Halloween, that night of frights, became my favorite holiday because I could put on a mask and walk among the blessed for a few brief, sweet hours. Such freedom I felt, walking down the street, my face hidden! Through the imperfect oval holes I could peer out at other faces, masked or painted or not, and see on those faces nothing but the normal faces of childhood looking back at me, faces I mistakenly thought were the faces everyone else but me saw all the time, faces that were simply curious and ready for fun, not the faces I usually braced myself for, the cruel, lonely, vicious ones I spent every day other than Halloween waiting to see around each corner. As I breathed in the condensed, plastic-scented air under the mask, I somehow thought that I was breathing in normality, that this joy and weightlessness were what the world was composed of, and that it was only my face that kept me from it, my face that was my own mask that kept me from knowing the joy I was sure everyone but me lived with intimately. How could the other children not know it? Not know that to be free of the fear of taunts and the burden of knowing no one would ever love you was all that anyone could ever ask for? I was a pauper walking for a short while in the clothes of the prince, and when the day ended, I gave up my disguise with dismay.

I was living in an extreme situation, and because I did not particularly care for the world I was in, I lived in others, and because the world I did live in was dangerous now, I incorporated this danger into my secret life. I imagined myself to be an Indian. Walking down the streets, I stepped through the forest, my body ready for any opportunity to fight or flee one of the big cats that I knew stalked me. Vietnam and Cambodia, in the news then as scenes of catastrophic horror, were other places I walked through daily. I made my way down the school hall, knowing a land mine or a sniper might give themselves away at any moment with the subtle metal click I'd read about. Compared with a land mine, a mere insult about my face seemed a frivolous thing.

In those years, not yet a teenager, I secretly read—knowing it was somehow inappropriate—works by Primo Levi and Elie Wiesel, and every book by a survivor I could find by myself without asking the librarian. Auschwitz, Birkenau: I felt the blows of the capos and somehow knew that because at any moment we might be called upon to live for a week on one loaf of bread and some water called soup, the peanut butter sandwich I found on my plate was nothing less than a miracle, an utter and sheer miracle capable of making me literally weep with joy.

I decided to become a "deep" person. I wasn't exactly sure what this would entail, but I believed that if I could just find the right philosophy, think the right thoughts, my suffering would end. To try to understand the world I was in, I undertook to find out what was "real," and I quickly began seeing reality as existing in the lowest common denominator, that suffering was the one and only dependable thing. But rather than spend all of my time despairing, though certainly I did plenty of that, I developed a form of defensive egomania: I felt I was the only one walking about in the world who understood what was really important. I looked upon people complaining about the most mundane things—nothing on TV, traffic jams, the price of new clothes—and felt joy because I knew how unimportant those things really were and felt unenlightened superiority because other people didn't. Because in my fantasy life I had learned to be thankful for each cold, blanketless night that I survived on the cramped wooden bunks, my pain and despair were a stroll through the country in comparison. I was often miserable, but I knew that to feel warm instead of cold was its own kind of joy, that to eat was a reenactment of the grace of some god whom I could only dimly define, and that to simply be alive was a rare, ephemeral gift.

As I became a teenager, my isolation began. My nonidentical twin sister started going out with boys, and I started—my most tragic mistake of all—to listen to and believe the taunts thrown at me daily by the very boys she and the other girls were interested in. I was a dog, a monster, the ugliest girl they had ever seen. Of all the remarks, the most damaging wasn't even directed at me but was really an insult to "Jerry," a boy I never saw because every day between fourth and fifth periods, when I was cornered by a particular group of kids, I was too ashamed to lift my eyes off the floor. "Hey look, it's Jerry's girl-friend!" they shrieked when they saw me, and I felt such shame, knowing that this was the deepest insult to Jerry that they could imagine.

When pressed to it, one makes compensations. I came to love winter, when I could wrap up the disfigured lower half of my face in a scarf: I could speak to people and they would have no idea to whom and to what they were really speaking. I developed the bad habits of letting my long hair hang in my face and of always covering my chin and mouth with my hand, hoping it might be mistaken as a thoughtful, accidental gesture. I also became interested in horses and got a job at a run-down local stable. Having those horses to go to each day after school saved my life; I spent all my time either with them or thinking about them. Completely and utterly repressed by the time I was six-teen, I was convinced that I would never want a boyfriend, not ever, and wasn't it convenient for me, even a blessing, that none would ever want me. I told myself I was free to concentrate on the "true reality" of life, whatever that was. My sister and her friends put on blue eye shadow, blow-dried their hair, and spent interminable hours in the local mall, and I looked down on them for this, knew they were misleading themselves and being overly occupied with the "mere sur-face" of living. I'd had thoughts like this when I was younger, ten or twelve, but now my philosophy was haunted by desires so frightening, I was unable even to admit they existed.

Throughout all of this, I was undergoing re-constructive surgery in an attempt to rebuild my jaw. It started when I was fifteen, two years after the chemo ended. I had known for years I would have operations to fix my face, and at night I fantasized about how good my life would finally be then. One day I got a clue that maybe it wouldn't be so easy. An older plastic surgeon explained the process of "pedestals" to me, and told me it would take *ten years* to fix my face. Ten years? Why even bother, I thought; I'll be ancient by then. I went to a medical library and looked up the "pedestals" he talked about. There were gruesome pictures of people with grotesque tubes of their own skin growing out of their bodies, tubes of skin that were harvested like some kind of crop and then rearranged, with results that did not look at all normal or acceptable to my eye. But then I met a younger surgeon, who was working on a new way of grafting that did not involve pedestals, and I became more hopeful and once again began to await the fixing of my face, the day when I would be whole, content, loved.

Long-term plastic surgery is not like in the movies. There is no one single operation that will change everything, and there is certainly no slow unwrapping of the gauze in order to view the final, remarkable result. There is always swelling, sometimes to a grotesque degree, there are often bruises, and always there are scars. After each operation, too frightened to simply go look in the mirror, I developed an oblique method, with several stages. First, I tried to catch my reflection in an overhead lamp: the roundness of the metal distorted my image just enough to obscure details and give no true sense of size or proportion. Then I slowly worked my way up to looking at the reflection in someone's eyeglasses, and from there I went to walking as briskly as possible by a mirror, glancing only quickly. I repeated this as many times as it would take me, passing the mirror slightly more slowly each time until finally I was able to stand still and confront myself.

The theory behind most reconstructive surgery is to take large chunks of muscle, skin, and bone and slap them into the roughly appropriate place, then slowly begin to carve this mess into some sort of shape. It involves long major operations, countless lesser ones, a lot of pain, and many, many years. And also, it does not always work. With my young surgeon in New York, who with each passing year was becoming not so young, I had two or three soft-tissue grafts, two skin grafts, a bone graft, and some dozen other operations to "revise" my face, yet when I left graduate school at the age of twenty-five I was still more or less in the same position I had started in: a deep hole in the right side of my face and a rapidly shrinking left side and chin, a result of the radiation I'd had as a child and the stress placed upon the bone by the other operations. I was caught in a cycle of having a big operation, one that would force me to look monstrous from the swelling for many months, then having the subsequent revision operations that improved my looks tremendously, and then slowly, over the period of a few months or a year, watching the graft reabsorb back into my body, slowly shrinking down and leaving me with nothing but the scarred donor site the graft had originally come from.

It wasn't until I was in college that I finally allowed that maybe, just maybe, it might be nice to have a boyfriend. I went to a small, liberal, predominantly female school and suddenly, after years of alienation in high school, discovered that there were other people I could enjoy talking to who thought me intelligent and talented. I was, however, still operating on the assumption that no one, not ever, would be physically attracted to me, and in a curious way this shaped my personality. I became forthright and honest in the way that only the truly self-confident are, who do not expect to be rejected, and in the way of those like me, who do not even dare to ask acceptance from others and therefore expect no rejection. I had come to know myself as a person, but I would be in graduate school before I was literally, physically able to use my name and the word "woman" in the same sentence.

Now my friends repeated for me endlessly that most of it was in my mind, that, granted, I did not look like everyone else, but that didn't mean I looked bad. I am sure now that they were right some of the time. But with the constant surgery I was in a perpetual state of transfiguration. I rarely looked the same for more than six months at a time. So ashamed of my face, I was unable even to admit that this constant change affected me; I let everyone who wanted to know that it was only what was inside that mattered, that I had "grown used to" the surgery, that none of it bothered me at all. Just as I had done in childhood, I pretended nothing was wrong, and this was constantly mistaken by others for bravery. I spent a great deal of time looking in the mirror in private, positioning my head to show off my eyes and nose, which were not only normal but quite pretty, as my friends told me often. But I could not bring myself to see them for more than a moment: I looked in the mirror and saw not the normal upper half of my face but only the disfigured lower half.

People still teased me. Not daily, as when I was younger, but in ways that caused me more pain than ever before. Children stared at me, and I learned to cross the street to avoid them; this bothered me, but not as much as the insults I got from men. Their taunts came at me not because I was disfigured but because I was a disfigured *woman*. They came from boys, sometimes men, and almost always from a group of them. I had long blond hair, and I also had a thin figure. Sometimes, from a distance, men would see a thin blonde and whistle, something I dreaded more than anything else because I knew that as they got closer, their tune, so to speak, would inevitably change; they would stare openly or, worse, turn away quickly in shame or repulsion. I decided to cut my hair to avoid any misconception that anyone, however briefly, might have about my being attractive. Only two or three times have I ever been teased by a single person, and I can think of only one time when I was ever teased by a woman. Had I been a man, would I have had to walk down the street while a group of young women followed and denigrated my sexual worth?

Not surprisingly, then, I viewed sex as my salvation. I was sure that if only I could get someone to sleep with me it would mean I wasn't ugly, that I was attractive, even lovable. This line of reasoning led me into the beds of several manipulative men who liked themselves even less than they liked me, and I in turn left each short-term affair hating myself, obscenely sure that if only I had been prettier, it would have worked—he would have loved me and it would have been like those other love affairs that I was certain "normal" women had all the time. Gradually, I became unable to say "I'm depressed" but could say only "I'm ugly," because the two had become inextricably linked in my mind. Into that universal lie, that sad equation of "if only . . ." that we are all prey to, I was sure that if only I had a normal face, then I would be happy.

　　　　　　　　The new surgeon in Scotland, Oliver Fenton, recommended that I undergo a procedure involving something called a tissue expander, followed by a bone graft. A tissue expander is a small balloon placed under the skin and then slowly blown up over the course of several months, the object being to stretch out the skin and create room and cover for the new bone. It's a bizarre, nightmarish thing to do to your face, yet I was hopeful about the end results and I was also able to spend the three months that the expansion took in the hospital. I've always felt safe in hospitals: they're the one place I feel free from the need to explain the way I look. For this reason the first tissue expander was bearable—just—and the bone graft that followed it was a success; it did not melt away like the previous ones.

The surgical stress this put upon what remained of my original jaw instigated the deterioration of that bone, however, and it became un-happily apparent that I was going to need the same operation I'd just had on the right side done to the left. I remember my surgeon telling me this at an outpatient clinic. I planned to be traveling down to London that same night on an overnight train, and I barely made it to the station on time, such a fumbling state of despair was I in.

I could not imagine going through it *again,* and just as I had done all my life, I searched and searched through my intellect for a way to make it okay, make it bearable, for a way to *do* it. I lay awake all night on that train, feeling the tracks slip beneath me with an odd eroticism, when I remembered an afternoon from my three months in the hospi-tal. Boredom was a big problem those long afternoons, the days marked by meals and television programs. Waiting for the afternoon tea to come, wondering desperately how I could make time pass, it had suddenly occurred to me that I didn't have to make time pass, that it would do it of its own accord, that I simply had to relax and take no action. Lying on the train, remembering that, I realized I had no obligation to improve my situation, that I didn't have to explain or understand it, that I could just simply let it happen. By the time the train pulled into King's Cross station, I felt able to bear it yet again, not entirely sure what other choice I had.

But there was an element I didn't yet know about. When I returned to Scotland to set up a date to have the tissue expander inserted, I was told quite casually that I'd be in the hospital only three or four days. Wasn't I going to spend the whole expansion time in the hospital? I asked in a whisper. What's the point of that? came the answer. You can just come in every day to the outpatient ward to have it expanded. Horrified by this, I was speechless. I would have to live and move about in the outside world with a giant balloon inside the tissue of my face? I can't remember what I did for the next few days before I went into the hospital, but I vaguely recall that these days involved a great deal of drinking alone in bars and at home.

I had the operation and went home at the end of the week. The only things that gave me any comfort during the months I lived with my tissue expander were my writing and Franz Kafka. I started a novel and completely absorbed myself in it, writing for hours each day. The only way I could walk down the street, could stand the stares I received, was to think to myself, "I'll bet none of them are writing a novel." It was that strange, old, familiar form of egomania, directly related to my dismissive, conceited thoughts of adolescence. As for Kafka, who had always been one of my favorite writers, he helped me in that I felt permission to feel alienated, and to have that alienation be okay, bearable, noble even. In the same way that imagining I lived in Cambodia helped me as a child, I walked the streets of my dark little Scottish city by the sea and knew without doubt that I was living in a story Kafka would have been proud to write.

The one good thing about a tissue expander is that you look so bad with it in that no matter what you look like once it's finally removed, your face has to look better. I had my bone graft and my fifth soft-tissue graft and, yes, even I had to admit I looked better. But I didn't look like me. Something was wrong: was *this* the face I had waited through eighteen years and almost thirty operations for? I somehow just couldn't make what I saw in the mirror correspond to the person I thought I was. It wasn't only that I continued to feel ugly; I simply could not conceive of the image as belonging to me. My own image was the image of a stranger, and rather than try to understand this, I simply stopped looking in the mirror. I perfected the technique of brushing my teeth without a mirror, grew my hair in such a way that it would require only a quick, simple brush, and wore clothes that were simply and easily put on, no complex layers or lines that might require even the most minor of visual adjustments.

On one level I understood that the image of my face was merely that, an image, a surface that was not directly related to any true, deep definition of the self. But I also knew that it is only through appearances that we experience and make decisions about the everyday world, and I was not always able to gather the strength to prefer the deeper world to the shallower one. I looked for ways to find a bridge that would allow me access to both, rather than ride out the constant swings between peace and anguish. The only direction I had to go in to achieve this was to strive for a state of awareness and self-honesty that sometimes, to this day, occasionally rewards me. I have found, I believe, that our whole lives are dominated, though it is not always so clearly translatable, by the question "How do I look?" Take all the many nouns in our lives—car, house, job, family, love, friends—and substitute the personal pronoun I. It is not that we are all so self-obsessed; it is that all things eventually relate back to ourselves, and it is our own sense of how we appear to the world by which we chart our lives, how we navigate our personalities, which would otherwise be adrift in the ocean of *other* people's obsessions.

One evening toward the end of my year-long separation from the mirror, I was sitting in a café, talking to someone—an attractive man, as it happened—and we were having a lovely, engaging conversation. For some reason I suddenly wondered what I looked like to him. What was he *actually* seeing when he saw me? So many times I've asked this of myself, and always the answer is this: a warm, smart woman, yes, but an unattractive one. I sat there in the café and asked myself this old question, and startlingly, for the first time in my life, I had no answer readily prepared. I had not looked in a mirror for so long that I quite simply had no clue as to what I looked like. I studied the man as he spoke; my entire life I had seen my ugliness reflected back to me. But now, as reluctant as I was to admit it, the only indication in my companion's behavior was positive.

And then, that evening in that café, I experienced a moment of the freedom I'd been practicing for behind my Halloween mask all those years ago. But whereas as a child I expected my liberation to come as a result of gaining something, a new face, it came to me now as the result of shedding something, of shedding my image. I once thought that truth was eternal, that when you understood something, it was with you forever. I know now that this isn't so, that most truths are inherently unretainable, that we have to work hard all our lives to remember the most basic things. Society is no help; it tells us again and again that we can most be ourselves by looking like someone else, leaving our own faces behind to turn into ghosts that will inevitably resent and haunt us. It is no mistake that in movies and literature the dead sometimes know they are dead only after they can no longer see themselves in the mirror; and as I sat there feeling the warmth of the cup against my palm, this small observation seemed like a great revelation to me. I wanted to tell the man I was with about it, but he was involved in his own topic and I did not want to interrupt him, so instead I looked with curiosity toward the window behind him, its night-darkened glass reflecting the whole café, to see if I could, now, recognize myself.

Fugitive Light, Old Photos

RICHARD MCCANN

At the morgue, the attendant showed us two Polaroids.

In one, my brother Davis was prone. In the other, he'd been turned face-up on a steel examining table. *Who combed his hair so neatly?* I wondered. *Who gave him that bright blue T-shirt?* But in the flashbulb's glare, his face looked mottled, the way a sleeper's face is sometimes marked by the imprint of his blanket, so that he seems to be bearing a harsh dream's souvenir.

"That's not my son," my mother said, putting the Polaroids down on the counter. She said she would have to see the body.

But the attendant returned to his desk—green metal, like government issue. He read from his clipboard: we couldn't see the body unless we had prior written permission, he said, since actual viewing was no longer the standard procedure. Then he resumed his work, watching *Soul Train* on a miniature TV.

I know I should have argued with him, as my mother wanted. I know I should have insisted.

But I wanted to see nothing further: not the tiled corridors, nor the refrigerated units, those rows of identical steel doors. After all, wasn't it enough to have cleared Davis's garbage-strewn apartment, to have disposed of the urine-soaked mattress on which he died, dragging it down three flights of stairs to his building's alleyway Dumpster? And afterward, when the police came to search his apartment for evidence, wasn't it enough to have hidden his used syringes at the bottom of a grocery bag, beneath old newspapers, like ordinary garbage? Davis was thirty-six. He had died of a drug overdose.

I signed the papers.

All the way home, I tried to reassure my mother. I told her, "That was really Davis whose picture we saw."

We had his body cremated. There is no body anymore.

Here is Davis at six, shrill with laughter, embracing our father's cocker spaniel, who is lying feet up on the lawn. Here is Davis at eight, conspicuous in the back row of his fourth-grade photo, burdened by the brown patch the doctor has affixed to his eyeglasses. And here is Davis at twelve, standing at the swim club, awkwardly shielding his pubescent body with a towel.

"You don't know this," my mother tells me. "But Davis was a blue baby. When he was born, there were critical seconds when he didn't get air."

We are sitting at her dining room table, beneath a bright ceiling light, sorting old black and white photos with scalloped borders. We are making a scrapbook of Davis's life. "Look," my mother says, handing me a photo of Davis as an infant toddling across a lawn of cut grass, holding an Easter basket.

"That's why he cried too much," my mother says. "The doctor came to my room after the delivery. He told me that because Davis was a blue baby, he could have serious trouble later on."

What does she want me to tell her? That Davis could not be

comforted because something terrible had happened to him in the abrupt moment between being taken from her body and delivered crying into her arms?

I could just as well remind her how Davis laughed with pleasure whenever our father called him Davy Crockett.

He was thin and graceless. His teachers labeled him a slow learner.

When I was angry at him, she made me recite: "Let me be a little meeker/With the brother who is weaker."

But I know what she wants. She is seventy-five. She tells me that I am her best friend, now that most of her friends have died.

She wants me to say, "He was a blue baby. A long time ago, there were critical seconds when he didn't get air." She wants me to caption these flimsy Kodaks—these proofs of happy impetuosities, of sudden Saturday outings, of picnics and festive hats fashioned from aluminum foil—so that she can mount them onto the huge black pages of the scrapbook she has bought.

Instead, I hand her the photo of Davis toddling across the lawn.

None of this—not even this snapshot, with its streaks of light—is the past I now recall. I see how Davis stares dazedly at the camera, as if he were drowsy and fretful in the noonday heat. And suddenly I want to draw him close, to offer him my protection.

"Look," I tell her. "By 'trouble,' I don't think the doctor meant that Davis was going to die of a heroin overdose."

She is silent, as if to tell me I have hurt her. We have not discussed the autopsy report she has received: *"Needle punctures involving right forearm . . . ," "Kidneys, 300 gms., no gross focal lesions, sections not remarkable . . . ," "Lividity. . . ."* Then she busies herself. "That isn't what I meant," she says. "I was just trying to explain a theory."

She holds a photograph beneath the table lamp and examines it. Then she chooses another. "I remember every detail," she says.

Don't, I tell myself. After all, it is only a snapshot of Davis in cutoff jeans, lying on our porch glider. It's only a snapshot of Davis washing our old two-tone Chevy.

But I am furious.

And suddenly, in a long drop, before I can stop myself, I am falling, weightless and unconstrained, through all the unphotographed moments of her rages and her terrors, toward memories that rise beneath me like hard earth. She comes to our room at night, searching the house for her cigarettes, whispering accusations . . . *"Why can't you ever . . . ," "I shouldn't have hoped . . . ," "If you would only . . ."* By morning she is sprawled in her beige slip on the basement daybed, her silver bracelets—her "lucky bangles," as she calls them—discarded in a crystal ashtray. She murmurs in her sleep . . . *"Don't let . . . ," "I never hated . . . ," "Not harmed. . . ."*

Sometimes, after school, we find her waiting in her Impala at the edge of the parking lot, her face obscured by the sun visor's deliberate black slash. When we open the car door and get in, sliding across the wide vinyl seat, we find her strangely girlish and tearfully apologetic. Other times, when she is not there, we walk home slowly, past a power station and across a divided highway, and then on through acres of identical subdivisions, afraid to say we think we'll find her drinking.

Listen, do you really want a theory so badly? Then here is my theory: You were supposed to be the mother, but you let your child die.

And again I am returned to those long, fatherless nights of our adolescence, when Davis and I sat on the back porch, beside a black iron railing, still waiting for the appearance of late-blooming constellations, as if our father's impassive face might appear to us among them.

Our mother sat in her bedroom, listening to a radio call-in show. "Dear hearts," the deejay whispered. "It's late. I know you're lonely."

Go to her, Davis and I would argue.

For a moment, when I look up, I am not sure who she is—this woman who sits beside me, sorting old photos; this woman who has hung a stained-glass Serenity Prayer in her kitchen window. *She is an old woman*, I tell myself. *She lives in an old woman's house.* There are her floe-blue plates, displayed on shelves along the wall. There are her tiered end tables, neatly arranged with bric-a-brac. There are her cut-glass dishes, filled with sugarless candies.

"I have to go," I tell her. It is late. Soon she will need to check her blood sugar.

I know she is disappointed. I know these photographs have awakened in her a story she has no one else to tell. But tonight, I cannot hear how as an infant Davis cried when anyone approached him. How he feared crowds so badly, she could not take him on the streetcar.

Tonight, I want no stories. Tonight, I want only the singular, precise moments of these snapshots—these snapshots reversed from negatives, these sensitive emulsions dependent upon even the briefest, most fugitive light. Tonight, I want only the singular, precise moments of everything that remains unfixed, unsorted, not yet pasted to its final page.

"All right," my mother says. "We can finish our scrapbook later." She starts to gather loose photographs from the table. "You haven't told me why you think he died," she says.

"Drugs," I tell her. "He died of a drug overdose."

"I know," she says. "But that isn't what I'm asking."

I tell her I will straighten the table. I cap the bottle of white ink we have used for writing captions; I wipe it with a paper towel. Then I set it inside an old shoe box, alongside the loose photos she has gathered. She carries the shoe box to her bedroom, to store in what she calls her "memory drawer."

When she comes back, she is carrying a large manila envelope. She says she has filled it with photos she thinks I'll want to have.

Then she sees me to the door.

For a moment, we pause beneath the yellow porch light. From there, the boxwoods that border the garage seem almost blue, dense with luminescence. "Good night," she says.

"Good night," I say. I walk to the car. But when I turn to wave good-bye, I see she has already closed the front door.

I get in the car. I switch on the dome light. I open the manila envelope.

It is not filled with photos of Davis, as I expected. Instead, it is filled with old photos I studied as a child for hours, drifting through them—long rainy Saturdays, sitting on the screened-in porch; whole summer afternoons, lying on the cool tiles of the basement floor—until I grew so mesmerized, I could scarcely recall my own name. Here is my mother at six, nervously stroking a spotted pony, her bangs cut short across her forehead. And here she is at fifteen, standing on the broad lawn of her parents' summer house, smiling at the suitor who has filled her arms with cut hydrangeas, in order to take her picture just this way. And here she is, in the photo I loved best, taken during her first marriage, when she was barely twenty. The photo is torn. But within it, she calmly regards herself in her dresser mirror, so that one sees her as she sees herself, reflected, a stargazer lily pinned to her dark hair. On its back she has written, "I looked like Merle Oberon."

But where is a photo of the night Davis was first arrested? I was there.

Two policemen had brought him back to the house. They said they'd caught him in a park having sex with a man for money. He was eighteen.

From where I stood on the living room threshold, everyone seemed so still and silent, I thought they would turn into a photo. *Click*, I thought. *Click*.

Then my mother leaned forward. "Get out of my sight," she told Davis.

What could I have said to him the last time we spoke, the night he phoned from jail—"Don't tell Mom," he made me promise—because his headaches had grown so fierce he thought he would pluck out his eyes?

Once, she was beautiful.

Once, a man gave her cut flowers.

We are all of us blue babies. At critical seconds, we all lack necessary air.

My mother shuts off the porch light. The lawn falls into darkness.

I put the key in the ignition and start the car.

But when I look up, I see my mother framed in her picture window, walking back through her living room, carrying the shoe box of old photos. She has changed into her housecoat. For a moment she disappears into the darkened doorway of her kitchen. Then she returns with a glass of water and seats herself at the dining room table.

She turns on the lamp. She leans forward. She opens the shoe box. She chooses a photo and lifts it into the sharp white light.

No, I warn her. *What you are doing is too difficult. Too difficult and wrong.*

But she works on. She studies the photo closely, as if the steady effort of her attention will force it to yield the mystery she imagines it holds. She examines it beneath a magnifying glass. What year is it for her, as she sits at her dining room table? What does she see now, outside that photo's glossy white border?

Watching her, I imagine her standing on the front lawn in a flowered sundress, holding a box camera, as years ago she must have. She wants to take a picture of her son.

Her sundress flutters in the spring wind. With one hand she balances the box camera. Then she extends her free hand toward Davis, who sits before her on the lawn.

"Davis," she coaxes. "Davis, come."

And when he stands at last and takes a toddling step toward her, she presses the shutter, and, through the viewfinder, she sees her own life walking precariously toward her, with his arms outstretched.

Don't die, I whisper.

But she can't hear me. She pastes the photograph onto the black page. She reaches into the shoe box. She chooses another. When she finishes the page, she turns it slowly; slowly, as if turning the page were the last thing she wanted to do.

Witness

CHRISTINA MIDDLEBROOK

It is difficult to remember being killed. When I do, my palms sweat, my stomach churns. I feel my voice go sobby. An image from the hospital comes to mind, my flowered L. L. Bean pajamas, and I fling my arms into an exasperated shrug. "Oh, God, it was horrible," I say to block further thought. My mind dives toward the groceries I've just brought in from the car or to a phone call I find I have to make, right now.

The very smell of disinfectant makes me want to leave the room.

I continue, nevertheless, to ask my friends, again and again, what I was like during the days after high-dose chemotherapy had reduced me to a shell. Their anecdotes catch my memory like the stray rosebush prunings that lie in wait for bare feet that walk over our perfect-seeming lawn. I am strangely unsuspecting. Thinking the grass clear of debris, I expect to have a matter-of-fact conversation. I expect the anecdotes to be just incidents recollected at a later date.

One thorn that lay in wait was hidden in a photograph.

Maggie graduated from high school in June 1993, three months after I was released from the hospital. Jonathan shot four rolls of film that day. As is our impatient custom, we took them to the one-hour photo joint the very next morning. We eagerly opened the first packet and saw some man fishing. A photo in the second packet showed a woman in a funny hat looking over a garden of tulips and daffodils.

We were quite annoyed. I hurried back to the photo joint, fretting that our packets would have already been collected by the weird couple on their fishing trip.

"These not yours?" the clerk asked.

"No, these are not mine. I don't know these people."

She frowned, looked at me, looked at the prints.

All white people look alike, I thought, and repeated, "These are not my photos. Mine are of my daughter's graduation, in a gym."

The clerk put aside the first packet, the one with pictures of the man fishing. Those clearly were not mine. Her frown deepened as she fingered through the next, the one with the woman and the garden.

"These not you?" she asked again, offering a print of a bald woman looking out her hospital window.

The pictures of the woman in the funny hat looking at a flower garden were shot, I suddenly realized, from my hospital room when Mary had come to visit. Neither Jonathan, who had taken the pictures, nor I recognized Mary or the makeshift February garden that proliferated outside my hospital window.

I have known Mary for fifteen years. The pots of spring bulbs interspersed among the low-maintenance institutional groundcover were there at my request. Before I entered the solitary confinement of my hospital room, I had been consumed with the worry that I would miss the blooming of the fruit trees on my street and of the hundreds of bulbs in my backyard. I had an indeterminate sentence: four to six weeks. I could not bear to miss the spring. But living things can carry funguses and molds, which might have killed me when my immune system was destroyed. Lovingly, my visitors placed pots of flowering bulbs outside my window. From my bed, on the other side of a seven-by fourteen-foot sheet of Thermopane, I directed them. I wanted the tall ones behind the short, and I wanted the colors to mix. This was my garden, my spring, for the duration. These tulips, daffodils, freesia, hydrangeas, and narcissus comprised the scene I looked at, daily, until I was well enough to go home.

Why didn't I recognize the garden, or Mary, when I saw the photo? Why hadn't the strings of get well cards hung on the wall, the television looming from the upper-right corner, the swinging arm of the bed table clued me in?

Remembering would be to risk reentering the experience. If I return to the scene the photograph portrays, I risk knowing, again, how it felt to have my body obliterated in order to survive. Strange as it sounds, the *I* I was, and perhaps now am again, would not take this risk. That *I* could not take in what the photos showed, just as the same *I* could not absorb the familiarity of the cards and pictures and garden I had used to decorate my hospital room.

Other bone marrow transplant survivors whom I had consulted before I began this ordeal consoled me with startling words. "Don't worry," they said, laughing, "you won't remember a thing. Your husband will, if he wants to, but not you." Could they have been right? What made me so quick to say I did not recognize this place?

On the day I was to be discharged, I sat in a wheelchair on the patio while Jonathan dismantled that garden, so lovingly maintained by family and friends throughout the February storms. He tells me now that he was startled when I said, near the end of my hospital stay, "I hate those fucking flowers!" and that when I got home I was going to burn everything I'd brought to the hospital with me.

My son James arrived that discharge day and was shocked not to find me in bed, my customary place. When he discovered me outside, sitting in a wheelchair and watching Jonathan toss tulips into the trash can, James and I held hands and cried.

"I'm going home, James. You must have left before my message. I'm going home today."

His voice cracked as he took my hand. "You're going home, Mom?"

I nodded.

"You weren't in your room, Mom," he cried. "I couldn't find you."

I understood from his face what he had just imagined. No one was in my room, and half-packed cartons were strewn about. His mother was not in the bed where, on his last visit only five days before, he had waited to empty the barf pans, one after the other, during the constant retching. Following medical protocol so quickly learned, he showed the vile contents to the nurse, then poured the inhuman slop down the toilet, a task no twenty-two-year-old son should have to perform for his mother.

"It was black, Mom, and smelly. Each time I threw one out I thought to myself, 'She is doing it. This is the cancer. This is the evil. She is throwing it up. I can throw it away.' "

I did not remember that he had been there.

He could not know, the morning of my release, that I had just eaten a hard-boiled egg and some bread. His image of me was frozen in illness.

"Did you think that I had died, James?" I asked his frightened face.

He nodded, strangled by tears.

I could feel his torture, the whole family's torture. They had thought that all of me, body *and* soul, was going to die. But *I* had known that if my body had to die, *I* was not going to accompany it.

I had not stayed inside my body to suffer the death of every fast-growing cell. My body was a poisoned wreck: all mucous membranes shed, the inside of my mouth and gastrointestinal tract filled with ulcers, eyelids glued shut with blepharitis. In the mornings I would open my eyes with my fingers. Fevers raged to fight the havoc wrought by high-dose chemotherapy. My urine turned bright red from the bleeding inside.

To save myself, *I*, the me of me, retreated to a far corner above the room. From there, I think, I turned my soul away to contemplate the firmament, to stare at the heavens, the stars, and the moon. I found a large psychic cloak and gathered my endangered identity within.

Who *I* am could not endure the torture of that room. Without the periodic witness like James or Jonathan, who knew who I was, *I* could not know myself. Not to know oneself is to die.

I know this is the phenomenon of multiple personality disorder and of catatonic states. Abused children, concentration-camp internees, soldiers under bombardment, all may split off from their bodies as I did. With sympathetic witness, I realize now, the condition is not fixed. I was blessed with sympathetic witnesses. I had twenty-four visitors who came regularly to my bedside and, unwittingly, held my identity for me when I dared not. They, my witnesses, chatted together at my bed and engaged in conversations about the world I used to inhabit, as well as about my misery. They waited patiently as I made my weary trips to and from the bathroom, forever wheeling the laden IV pole. They watched me open the mail I could not understand, played my telephone messages back to me, over and over. They watched me sleep my morphine sleep, tried to read the notes I wrote when I could not speak, jumped for the barf pan when the retching began.

But when none of my witnesses was there, I wasn't either. I did not dare stay in the room without them.

I know the day it happened, the moment I retreated to contemplate the firmament from outside that room. My friend John sat at my bedside that day, the second of high-dose chemotherapy.

"I'm beginning not to feel very good," I understated, dizziness and headache assaulting my brain. Suddenly the misery was too much. I can't remember whether John left after that or whether he was still there. I took the person he had come to visit and wrapped her in my arms. My body stayed in the bed, robotlike, to push a call button and get to the bathroom. My soul and *I* departed.

Stuff accumulated in that room. If I concentrate, I can describe it now, though I am astonished at how vigorously my mind avoids the scene. The refrigerator was stuffed with food, cans of juice, Popsicles, yogurt, and ice cream. The nurse told me to save them, in hopes that one day I would eat. Cards hung like laundry on a clothesline. On the first day I had instructed Jonathan how to string them. After three weeks I had accumulated a three-line wash.

In my naive determination, as I prepared for the transplant, I had compiled photo collages of friends and colleagues. I had not finished the job, and the photographs lay in stacks beneath the television. Miscellaneous medical paraphernalia, syringes, and tape, intermingled with hospital brochures, instruction sheets, and my mail, were on a counter. My drum, which I had hung on the wall directly at the foot of my bed, took on an ominous look. In the night the bear in its center bared her teeth at me. The windowsill was stacked with books I had thought I would read. Likewise, audio- and videocassettes remained in racks I had arranged near my bedside table. I taped posters to the doors that locked me in. The walls were festooned with loving messages from friends and colleagues (but nothing from my sister). After that second day, the day *I* picked up and left, they blurred into a Dilaudid haze.

A dietician came to lecture me about following a bacteria-free diet. A kind but uninformed volunteer returned time after time to show me a list of videos and a cart full of library books. I looked at her dully, politely saying "no thank you" until I could no longer speak. Each morning one of the hematology oncologists came to tell me about my blood. Nurses came with bags for my IV pole: the chemicals thiotepa, Cytoxan, and mitoxantrone; platelets and red blood cells to restore what the chemicals had killed off; glucose to feed me; diuretics to reduce the monstrous swelling of my body; unnamed drugs to protect my bladder from the chemical scourge; Xofran and Compazine to combat the constant nausea; Benadryl to clear up hives; Ativan for sleep; morphine and then Dilaudid to diminish the razorlike pain in my ulcerated esophagus and mouth and eyes and eustachian tubes; Antivert for dizziness; Acyclovir to battle herpes and shingles; medicines I can't remember for reasons I could no longer try to understand. I had twenty-six blood transfusions. Each nurse carefully explained the contents of each bag. I learned how to push the blue button for more painkiller. Robotlike, I discussed the dosages. I learned that a bolus is an added burst of painkiller. I learned how to take care of my festering mouth. I washed my gums with sponges five times a day, and gargled baking soda and the antifungal nystatin. Peridex, a disinfectant, turned my teeth yellow.

The staff was diligent in involving me, the me that acted as though *I* were present, in each procedure. They fiddled constantly with the tubes coming out of the triple-lumen catheter in my chest, never once making an injection or extraction without telling me what it was. I bless them for that, not because I could retain what they said, but because their words spoke to their sense that I was human, alive. They were witnesses too.

On the seventh day, after the constant drip of high-dose chemo-therapy into my veins, when the white blood cell count had dropped below one hundred and the red cell count was at the bottom, when the hemoglobin and platelets were destroyed, along with my hair, skin, and esophageal lining, technicians brought me my peripheral stem cells. These cells, the earliest initiators of cell growth, had been spun out from my blood during a total blood dialysis process called pheresis. This depleting process had taken place during the weeks before I entered the hospital. Now my own stem cells would rescue me. I remember a strange swishing of ice cubes as they removed the salmon-colored sacks from cold water. Four bags of microscopic stem cells were all that remained of my former self. The hospital guarded this sacred remnant in a refrigerator, just as I guarded, inside my psychic cloak, the tiny spark that is Christina.

Eight days after the stem cell rescue, fifteen days after I entered the fishbowl room, my own blood cells began to regenerate. The body began to fight back.

And why didn't *I* disappear forever during that hideous fight? I think because the witnesses called me back. Not knowing the psychic split that lay beneath the drug-induced stupidities, they treated me as they always had, with love.

Two neighbors from my childhood came from Chicago. They were Ayrie, my childhood bloodsister (we had cut our wrists and crossed them when we were eight years old) and Henrietta, her sev-enty-eight-year-old mother. In the three days of their visit, we remi-nisced about the years Ayrie and I spent in and out of each other's houses, about how the doors were never locked so we could walk in and out all summer long. At Ayrie's house we charred hot dogs over the gas burners and ate them with our fingers. At mine, we were not allowed to play in the living room. In the space between, we made a world with secret codes and elaborate clubs.

During my blood pheresis, another childhood friend, Julie, sat with me. She brought me books and Christmas-card pictures I had sent her of my children over the years. When my body began to shake uncontrollably, Julie climbed into bed with me as though we were still at summer camp. She wanted to keep me warm. My mother, brother, and sister never came to visit, to hold my childhood next to me. After Ayrie returned to Chicago, she persuaded my mother to leave a message on my hospital answering machine. My brother left a message at my house. But Ayrie and Henrietta were there. Julie was there. They knew me. They remembered.

There were other witnesses equally important: a friend standing at the foot of the bed wringing her hands; another sitting near my pillow in the night saying, "Yes, Christina, of course"; someone straightening the stuff around the room; a face bending over mine. They brought me messages from outside, told me stories of my other life. My masseuse came five times to tend the body *I* had abandoned. They asked again and again how I was and listened to the answer. I see them clad in sterilized yellow robes, one so cautious he wore a blue mask.

I moved in and out, sinking and resurfacing. I asked Jonathan when Sophie would come to visit.

"She has already been here," he explained.

From the unhappy expressions on my witnesses' faces, I understood that my words made no sense. *I* apologized. The witnesses soothed me. *I* drifted away. They continued tending me.

Sometimes, when I was alert enough to notice Jonathan's exhaustion, I braved having feelings about him. I fretted about his twice-daily round-trip commute over the congested Bay Bridge to be with me. Some mornings he was there before I woke. He returned, after work, to stay with me until I fell asleep. He slept in the armchair beneath the television set. I worried that he wasn't eating right. The worry was a vestige of my former self.

I apologized when Maggie, safely returned from the Yucatán, sat next to me during one of my long vomiting stints.

"I'm sorry," I kept repeating. "I'm sorry you have to see me this way."

"Don't worry, Mom," she told me. "I'm not looking at you." Also she spoke words from our other life, the life we'd had before. She wrote how, before cancer, I used to clutch my belly in laughter, not in pain. My daughter remembered that I could laugh. She held my sense of humor, kept it, for me.

Then I came back. It was a Saturday, three weeks after I had gone away. I had not thrown up for thirty hours. The only bag on my IV pole was filled with glucose. The triple-lumen catheter was no longer embedded in my chest. The night nurse came to take my five A.M. vital signs. I had no fever.

The February morning was still dark. *I* had known the day before that my body was better. *I* sensed it from my place, away, and experimented with the thought. *I* saw that I was sitting up. My stomach had finished its rebellion. I could swallow. Did *I* dare return? My ravaged body was calling for me. Three weeks is a long time to be separated. My soul danced around the shell in the bed, considering. Was it safe yet? Could I?

"I want to go home today," I told the night nurse. "I've been here long enough."

I dressed myself in street clothes, avoiding the sight of myself in the mirror. My mouth ate a hard-boiled egg and tasteless bread. It sipped mint tea. No retching. *I* was ready to pack up the room and flee, but my body was less enthusiastic. Two minutes out of bed and it had to lie down to rest. The weakness was astonishing. But my other part, the soul part, was determined. Now, reunited with my physical self, it demanded that I leave. "Get out!" it ordered me. "Get yourself out of here, quick."

I wept for days after I came home. I called each of the children and cried to them over the phone. I made Leah and James come for dinner. I told Maggie to move back in from her sojourn at her father's house. They sat by me, cautiously, waiting, it seemed, to see if I would break. I was too weak to stand up. Food had no taste. But I was home, in house and body.

The hardest task of recovery has been to tolerate my soul reentering this body that is mine. My heart beats too fast and my skin gets clammy when I think of what happened to my body as *I* was being cured. When I dare, I recall how it looked, lying beneath me. I see my cronelike skull, my bloated torso, my yellow teeth. I feel the itch of the affected skin, the confusion of the constant headache. I cannot swallow. I cannot think.

When we came home, I threw out everything that had been in that room with me.

Now that I realize, by way of the unrecognized photographs, that I made a split during the torture of my body, I am determined to remember more. I want the whole of my life back. I need a continuum from then to now. The experience returns in pieces. Jonathan mentions warm blankets. Leah writes me about my skin. Ethan speaks of the fragility of my voice over the phone.

Mary explains that when she visited, she had the remnants of a head cold and was not permitted to come into my room. Instead, she tells me, she came around to the patio window, where she looked at my bulb garden and threw me kisses through the window. Jonathan photographed us conversing by gesture. Those were the pictures I mistook for those of someone else.

I hear about conversations I had on the telephone. I invited Florence to join me for a cup of tea. I told John I would set an extra place at the table for him. Unless the witness was in the room with me, those events are lost. *I* was not there. I notice that the split occurs still. In the midst of a conversation, I cannot concentrate. Pain lurks. Do I dare feel it? What was I like? What did I say and do? As friends recount, my mind flees to another topic. I have to ask them to repeat.

"You'd leave messages on my answering machine that I couldn't understand because your voice was so frail. I'd really dread coming to the hospital. But when I saw you, I felt better. You were still you."

Sometimes memory comes rushing back. I remember Susan, with whom I have eaten lunch every Tuesday for eight years, sitting at my bedside drinking cappuccino from the hospital cafeteria. I remember Lynn determinedly tracking down aloe vera juice, which I insisted would end my vomiting. (It didn't.) I remember Susan being with me when the nurse came to tell me that my white cells were climbing. Suddenly I can remember a walk I took with Maggie and my IV pole outside the room. My white count had risen to 1,200. My immune system was strong enough for me to enter the hospital corridors. I remember seeing my flower bed from the corridor window. It was beautiful. I remember a nurse telling me, "Your garden is causing a lot of talk around this place!" Then the tears come and my throat constricts. I am back in the corridor, looking through the window to the patio. I am remembering the wreckage sealed in the room behind the patio window. She is so ugly. She is so sick. When my hematology oncologist asked me, at my first outpatient appointment, whether I would do it again, I was vehement: "no!"

I don't hate the relics of that room anymore. I can think about the things I collected for my stay. I have donated the photographs of all my colleagues to the C. G. Jung Institute of San Francisco. I can read the books, listen to the music, respond to the hundreds of cards, gifts, and letters. I am astonished by the realization that there were dozens of pots of bulbs in the garden outside my window.

Like the lucky soldiers in war, like some physically abused children, some concentration-camp survivors, *I* am still here. We lucky ones who have not gone mad have had witnesses who bore the truth when we could not. I think that's the only way the soul survives.

from *Paula*

ISABEL ALLENDE

Listen, Paula. I am going to tell you a story, so that when you wake up you will not feel so lost. The legend of our family begins at the end of the last century, when a robust Basque sailor disembarked on the coast of Chile with his mother's reliquary strung around his neck and his head swimming with plans for greatness. But why start so far back? It is enough to say that those who came after him were a breed of impetuous women and men with sentimental hearts and strong arms fit for hard work. Some few irascible types died frothing at the mouth, although the cause may not have been rage, as evil tongues had it, but, rather, some local pestilence. The Basque's descendants bought fertile land on the outskirts of the capital, which with time increased in value; they became more refined and constructed lordly mansions with great parks and groves; they wed their daughters to rich young men from established families; they educated their children in rigorous religious schools; and thus over the course of the years they were integrated into a proud aristocracy of landowners that prevailed for more than a century—until the whirl-wind of modern times replaced them with technocrats and business-men. My grandfather was one of the former, the good old families, but his father died young of an unexplained shotgun wound. The details of what happened that fateful night were never revealed, but it could have been a duel, or revenge, or some accident of love. In any case, his family was left without means and, because he was the oldest, my grandfather had to drop out of school and look for work to support his mother and educate his younger brothers. Much later, when he had become a wealthy man to whom others doffed their hats, he confessed to me that genteel poverty is the worst of all because it must be concealed. He was always well turned out—in his father's clothes, altered to fit, the collars starched stiff and suits well pressed to disguise the threadbare cloth. Those years of penury tempered his character; in his credo, life was strife and hard work, and an honorable man should not pass through this world without helping his neighbor. Still young, he already exhibited the concentration and integrity that were his char-acteristics; he was made of the same hard stone as his ancestors and, like many of them, had his feet firmly on the ground. Even so, some small part of his soul drifted toward the abyss of dreams. Which was what allowed him to fall in love with my grandmother, the youngest of a family of twelve, all eccentrically and deliciously bizarre—like Te-resa, who at the end of her life began to sprout the wings of a saint and at whose death all the roses in the Parque Japonés withered overnight. Or Ambrosio, a dedicated carouser and fornicator, who was known at moments of rare generosity to remove all his clothing in the street and hand it to the poor. I grew up listening to stories about my grand-mother's ability to foretell the future, read minds, converse with ani-mals, and move objects with her gaze. Everyone says that once she moved a billiard table across a room, but the only thing I ever saw move in her presence was an insignificant sugar bowl that used to skitter erratically across the table at tea time. These gifts aroused certain misgivings, and many eligible suitors were intimidated by her, despite her charms. My grandfather, however, regarded telepathy and telekinesis as innocent diversions and in no way a serious obstacle to marriage. The only thing that concerned him was the difference in their ages. My grandmother was much younger than he, and when he first met her she was still playing with dolls and walking around clutching a grimy little pillow. Because he was so used to seeing her as a young girl, he was unaware of his passion for her until one day she appeared in a long dress and with her hair up, and then the revelation of a love that had been gestating for years threw him into such a fit of shyness that he stopped calling. My grandmother divined his state of mind before he himself was able to undo the tangle of his own feelings and sent him a letter, the first of many she was to write him at decisive moments in their lives. This was not a perfumed billet-doux testing the waters of their relationship, but a brief note penciled on lined paper asking him straight out whether he wanted to marry her and, if so, when. Several months later they were wed. Standing before the altar, the bride was a vision from another era, adorned in ivory lace and a riot of wax orange blossoms threaded through her chignon. When my grandfather saw her, he knew he would love her obstinately till the end of his days.

To me, they were always Tata and Memé. Of their children, only my mother will figure in this story, because if I begin to tell you about all the rest of the tribe we shall never be finished, and besides, the ones who are still living are very far away. That's what happens to exiles; they are scattered to the four winds and then find it extremely difficult to get back together again. My mother was born between the two world wars, on a fine spring day in the 1920s. She was a sensitive girl, temperamentally unsuited to joining her brothers in their sweeps through the attic to catch mice they preserved in bottles of Formol. She led a sheltered life within the walls of her home and her school; she amused herself with charitable works and romantic novels, and had the reputation of being the most beautiful girl ever seen in this family of enigmatic women. From the time of puberty, she had lovesick admirers buzzing around like flies, young men her father held at bay and her mother analyzed with her tarot cards; these innocent flirtations were cut short when a talented and equivocal young man appeared and

effortlessly dislodged his rivals, fulfilling his destiny and filling my
mother's heart with uneasy emotions. That was your grandfather Tomás, who disappeared in a fog, and the only reason I mention him,
Paula, is because some of his blood flows in your veins. This clever
man with a quick mind and merciless tongue was too intelligent and
free of prejudice for that provincial society, a rara avis in the Santiago
of his time. It was said that he had a murky past; rumors flew that he
belonged to the Masonic sect, and so was an enemy of the Church, and
that he had a bastard son hidden away somewhere, but Tata could not
put forward any of these arguments to dissuade his daughter because
he lacked proof, and my grandfather was not a man to stain another's
reputation without good reason. In those days Chile was like a mille-
feuille pastry. It had more castes than India, and there was a pejorative
term to set every person in his or her rightful place: *roto, pije, arribista,
siútico,* and many more, working upward toward the comfortable pla-
teau of "people like ourselves." Birth determined status. It was easy to
descend in the social hierarchy, but money, fame, or talent was not
sufficient to allow one to rise, that required the sustained effort of
several generations. Tomás's honorable lineage was in his favor, even
though in Tata's eyes he had questionable political ties. By then the
name Salvador Allende, the founder of Chile's Socialist Party, was
being bruited about; he preached against private property, conservative
morality, and the power of the large landowners. Tomás was the cousin
of that young deputy.

Look, Paula, this is Tata's picture. This man with the severe features, clear eyes, rimless eyeglasses, and black beret is your great-
grandfather. In the picture he is seated, hands on his cane, and beside
him, leaning against his right knee, is a little girl of three in her party
dress, a pint-size charmer staring into the camera with liquid eyes.
That's *you.* My mother and I are standing behind you, the chair mask-
ing the fact that I was carrying your brother Nicolás. The old man is
facing the camera, and you can see his proud bearing, the calm dignity
of the self-made man who has marched straight down the road of life
and expects nothing more. I remember him as always being old—
although almost without wrinkles except for the two deep furrows at

the corners of his mouth—with a lion's mane of snow-white hair and an abrupt laugh filled with yellow teeth. At the end of his days it was painful for him to move, but he always struggled to his feet to say hello and good-bye to the ladies and, hobbling along on his cane, escort them to the garden gate as they left. I loved his hands, twisted oak branches, strong and gnarled, his inevitable silk neckerchief, and his odor of English Creolin-and-lavender soap. With inexhaustible good humor, he tried to instill in his descendants his stoic philosophy: he believed discomfort was healthful and that central heating sapped the strength; he insisted on simple food—no sauces or pot-au-feu—and he thought it bad taste to have too good a time. Every morning he took a cold shower, a custom no one in the family imitated, and one that when he resembled nothing more than a geriatric beetle he fulfilled, old but undaunted, seated in a chair beneath the icy blast. He spoke in ringing aphorisms and answered direct questions with a different question, so that even though I knew his character to the core, I know very little about his ideology. Look carefully at Mother, Paula. In this picture she is in her early forties, and at the peak of her beauty. That short skirt and beehive hair were all the rage. She's laughing, and her large eyes are two green lines punctuated by the sharp arch of black eyebrows. That was the happiest period of her life, when she had finished raising her children, was still in love, and the world seemed secure.

I wish I could show you a photograph of my father, but they were all burned more than forty years ago.

Where are you wandering, Paula? How will you be when you wake up? Will you be the same woman, or will we be like strangers and have to learn to know one another all over again? Will you have your memory, or will I need to sit patiently and relate the entire story of your twenty-eight years and my forty-nine?

"May God watch over your daughter," don Manuel told me, barely able to whisper. He's the one in the bed next to yours, an elderly peasant who has undergone several operations on his stomach but has not given up fighting for health and life. "May God watch over your daughter" was also what a young woman with a baby in her arms said yesterday. She had heard about you and come to the hospital to offer me hope. She suffered an attack of porphyria two years ago and was in a coma for more than a month. It was a year before she was normal again and she will have to be careful for the rest of her life, but she is working now, and she married and had a baby. She assured me that being in a coma is like a sleep without dreams, a mysterious parenthesis. "Don't cry anymore, Señora," she said, "your daughter doesn't feel a thing; she will walk out of here and never remember what happened." Every morning I prowl the corridors of the sixth floor looking for the specialist, in hopes of learning something new. He holds your life in his hands, and I don't trust him. He wafts through like a breeze, distracted and rushed, offering me worrisome explanations about enzymes and copies of articles about your illness that I try to read but do not understand. He seems more interested in the statistics from his computer and formulas from his laboratory than in your poor body lying crucified on this bed. He tells me—without meeting my eyes—"That's how it is with this condition; some recover quickly after the crisis, while others spend weeks in intensive therapy. It used to be that the patients simply died, but now we can keep them alive until their metabolism resumes functioning." Well, if that's how it is, all we can do is wait and be strong. If you can take it, Paula, so can I.

When you wake up we will have months, maybe years, to piece together the broken fragments of your past; better yet, we can invent memories that fit your fantasies. For the time being, I will tell you about myself and the other members of this family we both belong to, but don't ask me to be precise, because inevitably errors will creep in. I have forgotten a lot, and some of the facts are twisted. There are places, dates, and names I don't remember; on the other hand, I never forget a good story. Sitting here by your side, watching the screen with the luminous lines measuring your heartbeats, I try to use my grandmother's magic to communicate with you. If she were here she could carry my messages to you and help me hold you in this world. Have you begun some strange trek through the sand dunes of the unconscious? What good are all these words if you can't hear me? Or these pages you may never read? My life is created as I narrate, and my memory grows stronger with writing; what I do not put in words on a page will be erased by time.

Today is January 8, 1992. On a day like today, eleven years ago in Caracas, I began a letter that would be my good-bye to my grandfather, who was dying, leaving a hard-fought century behind him. His strong body had not failed, but long ago he had made his preparations to follow Memé, who was beckoning to him from the other side. I could not return to Chile, and he so detested the telephone that it didn't seem right to call, but I wanted to tell him not to worry, that nothing would be lost of the treasury of anecdotes he had told me through the years of our comradeship; I had forgotten nothing. Soon he died, but the story I had begun to tell had enmeshed me, and I couldn't stop. Other voices were speaking through me; I was writing in a trance, with the sensation of unwinding a ball of yarn, driven by the same urgency I feel as I write now. At the end of a year the pages had grown to five hundred, filling a canvas bag, and I realized that this was no longer a letter. Timidly, I announced to my family that I had written a book. "What's the title?" my mother asked. We made a list of possibilities but could not agree on any, and finally it was you, Paula, who tossed a coin in the air to decide it. Thus was born and baptized my first novel, *The House of the Spirits,* and I was initiated into the ineradicable vice of telling stories. That book saved my life. Writing is a long process of introspection; it is a voyage toward the darkest caverns of consciousness, a long, slow meditation. I write feeling my way in silence, and along the way discover particles of truth, small crystals that fit in the palm of one hand and justify my passage through this world. I also began my second novel on an eighth of January, and since have not dared change that auspicious date, partly out of superstition, but also for reasons of discipline. I have begun all my books on a January 8.

When some months ago I finished my most recent novel, *The Infinite Plan,* I began preparing for today. I had everything in my mind—theme, title, first sentence—but I shall not write that story yet. Since you fell ill I have had no strength for anything but you, Paula.

You have been sleeping for a month now. I don't know how to reach you; I call and call but your name is lost in the nooks and crannies of this hospital. My soul is choking in sand. Sadness is a sterile desert. I don't know how to pray. I cannot string together two thoughts, much less immerse myself in creating a new book. I plunge into these pages in an irrational attempt to overcome my terror. I think that perhaps if I give form to this devastation I shall be able to help you, and myself, and that the meticulous exercise of writing can be our salvation. Eleven years ago I wrote a letter to my grandfather to say good-bye to him in death. On this January 8, 1992, I am writing you, Paula, to bring you back to life.

My mother was a radiant young woman of eighteen when Tata took the family to Europe on a monumental journey that in those days was made only once in a lifetime: Chile lies at the bottom of the world. He intended to place his daughter in an English school to be "finished," hoping that in the process she would forget her love for Tomás, but Hitler wrecked those plans; the Second World War burst out with cataclysmic force, surprising them on the Côte d'Azur. With incredible difficulty, moving against the streams of people escaping on foot, horseback, or any available vehicle, they managed to reach Antwerp and board the last Chilean ship to set sail from the docks. The decks and lifeboats had been commandeered by dozens of families of fleeing Jews who had left their belongings—in some cases, fortunes—in the hands of unscrupulous consuls who sold them visas in exchange for gold. Unable to obtain staterooms, they traveled like cattle, sleeping in the open and going hungry because of food rationing. Through that arduous crossing, Memé consoled women weeping over the loss of their homes and the uncertainty of the future, while Tata negotiated food from the kitchen and blankets from the sailors to distribute among the refugees. In appreciation, one of them, a furrier by trade, gave Memé a luxurious coat of gray astrakhan. For several weeks they sailed through waters infested with enemy submarines, blacking out lights by night and praying by day, until they had left the Atlantic behind and safely reached Chile. As the boat docked in the port of Valparaíso, the first sight that met their eyes was the unmistakable figure of Tomás in a white linen suit and Panama hat. At that moment, Tata realized the futility of opposing the mysterious dictates of destiny and so, grudgingly, gave his consent for the wedding. The ceremony was held at home, with the participation of the papal nuncio and various personages from the official world. The bride wore a sober satin gown and a defiant expression. I don't know how the groom looked, because the photograph has been cropped; we can see nothing of him but one arm. As he led his daughter to the large room where an altar of cascading roses had been erected, Tata paused at the foot of the stairway.

"There is still time to change your mind," he said. "Don't marry him, Daughter, think better of it. Just give me a sign and I will run this mob out of here and send the banquet to the orphanage." My mother replied with an icy stare.

Just as my grandmother had been warned by the spirits in one of her sessions, my parents' marriage was a disaster from the very beginning. Once again, my mother boarded a ship, this time for Peru, where Tomás had been named secretary of the Chilean embassy. She took with her a collection of heavy trunks containing her bridal trousseau and a mountain of gifts, so much china, crystal, and silver that even now, a half-century later, we keep running into them in unexpected corners. Fifty years of diplomatic assignments in many latitudes, divorce, and long exile have not rid the family of this flotsam. I greatly fear, Paula, that among other ghastly prizes you will inherit a lamp that is still in my mother's possession, a baroque chaos of nymphs and plump cherubs. Your house is monastically spare, and your meager closet contains nothing but four blouses and two pairs of slacks. I wonder what you do with the things I keep giving you? You're like Memé, whose feet had scarcely touched solid ground before she removed the astrakhan coat and draped it over a beggarwoman's shoulders. My mother spent the first two days of her honeymoon so nauseated by the tossing Pacific Ocean that she was unable to leave her stateroom; then, just as she felt a little better and could go outside to drink in the fresh air, her husband was felled by a toothache. While she strolled around the decks, indifferent to the covetous stares of officers and sailors, he lay moaning in his bunk. At sunset the vast horizon was flooded with shades of orange and at night a scandal of stars invited love, but suffering was more powerful than romance. Three interminable days had to pass before the patient allowed the ship's physician to intervene with his forceps and ease the torment. Only then did the swelling subside, and husband and wife could begin married life. The next night they appeared together in the dining room as guests at the captain's table. After a formal toast to the newlyweds, the appetizer was served: prawns arranged in goblets carved of ice. In a gesture of flirtatious intimacy, my mother reached across and speared a bit of seafood from her husband's plate, unfortunately flicking a minute drop of cocktail sauce onto his necktie. Tomás seized a knife to scrape away the offensive spot, but merely spread the stain. To the astonishment of his fellow guests and the mortification of his wife, the diplomat dipped his fingers into his dish, scooped up a handful of crustaceans, and smeared them over his chest, desecrating shirt, suit, and the unsoiled portion of his tie; then, after passing his hands over his slicked-down hair, he rose to his feet, bowed slightly, and strode off to his stateroom, where he stayed for the remainder of the voyage, deep in a sullen silence. Despite these mishaps, I was conceived on that sea voyage.

Nothing had prepared my mother for motherhood. In those days, such matters were discussed in whispers before unwed girls, and Memé had given no thought to advising her about the libidinous preoccupations of the birds and the flowers because her soul floated on different planes, more intrigued with the translucence of apparitions than the gross realities of this world. Nevertheless, as soon as my mother sensed she was pregnant, she knew it would be a girl. She named her Isabel and established a dialogue that continues to the present day. Clinging to the creature developing in her womb, she tried to compensate for the loneliness of a woman who has chosen badly in love. She talked to me aloud, startling everyone who saw her carrying on as if hallucinating, and I suppose that I heard her and answered, although I have no memory of the intrauterine phase of my life.

My father had a taste for splendor. Ostentation had always been looked upon as a vice in Chile, where sobriety is a sign of refinement.

In contrast, in Lima, the city of viceroys, swagger and swash is considered stylish. Tomás installed himself in a house incommensurate with his position as second secretary in the embassy, surrounded himself with Indian servants, ordered a luxurious automobile from Detroit, and squandered money on parties, gaming, and yacht clubs, without anyone's being able to explain how he could afford such extravagances. In a short time he had managed to establish relations with the most illustrious members of Lima's political and social circles, had discovered the weaknesses of each, and, through his contacts, heard a number of indiscreet confidences, even a few state secrets. He became the indispensable element in Lima's revels. At the height of the war, he obtained the best whiskey, the purest cocaine, and the most obliging party girls; all doors opened to him. While he climbed the ladder of his career, his wife felt as if she was a prisoner with no hope for escape, joined at twenty to an evasive man on whom she was totally dependent. She languished in the humid summer heat, writing interminable pages to her mother; their correspondence was a conversation between the deaf, crossing at sea and buried in the bottom of mailbags. Nevertheless, as melancholy letters stacked up on her desk, Memé became convinced of her daughter's disenchantment. She interrupted the spiritist sessions with her three esoteric friends from the White Sisterhood, packed her prophetic deck of cards in her suitcase, and set off for Lima in a light biplane, one of the few that carried passengers, since during times of war planes were reserved for military purposes. She arrived just in time for my birth. As her own children had been born at home with the aid of her husband and a midwife, she was bewildered by the modern methods of the clinic. With one jab of a needle, they rendered her daughter senseless, depriving her of any chance to participate in events, and as soon as the baby was born transferred it to an aseptic nursery. Much later, when the fog of the anesthesia had lifted, they informed my mother that she had given birth to a baby girl, but that in accord with regulations she could have her only during the time she was nursing.

"She's a freak, that's why they won't let me see her!"

"She's a precious little thing!" my grandmother replied, trying to sound a note of conviction, although she herself had not yet actually seen me: through the glass, she had spied a blanket-wrapped bundle, something that to her eyes did not look entirely human.

While I screamed with hunger on a different floor, my mother thrashed about, prepared to reclaim her daughter by force, should that be necessary. A doctor came, diagnosed hysteria, and administered a second injection that knocked her out for another twelve hours. By then my grandmother was convinced that they were in the anteroom to hell, and as soon as her daughter was conscious, she splashed cold water on her face and helped her get dressed.

"We have to get out of here. Put on your clothes and we'll stroll out arm in arm like two ladies who've come to visit."

"For God's sake, Mama, we can't go without the baby!"

"Of course we can't!" exclaimed my grandmother, who probably had overlooked that detail.

The two women walked purposefully into the room where the newborn babies were sequestered, picked one out, and hastily exited, without raising an alarm. They could tell the sex, because the infant had a rose-colored ribbon around its wrist, and though there wasn't enough time to be certain that it was theirs, that wasn't vital anyway, all babies are more or less alike at that age. It is possible that in their haste they traded me for another baby, and that somewhere there is a woman with spinach-colored eyes and a gift for clairvoyance who is taking my place. Once safely home, they stripped me bare to be sure I was whole, and discovered a small birthmark in the shape of a sun at the base of my spine. "That's a good sign," Memé assured my mother. "We won't have to worry about her, she'll grow up healthy and blessed with good fortune." I was born in August, under the sign of Leo, sex, female, and, if I was not switched in the clinic, I have three-quarters Spanish-Basque blood, one-quarter French, and a tot of Araucan or Mapuche Indian, like everyone else in my land. Despite my birth in Lima, I am Chilean. I come from a "long petal of sea and wine and snow," as Pablo Neruda described my country, and you're from there, too, Paula, even though you bear the indelible stamp of the Caribbean where you spent the years of your childhood. It may be difficult for you to understand the mentality of those of us from the south. In Chile

we are influenced by the eternal presence of the mountains that separate us from the rest of the continent, and by a sense of precariousness
inevitable in a region of geological and political catastrophes. Everything trembles beneath our feet; we know no security. If anyone asks us
how we are, we answer, "About the same," or "All right, I guess." We
move from one uncertainty to another; we pick our way through a
twilight region. Nothing is precise. We do not like confrontations, we
prefer to negotiate. When circumstances push us to extremes, our
worst instincts are awakened and history takes a tragic turn, because
the same men who seem mild-mannered in their everyday lives can, if
offered impunity and the right pretext, turn into bloodthirsty beasts. In
normal times, however, Chileans are sober, circumspect, and formal,
and suffer an acute fear of attracting attention, which to them is synonymous with looking ridiculous. For that very reason, I have been an
embarrassment to my family.

And where was Tomás while his wife was giving birth and his
mother-in-law effecting the discreet kidnapping of her first grandchild?
I have no idea. My father is a great lacuna in my life. He went away so
early, and vanished so completely, that I have no memory of him at all.
My mother lived with him for four years, including two long separa-
tions—but sufficient time to bring three children into the world. She
was so fertile that she became pregnant if a pair of men's undershorts
was waved anywhere within a radius of a half kilometer, a predisposi-
tion I inherited, although, to my good fortune, the age of the Pill
arrived in time for me. With each birth her husband disappeared—as
he did at the sign of any major difficulty—and then, once the emergency was over, returned, beaming, with some extravagant present.
She watched the proliferation of paintings on the walls and Chinese
porcelains on the shelves, totally mystified at where all the money was
coming from. It was impossible to explain such luxuries when others at
the consulate could scarcely make ends meet, but when she asked him,
my father gave her the runaround—just as he did when she asked
about his nocturnal absences, his mysterious trips, and his shady
friendships. My mother had two children, and was about to give birth
to the third, when the whole house of cards of her innocence came
tumbling down. Lima awoke one morning to rumors of a scandal that

escaped the newspapers but filtered into every salon. It had to do with an elderly millionaire who used to lend his apartment to special friends for clandestine trysts. In the bedroom, lost among pieces of antique furniture and Persian tapestries, hung a false mirror in a heavy baroque frame—actually, a window. On the other side, the master of the house liked to sit with a select group of guests, well supplied with liquor and drugs, eager to enjoy the antics of the current, usually unsuspecting, couple in the bed. That night a high-ranking politician was among the invited. When the curtain was drawn for the voyeurs to spy on the unwary lovers, the first surprise was that they were two males; the second was that one of them, decked out in a corset and lace garters, was the eldest son of the politician, a young lawyer destined for a brilliant career. In his humiliation, the father lost control; he kicked out the mirror, threw himself on his son to tear off the women's frippery, and, had he not been restrained, might have murdered him. A few hours later every circle in Lima was humming with the particulars of the event, adding more and more scabrous details with each telling. It was suspected that it was not a chance incident, that someone had planned the scene out of pure malice. Frightened, Tomás disappeared without a word. My mother did not hear of the scandal until several days later; she was isolated by the demands of her series of pregnancies, and also by a desire to escape the creditors who were clamoring for payment. Tired of waiting for their wages, the servants had deserted; only Margara remained, a Chilean employee with a hermetic face and heart of stone who had served the family since the beginning of time. It was in these straits that my mother felt the pangs of imminent birth. She gritted her teeth and prepared to have the baby under the most primitive circumstances. I was almost three, and my brother Pancho was barely walking. That night, huddled together in the corridor, we heard my mother's moans and witnessed Margara scurrying back and forth with towels and kettles of hot water. Juan came into the world at midnight, tiny and wrinkled, a hairless wisp of a mouse, barely breathing. It was soon obvious that he couldn't swallow; he had some knot in his throat that wouldn't let food pass. Although my mother's breasts were bursting with milk, he was destined to perish of hunger, but Margara was determined to keep him alive, at first by squeezing drops from milk-soaked cotton, then later using a wooden spoon to force a thick pap down his throat.

For years, morbid explanations for my father's disappearance rattled around in my head. I asked about him until finally I gave up, recognizing that there is a conspiracy of silence around him. Those who knew him describe him to me as a very intelligent man, and stop there. When I was young, I imagined him as a criminal, and later, when I learned about sexual perversions, I attributed all of them to him, but the facts suggest that nothing so dramatic colored his past; he merely had a cowardly soul. One day he found himself trapped by his lies; events were out of control, so he ran away. He left the Foreign Service and never again saw my mother or any of his family or friends. He simply vanished in smoke. I visualized him—partly in jest, of course—fleeing toward Machu Picchu disguised as a Peruvian Indian woman, wearing a wig with long black braids and layers of many-colored skirts. "Don't ever say that again!" my mother screamed when I told her my fantasy. "Where do you get such crazy ideas?" Whatever happened, he disappeared without a trace, although obviously he did not hie himself off to the thin, clear air of the Andes to live unnoticed in some Aymara village; he just descended a rung in the immutable scale of Chile's social classes and became invisible. He must have returned to Santiago and walked the streets of the city center but as he did not frequent the same social milieu it was as if he had died. I never again saw my paternal grandmother or any of my father's family— except for Salvador Allende, who out of a strong sense of loyalty kept in close touch with us. Nor did I see my father again, or hear his name spoken aloud. I know absolutely nothing about his physical appearance, so it is ironic that one day I was called to identify his body in the morgue—but that came much later. I'm sorry, Paula, that this character must disappear at this point, because villains always are the most delicious part of a story.

My mother, who had been brought up in a world of privilege in which women were excluded from money matters, entrenched herself in her house, wiped away the tears of abandonment, and found consolation in the fact that for a time, at least, she would not starve; she had the treasure of the silver trays, which she could pawn one by one to pay the bills. She was alone in a strange land with three children, surrounded by the trappings of wealth but without a cent in her pocketbook and too proud to ask for help. The embassy, nonetheless, was alert, and learned immediately that Tomás had disappeared, leaving his family in bankruptcy. The honor of the nation was at stake; they could not allow the name of a Chilean official to be dragged through the mud, much less permit his wife and children to be put out into the street by creditors. So the consul was sent to call on the family, with instructions to help them return to Chile with the greatest possible discretion. You guessed right, Paula, that man was your Tío Ramón, your grandfather, a prince, and the direct descendant of Jesus Christ. He himself tells that he was one of the ugliest men of his generation, but I think he is exaggerating. We can't call him handsome, but what he lacks in good looks he more than makes up for in intelligence and charm. Besides, the years have lent him an air of great dignity. At the time he was sent to our aid, Tío Ramón was bone thin, had a greenish tint to his skin, a walrus mustache, and Mephistophelian eyebrows; he was the father of four children and a practicing Catholic, and not a spot on the mythic character he would become after he had shed his skin like a snake. Margara opened the door to this visitor and led him to the bedroom of her señora, who received him lying in bed surrounded by her children, still slightly battered by the youngest's birth but glowing with striking beauty and youthful ebullience. The consul, who had scarcely known his colleague's wife—he had always seen her pregnant, and with a remote air that did not invite closer contact—stood near the door, sinking into a swamp of emotions. As he questioned her about the intricacies of her situation and explained the plan to send her back to Chile, he was tormented by a stampede of wild bulls in the area of his chest. Calculating that there was no more fascinating woman alive, and failing to understand how her husband could have abandoned her—he would give his life for her—he sighed at the crushing injustice of having met her too late. She looked at him for a long moment, and finally agreed:

"All right, I will return to my father's house."

"In a few days a ship is leaving Callao for Vuh-Valparaíso. I'll try to obtain passages," he stammered.

"I shall be traveling with my three children, Margara, and the dog. I don't know whether my baby will survive the trip, this little one is very weak," and although her eyes were shining with tears, she refused to allow herself to cry.

In a flash, Ramón's wife and his children filed before his eyes, followed by his father pointing an accusing finger, and his uncle, the bishop, holding a crucifix shooting rays of damnation. He saw himself excommunicated from the Church and disgraced in the Foreign Service, but he could think of nothing but this woman's perfect face. He felt as if he had been blown off his feet by a hurricane. He took two steps toward the bed. In those two steps, his future was decided.

"From now on, I will look after you and your children. . . . Forever."

Forever. What is that, Paula? I have lost count of the days in this white building where echoes reign and it is never night. The boundaries of reality have been blurred; life is a labyrinth of facing mirrors and deformed images. A month ago, at this very hour, I was a different woman. I have a photograph from that day. I am at a party launching the publication in Spain of my most recent novel. I am wearing a silver necklace and bracelets and an aubergine-colored dress. My nails are manicured and my smile confident. I am a century younger than I am today. I don't know that woman; in four weeks, sorrow has transformed me. As I stood at a microphone describing the circumstances that led me to write *The Infinite Plan*, my agent pushed her way through the crowd and whispered in my ear that you had been taken to the hospital. I had a jolting presentiment that something fundamental had happened to change our lives. We had been together the day before, and you were very ill. When I landed in Madrid, I was surprised that you weren't at the airport to greet me, as you always have been. I dropped my suitcases at the hotel and, still reeling from the long flight from California, rushed to your house, where I found you vomiting and burning with fever. You had just returned from a spiritual retreat with the nuns from the school where you work forty hours a week as a volunteer helping underprivileged children, and you told me it had been an intense and saddening experience. You were beset with doubts, your faith was fragile.

"I go looking everywhere for God, but He slips away from me, Mama."

"God can wait for a while. Right now it's more urgent to look for a doctor. What's the matter with you, Paula?"

"Porphyria," you replied without hesitation. Since learning several years earlier you had inherited the condition, you had taken very good care of yourself, and regularly consulted one of the few specialists in Spain. When Ernesto found you so weak, he took you to the emergency room; they diagnosed flu, and sent you back home. That night your husband told me that for weeks, even months, you had been tense and tired. As we sat and discussed what we thought was depression, you were suffering behind the closed door of your bedroom; the porphyria was poisoning you, and neither of us saw it. I don't know how I went on with my obligations; my mind was on you, and in a break between interviews I ran to the telephone to call. The minute I heard you were worse, I canceled the rest of my tour and flew to the hospital. I ran up the six flights of stairs and located your room in this monstrous building. I found you lying in bed, ashen, with a disoriented expression on your face. One glance was enough to realize how ill you were.

"Why are you crying?" you asked in an unrecognizable voice.

"Because I'm afraid. I love you, Paula."

"I love you, too, Mama."

That was the last thing you said to me, Paula. Instants later you were delirious, babbling numbers, with your eyes fixed on the ceiling. Ernesto and I sat beside your bed all night, in a daze, taking turns in the one available chair, while in other beds in the room an elderly patient was dying, a demented woman was screaming, and an undernourished Gypsy girl with signs of a recent beating tried to sleep. At dawn I convinced your husband to go rest, he was exhausted from being up several nights. He kissed you good-bye and left. An hour later the true horror was unleashed: a spine-chilling vomit of blood followed by convulsions. Your tense body arched upward, shuddering in violent spasms that lifted you from the bed. Your arms trembled and your fingers contracted as if you were trying to hold on to something. Your eyes were filled with terror, your face congested, and saliva ran from your mouth. I threw my body on yours to hold you down, and screamed at the top of my lungs for help. The room filled with people in white, and I was dragged out of the room by force. I remember finding myself kneeling on the floor, then being slapped. "Be quiet, Señora; you must be calm or you will have to leave." A male nurse was shaking me. "Your daughter is better now, you can go in." I tried to stand but my knees buckled. Someone helped me to your bed and then left. I was alone with you and with the patients in the other beds, who were watching in silence, each deep in her own private hell. Your color was ghostly, your eyes were rolled back, dried blood threaded from your lips, and you were cold. I waited, calling you by all the names I had given you as a little girl, but you were far away in another world. I tried to get you to drink a little water. When I shook you, you looked at me with glassy, dilated eyes, staring through me toward another horizon, and then suddenly you were as still as death, not breathing. Somehow I called for help, and immediately tried to give you mouth-to-mouth resuscitation, but fear made me clumsy. I did everything badly. I blew air into your mouth erratically, any way at all, five or six times, and then I noticed your heart had stopped beating, and began to pound your chest with my fists. Help arrived seconds later, and the last thing I saw was your bed hurtling toward the elevator at the end of the corridor. From that moment life stopped for you. And for me. Together we crossed a mysterious threshold and entered a zone of inky darkness.

"Her condition is critical," the physician on call in the intensive care unit told me.

"Should I call her father in Chile?" I asked. "It will take him more than twenty hours to get here."

"Yes."

People began to come by: Ernesto's relatives, and friends and nuns from your school. Someone notified the members of the family scattered through Chile, Venezuela, and the United States. Shortly afterward, your husband arrived, calm and gentle, more concerned about others' feelings than his own, but he looked very fatigued. They allowed him to see you for a few minutes, and when he came back he informed us that you were hooked up to a respirator and being given a blood transfusion. "It isn't as bad as they say," he told us. "I feel Paula's strong heart beating close to mine," a phrase that at the moment seemed to have little meaning but now that I know him I can better understand. We spent that day and the next night in the waiting room. At times I drifted into an exhausted sleep, but when I opened my eyes I found Ernesto always in the same position, unmoving, waiting.

"I'm terrified, Ernesto," I admitted toward dawn.

"There's nothing we can do. Paula is in God's hands."

"You find that easier to accept than I do, because at least you have your faith."

"It's as painful to me as to you, but I have less fear of death and more hope for life," he replied, putting his arms around me. I buried my face in his jacket, breathing his young male scent, racked by an atavistic fear.

As it grew light, my mother and Michael arrived from Chile, along with Willie, from California. Your father was very pale. He had boarded the airplane in Santiago convinced that he would find you dead. The flight must have seemed an eternity. Devastated, I hugged my mother, and realized that although she may have shrunken with the years, she still radiates an aura of protection. Beside her, Willie is a giant, yet when I wanted a chest to lay my head upon, my mother's seemed more ample and comforting than his. We went into the intensive care room and found you conscious, and improved over the previous day. The doctors had begun to replace the sodium in your body—which you were losing in alarming amounts—and the transfusion had revived you. That illusion, however, lasted only a few hours; soon afterward, you became very agitated, and with the massive dose of sedatives they used to treat it you descended into the deep coma from which you have not awakened to this day.

"Your poor daughter, she doesn't deserve this. I'm old, why can't I die in her place?" don Manuel wonders from time to time, his voice barely audible.

It is so difficult to write these pages, Paula, to retrace the steps of this painful journey, verify details, imagine how things might have been if you had fallen into more capable hands, if they had not immobilized you with drugs, if . . . if. . . . How can I shake this guilt? When you mentioned the porphyria I thought you were exaggerating and, instead of seeking further help, I trusted those people in white; I handed over my daughter without hesitation. It isn't possible to go back in time. I must not keep looking back, yet I can't stop doing it, it's an obsession. Nothing exists but the unremitting certainty of this hospital; the rest of my life is veiled in heavy mist.

Willie, who after a few days had to return to his work in California, calls every morning and every night to offer support, to remind me that we love each other and have a happy life on the other side of the ocean. His voice comes to me from very far away, as if I had dreamed him and there was no wood house high above San Francisco Bay, no ardent lover now a distant husband. It also seems I have dreamed my son Nicolás, my daughter-in-law Celia, and little Alejandro with his giraffe eyelashes. Carmen, my agent, comes from time to time with sympathies from my editors or news about my books, but I don't know what she's talking about. Nothing exists but you, Paula, and this space without time in which we both are trapped.

In the long, silent hours, I am trampled by memories, all happening in one instant, as if my entire life were a single, unfathomable image. The child and girl I was, the woman I am, the old woman I shall be, are all water in the same rushing torrent. My memory is like a Mexican mural in which all times are simultaneous: the ships of the Conquistadors in one corner and an Inquisitor torturing Indians in another, galloping Liberators with blood-soaked flags and the Aztecs' Plumed Serpent facing a crucified Christ, all encircled by the billowing smokestacks of the industrial age. So it is with my life, a multilayered and ever-changing fresco that only I can decipher, whose secret is mine alone. The mind selects, enhances, and betrays; happenings fade from memory; people forget one another and, in the end, all that remains is the journey of the soul, those rare moments of spiritual revelation. What actually happened isn't what matters, only the resulting scars and distinguishing marks. My past has little meaning; I can see no order to it, no clarity, purpose, or path, only a blind journey guided by instinct and detours caused by events beyond my control. There was no deliberation on my part, only good intentions and the faint sense of a greater design determining my steps. Until now, I have never shared my past; it is my innermost garden, a place not even my most intimate lover has glimpsed. Take it, Paula, perhaps it will be of some use to you, because I fear that yours no longer exists, lost somewhere during your long sleep—and no one can live without memories.

Notes on Contributors

RICK MOODY is the author of the novels *Garden State*, *The Ice Storm*, and *Purple America*; a collection of stories, *The Ring of Brightest Angels Around Heaven*; and the coeditor of an anthology, *The New Wine: Contemporary Responses to the New Testament*.

JAMAICA KINCAID was born on the island of St. John's Antigua. She is the author of *At the Bottom of the River*, *Annie John*, *A Small Place*, *Lucy*, and *The Autobiography of My Mother*. She lives with her family in Vermont.

NATALIE KUSZ is the author of *Road Song*. Her work has won her both a 1989 Whiting Writers Award and the 1990 General Electric Younger Writers Award. She lives with her daughter in Cambridge, Massachusetts, and teaches at Harvard.

DON J. SNYDER is the author of *A Soldier's Disgrace: The Court Martial of Major Ronald Alley*, and two novels, *Veterans Park* and *From the Point*. "Winter Work" is included in his memoir, *The Cliff Walk*, published in 1997 by Little, Brown.

LAUREN SLATER is the author of *Welcome to My Country: Journeys into the World of a Therapist and Her Patients*. She is the director of AfterCare Services, a mental health and substance abuse clinic in East Boston, Massachusetts.

WILLIAM VAN WERT is the author of several recent books: *Memory Links*—a collection of essays—and the novels *What's It All About?*, *Stool Wives*, and *Don Quickshot*.

FRANCES MAYES's recent books are a memoir, *Under the Tuscan Sun*, and a book of poems, *Ex Voto*. "Talking Back" is from a work-in-progress about growing up in Georgia.

WILLIAM LOIZEAUX lives with his wife and second daughter in Hyattsville, Maryland. He has published fiction in anthologies and literary journals. *Anna: A Daughter's Life*, his first nonfiction work, was a 1993 *New York Times* Notable Book of the Year.

FLOYD SKLOOT has published two novels, two collections of poetry, and a book of essays about the illness experience, *The Night-Side* (Story Line Press, 1996), which includes "Healing Powers." He lives in Amity, Oregon.

JANE BERNSTEIN's memoir, *Loving Rachel*, has recently been reprinted by Chenoweth and Coyne. Her essays have been published in such places as *Ms.*, *Glamour*, *Poets & Writers*, the *New York Times*, and *Creative Nonfiction*. She is an associate professor at Carnegie Mellon University.

MAXINE SCATES is the author of *Toluca Street*, which received the Agnes Lynch Starrett Poetry Prize and the Oregon Book Award for Poetry. "The Dreaming Back" is part of a book-length collection of essays, *My Mother and Her Mother and Her Mother: Essays on Writing and Silence*.

REYNOLDS PRICE has published volumes of poems, plays, essays, translations from the Bible, and the memoir *Clear Pictures*, in addition to numerous novels, including *Kate Vaiden*, which won the National Book Critics Circle Award.

NANCY MAIRS is the author of several books, including *Ordinary Time*, *Voice Lessons*, and *Plaintext*. She lives in Tucson, Arizona, with her husband, George.

PATTON HOLLOW grew up in Athens, Ohio, and now lives in Cincinnati with his wife, Sylvia, and their two-year-old son, John. His work has appeared in *Epoch*, *The Gettysburg Review*, and elsewhere.

LAURA PHILPOT BENEDICT writes fiction, drama, essays, and screenplays from her home in Holland, Michigan. She has received a Writer's Fellowship from the West Virginia Division of Arts and

Humanities, as well as a Greenbrier County Artist Stipend Grant. Her latest project is a teleplay for West Virginia Public Television.

ALAN SHAPIRO's new book, *Vigil*, from which "The Vision" is excerpted, will be published this fall by the University of Chicago Press.

WILLIAM STYRON is the author of *Lie Down in Darkness*, *The Long March*, *Set This House on Fire*, *The Confessions of Nat Turner*, *Sophie's Choice*, *This Quiet Dust*, and *Darkness Visible*. He lives in Roxbury, Connecticut, and Vineyard Haven, Massachusetts.

CHRISTOPHER DAVIS is an associate professor of creative writing at the University of North Carolina at Charlotte. His first book of poetry, *The Tyrant of the Past and the Slave of the Future*, won the 1988 Associated Writing Program Award. His second collection is called *The Patriot*.

LUCY GREALY's essay "Mirrorings" received the National Magazine Award and was the basis for *Autobiography of a Face*. She has been a fellow at the Bunting Institute and the Fine Arts Work Center in Provincetown, and currently lives in New York City.

RICHARD MCCANN is the author, most recently, of *Ghost Letters* and the editor (with Michael Klein) of *Things Shaped in Passing: More "Poets for Life" Writing from the AIDS Pandemic*. He codirects the graduate program in creative writing at American University in Washington, D.C.

CHRISTINA MIDDLEBROOK is a Jungian analyst who lives in San Francisco with her husband and children. "Witness" is a chapter from her book *Seeing the Crab: A Memoir of Dying*, published by Basic Books in 1996.

ISABEL ALLENDE was born in Peru, raised in Chile, and now lives in California. She is the author of the novels *The House of the Spirits*, *Of Love and Shadows*, *Eva Luna*, and *The Infinite Plan*; the story collection *The Stories of Eva Luna*; and the memoir *Paula*.

About the Editor

KATHRYN RHETT is an assistant professor at Gettysburg College in Pennsylvania where she lives with her husband, writer Fred Leebron, and their two children. She has taught writing workshops at Johns Hopkins, the University of Iowa, the University of San Francisco, and the University of North Carolina at Charlotte. Her poetry has appeared in *The Antioch Review*, *The Gettysburg Review*, *Grand Street*, *The Ohio Review*, *Ploughshares*, and elsewhere. Her memoir, *Near Breathing*, was published in March 1997.